Britain's Fleet Air Arm in World War II

Britain's Fleet Air Arm
in World War II

Ron Mackay

Schiffer Military History
Atglen, PA

Cover and profile artwork by Steve Ferguson, Colorado Springs, CO.

LAND, SEA AND FIRE
In late 1942, Royal Navy 'H Force' carrier borne squadrons focused their strategic support in Operation Torch, the Allied landings in North Africa. In the ensuing six months, FAA aircraft ranged throughout the central Mediterranean, as depicted here in HMS *Indomitable*'s Seafire Mk.Ib's of 885 Sqdn. covering the withdrawal of 893 Sqdn. Marlet Mk.IV fighter-bombers from their strike on Volcano in the Ionian Islands, just off Sicily's north shore. Smoldering sulfur rises from the island's namesake in pale contrast to the harbor fires set by the Marlets.

Book design by Robert Biondi.

Copyright © 2005 by Ron Mackay.
Library of Congress Catalog Number: 2004108884.

Printed in China.
ISBN: 0-7643-2131-5

We are always looking for people to write books on new and related subjects. If you have an idea for a book, please contact us at the address below.

Published by Schiffer Publishing Ltd.
4880 Lower Valley Road
Atglen, PA 19310
Phone: (610) 593-1777
FAX: (610) 593-2002
E-mail: Info@schifferbooks.com.
Visit our web site at: www.schifferbooks.com
Please write for a free catalog.
This book may be purchased from the publisher.
Please include $3.95 postage.
Try your bookstore first.

In Europe, Schiffer books are distributed by:
Bushwood Books
6 Marksbury Ave.
Kew Gardens
Surrey TW9 4JF
England
Phone: 44 (0)20 8392-8585
FAX: 44 (0)20 8392-9876
E-mail: Bushwd@aol.com.
Free postage in the UK. Europe: air mail at cost.
Try your bookstore first.

Contents

Foreword

After a promising beginning as the Royal Naval Air Service in World War I, the Fleet Air Arm – or to give it the official Navy's title, 'The Air Branch of the Royal Navy' – became a military 'football' passed around between its parent Service and the Royal Air Force under whose operational control it fell from 1918-1937.

At the outbreak of World War II its aircraft establishment still reflected the perceived subordinate roles of gunnery spotting, reconnaissance and Fleet defence. Worse still was a serious dearth of both middle and senior-ranking aviators as well as aviation mechanics with which to operate and service the small number of aircraft, most of whom were technically no more than adequate for even surviving a modern air war.

Despite a series of reverses over the first three years of World War II stretching from Norway to the Far East, there also occurred several Actions such as the crippling of the Italian Fleet at Taranto in late 1940 and the Swordfish's fatal strike on BISMARCK that pointed the way to both the growing superiority of aircraft over warships (in particular the failing influence of the battleship as the prime weapon of naval warfare) and the attendant need to build up the FAA's strength for offensive operations.

A rapid expansion in officer personnel was achieved mainly through the ranks of the RNVR or 'Wavy Navy' whose 'citizen/sailor's' enthusiasm for by-passing King's Regulations and Admiralty Instructions was tempered but not subdued by the reduced numbers of 1939-1942 battle-hardened veterans still on hand, whose operational experience was passed on to the 'newcomers'. Additionally, by 1943 the aircraft designs on hand were equally more than capable of holding their own with their Axis adversaries – a fact that owes much to the excellent products emanating from the assembly lines of the Grumman and Chance-Vought Companies.

The safe shepherding of convoys in the Atlantic and Arctic, the crippling of TIRPITZ, the closing off of the English Channel around D-Day, and operations off Okinawa in 1945 – these actions were just a sample of the diverse duties undertaken and successfully fulfilled by the Royal Navy's 'Air Branch' By VJ-Day. The Fleet Air Arm's ranks could stand quietly but proudly alongside their land-based contemporaries in the knowledge that they had played a full part in subverting the nefarious aims of the Axis dictators.

CHAPTER ONE

'In the Beginning ...'

What was titled the Royal Naval Air Service in 1912 had already been experimenting with aircraft in various ways, but with the emphasis on floatplanes rather than wheeled designs. However, around 1912 a Cdr. Samson had already demonstrated the viability of take-offs from warships, when he flew a Short S27 off several warships with adapted foredecks.

The operation of floatplanes was regularly indulged in by the Royal Navy, up to and including World War I. Many were flown directly from their parent warship using recoverable wheel-trolleys that allowed for an easier take-off than was possible when taking off from the sea. On return, the vessel's derrick would lift the aircraft back on board. The sizeable wingspan of some of the floatplanes dictated the need for their wings to be folded in order for their proper stowage on board. (During 1913 the cruiser HERMES had conducted experiments involving the fore-going principles that proved their viability; this warship was sunk shortly after World War I began).

No less than ten vessels were commissioned by the Royal Navy following requisition or purchase from British merchant shipping stock during World War I to serve in the role of aircraft or floatplane support. EMPRESS, ENGADINE and RIVIERA carried floatplanes, while the former-named vessel was fitted with a flying-off ramp on the foredeck. ARK ROYAL, the third Royal Navy warship to bear this name, was the first of another five vessels to feature a ramp on the foredeck, although launching was made using a catapult; two cranes permitted the use of floatplanes in addition to wheeled-aircraft. BEN-MY-CHREE MANXMAN and VINDEX were similarly configured to handle land-based and floatplanes; one of the former-named vessel's S184 floatplanes successfully launched torpedoes against Turkish shipping in 1915. CAMPANIA, which had previously been a record-breaking Cunard passenger liner, was not only fitted with a ramp but was modified in the course of a second re-fit; this consisted of removing the forward funnel in favour of two funnels, between which the original short ramp could be extended. Finally, NIARANA and PEGASUS appeared towards the end of World War I.

Operations of aircraft in floatplane configuration cast up several basic problems for the Royal Navy. The very nature of the sea was the first, in that if its surface became too disturbed then floatplanes would experience great or even insuperable difficulties in operating. The second problem concerned the parent vessel; this would be forced to stop in order to effect the floatplane's recovery, which in turn would lay it open to attack, particularly by U-Boats. The original canvas-covered hangar was adequate in protecting aircraft from the worst effects of salt-water corrosion but was prone to structural damage caused by rough seas. More solid hangar structures appeared on the several specialist warships in service during World War I. However, the re-positioning of hangars from the above-deck location to one positioned below a suitable flight deck length was absolutely necessary as soon as the regular operation of land-based aircraft began to be made.

The Carrier Cometh

The development of the dedicated aircraft carrier as a viable element of Royal Naval operations, on which to recover aircraft as opposed to just launching them, can be primarily traced back to HMS FURIOUS. This warship was originally commissioned as a light battleship but the first stage in her conversion was in mid-1917, and then only in respect of her foredeck. The ramp constructed over this length was to be used for take-off only, which meant that the aircraft concerned had to be launched in circumstances that enabled them to touch down on land. Cdr. Dunning, who conducted the initial tests

Personnel gathered on the deck of FURIOUS are ready to rush forward and steady the Sopwith Pup being flown by Cmdr. Dunning on 2 August 1917. Five days later, his latest landing attempt ended in tragedy when the aircraft slewed to one side on landing and toppled overboard, with its pilot being drowned.

was of the opinion that it was feasible, given the fast pace of FURIOUS and the low landing speed of the Sopwith 'Pup' test-fighter, to regain the ramp safely. The first attempt on 2 August at Scapa Flow proceeded in order, even though the 'Pup' had to be sideslipped in order to clear the central superstructure. This 'first' in shipboard landings anywhere in the World encouraged further flights, but five days later, Dunning was drowned when he attempted an 'over-shoot', only for his engine to fail; the aircraft momentarily teetered on the edge of the ramp, before toppling into the sea. The unfortunate officer's enterprise had set the trend for future sea-borne aviation activities.

Between 1917 and 1918, work proceeded to progressively convert FURIOUS from its original cruiser concept to that of an aircraft carrier. A second ramp was fitted in place of the rear main gun turret, following which narrow 'passageways' were applied amidships along which aircraft could be manoeuvered forward for take-off. Hangars with operating lifts were located directly ahead of the main superstructure and towards the stern, with the latter lift offset to starboard. This upper deck layout would be retained until after World War I

when conversion to what would be recognised as a basic carrier outline was recommended.

ARGUS

The first vessel to appear in a full carrier outline, at least as regards her deck pattern, was a converted merchant ship originally intended for the Italians, the CONTO ROSSO – a supreme irony, when one considers the subsequent World War II service in the Mediterranean provided by what became ARGUS! Four years elapsed between her keel being laid in 1914 and commissioning in September 1918. The flush deck extended 535 ft. and was inclined upwards along the forward section as well as rounded down at the stern. The turbine engines drove four propellers to produce a maximum speed of 20.25 knots. The hangar provision was a generous 350 ft long and 20 ft. high, but the breadth was only 48 ft. compared with the overall 68 ft. beam. The absence of a fixed superstructure was countered by the presence of navigation points on either side and below the flight-deck level, along with a retractable chart-house positioned along the forward deck centerline. Post-World War I modifications included bulges on the lower hull

Left: The Blackburn Dart torpedo-bomber was accepted into FAA service during 1923 and the assigned seventy aircraft served until 1935. This aircraft is releasing a torpedo from between its sturdy landing gear supports. Right: The early FAA designs produced by Blackburn would have earned a prize for some of the ugliest, un-aerodynamic looking aircraft. The Blackburn Blackburn was intended to operate in a spotter/reconnaissance role, with the high cockpit position providing good visibility on take-off and landing. Two portholes on either fuselage side were used by the Observers. The aircraft joined the FAA in the same year as the Dart but was phased out in 1931.

and levelling-out of the forward flight deck, as well as the fitting of twin catapults. The warship was also used by the National Physics Laboratory (NPL) to test out the feasibility of a fixed superstructure for the latest carrier EAGLE, and the effect of the wind currents upon the deck (and therefore upon aircraft movements) that might arise from the presence of the structure.

HERMES

Even as FURIOUS and ARGUS were being developed or constructed, the first custom-built RN carrier was on the Armstrong Whitworth shipyard stocks from January 1918. The Admiralty's current view of the use of aircraft in a primarily reconnaissance role was reflected in this warship's

development; she was to bear all the aspects of a light cruiser as regards her speed, structure and machinery, and operate as part of a cruiser Squadron. In addition the fixed superstructure on the central starboard area of the flight deck would set the trend for Royal Navy Fleet carrier design from this stage onwards. Her aircraft-carrying capacity was modest, being originally set at twenty and reducing to a mere twelve by 1939. The potential imbalance created by the superstructure on a light cruiser hull was only corrected by the permanent flooding of specific portside bulge compartments; this action was one among several similar measures affecting the flow of oil fuel through the ship's tanks and the permanent filling of specified watertight compartments on this side of the carrier! This carrier was commissioned in 1923.

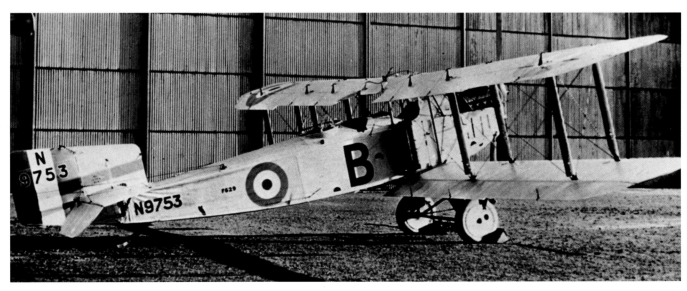

The Fairey IIID served in the same spotter/reconnaissance role as the Blackburn between 1924-1930, and was adapted to operate off water as well as land. Power was provided either by a Rolls-Royce Eagle VIII producing 375 hp, or – as in the case of the batch that included this airframe – the Napier Lion IIB, V or VA, up-rated to 450 hp.

Above: FURIOUS was originally designed as a battleship, but a flight deck was built in place of her forward main gun turret. The warship was commissioned in June 1917 but a deck was then fitted to the rear section of the hull and link-ramps placed around the central superstructure with which to move aircraft fore and aft. This arrangement was changed in 1925 when the superstructure was deleted and a complete flush flight deck inserted above the hull length.

Below: A torpedo is being dropped by a Blackburn Ripon, one of the D Flight contingent based at Gosport near the huge Naval Base of Portsmouth, and home to the Navy's Torpedo School. A total of ninety-two Ripons was constructed, and the design began to replace its Dart stable-mate in 1929, serving the FAA over the ensuing six years.

Gosport is also the location for this formation take-off by Blackburn Baffins, which took over from the Ripon in 1935. The Baffin possessed an overall performance that was little better than its predecessor, and was soon relegated from front-line service in 1937 by the Fairey Swordfish.

Early Landing-on Developments

Once the concept of land-based aircraft conducting operations from an aircraft carrier had been firmly embraced, the Admiralty had to consider how a safe landing procedure could be established. The very low landing speeds of the machines initially in service meant that little was required in the way of arrest-equipment. Tests conducted on FURIOUS, using sandbag-weighted wires set out longitudinally and in a forward-converging pattern, and which were engaged by hooks fitted to the aircrafts' axles, had further led the authorities to believe the system was hardly necessary, although it was retained. Flexible lateral flaps set into the deck were also tested, but the degree of damage to the aircraft landing gear was deemed too great to justify their further use. It was to be 1931 before the initial step towards the lateral-mounted friction-type or hydraulic wire system that was to become a standard feature of all future carrier operations was taken. (A secondary and equally vital benefit arising from the use of arrester equipment, especially as the speed factor increased, was the security of other aircraft already parked on the deck, since these would be immune from being run into – provided the aircraft's hook properly engaged the wire!).

Carrier Defensive Armament

The original concept of the aircraft carrier as being constructed on the lines of a cruiser, and therefore serving as part of a cruiser Squadron, dictated the nature of its armament. The 8-inch weapon applicable to this class of warship was initially regarded as necessary in order to combat counter-attacks by enemy warships, especially should the carrier find itself isolated from the remainder of its Squadron. To a lesser extent, the heavy weapons were required to fight off aerial attacks. However, by the mid 1920s, the scheme was cancelled, and the heaviest caliber armament borne by Royal Navy carriers was to be the 6-inch guns fitted to EAGLE, along with six 5.5-inch weapons fitted to HERMES. Otherwise, the 4.7-inch

The first custom-built RN carrier was the HERMES, which was commissioned in 1923. The low height of the hull, and flight deck is further accentuated by the massive island superstructure. Note the twin pillar supports for the afterdeck, which is also raised in a shallow curve. The carrier's maximum aircraft complement was twenty, but she had none on board when Japanese Naval aircraft sank her off Ceylon (Sri Lanka) on 9 April 1942.

A Fairey IIIF (Mk.IIIB), powered by a 570 hp Lion XIA, is perched precariously on the short launch-ramp mounted on top of the battleship BARHAM's No.3 gun turret. A spare pair of floats is stowed beneath the after mast. BARHAM was torpedoed in the Mediterranean in November 1941 and blew up with heavy loss of life.

The Fairey Flycatcher was adapted to floatplane configuration as seen here. Note the large spinner fairing that was normally absent from the standard airframes, and the wheels projecting just below the float base that enabled the variant to act in an amphibian role. However, the wheels did cause an inordinate amount of drag when attempting a take off on water!

gun was the maximum calibre gun fitted on any of the seven carriers constructed during World War I and the inter-War years. Anti-aircraft defence was further catered for by the inclusion of 2- and 3-pounder guns and in the case of ARK ROYAL, .50 Vickers machine guns.

The scale and quality of the revised defensive armament was respectively no more than adequate and of questionable value. The heaviest calibre weapon was the 6-inch borne by EAGLE; nine of these were supplemented by five 4-inch guns and four 3-Pdrs. Before ARK ROYAL was commissioned in 1938, this figure was the largest on Navy carriers, apart from FURIOUS, which mounted ten 6-inch, six 4-Pdrs. and four 2-Pdrs. The two COURAGEOUS class warships had sixteen 4.7-inch guns only, while HERMES carried a derisory total of six 5.5-inch and three 4-inch weapons! ARK ROYAL, by comparison, was comprehensively decked out. Eight 4.5-inch turrets, each with pairs of guns straddled both sides of her center deck, with six of the 2-Pdr. mountings placed around or opposite, the main superstructure. Finally, another thirty-

two Vickers-manufactured .50 machine guns were grouped towards the four corners of the flight deck.

The heavier and medium-caliber guns down to the 3-Pdr. possessed a reasonable punch but their rate of fire was not very high, in addition to which their ability to track aircraft was very poor. That left the 2-Pdr.pompom and the Vickers .50 machine gun. The former-named weapon was to be immortalised during World War II as the 'Chicago Piano' for its tremendous fire-rate, as captured in numerous wartime newsreels – regardless of its very moderate success-rate in practice! As for the Vickers .50 machine gun, it was regarded as a very temperamental weapon with poor directional sighting as a principal serious failure. The availability of cannon-caliber designs from Switzerland (Oerliken) and Sweden (Bofors) was only latterly taken up by the Admiralty, and then only under the impetus of wartime demands for more efficient defensive means with which to combat the Axis bombers and particularly the dive-bombers.

CHAPTER TWO

The Locust Years
1918-1939

Washington Treaty Stipulations/Limitations

The scaling-down of military Forces after World War I extended to the Navies of the major or – in the case of the United States and Japan – emerging Powers. In a move that could not have pleased the proponents of the battleship as the kernel of Naval power, such warships were to be greatly reduced in numbers, with numerous warships already in service or in the process of construction being scrapped. On the other hand, the conversion of warships from battleship or battle-cruiser configuration to that of aircraft carrier was permitted, albeit within overall tonnage limitations for each nation.

In the case of Britain, the United States and Japan, the overall tonnage figures were based on a 5:5:3 proportion; the larger totals reflected the perceived need for the Anglo-American Navies to secure their interests in oceans other than the Pacific, which was regarded as Japan's sole area of nautical influence. The overall total of 525,000 tons included a specific allocation of 135,000 tons devoted to aircraft carrier development. In all instances an individual warship tonnage of 27,000 tons was to be applied, but an illogical aspect of the limitation-factor was the 'allowance' for two carriers displacing up to 36,000 tons, including an armor maximum of 3,000 tons. Whereas the American LEXINGTON and SARATOGA were constructed up to this limit, and Japan commissioned the KAGA and AKAGI around the 30,000-ton figure, the Royal Navy did not follow suit. By 1922, the total carrier and seaplane displacement figure was only 44,580 tons spread among four warships. The arrival of HERMES and EAGLE raised this total to 80,580 tons, while even the introduction of the COURAGEOUS Class carriers left this figure standing at 124,580 tons. By the time the ARK ROYAL with a 22,000-ton displacement figure was commissioned in 1938 the provisions of the Washington Treaty had been left behind, given

the political and military tensions currently existing around the world.

Carrier Force Expansion

The retention of FURIOUS and ARGUS after World War I and the introduction into service of HERMES in 1923 proved to be an adequate complement of carriers when related to the current small number of aircraft on hand. FURIOUS had by then been properly configured to full carrier status by the removal of her central superstructure and the fitting of a main flight deck along with an auxiliary flying-off deck placed on the forward hull deck; Two hangars were also applied, the access lifts of which were positioned forward for the upper hangar (whose floor formed the rear of the auxiliary flying-off deck) and aft for the lower hangar. Navigation and flying control were monitored from two small 'bunkers' located on the starboard and port sides of the extreme forward edge of the main flight deck. In addition a retractable charthouse was placed in the forward deck centerline. (A small island structure would be added on the starboard side directly behind the rear of the forward lift in 1939).

EAGLE

By the end of the 1920s, no less than three new carriers had been commissioned. The first of these was EAGLE, which was another adaptation, in this instance the battleship ALMIRANTE COCHRANE ordered by the Chilean Navy in 1913. However it was fully five years before the decision to proceed with the warship's development as a carrier was taken. The flight deck beam of 95 ft. was tapered towards the bow and stern with the former section coming to a point in the same manner as FURIOUS and ARGUS. Two lifts accommodated aircraft movements into and out of the single

Up to 1924, the FAA fighter designs were all adaptations of RAF aircraft. The ten-year service span of the first custom-built FAA fighter, the Fairey Flycatcher, lasted from 1924-1934. The aircraft seen here operated from Leuchars in eastern Scotland, which was used as a holding Base for FAA aircraft assigned to the Home Fleet.

hangar that extended 400 ft., almost two-thirds of the 652 ft. flight deck length. The original single funnel was expanded to two units centered within the long island structure. The Navy's latest carrier was finally commissioned in February 1924.

COURAGEOUS and GLORIOUS

EAGLE's battleship lineage was to result in a warship whose weight restricted her maximum speed to 24 kts. (knots). By contrast, the two COURAGEOUS Class carriers brought into service in 1928 and 1930 did not suffer from what was a basic disability, either when operating aircraft or manoeuvring to avoid U-Boat attacks; both weighed in at 26,100 tons (deep load) and would be capable of a 30.5 kt. maximum speed provided by the 90,000shp Parsons geared turbines output. These latest additions were sister-ships of FURIOUS in their original conception and construction as 'large light cruisers', having served in this role between 1917 and 1923, and were only submitted for conversion in the immediate aftermath of the Washington Naval Treaty of 1922.

The conversion followed the basic pattern applied to FURIOUS with total removal of all fittings down to the main deck. The twin-hangar arrangement was continued, as was the under-lapping of the main flight deck's forward section in relation to the lower auxiliary flying-off deck. However, the rear section of the main flight deck was later extended back to

the stern in the case of GLORIOUS; this adaptation clearly contrasted with FURIOUS and COURAGEOUS, whose flight decks remained under-lapped in relation to the hull stern.

A common feature on all three carriers was the rounded shape of the main flight deck's forward rim that provided enhanced aerodynamic conditions for the aircraft. The single noticeable external difference on both carriers compared to FURIOUS was the island superstructure. This was smaller and neater in layout compared to either HERMES or EAGLE with the single funnel extending above the bridge; GLORIOUS, at least, also had an extending navigation platform that folded back against the funnel's inside surface when not in use.

ARK ROYAL

In 1935, the Royal Navy's order for its latest carrier was placed. This time around, however, the warship would be built from the very beginning with its operational role in mind, namely the launch and recovery of aircraft. Although HERMES had also been envisaged in the carrier role when ordered, its design layout reflected the Admiralty's intention to use it as part of a cruiser Squadron. This contrasted with ARK ROYAL, which was constructed from the very start as a pure aircraft carrier. Whereas all its predecessors' main strength deck was that of the hull, with the flight deck playing a subsidiary role in this respect, the ARK's actual flight deck assumed this primary

This example of a Flycatcher floatplane is pictured over-flying warships moored at Gibraltar sometime during the early-1930s. The carrier ARGUS (also known as the 'Flat Top') is anchored in the foreground. The battle cruiser in the center right of the picture is HOOD, destroyed with all but three of her crew by BISMARCK on 24 May 1941.

Clear evidence that the RAF retained virtually unfettered control of the Fleet Air Arm up to 1937 is provided by this photograph taken on COURAGEOUS between 1929-1932. W/Cdr. Collishaw (Senior RAF Officer and Flag Officer's Staff Officer) is seated fifth from left, second row. The few FAA personnel are lost among their 'Junior Service' contemporaries!

function. The sole concession to this principle involved the three lifts, all having to be offset in relation to the deck centerline in order to retain a full strength factor.

The flight deck extended 800 ft. from bow to stern and was provided with a generous-sized 'round-down', while the lifts serviced two hangars with the upper one 124 ft. longer than its 452 ft. 'twin'. A departure from previous overall layout was the total enclosure of both the bow and the stern. The hull was provided with a 4 1/2–inch armour belt amidships and a 3 1/2-inch cover over the engine boilers and magazines. The hull skinning was double-layered to provide additional strengthening against torpedo hits. The Parsons geared turbines fitted to ARK's four predecessors were in this instance capable of an enhanced 102,000shp output that could propel the 27,700 tons (deep load) carrier at a 31 kt. maximum speed.

Naval Doctrines – Surface Ship against Aircraft

Bombs

The conclusion in 1918 of what was sadly not to prove 'The War to end all Wars' left the major Navies of the World with the feeling that future activities would still be centered on the battleship as the major sea-borne weapon of use. The advent of aircraft for military aviation purposes in little or no way disturbed the thought-patterns of My Lords of the Admiralty or their contemporaries elsewhere; there appeared to be no feasible way in which air-mounted weapons could be even brought to bear against, let alone prove a mortal threat to, the 'Dreadnoughts' or indeed any size of warship. (In America, Billy Mitchells' bombing experiments again the former German battleship OSTFRIEDLAND, although successful in sinking the warship, had been conducted against a static rather than a mobile target, while the calibre of the bombs used, although sizeable, were not typical of the ordnance on hand.

Indeed, the bombs in current use throughout the military aviation world between the two World Wars were of small size as well as bereft of real armour-piercing capability, while the available aircraft operating off aircraft carriers could not support truly large bombs, let alone transport them for any distance. A 1937 assessment of FAA bombing results had revealed that around eleven bombs dropped by dive-bomb method and an increased factor of nearly three times that figure for high-level bombing was required to achieve a single hit.

A pair of Fairey IIIF (Mk.II) float-planes fly above Lin Kungtao, China, sometime during the 1920s. Both were assigned to 440 Flight and served with HERMES. Note the very exposed crew positions, and the square shape of the fin compared to the Mk.III successor, which featured a curved leading edge; however, some Mk.II airframes were similarly modified to Mk.III standard.

A Fairey FIII with a fine chequerboard pattern on the vertical fin and elevators is taking off to port of the flight deck centerline. The 1700 serial number sequence partially visible on the rudder indicates this is a IIIB variant of the spotter-reconnaissance design, of which one-hundred sixty-six were constructed.

(In Germany during the late 1930s, a Major Harlinghausen would draw similar conclusions in presenting the bomb as very much the 'poor cousin' of the air-dropped torpedo when it came to crippling or sinking vessels, and his views would gain acceptance within the *Luftwaffe* High Command.).

Naturally, assessments could never replace practical experience, and the bomb was still to play its part in sinking warships during World War II. The dive-bombing technique would display a higher strike-rate than forecast in 1937, with both positive and negative impact upon the Royal Navy – KOENIGSBERG and TIRPITZ falling into the first, and ILLUSTRIOUS, FORMIDABLE and INDOMITABLE into the second, category respectively. As regards level-bombing, the increasing calibre and explosive content of this form of ordnance was to strike home with telling effect, particularly against static warships. The sinking or fatal crippling of several *Kriegsmarine* capital ships by RAF Bomber Command was a case in point.

Torpedoes

The Royal Navy's successful use of air-dropped torpedoes in the Mediterranean during 1915 was probably dismissed as posing a threat, since the vessels concerned were of very moderate tonnage and had no hull armour provision. In addition, the weight of a torpedo was such that the same limitations on take-off and range capability applied to Naval aircraft as in the case of bombing operations. However, the use of Naval aircraft for offensive purposes was only regarded as suspended until such time as design technology produced the necessary means, rather than being regarded as a scenario that was never likely to arise – at least in the minds of the

'Battleship Brigade' proponents among the major Navies of the world!

The efficacy of the torpedo as a strike weapon was being regularly displayed from around the mid-1920s onwards when exercises were conducted, for example, in the Mediterranean, EAGLE's aviators were adjudged to have hit QUEEN ELIZABETH with up to five torpedoes, while the carrier fighters had thoroughly 'strafed' the battleship's decks by way of hindering the AA gunners' counter-fire. During 1931, Ripons from GLORIOUS took on the battleships ROYAL SOVEREIGN, RESOLUTION and RAMILLES. Fourteen torpedoes were dropped, the majority aimed at RESOLUTION; four hits were recorded along with one on RAMILLES. The reaction from above was to the effect that the Ripons would never have got within dropping range before being summarily dealt with by the AA gunners!

Next year, a major exercise involved attacking the Fleet at anchorage in a Greek bay. The Dart torpedo-bombers based on the two COURAGEOUS Class carriers dropped nearly sixty 'tin-fish' in two days, and were credited by the exercise 'umpires' with making twelve strikes on the four battleships present, with one (RESOLUTION) absorbing seven. However, the overall assessment of the exercise was to the effect that all the warships had suffered up to 30% loss in maximum speed, but none had been sunk!

Of course, neither the destructive effect of the torpedoes nor the AA guns could be fully confirmed under such passive circumstances, but the mere fact that the assaults had borne such a degree of success should have alerted the Admiralty to the looming vulnerability of their warships, even with the presence of AA defences,' This was especially the case should

Three Hawker Nimrods from No.800 Sqdn. are photographed over-flying COURAGEOUS. The blue diagonal fuselage bands indicate assignment aboard the 'parent' Fleet carrier. The Lead aircraft also bears a colored vertical stabiliser, which denotes either a Flight or Sqdn. CO's machine.

This Hawker Nimrod has made an awkward landing on a carrier deck and great pressure had been placed on the starboard landing gear strut. The Officer in the left foreground appears to be at some risk if the aircraft continues to swing in his direction!

a large enough Force of attackers be on hand to indulge in anti-AA 'swamping' tactics by approaching from various directions.

RAF Control of the FAA

The independent entity now known as the Fleet Air Arm did not arise until the onset of World War II. Prior to that time, basic control had rested in the hands of the 'Junior Service', the RAF, following the conclusion of World War I. The Admiralty retained a degree of involvement in terms of the personnel, in that all Observers came from Naval ranks along with 25% of the pilots. The monopoly on Observer selection further summed up the Navy's continuing attitude on aircraft use as being principally in the spotter-reconnaissance role.

This all-round unsatisfactory arrangement persisted until 1936-1937 when Sir Thomas Inskip propounded the case for the Navy to assume control of its Air Arm. However, when this recommendation was put into practice two years later, the Admiralty was not granted priority in coastal and long-range maritime protection; these operations were currently assigned to the RAF's Coastal Command, and continued to be so in the

future. Another dangerous anomaly, until the arrival of effective dedicated Naval fighter designs, lay in the fact that aerial protection of the Home Fleet was primarily laid to the RAF. This situation assumed perfect and prompt liaison between the two Services at all times. The short endurance of RAF fighters between 1939-1942 meant that enemy aircraft assaults had to be anticipated (there being little or no shipboard radar sets on hand with which to pick up incoming hostile 'traffic') and fighters quickly despatched; the alternative of 'standing patrols' over main Fleet movements just could not be fulfilled on the joint grounds of lack of aircraft numbers and excessive fuel expenditure. A lack of radio links between Naval ships and RAF aircraft further added to the difficulties in implementing the Plan. (The Norwegian Campaign highlighted the basic farce of this scheme when RAF participation in direct Fleet protection came to nought, thanks to the excessive range factor).

Aircraft Development

Aircraft design-pattern during the first two to three decades of flying maintained an overall dependence on biplane layouts,

A Hawker Osprey Mk.I is attended to by deck handlers as the pilot walks away past the left-side stabiliser. Red, white and blue National markings are applied to the rudder, but the fuselage band (applied in black to denote assignment to EAGLE) is angled forward instead of backwards. The carrier was serving in the Far East at this time.

The two Osprey Mk.II reconnaissance aircraft seen here have consecutive serial numbers, which are applied to the rear fuselage and rudder. Note how the numbers on the fin are outlined against the red and blue sections of the National marking. Both aircraft belong to No.803 Sqdn., which operated the Osprey between 1933-1939 when the Blackburn Skua displaced them.

with fixed undercarriages and fabric-covered surfaces. The wholesale advance to monoplanes with retractable undercarriages and metal skinned surfaces did not really take hold among the aviation fraternity until well into the 1930s. The delay in this seemingly necessary seed-change, if aircraft were to increase their ability to fly faster and further with greater loads, was to affect military aviation as much as its civil counterpart.

The Royal Navy's inventory of aircraft for its fledging Air Arm, titled the Naval Air Arm and assigned to the control not of the Navy but of the RAF, was totally inadequate in quantity – if not also in quality as regards some of the designs at its disposal – during the greater bulk of the inter-War period. Of course, the end of World War I swiftly led to a drastic run-down in the technical and human logistical structure of the Armed Services, a procedure that did not exclude the Royal Navy, and therefore could explain this basic post-War situation of minimal strength.

Two particular aviation Companies (Blackburn and Fairey) played a leading role in the construction of designs specified by the Admiralty at this time. The former concern lent itself, albeit unconsciously, to producing some of the ugliest, if not to say most un-aerodynamic machines ever to take to the air, the Blackburn and the Dart being the designs in question. There were three strands of operational activity to

be catered for, namely reconnaissance, and Fleet 'spotting', torpedo/bombing operations and fighters.

1.) Reconnaissance

The primary, perceived role for FAA aircraft, namely reconnaissance, was taken up by the Avro Bison, whose appearance vied with the Blackburn in ugliness; the Blackburn also commenced service in 1923. The massive fuselages on both designs with their large side windows for observation purposes contributed greatly to the 'ugliness' factor. The following year the Fairey IIID made its appearance, tasked with the same basic duty. Although all three featured almost the same wingspan and fuselage dimensions, the FIIID presented a much neater overall outline. It was also the only one of this trio capable of operation as a seaplane. By 1928 a more advanced FIII variant was coming into service in the form of the FIIIF, which was intended to displace the FIIID and the Avro Bison, a process that was completed by 1930. The FIIIF was by far the most graceful among its spotter-reconnaissance contemporaries; on the other hand both FIII variants suffered one disability, in that the crew of three were positioned in open cockpits compared to the partially or totally enclosed locations for all crewmembers but the pilots on the Bison and Blackburn.

A floatplane version of the Hawker Osprey Mk.I is hoisted on board its parent warship anchored in the Firth of Forth (As identified by the massive cantilever Forth Railroad Bridge in the background). The aircraft's silver finish provides a superb background for the roundels, fin-flash and aircraft serial/ individual aircraft number.

The FIIIF served for a full eight years, by which point the Blackburn was long retired (1931) and the spotter-reconnaissance function was being shared, although in a diminishing manner, with yet another Fairey design, the Seal. However, the Seal prototype had in fact been a converted FIIIF airframe, and was originally envisaged as being the Mk. VI variant of the FIIIF. To some degree, the Royal Navy seemed firmly wedded to the biplane concept even as the war clouds began to loom up during the mid-1930s, a position that is evidenced by the ordered replacement for the Seal, the Fairey Swordfish. This was yet another biplane design, whose impact upon the conduct of the War at sea would prove vital, in spite of the aircraft's apparent obsolescence from 1939 onwards

Although floatplanes had formed a prominent segment of RNAS operations during World War I, the Service was then destined to function without a specifically designed floatplane up to 1936, when the Supermarine Company's Walrus appeared upon the scene. This chunky biplane with its Pegasus engine mounted in 'pusher' configuration between the wings was to claim a place in Royal Navy historical annuls not far short of that to be earned by the Fairey Swordfish. The original spotter-reconnaissance role was extended to encompass air-sea rescue duties, with the RAF the principal exponent of this equally vital function. It would be 1944 before its replacement, the Sea Otter (in many respects a 'cleaned-up' Walrus), arrived

on the scene. The Walrus, known as the 'Shagbat' among the FAA fraternity during World War I, proved an excellent choice for its declared function, since it possessed a range of 600 miles while cruising at 95mph, and an operational ceiling of 18,500 ft.

The final aircraft to occupy a spotter-reconnaissance slot was the Seafox, another Fairey production. This neat aircraft, which entered service during 1937, was designed for operation from catapult-equipped warships, with cruisers in specific mind. One example would also feature in the first major ship-to-ship action between the Royal Navy and the *Kriegsmarine*, namely the GRAF SPEE action off the River Plate in December 1939. However, unlike the Walrus, it was never land-based, whereas the Supermarine design was fitted with a retractable undercarriage. The emergence of escort carriers from late 1942 onwards saw the Navy dispense with the Seafox's services by mid-1943.

Range and endurance are principal requirements for all types of military aircraft, particularly in the reconnaissance role. As regards range, the Seafox possessed a standard capability of 440 miles, while the Walrus extended this figure by a further 160 miles. In terms of endurance, the Fairey FIIIF could maintain flight for between three and four hours. On the other the IIIF's Fairey stable-mate the Seal, pushed this specific performance figure up to 4 1/2 hours, as did the Seafox.

Another Hawker Osprey Mk.I floatplane displays its bulky but still streamlined outline to the camera aircraft. The Osprey served with a total of six FAA Catapult Flights and two Flights based on carriers during the 1930s and in fact was only declared obsolete in 1940. Total numbers constructed came to 131 in all, including two prototypes.

S1700 is a Hawker Osprey Mk.III that has been fitted with a pair of small floats placed under the outer wings in order to increase aircraft stability during landing and take-off. The central float has a small skid under the rear end, while the beaching gear possesses generous-sized wheels. A total of forty-nine Ospreys Mk.III were constructed.

2.) Torpedo/Bombing Operations

The offensive capability of Naval aircraft was destined to be split between the carriage of bombs and torpedoes. The range of standard ordnance capable of being lifted off carrier decks during World War II generally did not extend beyond a maximum of 1,000 lbs., although 1,600 lb. armour-piercing bombs were to be hauled by the Fairey Barracuda. However, these weapons were just not on hand prior to the outbreak of the Conflict.

The maximum load of the Fairey FIIIF for example was limited to 500 lbs. In the case of the dedicated attack aircraft most were able to lift individual bombs up to 550 lbs. A bomb of this capacity could inflict serious or even mortal damage on thin-hulled warships such as destroyers and cruisers, but their effect upon the hulls of battleships was likely to range from minimal to nil. The introduction of the airdropped torpedo, in contrast, was to raise the spectre of inferiority for all classes of warship when it came to surviving assaults from this weapon.

The Blackburn Company dominated the scene in this technical respect between the World Wars, producing four distinct designs for the torpedo-dropping role. The Dart entered service in 1923 and was only declared obsolete in 1935. The Napier Lion IIB engine fitted to both the Dart and the Blackburn was housed in a large, blunt-ended cowling and

surely contributed to the maximum speed factor of 100 mph for the former. The second and third types intended for torpedo operations – the Ripon and Baffin – bore progressively slimmer fuselages and neat engine mountings, with the latter switching from the in-line Napier Lion to the Bristol Pegasus un-cowled radial that raised maximum speed to 136 mph. The Ripon appeared in 1929 and could lift torpedo or bomb loads extending up to 1,650 lbs. in total. Maximum speed was 118 mph at 15,000 ft., and endurance was three hours. The design was superseded by the Baffin in 1935, whose air-cooled Pegasus motor was a Company change-over from the Napier Lion. A maximum speed increase to 136 mph and range of 450 miles along with a capacity for a 1576 lb. torpedo or 1590 lbs. of bombs, were features of the Baffin.

The final Blackburn design was the Shark, whose Armstrong-Siddeley Tiger VI produced 700 hp to produce a maximum speed of 152 mph, and which also entered service during 1935. However, unlike its predecessors the Shark's planned role was to be expanded from simple torpedo operations to also acting in the spotter-reconnaissance function. This was a clear indication of the Admiralty's continuing desire to possess aircraft that could be operationally versatile, but it was a desire that would result in designs that proved to be partial or even total failures, with tragic consequences for many of their crews. Maximum speed rose to 152 mph, while range

Osprey Mk.III/S1699 is photographed with its tail mounted on a fixed plinth. The aircraft's attitude provides a good indication of how close the propeller blades are to the ground. This airframe along with S1700 and S1701 featured the use of stainless steel in its construction. Ospreys Mk.I to III were powered by the Kestrel IIMS engines, but the Mk.III's Fairey Reed metal propeller displaced the Watts wooden propellers applied to the other two Marks.

was quoted as 625-792 miles, with or without a bomb or torpedo load respectively. The endurance figure was established as being a fraction under five hours.

The Fairey Swordfish has already been mentioned in the section dealing with spotter-reconnaissance aircraft provided for the FAA. However, its true value to the Navy during the ever-looming World Conflict would be to operate so effectively in the first-stated element of the torpedo-spotter-reconnaissance role demanded of it. The private Fairey venture known as the TSR I featured a smaller overall outline compared to its TSR II successor, but was destroyed within months of its first flight in 1933. What evolved as the T.S.R. 2 'Swordfish' was successfully flown and tested during 1934, following which production commenced, culminating in the first deliveries to the Navy in early 1936. The all-fabric covered machine could mount a single 1,610 lb. torpedo while ranging 546 mph; the range factor almost doubled on reconnaissance sorties, but only with the assistance of a 236 Gall supplementary fuel tank located in the rear cockpit area.

The respective maximum and cruising speeds of 139 and 104-129 mph promised mortal problems for the three-man crew if faced by fighters or heavy AA fire. On the other hand the Swordfish's superb manoeuvrability would prove a valuable counter to the worst that enemy aerial or surface gunfire could throw in its path. The slow-speed flying performance was first-class, and added to the pilot's confidence particularly when taking-off and landing-on a carrier, including the escort carriers with their minimal deck dimensions compared to their 'Big Brother' Fleet examples!

(The ultimate irony in referring to the Swordfish's comprehensive operational use in World War II lies in the fact that it was an obsolescent design even in 1939, which was forced to soldier on until replaced in service. In addition, it outlived its intended direct replacement aircraft, the Fairey Albacore, and kept pace with its immeasurably more advanced torpedo-bomber contemporary, the Grumman Avenger during the latter course of World War II).

3.) Fighters

The role of the fighter within Navy circles was initially regarded as one of pure defence for its parent carrier and the warships in the immediate vicinity. The Fairey Flycatcher, along with the Nieuport Nightjar and Parnall Plover already in service, commenced this duty in 1923 and replaced both the afore-mentioned contemporaries within twelve months. Over the ensuing eight years the stocky but manoeuvrable aircraft comprised the entire Fleet fighter strength, both afloat and on shore across the length and breadth of the British Empire. It was also fitted with floats and used either in an amphibian role (with wheels mounted on the floats) or fired off catapults.

The fighter that began to displace the Flycatcher around 1932 came from the Hawker stable, and possessed much of the features of the Company's Fury ordered by the RAF. The Nimrod's all-metal structure and partial metal exterior was something of an advance from the Flycatcher's wood/metal construction although the Fairey aircraft also possessed a degree of metal external skinning. More important was the maximum speed increase up to 181 and 195 mph at 13,000 ft. for the Mks.I and II, compared to less than 120 mph at a similar altitude for the Flycatcher. The climb-rate was similarly boosted from around 1,000 ft. per minute (Flycatcher) to 1650 ft. per minute (Nimrod). On the other hand the Flycatcher's endurance was estimated at 1 hr. 50 min. compared to 1 hr. 40 min. for the Nimrod. Armament on both aircraft consisted of twin Vickers machine guns synchronised to fire through the propeller.

Coming into service at the same time as the Nimrod was the Osprey, a Navalised version of the RAF's Hawker Hart two-seat bomber. However, the Navy intended the Osprey to be utilised in a combined fighter-reconnaissance role. This was not surprising, since overall performance was similar to the Nimrod in terms of maximum speed and climb-rate, while it enjoyed a greater endurance of 2 hrs. 15 min.

Although the Royal Navy aviation planners could be accused of lagging behind their contemporaries in the RAF in terms of converting from biplane to monoplane designs, they did not totally ignore this vital factor for future operations. Specification O27/34 resulted in the Blackburn Skua entering service during 1938, while a four-gun turret version named the Roc turned up briefly in 1940 before mercifully being relegated from front-line operations.

The basic nail in the Skua's operational 'coffin' was contained in the Specification requirement itself, which called for a combined fighter and dive-bomber function. The whole essence of any fighter's function is to fly at the same or greater speed than its adversaries as well as manoeuvring well, both in attack and defence. Dive-bombing, by contrast, requires a sturdy airframe with particular emphasis on resisting the great stress placed on the airframe during recovery from a dive. The result was a hopeless compromise at least from the Skua's perceived use as a fighter, since the maximum speed was a pedestrian 225 mph – not greatly in advance of the Osprey, and a full 20 mph lower than the latest biplane design (the Sea Gladiator) that displaced the Nimrod fighter a matter of months following the Skua's service debut! Certainly, the Blackburn aircraft would provide a solid return for the FAA during the first three years of World War II – but not as a fighter. The 4 1/2-hour endurance and range of 760 miles provided a good base for operations as a dive-bomber or patrol aircraft, although the maximum bomb weight that could be carried under the central fuselage was only 500 lbs.

The Blackburn Roc fighter was even more of a farce. For a start its armament was totally contained in the Boulton-Paul turret behind the pilot, in addition to which its maximum speed was just 194 mph. The few Rocs that were embarked on FURIOUS during the Norwegian Campaign constituted the sole example of active service for the aircraft during World War II; withdrawal from front-line units swiftly occurred and training and target-towing activities took up the remainder of its military career. (The fact that the Roc is an mythical species of bird only adds an ironic footnote to the aircraft's blighted history!).

This Osprey Mk.IV airframe has exchanged its Rolls-Royce Kestrel V for a Hispano-Suiza unit. The aircraft toured Spain during 1935 with Spanish registration letters EA-KAJ that can just be discerned beneath the British registration fuselage detail.

Blackburn Sharks of No.820 Sqdn. are preparing to launch off COURAGEOUS while Blackburn Baffins are ranged further aft. This carrier and her sister-ship GLORIOUS could accommodate up to forty-eight aircraft. FAA and RAF personnel generally served as deck handlers up to 1937 when the FAA came under Royal Navy control once again.

A Blackburn Shark of No.810 Sqdn. displays its mainly aluminium doped airframe, with a black stripe running the length of the top fuselage. Diagonal color band is blue, denoting service between April and September 1937 on board COURAGEOUS. The large landing gear struts and wheels could comfortably absorb heavy deck landings.

Swordfish Mk.I from No.823 Sqdn. pass in review over the Royal Yacht VICTORIA AND ALBERT. The event was the 1937 Naval Review at Spithead that celebrated King George VI's Coronation. The yellow fuselage with black trim denotes service on board GLORIOUS. Black/white stripes on nearside aircraft fin indicate a Flight Leader. The crews are standing to attention but would not be much warmer when sitting down!

Finally, waiting in the wings during the initial period of World War II was the Fairey Fulmar, the subject of Specification O.8/38 and intended to serve as a Fleet Fighter. The term 'Fleet' certainly did not apply to the aircraft's speed factor following its entry into service during the latter half of 1940, but at least its slim-line monoplane layout and eight-gun battery presented the Fleet Air Arm carriers, other warships and convoyed merchantmen with a reasonable form of defensive cover against marauding Axis aircraft.

FAA Unit Structure

Between 1918 and 1923 the few Naval aircraft units still on hand bore RAF Squadron. Numbers. No.203 Sqdn. created in early 1920 operated first Sopwith Camels and then Nieuport Nightjars; No.205 Sqdn. simultaneously came into being with its Parnall Panthers acting in the Fleet Reconnaissance role while No.210 Sqdn. was allocated torpedo-training duties with its Sopwith Cuckoos, that in turn gave way to Blackburn Darts two years later. Finally, an element of No.205 Sqdn. separated and evolved into No.3 Sqdn. whose Westland Walruses served

as Fleet 'spotters'. The water-based section of the 'aerial' Navy was not ignored, with the School of Naval Co-operation at Calshot using Short S194s and then Fairey IIIDs.

This truncated Force was probably regarded as adequate at the time, since only FURIOUS and ARGUS along with two seaplane carriers were currently on hand for the entire Air Arm function at sea; operational Bases had been reduced to the same number – four – with Leuchars in Scotland and Gosport in England retained for land-based aircraft and Calshot and Lee-on-Solent used for seaplane operations.

The changeover from a Squadron structure to a smaller one, known as a Flight and each consisting of just six aircraft, occurred in 1923. The numerical sequence was based on multiples of 400; numbers 401 to 420 denoted Fleet Fighter Flights, Nos.421 to 440 Fleet Spotter Flights and Nos.441 to 460 Fleet Reconnaissance Flights and 460 onwards all Fleet Torpedo Flights. Although over sixty numbers were involved within this total allocation, no more than twenty-seven would be utilised between their introduction and the ensuing changeover to a new Squadron number system during 1933.

This time round, the numbers commenced at 800 to avoid confusion with the RAF. Nos.800 to 809 went to the fighter-equipped units, Nos.811 to 820 to torpedo-bomber units and 821 onwards to those operating in the spotter-reconnaissance role. Each unit complement figure was raised from six to between nine and twelve, which was a reflection of the number of carriers then on hand (six) as well as their general ability to accommodate at least two if not three or even four Sqdns. (The lowest figure was twenty, shared between ARGUS and HERMES while the two COURAGEOUS class carriers could take forty-eight aircraft).

Carrier Hangar Design

The original internal stowage of aircraft on the Navy's carriers faced a lateral limitation in hangar layout. This was caused by the existence of the 'uptake' ducts for the ship's engines that were positioned on either side of the outer hull sides as in the case of ARGUS and FURIOUS. The duct outlets were so located that the engine-smoke emissions were kept clear of the flight deck in order to cut down the risk of turbulence and poor visibility affecting take-off and landing operations.

The fitting of an 'island' structure on all Navy carriers from HERMES and EAGLE onwards allowed for an expanded lateral spread in the hangar layout of these warships along with the two COURAGEOUS Class vessels. The longitudinal strength member of the hull was the hangar deck in all four instances, while the flight deck served as a relatively lightweight aircraft platform, with little ability to absorb bomb damage. The Admiralty acknowledged this potentially fatal limitation before commissioning the first of the seven major carriers operating during World War II. ARK ROYAL's flight deck was not only the largest in length at 800 ft., but also formed the hull's principal strength member, beneath which two hangars were positioned; both were 60 ft. in width and 16 ft. high, with the upper hangar 116 ft. longer than the 452 ft. lower unit. The three lift wells formed a triangular layout extending on either side of the island, and were positioned off-center in order to maintain the flight deck's strength factor.

The ever-present risk of being attacked by land-based bombers when operating in confined waters such as the North Sea and Mediterranean – both preserves for centuries of the Royal Navy – directed attention towards a comprehensive

A group of officers are gathered around the fuselage and in the cockpit of a Swordfish Mk.I from No.821 Sqdn., whose blue/red/blue color band relates to service on board ARK ROYAL. An additional horizontal color band extends on either side of the 'Type A' roundel and probably denotes a Flight or Sqdn. CO's aircraft.

armour system for the new ILLUSTRIOUS Class of carrier, the first of which bore the Class title and was laid down in 1937. The hangar area (458 ft. by 62 ft. by 16 ft.) was provided with 4 1/2-inch sides and fore-and-aft bulkheads as well as a 3-inch roof integrated into the flight deck; the hangar floor was also armoured to a depth of 3-inches. A lesser-armoured layer of 1 1/2-inches was applied to the non-hangar ends of the flight deck and the hangar deck ends bore a 1-inch thickness of armour. The armour provision did not extend to the lift surfaces due to the inordinate weight factor that would have adversely affected their operation. (The ARK's steering compartment was also furnished with 3-inch armour protection).

The fourth carrier INDOMITABLE featured a double-hangar layout with the lower hangar extending for the last 168 ft. of the upper hangar length, and the latter's height reduced from 16 ft. to 14 ft. The resultant increase in aircraft capacity from thirty-six to forty-eight was balanced by the reduction in side armour thickness to 1 1/2 inches The value of all this armour provision was to pay off during World War II, with the three carriers so affected by bomb strikes all surviving the experience even if they were rendered out of commission for many months.

Fuel/Ordnance

The sizeable quantities of fuel and ordnance required to be housed in Royal Navy aircraft carriers posed a specific safety question – how to store the material in such a manner that both were readily accessible for use while also ensuring that the vessel's own security was maintained. The volatility of fuel tanks was arguably increased as their content was reduced through usage, thanks to the resultant accumulation of vapour that usually occurred within the increasing air pocket. Seawater has a heavier density than aviation fuel and was fed into the tanks to (hopefully) obviate the chance of vapour build-up as the fuel content was used up. A second safety measure was introduced by surrounding the tanks with seawater.

The parallel question of safe ordnance stowage was addressed by placing the magazines as far away as possible from the open area of the hangar. This measure was as good a safeguard against hits from bombs or torpedoes as could be achieved. However, in the event of a direct bomb strike or strikes onto or into the carrier's interior, there was little or nothing that could prevent either a critical or fatal degree of destruction should bombs and/or ammunition be set off when present either in the hangar or up on the flight deck

Flight Deck Handling of Aircraft

Although aircraft take-off and landing speeds progressed steadily upwards between the two World Wars, the absolute

This is a bow-on angle picture of EAGLE that provides an indication of her original battleship structure, including the pointed forward edge of the flight deck. The carrier's gross weight of 21,850 tons was virtually identical to the two COURAGEOUS Class carriers introduced several years after EAGLE. On the other hand she accommodated just half the forty-eight aircraft complement of her contemporaries.

necessity for some form of viable arresting apparatus with which to bring machines to a safe and intact halt only fully emerged as the 1930s were entered. The original longitudinal and converging layout of wires that were to be picked up by hooks attached to the aircraft's axles proved to be marginally efficient and was abandoned early on. In 1931-1932, experiments were carried out using three varying designs configured in a lateral as opposed to longitudinal manner. Only the third differed from the other two friction-based systems, in that the wires were controlled hydraulically and were self-correcting and in that the wire engaged by the aircraft's arrester-hook returned to its original position.

The benefit of this 'arrest' action applied not only to the aircraft so involved but also to aircraft already positioned further up the flight deck, in that the risk of a collision through a failed landing was at least minimised if not prevented altogether. Flexible safety barriers were generally on hand ahead of the final arrester wire in order to further prevent such accidents, but although largely effective, there were to be occasions where even this secondary measure did not succeed. Nevertheless the introduction of proper arrester equipment was a solid advance in ensuring safe and speeded-up flight deck procedures for flying operations.

A Swordfish Mk.I believed to be from No.811 Sqdn. is snapped just at the point of lifting off and crossing the forward flight deck of a Fleet carrier. The photographer's location and the existence of the homing beacon on the carrier's mast-top suggests he is standing on the lower flight deck of FURIOUS.

Swordfish K8395 was one of a number fitted out with floats. Aircraft is mounted on a wheeled attachment positioned in the center of its floats, and appears ready for take-off from its carrier's flight deck. The drag effect of the floats in flight must have furthered reduced the already modest maximum speed performance of the 'Stringbag'!

Two 'Stringbags' from No.813 Sqdn. are photographed from a third Swordfish. The unit was embarked on EAGLE at this time and bore the black diagonal band on the fuselage that identified the carrier. The Sqdn.'s aircraft were numbered from 580 to 590 and the black-finned aircraft denotes the example allocated to the Sqdn. CO.

No.813 Sqdn. changed its codes from a number sequence to E4 in July 1939. Aircraft H is being hoisted on the flight deck of EAGLE. The aluminium finish is still in use but the black diagonal band identifying the Sqdn. as being embarked on the carrier has been deleted.

The question of swift handling of aircraft both on launch and recovery was of prime importance. The absence of arrester wires as well as a flexible crash barrier to permit a safe 'deck park' for already-landed aircraft, affected recovery operations in particular, since the aircraft handlers had to get each aircraft safely onto the lift and out of the way to ensure the safe arrival of the following machine should its pilot make an extended landing. The resultant time-span between each pair of movements could extend up to several minutes even under sound weather conditions and efficient operation by the deck personnel, so that the rear element of a medium or large Force could be left dangerously short of fuel before their turn to land was on hand.

The need for the aircraft carrier to turn into wind meant that the warship, which was seen as a support element of any Fleet movement, was all too often detached from the formation should the wind direction be materially different from the latter's steaming course. A second danger followed on from these course deviations; this was the added vulnerability of the carrier, even with a destroyer escort, to either U-Boat attack or a similar assault from surface warships such as cruisers.

The FAA aircrew faced a primary hazard that was largely absent from landing approaches made onto airfields. The relatively narrow width of flight decks and the sometimes wayward motion of the carrier, particularly in heavy sea or swell conditions, allowed for little or no latitude should a landing aircraft be thrown off its final approach or skid on landing. With this in mind, retractable palisades were fitted along the after section of the flight deck.

Although it was naturally laid to the pilot to land his aircraft safely, the increasing speed of approach of designs entering service, particularly in the run-up to World War II, led to the introduction of the Deck Landing Control Officer (DLCO). Equipped with hand-held 'bats' and located on the port-after section of the flight deck, this individual's duty was to indicate to a pilot whether his line of approach was correct. This was achieved by extending his arms and lifting them up or down to indicate whether the aircraft's vertical attitude was too low or high, while angling both arms right or left to indicate the aircraft's horizontal attitude. (A 'left-hand down' action for example indicated that the pilot should lower the starboard wing. U.S. carrier DLCOs conversely acted as a mirror image of the approaching aircraft, an action that could be dangerous if not lethal for those FAA pilots landing 'away from home' as it were!). A too low approach speed was indicated by the bats being circled in towards the DLCO. A horizontally extended right arm confirmed that the pilot was making too fast an approach. Finally, crossed 'bats' in front of his body as the aircraft was about to over-fly the carrier's 'round-down' was the DLCO's signal for a (hopefully) sound touchdown; in the event of what was judged to end in a bad landing the DLCO would raise his right-hand 'bat' and make a vigorous circular motion as a sign to 'go around' – advice that was not always followed by the pilot in question!

The need for a form of 'booster' equipment to ensure the safe take-off of an aircraft, especially when the flight deck length was restricted – for example in the case of a partial or full launch of the carrier's aircraft complement – was ultimately

A Swordfish that is adapted to a floatplane configuration is running up its Pegasus engine and will soon advance down the slipway of the Naval shore Establishment of Portland on the English Channel, at which stage the wheel-mountings will be detached from the floats. The national markings prior to World War II were restricted to Type A fuselage and upper wing roundels.

The Supermarine Walrus was ordered in 1935 after two years of prototype trials and a total of 740 were constructed before production ceased in 1944. The aircraft was powered by a Bristol Pegasus rated at 775 hp and mounted in a distinctive 'pusher' manner between the wings.

Three Swordfish from No.810 Sqdn. are identified as currently embarked on COURAGEOUS by the diagonal fuselage bands whose color is blue. They are further identified as belonging to this unit, to whom the number range (523-537) was allocated between 1936 and September 1939. In that year No.810 Sqdn. was re-assigned to ARK ROYAL.

to be met by the fitting of catapults. This device had originally come into service with the U.S. Navy using compressed air as well as powder. The Royal Navy was well behind in utilising catapults and first introduced them on cruisers and battleships for these warships' 'spotter' aircraft. The ARK ROYAL was the first carrier to possess catapults from the very beginning; the two COURAGEOUS Class carriers then in service had also been provided with twin catapults during the course of re-fitting in the mid-1930s. However, the launch procedure was slower when applied to a sequence of aircraft launches, this being due to each aircraft having to be settled upon a 'cradle' frame that threw its load into the air when the forward end of the catapult channel was reached.

Return of the FAA to Naval Control

The full implementation of the Inskip Report's recommendation for a full transfer of control over Naval flying activities from the RAF to the Navy was only made a mere three to four months before the onset of World War II. The Admiralty took charge of sixteen front-line and eleven second-line Sqdns. as well as eleven catapult Sqdns. Five of the seven carriers were fully commissioned with the remaining pair reduced to training status. In support in Britain were five airfields in current operational use with four more either about to be assigned to the Fleet Air Arm or under construction.

The small size of the Fleet Air Arm in relation to its worldwide operational brief was a serious enough technical and strategic deficiency. However, even more serious at least in the short term, was the dearth of trained support personnel remaining within the Force's ranks. A good proportion of the RAF ground crew elected to remain in their Service, along with the pilot element provided by the Junior Service. The middle and senior ranking officer cadre did not possess too many individuals who had come up through the ranks of the FAA since 1918; the career prospects for those personnel who might have elected to remain with the Navy away back then were probably regarded as poor to nil. This contrasted with the potentially better promotion prospects within the newly created RAF. The lack of aviation personnel stationed at the Navy's school and weapons-training establishments between the Wars not only prevented any liaison structure between the Air Arm and the other Navy Branches, but also reinforced the sense of its isolation from, and reduction to a subsidiary element within, the mainstream of Naval operations. In essence, the Naval vessels would afford their own survival prospects through their defensive armament, with little or no support required from the aviation Department. The 'Battleship Brigade' mentality was still alive and well at Admiralty HQ!

CHAPTER THREE

The Lengthening Odds
1939-1940

'Phoney War – What Phoney War?'

Although World War II on land had erupted into violent action from the beginning with the German assault upon Poland, a virtual state of inertia took hold on the Western Front. Activity here was largely limited to patrol and counter-patrol sorties – although the French Army did make a wholesale incursion into enemy territory for a few days in September, before making an equally wholesale retreat back to their own front-lines! The ensuing eight months in the West witnessed a stalemate situation that earned for itself the title 'Sitzkrieg' in Germany, 'Drole de Guerre' in France and 'Phoney War' in America. The position in the Atlantic and North Sea provided a sharp and mortal contrast with the Land Campaign from the very start of the Conflict. U-boats had begun their deadly rain of destruction on Allied shipping right away, while several surface warships such as the GRAF SPEE, having sailed from Germany in late August 1939, were ranging the broad ocean expanses in search of suitable commercial prey.

The vast spread of the British Empire placed a constant strain on the nation's Armed Forces as War again enveloped Europe, and ultimately much of the Globe. The Royal Navy had retained the majority of its aircraft carriers in Home Waters, with only GLORIOUS and EAGLE currently 'on Station' in the Mediterranean and the Far East respectively. The Home Fleet was currently utilising the services of ARK ROYAL and COURAGEOUS, while HERMES was being re-commissioned following a refit. Of the two remaining carriers, FURIOUS was involved in training exercises in Scotland and ARGUS was reduced to 'reserve' status in Portsmouth.

The Royal Navy's initial attempt to combat the U-Boat threat included the use of the two available aircraft carriers as central pivots in anti-submarine 'hunting' Groups operating off the two main Atlantic Approaches to Britain. This scenario

was seriously flawed in two respects. First, the limitations of the 'Asdic' detection equipment meant that U-Boats were not even likely to be automatically picked up, let alone challenged and dispatched by the escort vessels. Secondly, the allocation of escorts to each carrier (four) was barely adequate to protect their charges from attack, especially when – in the case of COURAGEOUS at least – half this force was on 'stand-by' to go to the assistance of vessels in distress within the area covered!

Within a mere two weeks of hostilities commencing the vulnerability of these warships to counter-attack was harshly revealed. ARK ROYAL was near-missed by a torpedo fired by U-39 on 14 September, and three days later its fellow carrier incurred a mortal blow. COURAGEOUS was cruising off southwest Ireland, and was turning into wind to land-on her Swordfish; only two escorts were currently in position as the other pair had responded to SOS signals. Barely had the aircraft landed and the crew dispersed to the wardroom when two out of a salvo of torpedoes released by U-29 smashed into her port side. The combination of her forward motion coupled with the extensive damage to her hull induced a deadly spiral effect that saw her slip under the relatively smooth Atlantic surface. Over 500 sailors and airmen were drowned and all of Nos.811 and 822 Sqdn. Swordfish was lost. The seeming ability of a U-Boat to penetrate the combined screen of destroyer escorts and circling anti-submarine aircraft and deliver its attack unimpeded was probably the most pertinent reason for the Admiralty's immediate suspension of these Group patrols.

For one of the surviving pilots, Lt. Charles Lamb, today's experience was the first in a succession of similar incidents during World War II. There was an ironic twist to the naval aviator's survival on this occasion. Several hours before the carrier was struck Lamb's crew had taken off in response to an SOS call from a passenger liner under direct threat from a U-Boat. His square search completed, Lamb turned back for the expected rendezvous with COURAGEOUS, only to find an open expanse of Atlantic water instead! A square search pattern over the ensuing 1/2 hour had almost run its course and consumed most of the aircraft's remaining fuel when a distant humped shape was initially taken for a U-Boat. This was headed for in the hope of at least taking the submarine down with their Swordfish, still carrying its depth charges, but which was now faced with 'ditching'. Then, the 'U-Boat' materialised into COURAGEOUS and Lamb managed to turn his dive into a glide. Such was his apprehension at running out of fuel (the fuel gauge had been on the 'empty' mark for several minutes) that he ignored the batsman's frantic signals to 'abort' his landing attempt; the carrier was still turning into wind and Lamb's approach was therefore cross-wind, rendering the aircraft liable to hit the deck at a crab-wise angle. As it so happened, the Swordfish safely engaged a wire and halted properly. The subsequent sinking of the carrier provided Lamb with a far better prospect of survival compared to his and his crew's chances of being picked up from the 'ditching' that had loomed up only a short time before!

ARK ROYAL's good fortune in evading a torpedo attack on 14 September 1939 was to be but the first in a string of 'near-miss' incidents that would weave a legend-like pattern around the carrier over the ensuing two years of her operational

career, and leave 'Lord Haw-Haw' (William Joyce, the foremost Nazi propaganda broadcaster in World War II) continually raising the question; "Where is ARK ROYAL, Mr. Churchill?" The ARK was in the company of two battleships REPULSE and RENOWN, all three having sailed into the North Sea from Scapa Flow. On 26 September, the rendezvous with a Hudson from RAF Coastal Command occurred simultaneously with a number of 'bogeys' appearing at altitude. These took the form of He 111s of I./KG 26 '*Loewengeschwader*' along with four Ju 88s.

The latter-named bombers made dive-bombing runs on ARK, but prompt evasive action by the helmsman ensured what were SC500 explosive bombs missed. However, Adolf Francke, one of the pilots of what were Ju 88s of I./KG 30 '*Adlergeschwader*' reported that his bombs almost certainly struck home. A subsequent *Luftwaffe* reconnaissance effort picked out two warships that were in fact cruisers, but were mistakenly taken to be the two battleships; this misnomer naturally led to the conclusion that ARK ROYAL had in fact been sunk. In the event, it was just as well the carrier's deck had not been struck on her unarmored flight deck, while the concussive effect of near misses could have rendered a varying degree of damage to her hull.

Immediately preceding the bombing assault on ARK ROYAL, a Skua of No.803 Sqdn. had been one of a number scanning the zone around the Fleet for any German aircraft in

The Fairey Seafox came into FAA service during 1937 to perform a spotter-reconnaissance role, a duty it fulfilled until 1943. This example still bears the pre-war silver finish that would give way to full camouflage in 1939. One of its most notable actions was during the Battle of the River Plate in December 1939. The aircraft from No.718 Sqdn. based on the cruiser AJAX acted as a gunnery 'spotter' during the contest between the Royal Navy and the German 'pocket battleship' GRAF SPEE.

The silver finish on FAA aircraft swiftly disappeared under camouflage coating with the outbreak of hostilities in September 1939. This Seafox assigned to the Armed Merchant Cruiser ASTURIAS has been sprayed in Dark Slate Grey and Extra Dark Sea Grey on all top surfaces other than the lower wings, which bore a Light Sea Grey variation in place of Dark Slate Grey. The undersides were in Sky.

general and 'shadowers' in particular. The latter function was being performed by tandem-engine Do 18 flying boats, and it was one of these machines that had the misfortune to encounter the above-mentioned fighter flown by Lt. McEwen, who promptly attacked and shot it down. This was the very first *Luftwaffe* aircraft to fall to RAF or FAA opposition in World War II

The Skua's first successful combat action was in stark contrast to the design's operational debut on 14 September. Three aircraft from No.803 Sqdn. had answered the SOS call from a freighter under attack by U-30. When the formation reached the scene it was to find the Germans in the process of shelling their target. The U-Boat was dived upon and the bombs released with lethal effect – not for the submarine but for two of the Skuas! Both pilots had descended to minimum level before releasing their loads, whose explosive effect fatally damaged the control surfaces and forced each to seek a hasty and fortunately successful 'ditching'. The airmen managed to swim over to the freighter whose crew had already abandoned ship but their relief at gaining a deck under their feet was short-lived. It so happened that U-30 surfaced again and sent a boarding party onto their prey. In the course of the search, the FAA personnel were discovered and escorted back to U-30 for ultimate delivery to a POW camp. (This was the same day

ARK ROYAL had survived a torpedo attack but her airmen involved in this incident did not parallel their carrier's good fortune!).

South Atlantic Action

Between September and early December 1939, a steady string of Allied merchant shipping losses was recorded in the Atlantic. These losses were credited not to U-Boats but to surface raiders, which included the pocket battleships DEUTSCHLAND and GRAF SPEE. These were plying their trade in the northern and southern reaches of the Atlantic respectively. The latter-named warship had nine sinkings to its credit by the year-end and had evaded all the efforts of Force K that included ARK ROYAL to find her. However, the Royal Navy's bid to track her down finally bore fruit on 13 December off the Uruguayan coast.

The intercepting Force of three cruisers (EXETER, AJAX and ACHILLES) operating out of the Falkland Islands formed the intercepting Force. However, the mix of 8-in and 6-in guns carried by EXETER and the other warships respectively were badly out-gunned and out-ranged by the 11-inch weapons mounted on GRAF SPEE. The German guns fired a 661 lb. shell over twenty-two miles while even the 256 lb. shell fired by EXETER fell four miles short of this. Early strikes on

Pilots man their Blackburn Skuas at a Royal Naval Air Station (RNAS) early in World War II. The ground crew are turning the propeller blades in order to rid the engine cylinders of oil accumulation prior to start-up. A thirty lb. practice bomb is mounted under the port wing on the nearest aircraft. The Skua entered service in 1938 as the FAA's first monoplane design, and was operated both as a dive-bomber and fighter-reconnaissance aircraft up to 1941.

EXETER rendered her two Walrus 'spotters' out of action. AJAX managed to launch one of her two No.718 Sqdn. Seafoxes, and Lts. Lewin and Kearney set about their duty of 'spotting' for the cruisers' guns, while keeping an eye open for the Arado 196 adversary carried by the German warship.

In the course of the running battle extending over some ninety minutes, EXETER was effectively disabled as regards her entire firepower and retired from the scene. AJAX lost the use of all but one of her turrets, but kept the pressure on GRAF SPEE along with her sister light cruiser, despite the massive disparity in striking power and range. In the event, sufficient damage had been inflicted on GRAF SPEE to induce her Captain, Hans Langsdorff, to seek temporary refuge in Montevideo in order to repair his vessel.

Four days later, as AJAX, ACHILLES and the 'County' Class cruiser CUMBERLAND steamed off Montevideo in anticipation of the German warships' expected exit, Lt. Lewin was again launched and prepared for another 'spotting' operation. However, as he approached the GRAF SPEE's location, he was able to confirm that no further action was necessary, Capt. Langsdorff having 'scuttled' his ship; the flashes Lewin had taken for gunfire were in fact the 'scuttling' charges being activated. The Seafox's part in the action had undoubtedly been vital in accurately sustaining the assault upon what was a technically superior fighting vessel compared to its RN adversaries. In so doing, Lewin and his machine had fulfilled the task that the Admiralty has originally envisaged as the basic if not sole reason for introducing aircraft into its

Three Blackburn Rocs fly a 'Vee' formation sometime during 1939-1940. The rear mounted gun turret held four .303 machine-guns, and the fuselage 'spine' behind the turret retracted to allow the gunner to fully train his guns.

Fleets in the first place! (Ironically, GRAF SPEE's demise had occurred in the same South Atlantic region where in 1914 Admiral von Spee's warships had destroyed Admiral Craddock's Force at Coronel, before falling victim in turn to a second British Force led by Admiral Sturdee!).

Raiders – the Elusive Menace

There was a third strand to the *Kriegsmarine* initial Campaign against Allied merchant shipping, which was of a more insidious nature and accordingly more difficult to identify compared to the U-Boats and surface warships. Whereas the latter could be physically identified, the armed raiders converted from merchant hulls enjoyed an anonymous outline that allowed them to steal up upon their prey before raising the Nazi ensign and commencing what was all too often a one-sided action.

The Navy had deployed all but one of its available carrier force to cover the major trade routes, including ARK ROYAL, whose narrow escape from being torpedoed in the Western Approaches saw her sent into the south Atlantic along with the battleship RENOWN. HERMES plied the routes spread between the West Indies and later those off West Africa. GLORIOUS was operating in the Red Sea while EAGLE was dispatched further south to interdict the routes to and from the East Indies. As it happened the basic brief was to hunt down known surface warships or to trap any merchant vessels attempting to get to Germany through the British blockade. During the first seven months of World War II, just one vessel was intercepted and caught during November 1939 when Force K that included ARK ROYAL detained the UHRENFELS.

However, the first five out of seven of the heavily armed specialist vessels were on the high seas by mid-1940 and over the next two years would exact a painful toll in Allied shipping. Their main armament of between six and eight guns supported by torpedo tubes made them serious opponents for warships up to cruiser class, while the Royal Navy's Armed Merchant Cruisers (AMC), all converted liners, were hopelessly out-gunned and liable to become victims themselves in any encounter. Apart from encouraging all vessels to sail in convoy, the search went on for the various supply rendezvous locations that allowed the enemy craft to remain at sea for extended periods.

By late 1942, at least five of the nine vessels so configured had been destroyed in individual actions, but one of these – KORMORAN – exacted a very high price. On 19 November 1941 HMAS SYDNEY challenged her, but as the Navy warship steamed close by, the German raider dropped her Dutch 'disguise' and opened fire. Even though SYDNEY was certainly at 'action stations' the ensuing battle left her severely battered, in flames and fading across the horizon according to German survivors. Not one Australian sailor survived to tell the tale, although the damage to KORMORAN was such that she was later scuttled off the Australian coastline.

Norwegian Campaign

First Counter-Strike
The 'Phoney War' for the Allies came to an intermediate conclusion on 9 April 1940. This was the day that the Nazi

This is the first production Roc (L3057) out of 136 airframes delivered between February 1939 and August 1940 and photographed prior to being camouflaged. Note the vertical angle of the main landing gear when the aircraft is on the ground.

Another Roc is photographed after camouflage has been applied. Note the large ventral fin fairing fitted around the tail wheel. The entire vertical fin is taken up with the National marking, while the fuselage Type B roundel is surrounded by an enlarged yellow rim. The aircraft's serial number has either been over-sprayed or not yet applied.

Forces invaded Denmark and Norway. In the House of Commons, the Prime Minister was quoted as saying that 'Hitler has missed the Bus' in respect of his latest military venture. This somewhat clumsy and pedestrian observation was to be savagely thrown back in the face of Chamberlain and his Cabinet as the *Wehrmacht* swept onwards and consolidated its positions particularly within southern Norway.

The Royal Navy had just commenced a programme of mining the waters encroaching upon the Norwegian coastline by way of hindering the Nazis regular cargoes of Swedish iron ore shipped from Narvik. Now the effort of its available warships would address the question of how to thwart, if not turn back, the German assault. Already, at the very onset of the enemy assault and before any counter-action could be launched, the *Kriegsmarine* managed to escort *Wehrmacht* units in the soldiers' successful seaborne bid to secure the ports of Bergen, Trondheim and Narvik spread along the length of Norway's coastline. This 'sleight of hand' action by the Germans set the trend for what was to prove a continuous Allied failure to respond in time, particularly on land, so leaving its Forces to be 'second-guessed' throughout the entire Campaign.

The distance from airfields in northern Britain to Norway was too great for fighter support to be provided and so this primary duty fell to the Fleet Air Arm. However, just one aircraft carrier FURIOUS, was on hand in Home Waters at this critical time, and she was re-fitting in Scotland. In fact fully two weeks was to elapse before any form of fighter cover could be granted either the Royal Navy or the Allied Expeditionary Force. The carrying capacity of FURIOUS was now limited to eighteen since her re-armament in 1938 that had restricted flight operations to her upper main deck only. She therefore headed out to Norway with just two Swordfish-equipped Sqdns. Nos.816 and 818.

At least one sound strike was made by the Fleet Air Arm during this time. The FAA airfield at Hatston in the Orkney Islands lying north of Scotland contained the Skuas of Nos.800 and 803 Sqdns. They were normally embarked on ARK ROYAL, but she was currently berthed at Alexandria in Egypt. Sixteen crews took off on 10 April for an attack on enemy warships located in Bergen harbor. Although the target was at the aircrafts' maximum range, the lengthy flight was accomplished successfully by all but one of the formation. More importantly, three of the 500 lb. bombs struck the light cruiser KOENIGSBERG along her forward length, causing her to burst into flames, list to starboard and finally break in two following an internal explosion. This success was achieved at the cost of a single Skua and its crew.

The Swordfish from FURIOUS experienced a reverse degree of fortune next day when their torpedoes launched at destroyers in Trondheim 'grounded' due to the shallow depth; the reported presence there of the heavy cruiser HIPPER turned out to be false. Over the next two days, in appalling snow and sleet weather conditions, the Swordfish attacked shipping in Narvik and inflicted damage on several commercial or naval vessels. Aircraft serviceability was almost halved (eighteen down to ten) by 13 April. A notable sortie occurred this day when the battleship WARSPITE and nine destroyers entered Narvik fjord and decimated the destroyer Force moored there.

The stubby but purposeful outline of a Martlet Mk.I is seen as the pilot prepares to move out of the aircraft's dispersal. Aircraft is camouflaged dark green/earth brown on top with a 'Sky S' fuselage band. The port wing underside is sprayed black and the Type A roundel bears a thin yellow edge as a contrast. The initial batch of Martlets was originally intended for France but was diverted to Britain following the military collapse of that unfortunate nation.

The veteran battleship WARSPITE is in the process of deploying her assigned Walrus floatplane. The engine is running and the pilot is getting into position to detach the crane jib from the lifting cable. The lower wings support a greater than normal range of racks. Note the salt-water wear on the floats. Picture taken at Scapa Flow, the major RN Base in the North of Scotland.

This Skua was assigned to No.806 Sqdn. and bears the unit code/aircraft letter (L6:G) at the rear of the vertical fin. The camouflage demarcation line is located along the upper fuselage and Type B roundels replace the usual Type A pattern. The Sqdn. was formed in February 1940 and embarked on ILLUSTRIOUS up to the year-end.

To this scale of destruction was added U-64, struck and sunk by two bombs released by the Observation Swordfish floatplane belonging to WARSPITE and flown by P/O Rice.

Luftwaffe assaults on the Royal Navy contingent reaped some success in sunken or badly damaged warships, and on 18 April FURIOUS sustained serious damage to her port turbine blades, caused by two large bombs released from a He 111. The effect of these near misses was to throw the unit out of alignment and so force a maximum speed limitation of twenty-five knots. This reduction was not too critical however, especially when given the extremely modest take-off and landing performance of her current complement of Swordfish biplanes. More worrying for the airmen during the entire operational spell was the prospect of losing sight of their carrier, on return from a sortie and therefore running short of fuel, due to the onset of a blizzard. Conversely, the same unpredictable weather condition probably saved FURIOUS from the attentions of the *Luftwaffe* on these occasions, since the vessel could be tucked out of the bombers sight.

Reinforcements Arrive

The elderly carrier remained 'on station' for the ensuing eight days following the bomb damage incident when she was relieved by ARK ROYAL and GLORIOUS on the 24th. The situation in respect of FAA fighter cover was scarcely any better, however, since the Sea Gladiators of Nos.802 and 804 Sqdn., only eighteen of which were embarked on the latter vessel, basically provided this service. The eighteen Skuas of Nos.800 and 801. Sqdns. embarked on ARK ROYAL were supplemented by five of their turret-equipped contemporary,

the Blackburn Roc (Ironically bearing the name of an Eastern legendary species of bird!). Based on the Skua layout, the Roc featured a slightly broadened fuselage to accommodate a four-gun Boulton-Paul turret, but had no forward-firing weapons. Its maximum speed of just less than 200 mph was even more inhibiting than the 225 mph figure attainable by the Skua! Both were to function in a fighter role, but were only likely to be effective against aircraft of a similar or inferior performance, such as the Ju 52 transport, Ju 87 dive-bomber or the Arado 196 floatplane. None of the three-named FAA designs stood much chance up against the Bf 109 or Bf 110, and were even hard-pressed to combat the German twin-engine bombers. GLORIOUS also carried No.263 Sqdn.'s eighteen Gladiators, which were launched to operate off an iced-over lake at Lesjaskog south of Trondheim.

While the Sea Gladiators provided immediate air cover for the Navy warships, patrols over the Norwegian coast were flown by the Skuas in response to the Army's request for air cover against enemy bombing raids. Although the He 111s and Ju 88s encountered largely suffered minimal degrees of battle damage, several were not so fortunate. Capt. Partridge a Royal Marine pilot with No.800 Sqdn. did succeed in downing a He 111, although return fire disabled his Skua and forced him to crash-land. Setting fire to their aircraft the two airmen waded through deep snow to a small hut. Soon after settling down inside, they were joined by three other airmen – wearing *Luftwaffe* uniforms and survivors from Partridge's He 111 'kill'! The following morning a Norwegian patrol arrived and took the Germans away.

FURIOUS, with her deck cranes in the raised position and an absence of aircraft on deck, is beating her way through a strong running sea. The carrier was to see service in the North Atlantic and Mediterranean until late 1944. The raised angle of the forward flight deck is clearly depicted here.

Lt. Hay, also Royal Marines and flying a No.801 Sqdn. Roc, utilised his superior altitude to close on an unwary Ju 88. Sadly, when he attempted to slew his aircraft so that the turret could be deployed, all four .303 machine guns jammed, leaving a startled but thankful German crew to accelerate away. On a previous sortie involving Lt. Squires in a second Skua, Hay had followed Squires in to attack a He 111 from behind. All three aircraft dropped to sea level, and Squires, having completed his firing pass then made a fatal error. He pulled up, thereby exposing his aircraft's undersides to the enemy gunners, and an accurate burst of fire smashed into the Skua, which crashed into the sea killing both airmen. Hay, in contrast, kept sniping away at his target until it faltered and also impacted with the sea.

The two carriers' first spell of operational duty was conducted off central Norway in support of Allied Forces landed at Aandalsnes and Namsos, in what was a short-lived and vain attempt to recapture Trondheim positioned between these two towns, and so throw back the Wehrmacht's northern advance. Both remained 'on Station' for what was a mere period of days, due to the swift decision to evacuate the Allied troops by the end of April, and to concentrate on re-capturing and holding Narvik in the far north. In that time, while both carriers were 'standing off' anything up to 100 miles from the Norwegian mainland, the Skuas maintaining regular patrols over the coast as well as Aandalsnes and Namsos. In addition both the Skua and Swordfish Sqdns. carried out dive-bombing assaults on Vaernes airfield and Trondheim harbor in particular, while the Swordfish also made regular anti-submarine sorties.

The *Luftwaffe* presence was constant and menacing, with Bf 109s a particular hazard to the FAA aircraft and crews. Losses to this source totalled five on 25 April while an equal number of aircraft were lost in other circumstances. ARK ROYAL enjoyed even more fortune than FURIOUS had when bombed on 18 April. The ARK was near-missed by an SC250 that plummeted into the sea yards away from the fragile hull, but failed to detonate. Two days later, the carrier was homeward bound to Scapa Flow, having added another chapter to the saga of 'Lord Haw-Haw' the leading Nazi propaganda announcer and his constant jibe, "Where is ARK ROYAL, Mr. Churchill?" It was to be another eighteen months before the jibe would bear its sad fruit, when the carrier was sunk in the Mediterranean.

The decision to withdraw the Army troops attempting to take Trondheim was taken the same day (1 May) that GLORIOUS, having previously returned to Scapa Flow for replenishment, again took up her station off the region to provide a welcome measure of support for the hard-pressed aviators on ARK ROYAL. The *Luftwaffe* bombers, by now operating out of southern Norwegian airfields, were making regular attacks against the warships as well as the evacuation points around Aandalsnes and Namsos. Although the Sea Gladiators were flying constant air cover, it was usually the case that the twin-engine bombers could make their bombing runs and then clear away with relative impunity.

The Ju 87 Stuka was also on hand but the general bombing effort made by this precision dive-bombing design thankfully did not bear too much fruit, and one was shot down by the GLORIOUS Sea Gladiators on 1 May. On the other hand, the occasions when bombs impacted very close to the carriers did not do any good to their hulls. The Navy AA gunners did their utmost to increase the deterrent effect against the bombers but the risks to the Sea Gladiators or Skuas assigned to protect their warships inevitably rose as the fighters challenged the bombers. This proved to be the case even when signals from the aircraft indicated their 'friendly' status, as happened to

Sub-Lt. Brokensha of No.803 Sqdn. The 4.7-inch gunfire from the warships protecting the Namsos evacuation below still persisted, until the aircraft received fatal damage that forced its crew to bale out; both airmen were fortunate to be subsequently plucked out of the sea by a destroyer.

The presence of the first Type 79 and 279 Radar sets on several warships proved to be of basic benefit in providing the range, bearing and estimated altitude of approaching formations. The latter factor (height) however was the most indefinite, and confusion in determining the difference between the enemy bombers and the fighter Sqdns. sent to intercept was rampant, and probably created the grounds for 'friendly fire' incidents as recorded in Brokensha's case. An even more inhibiting factor militating against sound and timely radar warning was the mooring of the warships in the fjords, where the high landscape seriously restricted the signal quality emanating from the sets. .

Two tactical lessons leaned from the initial spells of duty off Norway affected the carrier group formations. They were steaming in too close a pattern and so increasing the chances of a hit or hits from aircraft releasing their bombs in a 'stick' sequence. There again each length of the 'zigzag' evasive action was reported by the airmen to be of too little value in unsettling the enemy bomb-aimers' sighting action. Both these situations could be corrected, unlike the final observation – that the warships provided perfect aiming-points on clear evenings when silhouetted against the setting sun! These various issues only further highlighted the point that the practicability of operating aircraft from carriers in close proximity to a quantitative and qualitative superior adversary

was already becoming evident at this initial stage of the Campaign.

Both GLORIOUS and ARK ROYAL, having re-armed and re-provisioned in Greenock and Scapa Flow, again returned to the fray during the course of May and into early June, but this time up off the Narvik region in support of the Allied Expeditionary Force. GLORIOUS arrived back on station on 18 May with the added duty of 'ferrying' the Hurricanes of No.46 Sqdn. who were due to fly off and land at Bardufoss. However, the airfield was not yet in commission for such modern aircraft and GLORIOUS steamed back to Scapa Flow on the 22nd along with ARK ROYAL and FURIOUS; the latter carrier made a similar 'ferrying' effort to fly-off No.263 Sqdn., also to Bardufoss – the second time this Gladiator-equipped unit was to operate out of Norway – and these lighter machines were more able to accommodate the still rough and ready nature of their new airfield.

GLORIOUS had also delivered six Walrus floatplanes to Harstad in the vicinity of Narvik. These lumbering aircraft belonging to No.701 Sqdn. were to be used for reconnaissance and communications sorties. The penultimate spell of Norwegian duty for GLORIOUS commenced within twenty-four hours of her arrival in Scapa Flow and this time round on the 26th. S/Ldr. 'Bing' Cross led his Hurricanes not to Bardufoss but to a more basic strip at Skaanland. (Barely two weeks later the surviving fighters and pilots of this unit were to be re-united with GLORIOUS in the most tragic manner.).

The re-capture of Narvik was accomplished on 28 May, but by then the overall Allied military situation not only in Norway, but further south in France was deteriorating rapidly.

This formation of fighters considered for FAA operations depicts the varying fortunes of the three designs involved. The Martlet on the right was to prove an effective operational performer up to the end of hostilities. The Fulmar was a useful 'stand-in' between 1939 and the introduction of more nimble fighters beginning with the Martlet and Sea Hurricane. The F2A Buffalo (Behind the Fulmar) proved to have an overall performance that was dangerously deficient compared to its Axis adversaries, and did not enter front-line service with the FAA.

Consequently, the decision had already been taken to evacuate Narvik, and with it, the last toehold in Norway, four days previous. In effect the town was only being secured in order to then destroy all its important iron ore and harbor facilities.

Loss of HMS GLORIOUS

As the fatally flawed Norwegian Campaign drew to a close, the Royal Navy units operating off the northern coastal region of that country were busy covering the evacuation of Narvik The Fleet Carriers ARK ROYAL and GLORIOUS completed what would be their final 'shuttle' to and from Britain on 1 June but only the former carrier continued to provide direct aerial cover along with the RAF Gladiators of No.263 Sqdn. and the Hurricanes of No.46 Sqdn. The small contingent of six Sea Gladiators along with the same number of Swordfish now on board GLORIOUS was deemed too marginal for the benefit of anything other than the carrier itself. Consequently, the vessel maintained a cruising status further out from the main Fleet's location. Towards the end of her spell of duty (6th), GLORIOUS was permitted to launch a Swordfish sortie against the HQ of *Gen.* Deitl, commanding the German Force

at Narvik, but bad weather conditions forced the crews to turn back

However, by 7 June the cruiser DEVONSHIRE and GLORIOUS were detached ahead of the remaining warships, proceeding independently back to Britain. The former-named warship's complement included the Norway's King Haakon and his Government, hence the reason for its dispatch. In the case of the aircraft carrier, Capt. D'Oyly-Hughes was given sanction to sail alone on the officially stated grounds, namely a shortage of engine fuel. However, a second reason reportedly quoted by D'Oyly-Hughes in support of early withdrawal was the need to prepare for court-martial proceedings against the two senior Commanders of his aircraft complement following arrival at Scapa Flow!

A post-War TV documentary about GLORIOUS raised this point among others. Comm. Heath, along with Lt. Comm. Slessor, had faced sustained criticism from D'Oyly-Hughes over many months. The former-named officer was currently under house arrest at Scapa Flow following a final disagreement with his Captain during GLORIOUS's penultimate spell of duty off Norway, but Slessor's services

A Walrus amphibian is photographed just as it is cast free of the catapult mounting. Known as the 'Shagbat' within the Fleet Air Arm, the Supermarine aircraft served the FAA throughout World War II, both in the reconnaissance and gun-spotting roles.

were retained during the final operational period. The programme also queried the fuel-shortage reason by making a calculation of the fuel already consumed during the carrier's current spell of operations off Norway; the result was a remaining fuel-state that was far from critical on 7 June. However, this is an assertion, not a proven fact, since all log records went down with the vessel.

The question of salvaging the surviving RAF fighters by flying them on board created no problems for the Gladiator biplanes. The higher-performance Hurricanes were a different matter, since their landing speed in particular was deemed much too fast for landing on a carrier, especially since no arrester gear was fitted. Reducing tire pressure and placing sand-weighted bags in the rear fuselages, the Hurricanes took off on 7 June and headed out for GLORIOUS in what was regarded as a 'do or die' effort. To everyone's astonishment, all ten of the RAF pilots carried out not only proper but also very comfortable landings. This singularly daring action apparently opened the Admiralty's eyes to the use of current and future monoplane fighter designs operating off carrier decks.

Above: A 'Wren' radio mechanic is carrying out an equipment test in the Observer's cockpit section of a Swordfish. The repeater dials on the port side monitor the aircraft's speed and altitude, while the mounting for the Type O-3 compass is directly above. The padding belongs to the top of the Telegraphist/ Air Gunner's (TAG's) seat.

Below: A group of pilots are gathered round the port-lower wing of a Gladiator while studying a map. The Gloster Gladiator had originally entered service with the RAF and the Sea Gladiator was the Naval version representing the FAA's frontline fighter up to the onset of World War II. This particular example is missing its sliding cockpit canopy.

The next morning, the RAF pilots were surprised, if not quietly perturbed, to note that all the FAA aircraft had been, or were being, 'struck down' into the hangars, while the ordnance was also being stowed away. One Swordfish and a Section of Sea Gladiators were at 'Readiness' but not 'ranged' on the flight deck. This total lack of aerial surveillance, when applied to the possible presence of the *Kriegsmarine*, was to reap a tragic reward on the afternoon of 8 June.

The battle cruisers SCHARNHORST and GNEISENAU had sailed from Germany several days before with the briefed intention of attacking the main British base at Harstad. However, Admiral Marschall was of the growing opinion that little of value would be encountered there, whereas the interdiction of the sea route between Norway and Britain would prove a much more fruitful source for targets, after air reconnaissance had indicated a regular westward flow of shipping traffic. His Force therefore took up a northwesterly course and was astride the route by the morning of 8 June. Several vessels had been intercepted and sunk before the battleships – by now bereft of their destroyer escort that had been detached to refuel in Trondheim – then made a tragically un-planned, interception with the RN carrier during the afternoon as they held a northerly course towards the Harstad region. The sharp eyes of a lookout on one of the capital ships noted the momentary burst of smoke issuing from the carrier's funnel far away on the southeastern horizon.

GLORIOUS was proceeding at seventeen knots, along with the destroyers ARDENT and ACASTA, both of whom were to be lost in gallant defensive efforts, although the latter landed a single torpedo strike on SCHARNHORST. Within a short period of opening fire with their main 11-inch armament, both warships had landed devastating punishment on the hapless carrier. One of the RAF pilots recalled the gallant but vain efforts of the crew to get their available aircraft up on deck and away, before the hangar deck was penetrated and set ablaze. (What the one 'Readiness' Swordfish could have achieved – even assuming that it was fitted with a torpedo – was very debatable, and could scarcely have materially altered the overall situation).

A sizeable proportion of the personnel survived the final demise of GLORIOUS, which only heightened the tragedy that spanned the ensuing three days. A wireless signal had been got away stating that 'two pocket Battleships were making an attack'. However, no RN rescue vessels ever subsequently appeared, and a scale of human attrition (similar to that suffered five years later by the survivors from USS INDIANAPOLIS, torpedoed after delivering the first Atom Bomb to Tinian) inevitably occurred with death from exposure to the frigid conditions ever existing within the Arctic Circle being a prime factor. Less than 4% of the Naval and RAF personnel, a figure that included two of the RAF pilots on board the carrier, survived to be picked up around 11 June either by a Norwegian commercial vessel or German seaplane; the loss of life on the two destroyer escorts was equally severe. (The first knowledge of the sinking came via a German broadcast on 9 June, but the exact location of the incident was claimed to be unknown and

The Grumman F4F fighter seen here was one of a batch originally ordered by France, but diverted to Britain following that Nation's defeat in June 1940. The aircraft still bears the French application of the national marking on its rudder rather than the British equivalent of placing this on the fin, which contrasts oddly with the British fuselage roundel. The latter is itself an adaptation of the Type A1 roundel introduced during the second half of 1940. The overall finish is a glossy blue.

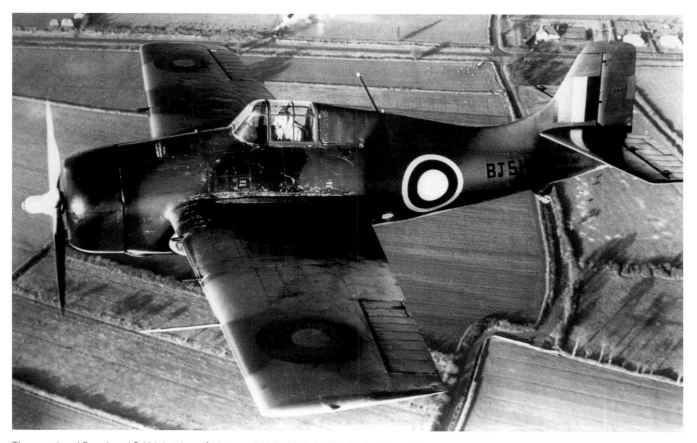

The re-assigned French and British batches of what was initially titled the Martlet (and later the Wildcat) in FAA service were operational by later 1940. This example bears a full camouflage pattern and Type A1 fuselage and fin markings. The Type B wing roundels are adapted Type As with the white center band over-sprayed.

the subsequent air/sea search patterns revealed no trace of the survivors, although several sailors did see aircraft over-fly their rafts.)

The Official Admiralty Files on the loss of GLORIOUS are stamped 'Not to be opened until 2041', a fact which immediately raises suspicions of a cover-up. The presence in the immediate area of DEVONSHIRE, which was under orders to maintain strict radio silence, and the stated receipt of the GLORIOUS transmission by sailors in her Radio Room, further adds to the 'cover-up' theory in some circles. Was the safety of King Haakon and his Government deemed essential, even at the cost of the crews of three Royal Navy warships, in that no attempt was made to go to the rescue? Worse still, was the apparent fact that no action was taken by the cruiser's Captain to pass on the signal details, however garbled these might have been, even although he broke radio silence on another matter next day (9th).

The Naval Historical Branch spokesman has asserted in the previously mentioned TV documentary that the signal from GLORIOUS was received in a garbled and therefore un-confirmed form. He also refutes the statements by several of

the surviving witnesses as to the signal's clear receipt on DEVONSHIRE. This, along with the 100 years restriction-rule, further fuels the speculation regarding some form of 'cover-up'. What is undeniable, is that a major RN warship, along with its equally valuable crew, had been lost in apparently questionable circumstances, at what was for the British Nation an already parlous period in her Naval and Military History. The incident also formed a tragic postscript to the entire ill-planned Allied counter-Campaign against the Nazi advance into Scandinavia.

Ebb Tide of Failure

Carrier activity off Norway during the Campaign was fated to culminate in a disaster for the Skua-equipped units on board ARK ROYAL. The torpedo damage to the battle cruiser SCHARNHORST on 8 June had forced a retreat back to the port of Trondheim. A joint assault on the warship was laid on for 13 June, with RAF Beauforts and Blenheims adding to the Skuas efforts. The crews of No.800 Sqdn. had participated in the successful attack on the cruiser KOENIGSBERG in Bergen harbour on 10 April. Now embarked on ARK ROYAL along

The ARK ROYAL was the Royal Navy's first custom-built modern carrier and provided valuable service in the Atlantic and Mediterranean for over two years until its loss in November 1941. This view of her flight deck shows it dotted with Swordfish. The carrier was unique in having three lifts, and the central one is seen in the lowered position. Also clearly defined are the two accelerators extending along the outer edges of the forward flight deck.

with No.803 Sqdn., they prepared for this latest sortie and duly took off, each aircraft carrying a 500 lb. bomb.

The *Luftwaffe* fighters, in stark contrast to the April sortie, were present in numbers and entrenched on airfields around Trondheim. Worse still, were the absence of cloud cover and a protracted approach of some 100 miles over the Norwegian mainland before reaching the target. (Why this latter feature of the sortie should have risen is unclear since Trondheim lies almost on the coastline). The absence of the RAF aircraft only added to the looming tragedy, as the Bf 109s and the flak guns challenged the fifteen Skuas pitching over into their dives. The likelihood of even damaging SCHARNHORST with its immeasurably heavier armour provision than KOENIGS-BERG, was questionable; in fact just one of the bombs struck home – but did not explode!

Eight of the Skuas were taken down in the course of the attack, a figure that included the Sqdn. COs, Capt. (Royal Marines) Partridge of No.800 and Cdr. Casson from No.803. Eight days later, the handful of Swordfish from Nos.821 and

823 Sqdns. dispatched from Hatston in the Orkney Islands lost two of their number in the course of challenging SCHARNHORST's passage further south to Kiel; their torpedoes would have inflicted serious damage had they struck home, but the crews' inevitable inexperience was a major factor in the lack of success.

In Home Waters

Although the Fleet Air Arm's primary effort in home waters up to June 1940 was directed from its carrier base, operations were also conducted from its Shore Bases. This was particularly the case from the inception of the Nazi Invasion of France, Belgium and Holland on 10 May. No.826 Sqdn. based at Ford on the south coast of England had been re-equipped with the new Fairey Albacore during March, and was fully operational when the German Campaign opened across the Channel. During May, its crews carried out the interdiction of road and rail communications as well as striking at German shipping. A switch during June to Bircham Newton a Coastal Command airfield in East Anglia, saw the Sqdn. placed under the Command's direction up to November.

During this period of detachment, the revised brief was to lay mines and continue bombing strikes against shipping off the enemy coastline between southern Denmark and northeast France. In addition a succession of East Coast convoys were granted cover. No.829 Sqdn. was converted to the Albacore in June at Lee-on-Solent, followed by No.828 (September at Ford) and No.827 Sqdn. (October at Yeovilton). The first-named unit then transferred to St. Eval and St. Merryn in southwest England from where operations were conducted against the key seaport of Brest among other targets, all under Coastal Command control. No.827 Sqdn. was similarly moved within the British Isles, this time to the Hebrides off western Scotland, from where anti-submarine sorties were flown.

Swordfish Sqdns. also shared the duties of mine laying and the bombing of French, Belgium and Dutch seaports in the eastern stretch of the Channel, once the Germans had occupied these. No.812 Sqdn. led the way in this ever-hazardous activity, even when flown at night, and continued on until March 1941. No.825 Sqdn. was based at Detling in Kent from the same May 1940 period. Both units were transferred to Coastal Command control during this time. No.825 Sqdn. shared its Detling airfield with the Skuas of No.801 Sdqn during the Dunkirk Evacuation. The Skua crews carried out their aircrafts' design requirements of dive-bomber and fighter to the best of their ability, but suffered a number of casualties, as did the equally vulnerable Swordfish personnel.

The Battle of Britain

The need for an adequate pool of fighter pilots with which to challenge the *Luftwaffe* during the cataclysmic summer of 1940 was to prove a major problem for the RAF, compared to the availability of actual numbers of fighters. Even as the final evacuation from Dunkirk was just completed, the Fleet Air Arm was being combed for volunteers that took the form of airmen still under training. Thirty-eight Naval personnel were involved, and this figure was supplemented in late June by a further thirty: the latter cadre was later reduced in July by ten, whose service in the Mediterranean was deemed to be of greater priority.

The transition for those pilots already in operational service from the current crop of FAA aircraft to the Spitfire or Hurricane must have been noticeable. It is also likely that the survivors of the Battle must have recalled their time flying alongside the RAF with some regret. This would have particularly applied in the case of those pilots being re-assigned to fly the Skua or even the Fulmar, both of whose overall performance lagged way behind both RAF fighters!

Several names stand out among the FAA contingent assigned to RAF Fighter Command. Three of these were destined to operate with the controversial 'Duxford Wing' whose charismatic Commander was S/Ldr. Douglas Bader. Sub-Lt. 'Dickie' Cork joined Bader's No.242 Sqdn. along with Sub-Lt Gardner and Midshipman Paterson, while Sub-Lt. 'Admiral' Blake was posted to No.19 Sqdn. based nearby at Fowlmere. Cork was regular Royal Navy, while Gardner and Blake were Royal Naval Volunteer Reserve (RNVR) officers, but all three had recently passed out of No.7 Operational Training Unit (OTU), Hawarden. Paterson's operational career was short-lived as he was killed during a convoy patrol, but two of his three more fortunate companions went on to achieve 'ace' status.

Cork in particular found himself flying in Bader's Section and opened his account on 30 August with credit granted for a Bf 110 'kill' as well as a He 111 'damaged' when a *Luftwaffe* thrust at North weald was turned back. During the first full daylight raid on London (7 September) he shared another Bf 110 with Bader. Cork provided a good account of the Wing's involvement in the 15 September action, forever commemorated as 'Battle of Britain Day'. The morning incursion was met by an increasing number of RAF units, and culminated over London in the appearance of the five Sqdns. within the Duxford Wing.

Cork recalled how Bf 109s 'jumped' his unit. While taking avoiding action, he ran across a Do 17, which he engaged and ultimately claimed as shot down. By the official conclusion of the Battle on 31 October he was credited with four full and two shared 'kills' This remarkable airman would continue to make his mark upon the enemy over the next two years, but this time in his natural Naval environment. He gained the award of the Distinguished Flying Cross (an RAF medal) for his service during the Battle of Britain – this was later replaced by the Royal Navy's Distinguished Service Cross, at the insistence of the Admiralty!

Gardner and Blake also achieved 'ace' status during the Battle. Gardner opened his account with a He 111 during July, which he downed in the course of a prolonged tail chase out over the North Sea. Bombers appeared to be his favourite option as he had four 'kills' with a fifth shared as well as a 'probable. Blake's final tally was four 'kills' and one shared but while acting as a Sqdn. 'weaver' on 29 October he was picked off and killed by Bf 109s. Blake's sad fate was to be shared by seventeen of the Naval volunteers, among whose number was another 'ace'. He was Sub-Lt. Dawson-Paul flying with No.64 Sqdn. He ran up a total of seven full 'kills' during July, but the final example on the 25th ended in his own loss to a Bf 109. He was picked up by a German vessel in the Channel but expired several days later.

The Wildcat – A Technological 'Breath of Spring'

Prior to 1940 the Admiralty had sought out British aviation Companies for its aircraft, with Blackburn and Fairey well to the forefront. The results to date had been no more than adequate but the first chink of light in transforming the FAA from a Force fighting on the technological back-foot to one matching if not exceeding its adversaries' capabilities was about to emerge as 1940 was in its latter stages. The Grumman Company had received a contract in 1939 to construct a fighter design that became known as the Wildcat. Further orders had been solicited from France and Britain and the resultant export quotas for 81 and 100 airframes respectively bore the designations G-36A and G-36B. The French aircraft were fitted with the Twin Wasp R-1280-G205A engine and the British version with the Pratt and Whitney S34-G; both were fitted with fixed wings. The collapse of France prior to the G-36B's delivery resulted in the entire batch being diverted to Britain, where the name Martlet was bestowed upon these Mk. I machines.

The stubby monoplane with its mid-wing location and two-speed, two-stage engine supercharger was a revelation in terms of its maximum speed, climb-rate and range compared to what was currently on hand in FAA service; the 'Gladiator' biplanes and 'Roc' monoplane fighters were markedly inferior in all these performance aspects while even the 'Fulmar', though a sound enough design, was not as good as this new American machine.

Another advanced and welcome feature introduced by the Martlet lay with the launching procedure, in that it could be dispatched off the deck without having recourse to the collapsible 'cradle' that perforce had to be used for current British designs. Instead, a hook under the forward fuselage provided the attaching point for a wire strop, whose other end was linked to a shuttle placed in the catapult slot. Now not only could a faster rate of launch be achieved but also the tail-down attitude at take-off provided maximum lift compared to the tail-up position when aircraft were dispatched using the 'cradle'.

There were some problems experienced by the pilots of No.804 Sqdn, which was the first unit to convert onto the Martlet closely followed by No.802 Sqdn. The landing gear retracted into the fuselage and therefore provided a narrow

The rain-swept and treeless geography of the Orkney Islands off northern Scotland form a cheerless background for these two sailors who are completing the loading of a torpedo under a Swordfish Mk.I. The presence of just the pilot and metal 'X' shape on the weapon's nose indicates this is just a practice sortie. The Swordfish's Fairey-Reed metal propeller did not provide a variable pitch function.

wheelbase that could result in the wing tips striking the ground in the worst instances of rough ground handling or high sea winds when the fighter was parked out on deck. A lack of auto-boost left the pilot with no option but to physically adjust the boost lever throughout a flight's duration. Carbon monoxide seepage was experienced and a violent draught struck the cockpit area when the canopy was opened in flight.

Visibility over the engine cowling was also not too good while the 'blanking out' effect on the rudder during take-off and landing kept the pilots on their toes – or rather their rudder pedals! (This latter problem on the Mk. I was eased on subsequent variants through replacing the miniscule 'solid' tail wheel and support with an extended support and larger inflatable tire; the basic effect was to lift the aircraft into a more horizontal angle of attack on take off and simultaneously bring more of the rudder surface into play).

There seems to be a contradiction with the choice of what was a high performance monoplane fighter by the Admiralty, or rather the date at which the decision was made. In the past, authors have inferred that it was only the 'ad hoc' landing of the RAF Hurricanes on GLORIOUS in June 1940 that persuaded the Royal Navy Chiefs that such aircraft designs could be safely operated from their carriers. If this is true, then the order for the Martlet should logically only have occurred subsequent to this time. However, it appears that the original order was placed before the GLORIOUS incident occurred! (At the very least the decision to accept the French batch for FAA service must have been made extremely quickly, since France capitulated a mere two weeks following the sinking of GLORIOUS on 8 June).

CHAPTER FOUR

Battle of the Atlantic 1940-1942

False Tactical 'Dawn'

"If Blood be the price of Admiralty, Lord God, we have paid in full." These two lines are the culmination of a short poem that addresses Britain's centuries-old dependence upon the oceans for its continued economic existence. It is a basic fact that the principal threat to Britain's very survival during both major Conflicts of the 20th Century, particularly between 1939-1945, did not come from the air but from the sea – or rather from under the sea – in the shape of the *Kriegsmarine*'s formidable U-Boat Fleet. It was Churchill's heart-felt assertion that what evolved as the 'Battle of the Atlantic' was the single-most Campaign that gave him the most anxious moments and most sleepless nights during his five year Wartime Premiership. He was right to address his concerns in this specific direction; the free and un-fettered passage of trade vessels bringing their vital loads across from the New World (and by extension along the sea routes linking Britain with its Empire sources of supply) was absolutely critical to the Nation's ability to sustain the fight against the Axis Powers, let alone see its ultimate successful conclusion.

By 1939, the Royal Navy's concentration on combating the U-Boat menace was centered on a sonar device originally examined and recommended by the Anti-Submarine Detection and Investigation Committee and bearing its initials ASDIC. The bright prospects for blunting submarine assaults by the wholesale use of this detection equipment was all too soon found to be regularly compromised in practice. The varying water density and temperature of the sea depths tended to refract the sonar signal; even when the signal did strike home directly on an underwater object, the 'return' could not differentiate between the metal surface of a submarine and other objects of a similar scale-size, such as a whale. Worse still, was the total inability to detect a submarine running on

the surface; this method of attack-approach and evasion was to be used with lethal effect during the first 1940-1941 'Happy Time' for the U-Boat crews, with an emphasis on nocturnal attacks delivered against the convoys.

The Dark Abyss

The 'Battle of the Atlantic' covered the entire span of World War II, but the numbers of U-Boats on hand to open the Campaign were relatively small; even so, a steady number of merchantmen, regardless of whether or not they were part of a convoy, were culled from the Allied ranks between September 1939 and the following spring. Just six Type VII, six Type VIIB and five Type IX vessels were on operational hand in the Atlantic, along with 17 Type VII and one Type VIIB in the North Sea. The Type VIIB possessed 108 tons of fuel against sixty-seven tons for the Type VII, and carried three more torpedoes than the eleven borne by the Type VII; it also was equipped with a stern torpedo tube. The Type IX by contrast had 4,000 hp diesels against 2320 and 2800 for the other two respective Types, while its top speed was 18.2 knots on the surface (compared to 16 and 17.2 knots). Total fuel capacity was greatly extended at 154 tons as was the offensive capacity at twenty-two torpedoes. Losses between September 1939 and April 1940 totalled thirteen in the Atlantic and four in the North Sea.

Up to June 1940, the avenues of approach to the Atlantic were somewhat restricted for the *Kriegsmarine* U-Boats, since the crews were forced to sail out across the North Sea and skirt to the north of the British Isles before coming within range of their targets. This limitation also adversely affected the length of full operational time 'on station'. The unexpected fall and subsequent occupation of France in June 1940 drastically altered the tactical and strategic picture at sea in

SPRINGBANK was one of four merchantmen commissioned into the Royal Navy. Known as Fighter Catapult Ships (FCS), each embarked up to three Fulmar fighters provided by No.804 Sqdn. The aircraft were intended to drive off or shoot down Fw 200 *Kondor* 'shadowers' that sought out convoys and guided U-Boats into their path. Since shipboard recovery was impossible the pilots had the option of baling out over the convoy or heading for the nearest available friendly airfield.

the Germans' favour. The development of the Naval Bases at Brest, St. Nazaire and Lorient on France's Biscay coastline formed the main launching ramp for U-Boat operations. The crews could now sail out into the broad sweep of the Atlantic with almost total immunity from British sea-borne or airborne counter-measures. In addition, this direct and shortened route compared to the pre-June equivalent bestowed a reverse increase in time spent 'on Station'.

Deployment of the *Luftwaffe* in the form of the Fw 200 *Kondor* further added to Britain's problems. These four-engine 'militarised' variants of Kurt Tank's civil airliner soon began to take a regular toll of shipping. The loads of 250 kg. bombs with which these aerial buccaneers were supplied were responsible for sinking nearly one hundred merchant vessels totalling 363,000 tons between August 1940 and February 1941. The basic lack of AA weaponry permitted a low-level approach to be made, from which altitudes the prospect for hitting their targets were greatly increased.

From the beginning of 1941 they were also used to monitor the course of any convoys they came across, by circling and sending out position radio signals onto which the U-Boats could 'home'. Finally, the aircrafts' range was such that direct flights between their main airfield at Bordeaux-Merignac in southwest France and southern Norway became the norm for the crews. This meant that when used in a direct assault role, the *Kondors* could easily remain out of range of fighter attack from units operating out of Britain's airfields.

At this parlous stage in World War II, convoy air cover was initially the sole province of RAF Coastal Command. The twin-engine Lockheed Hudson could provide short-range protection, while the four-engine Sunderland flying boat was

capable of ranging out towards the middle of the North Atlantic Aircraft based in Canada provided escort cover for a similar range to that of the Command's twin-engine types, with the Hudson among those in the forefront. This grave distance factor left an aerial 'black hole' in the central Atlantic, that provided the U-Boats with ample opportunity to dictate the pace and scale of their assaults against the convoys. Royal Navy escort strength had been seriously depleted in particular during the Evacuation of Dunkirk, but even had this not occurred, their numbers would still have been below par for the task at hand in the Atlantic. The new Classes of escorts in the form of corvettes and frigates were coming 'on stream' but a full two years was to elapse before a basic sufficiency in seaborne protection would arise for the hapless merchant vessels and their civilian crews.

The initial period of the reinforced U-Boat Campaign became known as the 'Happy Time' for the Germans. The odds were all in their favour, given the numerical and technical poverty existing among their adversary's ranks. A typical example occurred during the passage of Convoy SC7 heading for Britain in mid-October 1940. The initial contact by one U-Boat took out two of the thirty-four merchantmen – a portent of things to come the following night By then, five more U-Boats, including one captained by Otto Kretschmer, had closed on the convoy and a further eighteen vessels were sunk, with the three escorts on hand being able to do little or nothing against the slaughter.

In the case of Kretschmer, the British ASDIC system was rendered totally useless; the German penetrated the convoy ranks, having trimmed his U-Boat with the superstructure just protruding above the surface, and was accordingly immune

A Hawker Hurricane is pictured positioned on the bow-mounted ramp of a Catapult Armed Merchantman (CAM)-Ship. The Hurricanes forming the Force of fighters assigned this particularly hazardous role belonged to the Merchant Navy Fighter Unit (MSFU) and were flown by RAF pilots.

A Hawker Hurricane is being fired off the bows of a Catapult Armed Merchantman (CAM)-Ship. The absence of regular carrier support between 1940 and late 1942 on the Atlantic convoy routes resulted in this second counter-measure that was intended to combat the Fw 200 'shadowing' aircraft or any other *Luftwaffe* attackers. Thirty-five Cam-Ships were introduced between May 1941 and the last operation conducted by one of these vessels occurred in July 1943.

from all detection, while he went about his individual task of culling no less than seven vessels from SC7. The other four U-Boats had adopted a similar action around the convoy fringes and became equally elusive shadows for the ASDIC operators. (The action had taken place within flying range of Britain, but just one 'contact' was made by a Sunderland, which damaged but failed to sink the U-Boat involved).

The mounting merchant shipping losses between July 1940 and the year-end were of a scale that could easily have resulted in Britain's inability to continue the Battle against Nazi Germany had the situation not been at least stemmed. A temporary lull in the first month of 1941 thanks to the onset of the Atlantic winter weather was soon over-taken by the resumption of loss-scales that totalled in excess of 1 3/4 million tons by the high summer. A marginal balancing of the odds occurred in March when no less than three leading U-Boat Aces – Kretschmer, Schepke and Prien – were lost in the course of a single convoy action.

However, the supply of fifty World War I U.S. Navy destroyers to the Royal Navy, and the first Air-to-Surface Vessel (ASV) radar sets mounted in Coastal Command aircraft as well as escort vessels, coupled to the fact that German U-Boat production was not as high as might have been anticipated, were factors that began to swing the Battle momentarily in Britain's favour as 1941 progressed towards its conclusion. In addition, by mid-1941 the United States began to patrol the convoy routes not only from its own shores but also from Iceland following the establishment of bases there, supplementing the British Forces already in place.

Air-to-Surface Vessel (ASV)

The advent of ASV radar equipment was of vital importance to the tracking down and destruction of U-Boats. The first Mk.I sets mounted in Hudsons provided the minimum of benefit however; the screen presentation was steadily swamped by what was known as 'surface clutter' from the sea, culminating in no vessel 'contact' at all when still over three miles from a potential target flying at 3,000 ft. and over four miles when down to 200 ft.! At least the equipment was useful for 'homing in' upon the convoy assigned for escort cover by the aircraft.

ASV Mk.II by contrast, held the advantage over its predecessor in that its range capability was enhanced even though the 'clutter' limitation was not materially dispersed, and indeed would affect all variants. The new equipment entailed two sets of external aerials, one aligned along the top fuselage for forward scanning and a second placed on both fuselage sides to provide the equivalent lateral cover. Now, vessels including submarines could be picked out between twelve and twenty miles depending on whether they were head-

on or side-on respectively when flying at 2,000 ft.; the 'clutter' factor took full effect at five miles however. In addition the fixed nature of the aerials dictated that the detection process involved use of one or other of the aerials sets, but not both simultaneously.

The basic problem with both ASV systems was the inability of the available set valves to generate sufficient power and therefore frequency above 200 megacycles with which to produce the necessary fine radiation beam. The benefits of ever-higher frequency would (hopefully) not only reduce the size of, if not totally dispense with, the drag-inducing external aerials but could result in an internally-mounted rotating aerial with which to maintain all-round 'scanning' cover.

This hope materialised during 1940 when two scientists Randall and Boot brought out a high-power 'magnetron' oscillator generating 500 watts at 3,000 megacycles. The resultant wavelength of ten centimetres was a quantum leap compared to the 1.5 meter wavelength available from the ASV Mk.I and II sets. And so the 'centimetric' radar system had been created, albeit with disappointing results for Coastal Command in the interim period up to late 1942. Instead, priority was granted to the creation of Airborne Interception (AI) equipment for RAF night fighters as the 'Blitz' of 1940-1941 intensified, while Bomber Command was later granted a similar priority for the introduction of its 'H2S' Plan-Position Indicator sets over the ASV requirements of its sister-Command.

First Counter-Measures

The involvement of the Fleet Air Arm in the Battle did not basically occur until mid-1941, and then only involved a minimal scale of activity. The Navy's Carrier Force was stretched very thin during 1941, and was deployed across several Theaters of Operations, including the Mediterranean Sea and Indian Ocean. ILLUSTRIOUS was knocked out of action in January and FORMIDABLE the following May. The newly-commissioned VICTORIOUS was retained on Home Fleet service and EAGLE along with ARK ROYAL opposed the Axis Air Forces in the Mediterranean. Finally, HERMES, was plying her 'trade' around the East African coast.

The absence of carrier-borne aircraft with which to combat the U-Boats and their KG 40 supporting aircraft in the Atlantic led the British authorities to look for any means, however, limited, to strike back. The specific menace of the Fw 200 bombers was addressed first, since their value in sinking vessels or maintaining contact with convoys onto which the U-Boats could be 'homed' was of great benefit to the Germans. The equally pressing issue of Fleet Air Arm provision for direct convoy protection against the U-Boats would have to wait until the advent of the escort carrier in late 1942.

Fighter Catapult Ships

Two schemes were set up during 1941, each of which involved the catapulting of aircraft. The first of these involved five ships, four of which were merchantmen commissioned into the Navy; the fifth was PEGASUS, which was a re-named ARK ROYAL, the World War I seaplane tender. No.804 Sqdn. had languished in the Orkneys since its brief operational spell in mid-1940, in the course of which the unit converted from Skuas to Grumman Martlet fighters The Martlets were now surrendered for a mix of Fulmars and Sea Hurricanes as the pilots trained-up on catapult techniques in southern England.

By May, aircraft and crews had been embarked on the four surviving vessels – PATIA had been sunk before coming into service – and were ready for action. MICHAEL E took a pair of Sea Hurricanes to sea but was sunk four days out on 31 May, having achieved a single 'action' launch. Her contemporaries ARIGUANI, MAPLIN and SPRINGBANK, all of which were designated Fighter Catapult Ships (FCS), followed suit and joined the Battle within weeks. (SPRINGBANK's catapult was a discarded cordite-operated unit from the cruiser KENT and was mounted transversely behind the funnel. The other vessels featured catapult units mounted along the forecastle length and using rocket-power for launching).

The bow location for all of the FCS vessels other than SPRINGBANK left each fighter fully exposed to the corrosive effects of salt water even when sailing in calm weather (a none

too prevalent experience in the Atlantic at any stage of the year). Added to the problems of maintaining the machines in even basic mechanical order was the physical danger to the mechanics as they clambered up onto the catapult frame and attempted to carry out work on the gun bays or surrounding areas of the wings; it was all too easy to slip as a result of the vessel's unpredictable motions, while the handling of larger parts such as wing and fuselage panels could and did result in their loss due to the wind tearing them loose from the mechanics stiff (and probably also frozen) hands.

The obvious operational flying limitations were twofold. First, its 'parent' ship could not recover each aircraft. Second, the pilot – or crew in the Fulmars' case – was faced with baling out unless the action occurred close enough to Allied airfields. In fact, the number of 'action' launches was just ten between June 1941 and May 1942 when MAPLIN was the last of the merchantmen contingent to be withdrawn from FCS service. In this time SPRINGBANK was sunk during September, but the scale of action, although small, had resulted in all ten enemy aircraft being driven off, with two of the Fw 200s destroyed.

The vessel and pilot concerned on both successful occasions was MAPLIN, whose Sea Hurricane flown by Lt. (A) Everett, RNVR (A winner of the Grand National Steeplechase in 1929) was launched on 18 July and 3 August. The July sortie saw Everett failing to intercept his target before one of the bombs struck home; almost immediately, a major portion of one wing was torn off the enemy aircraft by gunfire

A Fulmar Mk.II has been positioned on a catapult unit and, although not under power, appears ready for launch according to the raised flag yielded by one of the two men standing at the top left of the picture. Picture was taken no earlier than mid-1942, judging by the revised CI National markings on fuselage and vertical fin that were introduced at this period of World War II.

directed not from the Hurricane but from the ship's gunners! The convoy was close enough to the mainland for Everett to navigate his way there. The second *Kondor* loss was credited to Everett in circumstances that were unlucky for the *Luftwaffe* airmen. MAPLIN was approaching her rendezvous with a convoy when the *Kondor* was spotted and engaged. A protracted tail-chase ensued, which ended in the *Kondor* being dispatched in flames, and Everett returned to his ship, near which he safely 'ditched' instead of baling out.

Merchant Navy Fighter Unit

The parallel 'emergency' defensive measure was also catapult-based but involved the RAF. A 'pool' of Hurricanes was created in May 1941, whose pilots operated off the ramps placed on the bows of thirty-four selected merchantmen. The Merchant Ship Fighter Unit (MSFU) began to take over the FCS role during 1941, and continued on until well into 1943.

The art of catapult launching of any style was not a normal part of an RAF pilot's training, nor after the return of the Fleet Air Arm to the Navy in 1939 was service at sea part of his training brief. The Hurricanes Mk.I assigned to the MSFU were fitted with catapult spools and had their fuselages strengthened to absorb the increased stress occurring during the firing-off process. Training in the launch technique was made on an airfield-based seventy feet ramp involving an average of three launches. Then further flights were made from the airfield runway in order for the pilot and the Fighter Direction Officer (FDO) to operate together; the latter individual would use either visual or radar means of guidance. This duo were finally linked up with a second pilot (also trained-up with the FDO) as well as three RAF and one RN mechanic to form a team for operational assignment.

The launching procedure from the portside and bow-mounted ramp was preceded by the CAM-ship hoisting a signal Flag to indicate her intention following this request from the FDO to the ship's Master. The Catapult Directing Officer (CDO) would ensure the free running of both the aircraft and the trolley on which it was mounted by confirming the stowage of the front spool holding-back clamps, trolley securing bar, front locking bolt keep back pins and the tail securing bar, after these had all been detached. By then the pilot was in the cockpit with the engine switched on and revved up to full power.

Communication between the CDO and the Master to indicate all was ready was made by using hand-held flags, since the noise-factor was too great for voice communication to be used. The pilot reacted to the CDO's vigorously waved flag indicating he was ready to operate the rocket-firing switch by opening and locking his throttle, then raising one hand and lowered it sharply when he was braced for the take off. The

The centuries-old tradition of the daily 'tot' of rum to Naval personnel is in the process of being indulged here. Those sailors who did not drink alcoholic beverages were granted an allowance of 'thruppence' (a three-penny bit) in English money in lieu. The tradition was sadly (for regular partakers at least!) discontinued after World War II.

firing-switch activated the charge of thirteen rockets that thrust the fighter into the air – and that was all there was to it!

On occasions the rockets either did not fire or, worse still, only partially operated. In the former instances the CDO would immediately wave a red flag and check his equipment for circuit breaks, loose safety links or badly adjusted points. Partial operation of the rockets could leave the Hurricane staggering into the air or even being shot into the sea, while there were occasions where rocket explosions caused injuries to those personnel in the immediate vicinity of the ramp.

CAM-ship operations were initially conducted with the trans-Atlantic convoy routes in mind. The scale of interceptions of *Luftwaffe* aircraft was not large, but this basically negative feature of operations concealed the fact that the driving away of these 'surveillance' machines enabled the convoy in question to take a subsequent evasive course. This action in turn could at least reduce the chance either of renewed interception from the air, or by the elements of a lurking U-Boat 'Wolf-Pack' whose crews were probably dependent upon regular radio-signal directions from the circling Fw 200s, Ju 88s or Bv 138s.

On 1 November 1941 for example, F/O Varley, one of the pilots of No.14 MSFU on board EMPIRE FOAM was alerted when an Fw 200 was sighted ahead of the convoy. Within a matter of three minutes he was airborne, only to discover that his prey had disappeared out of sight. The Fw 200 was again sighted several minutes later, this time low down and astern of the convoy, whereupon Varley decided to orbit in this rear position on the assumption that his adversary was acting in a 'decoy' function for other aircraft.

Varley's theory appeared to gain credence when Sub-Lt. Gostelow (CDO) called over the radio to report a 'bogey' approaching from ahead, followed by the sight of a corvette

A Walrus has just been fired off the catapult of what appears to be an auxiliary vessel, probably an Armed Merchant Cruiser. Between 1935-1945 the majority of the sixty-four first-line warships (other than carriers) and the twelve AMCs equipped with catapults embarked the Walrus as their aircraft complement.

firing its AA armament. The four-engine aircraft turned out sadly for Varley to be a B-24 Liberator, whereupon he resumed his orbiting flight! Finally, having been airborne for almost two hours, Varley decided to vacate his Hurricane close to a destroyer, whose crew fished him out of the mercifully calm Atlantic barely minutes after he had struggled out of his parachute harness and clambered into his one-man dinghy.

The occasional 'kill' was recorded during the time the CAM-ships were operating prior to the disbandment of the MSFU in July 1943. The Gibraltar run witnessed several successes including EMPIRE MORN's P/O Saunders on 14 June 1942 and EMPIRE HEATH's F/O Taylor on the following 1 November, both victims being Fw 200s. By July 1943 the number of CAM-ships was down to five, two of which were still available for escort duties from Gibraltar on the 23rd when a convoy departed northward to Britain.

Three days out, two reports of 'bogies' materialised into first a Fw 200 and then a B-24; the latter was signalled to engage the Fw 200 but the combat resulted in the destruction of the enemy 'shadower' closely followed by its RAF adversary. Soon after a second Fw 200 loomed up to circle the convoy. F/O Stewart's Hurricane was launched from EMPIRE

DARWIN and within minutes had put paid to the Fw 200's operational career.

One hour later, EMPIRE TIDE's F/O Flynn was similarly 'fired-off' in pursuit of the latest Fw 200 to challenge the convoy's progress as it flew laterally across the convoy's heading. Flynn's rate of closure was equally swift but the ensuing combat was much more protracted and involved six passes. Concentration on the cockpit was followed by strikes against the various gun turrets and mountings. Smoke vomited from one engine during one pass but the Fw 200 took no evasive action during the entire encounter; on the other hand its gunners landed heavy strikes on Flynn's left wing and holed his canopy. The last seen of the 'shadower' it was emitting a heavy smoke trail from the stricken port-inner engine and losing altitude. This 'swansong' for CAM-ship operations was happily capped by the recovery of both RAF pilots thanks to the convoy escorts.

The BISMARCK Action

The several Capital ships commissioned by Germany during World War II not only constituted a parallel threat to Britain's sea-borne trade routes, but for the bulk of World War II would by their very existence tie down an inordinate degree of Royal Navy resources in specific locations, such as Scapa Flow, thereby denying their use elsewhere. The '*Panzerschiffe*' DEUTSCHLAND and GRAF SPEE and battle cruisers SCHARNHORST and GNEISENAU had already displayed their fearsome firepower during anti-convoy forays into the open seas between September 1939 and early 1941. Now, by May 1941, Germany's mighty BISMARCK was ready for operations, as she deployed from the Baltic up along the Norwegian coast accompanied by the cruiser PRINZ EUGEN. The likelihood that these two warships would attempt a joint sortie to interdict the northern convoy routes in the company of SCHARNHORST (Currently berthed in Brest with the crippled GNEISENAU) could not be discounted, although this scheme had been previously cancelled.

The first confirmed sighting of the new battleship was made by a PRU Spitfire pilot F/O 'Babe' Suckling flying out of the northern Scottish airfield at Wick on 21 May. His films showed the pair of *Kriegsmarine* vessels anchored at Karsfjord close to Bergen. The subsequent sorties by Coastal Command aircraft next day were thwarted by inclement weather. The Admiralty's concern that the weather conditions might have cloaked the enemy warships' departure was confirmed by the day's end. A Martin Maryland reconnaissance aircraft based at Hatston managed to get through despite the extremely poor weather conditions, to find the fjord bereft of shipping – the Fox was out!

Admiral Luetjens and BISMARCK's Captain Lindemann had the choice of breaking out either between the Faeroe Islands and Iceland, or further north through the Denmark Strait sandwiched between Iceland and Greenland, and the latter course was selected. Two 'County' Class cruisers, SUFFOLK and NORFOLK were patrolling the Strait, and Admiral Tovey dispatched the battle cruiser HOOD and the newly commissioned battleship PRINCE OF WALES to forge ahead of the Main Fleet, as all steamed out of Scapa Flow. The Navy's latest ILLUSTRIOUS Class carrier VICTORIOUS was an element of the Force, but was still 'working up' and possessed just nine Swordfish of No.825 Sqdn. and six Fulmars.

The enemy warships were picked up and 'shadowed' by the two 'County' Class cruisers, who duly reported the course and speed to the pursuing pair of Capital ships. The latter finally made visual contact in the early hours of 24 May and the action commenced. BISMARCK had given way to PRINZ EUGEN, an act that has been claimed was the reason for Admiral Holland on board HOOD ordering all fire from both Capital ships to be concentrated on the lead warship in the (mistaken) assumption it was the German battleship. Within a matter of minutes this assertion became tragically irrelevant, when a third enemy salvo struck home and literally blew the warship known as 'the Pride of the British Navy' out of the water, leaving just three of her complement of 1,419 alive. PRINCE OF WALES then received the un-fettered attention of both enemy warships and suffered heavy damage, including one hit that killed all but two personnel on her bridge, before pulling out of the action. However, three hits on BISMARCK had caused two fuel tanks to leak and the warship to go down marginally by the head – the first nail in her coffin.

Admiral Tovey's Main Fleet was well to the south east at this point but by the late evening his Force was close enough for the Swordfish on VICTORIOUS to be dispatched. Leading the Sqdn. was Lt-Cdr. Eugene Esmonde, in a take-off that was fraught with danger, due to a vertical deck pitch of anything up to 50 ft in variation! All aircraft got away safely, and fought

The Fleet Air Arm carried out shore-side deck-landing training at airfields, a process that was given the title of Airfield Dummy Deck Landings (ADDLs). In this picture the DLCO has lowered his bats, which is a good indication that the Fulmar pilot has made a sound landing approach.

This is the very first escort carrier to enter RN service during World War II. The vessel was originally the German merchantman HANNOVER but was converted and named HMS AUDACITY. The spartan hull outline lacked a superstructure and there were no hangar facilities, so all aircraft servicing was carried out in the open air. The carrier was sunk on only its second Gibraltar convoy-run in December 1941.

their way through recurring rain and sleet showers. The formation, having lost its way in the cloud after initially picking out their target, and then being re-directed by NORFOLK, finally broke cover over what turned out to be a U.S. Navy cutter sailing in the immediate vicinity of BISMARCK. The gunners on the German warship were accordingly alerted and ready for the assault.

The three 'V-formations' of torpedo-bombers headed into a veritable wall of gunfire, with the AA weaponry reportedly supported by fire from the BISMARCK's main armament. The violently evading warship got clear of all but one of the torpedoes, with the exception striking home impotently against the main armour belt amidships. (The erratic motion of the warship coupled with a tendency to greatly over-estimate the Swordfish speed, probably explains the German AA gunners' lack of success in bringing down any of the attackers).

Despite having never made a night landing on a carrier in good conditions, let alone the rain and running sea that existed here, all nine Swordfish crews regained the deck of VICTORIOUS safely, unlike the two 'shadowing' Fulmars that were finally forced to 'ditch'. However, one of the two-man crews, having found themselves in a dinghy surrounded by the grim wastes of the Atlantic – a seemingly terminal situation – enjoyed the greatest of good fortune when subsequently ran across by a British merchantman! Their companion Fulmar and crew were not so fortunate.

The surviving Fulmar crew's good fortune was mirrored in even greater measure by Lt. Jackson of No.825 Sqdn. His crew were dispatched along with others next day to make a search for BISMARCK following the battleship's success in breaking free of her cruiser 'shadowers'. VICTORIOUS was not found at the end of the sortie and the pilot was about to

The deceptively calm surface of the North Atlantic forms a backcloth to the Swordfish from No.825 Sqdn. based on VICTORIOUS. These aircraft and their crews would deliver the first major attack on the German battleship BISMARCK during the late evening of 24 May 1941. By the time the attack Force took off the carrier deck was pitching by as much as forty or fifty ft. but all the crews returned safely on board.

'ditch' when a lifeboat was sighted nearby. The aircraft was put down in close proximity to the floating 'miracle' that turned out to be a waterlogged remnant from an Allied merchantman. The boat was baled out as best as possible, the sail equipment still on board was hoisted and an easterly course taken up. This was, unbeknown to the three airmen, the start of a nine-day odyssey, often through heavy seas, rain and sleet, that would leave them in grave danger of expiring thanks to the diminishing food and water supplies, while one member's legs were displaying ominous signs of gangrene. Then, their path crossed that of an Icelandic fishing boat – a sight that made Jackson momentarily imagine he was hallucinating – but it took the last of several Very lights to attract the crew's attention, whereupon they were hauled aboard and tended to.

A few hours after the Swordfish attack, BISMARCK evaded the radar surveillance of SUFFOLK and for the next thirty-three hours was 'lost' before being again picked up by an RAF Catalina of No.209 Sqdn. By then Tovey's Force, due to a misinterpretation of his adversary's intentions, was well behind its quarry and in danger of running short of fuel, while 'Force H' coming up from Gibraltar was equally hard-pressed to catch BISMARCK and engage her on the surface before she came within range of *Luftwaffe* air cover. ARK ROYAL's presence within 'Force H' was now to have a crucial bearing on the subsequent events of the overall action. The Swordfish of Nos.810, 818, and 820 Sqdns. first of all took over the 'shadowing' duty after the RAF Catalina was damaged by AA fire, and then prepared for a torpedo assault on the afternoon of the 26th. Low cloud and poor visibility faced the crews selected for the attack, as they headed off towards their target.

Unbeknown to the aviators was the order passed to the cruiser SHEFFIELD to close up and 'shadow' BISMARCK. The basis for a military 'own goal' now arose as the pilots broke cloud-cover and made their attack runs against a warship picked up by the ASV equipment carried by some Swordfish. The majority of the torpedoes were already released when the dreadful fact was realised that the 'BISMARCK' was in fact their own cruiser! What transpired was a stroke of good fortune, ironically due to technical failure on six of the eleven of the weapons actually dropped. The torpedoes had been fitted with magnetic pistols, which in the instances mentioned did not stand up to impact with the sea and duly detonated, while the five that entered the water and ran were thankfully evaded by SHEFFIELD.

The thoroughly chastened airmen landed back on ARK ROYAL's deck and their aircraft were soon prepared for a second sortie. This time around contact pistols were fitted to the torpedoes and the fifteen crews headed out across the storm-tossed sea. The adverse cloud conditions caused at least one

aircraft to lose its course to the target; however the Observer knew where SHEFFIELD was, directed his pilot to her position, and obtained the necessary compass course through use of his Aldis Lamp. There was no mistaking the bulk of BISMARCK even in the fading light as her gunners threw up a curtain of fire against their attackers, fortunately with equal lack of success as with the VICTORIOUS contingent. Only two of the torpedoes made contact, with one making no impression against the main armour belt. The second found what can be regarded as the 'Achilles heel' of any warship however effectively armoured – the propeller shaft and blades and rudders. The latter units were jammed by the explosive effect and only one was subsequently freed; consequently, the massive battleship no longer answered to a proper steering action. Luck had finally turned the pursuit in favour of the Royal Navy, as BISMARCK commenced an erratic course pattern that swung her inexorably away from the promised safety of her revised landfall at Brest. (Her original destination had been St. Nazaire, whose giant dry-dock would have accommodated the battleship for the necessary battle-damage repair).

The following morning, having survived regular torpedo attacks from several Royal Navy destroyers, the BISMARCK's crew faced up to the heavy guns on DUKE OF YORK and RODNEY. The resultant battering borne by the German warship over nearly two hours destroyed her superstructure and inflicted terrible casualties but left her still afloat. An acute shortage of fuel forced the withdrawal of the British battleships, whereupon NORFOLK and DEVONSHIRE closed with the burning hulk and fired a succession of torpedoes that reportedly finished the task. Swordfish from ARK ROYAL had been launched but were not called to participate in the action.

The demise of BISMARCK, although credited to a combination of air and sea-fired weapons, was the latest pointer in the battleship's continuing relegation from its hitherto supreme status within the Navies around the World. The aircraft carrier was fast assuming that premier role as World War II evolved, and the major sea actions between 1941-1945 would be almost exclusively dependent on air power as their chief weapon. Battleships would still feature in actions, but generally in a shore bombardment role rather than facing up to one another on the high seas.

'In the Valley of the Shadow'

The date is 12 February 1942, and the location is the storm-tossed English Channel accompanied by low scudding cloud formations. In between is sandwiched a six-plane Swordfish formation in two sub-flights, heading south towards the French coast and a horde of winking lights that emanate from the flak batteries on the enemy battleships and their escorts. All around the biplanes are numbers of Bf 109s and Fw 190s whose attacks are barely contained by the single VGO machine guns wielded by the TAGs as their pilots grimly hold a plodding course. The odds against survival, let alone bringing their torpedoes to bear, are mounting inexorably as they close in upon the warships.

The Swordfish actually penetrate the outer ring of escorts but almost immediately the Lead aircraft loses part of a wing to flak; its torpedo is launched but then the 'Stringbag' bursts into flames that consume it and its crew. Lt/Cdr Eugene Esmonde (Sqdn. CO) has made his final sortie. Although other torpedoes are confirmed launched not one reaches its target, while all six aircraft are shot down. In the meantime the *Kriegsmarine* warships steam on grandly through the Channel gloom on course for Kiel, Germany.

The foregoing action was arguably the most gallant albeit tragic example of increasingly desperate counter-measures during what became known as 'the Channel Dash'. Since March 1941 when SCHARNHORST and GNEISENAU had arrived in Brest, (followed by PRINZ EUGEN in May) the three warships had been under constant surveillance by aircraft

and submarine. The British were aware of the planned 'breakout' but could not have imagined the daring and risky option of an eastwards passage through the narrow English Channel.

'Fortune did favor the Brave' on the evening of 11 February 1942 thanks to radar failure on the surveillance Hudson, and a submarine's equal failure to pick up the ships' movements. This was followed by hours of darkness that enabled the Germans to traverse almost the entire Channel length before their accidental discovery by a pair of Spitfires late the following morning revealed the shocking fact. Now the plans for a coordinated Royal Naval and RAF assault basically fell apart to give way to a series of hastily drawn up attacks by naval units and RAF Bomber Command. The warships landed no torpedo strikes while the inadequate weight and quality of the RAF bombs combined with the low cloud base ensured an even greater failure, since many of the aircraft never even sighted their targets!

No.825 Sqdn. led by Esmonde had participated in the Bismarck Action, and now the crew were ready at Manston airfield in Kent. The weather conditions were the same as when

The CO of No.825 Sqdn., Lt/Cdr. Eugene Esmonde stands second from left on this photograph. He was destined to win a posthumous Victoria Cross during a gallant but failed bid to sink the German Capital ships SCHARNHORST, GNEISENAU and PRINZ EUGEN as these escaped up the English Channel from Brest in February 1942. Lt. Percy Gick (extreme left) was the Sqdn. Senior Pilot and later served on the escort carrier VINDEX as Commander (Flying).

This is a good close-up view of a Swordfish Mk.I bearing the standard armament of a single eighteen inch torpedo. The wing rack for carrying small bombs or smoke floats is a point of note. The fuselage paintwork is well worn directly behind the lower engine cowling. The presence of the pilot only indicates a non-operational sortie.

The yellow letter P in a yellow circle normally denotes a prototype British military aircraft. In this instance MA760 was actually the first production airframe for the Seafire Mk.IIC variant. This aircraft was retained by the manufacturers and used as a test-bed for the folding wing pattern later applied from the Seafire Mk.III onwards.

BISMARCK was attacked on 24 May 1941: then all the attackers had returned to VICTORIOUS, but this positive scenario was to be cruelly reversed today. Although a strong Spitfire escort was planned, only a handful actually made the aerial rendezvous – not surprising in these climactic circumstances. And so the ill-fated Swordfish crews headed out towards their martyrdom. Only five of the eighteen airmen survived their immersion in the icy waters to be rescued by MTBs.

The shock to the British Public arising from this incident was heightened three days later by the news of the Fall of Singapore. In the case of the 'Channel Dash' at least the long-term strategic disadvantage accruing from what was a German tactical success soon became apparent. Instead of an open-ended access to the Atlantic convoy routes from the French seaports, the enemy Capital ships found themselves again 'boxed in' by the presence of the British Home Fleet from its bases in northern Britain. As it was, sea mines laid by the RAF off Holland ahead of the German Force on the 12th ensured that both GNEISENAU and PRINZ EUGEN received serious damage; in the case of the former warship it reached Kiel but never regained full commission status and became derelict. SCHARNHORST joined TIRPITZ in Norwegian waters but both vessels basically remained there until destroyed in December 1943 and November 1944 respectively, having achieved virtually nothing positive.

Lt/Cdr. Esmonde and his fellow aviators, although achieving nothing on 12th February, did uphold the centuries-old Royal Navy tradition to 'engage the enemy more closely'. Even the Germans later commented on the signal gallantry of, 'the British airmen in their mothball group of ancient aircraft'. The subsequent award of the Victoria Cross, Britain's supreme military medal, to Esmonde (whose body was recovered two months later from the Thames Estuary) was a fine if poignant postscript to what transpired that terrible day over the English Channel.

AUDACITY

The pressing need for British Naval airpower to extend out over the oceans in general and the north Atlantic in particular in sufficient numbers of carriers was being addressed in the course of 1941. Both Britain and America would expand into this specific field of military technology, but the latter Nation serving as the 'Arsenal of Democracy' would prove to be by far the greater provider. This was hardly surprising, given the even vaster extremities of the Pacific Ocean that formed its western 'back door' and sphere of influence.

The concept of the auxiliary carrier, whose construction was commercial in form but adapted to the field of aviation, first bore fruit for the Royal Navy in late-1941. In one of World War II's ironic twists, the vessel chosen for conversion to a carrier was a captured German merchantman HANNOVER. The conversion work spanned the first five months of the year and was simple almost in the extreme. For a start the flight deck length of 450 ft. seemed barely adequate for the slowest Naval aircraft type on hand, the Swordfish, let alone the Hawker Hurricane or Grumman Martlet, that constituted the original and revised designs respectively mooted for operations.

Even more constricting was the absence of a hangar, which reduced the operational element of the flight deck down to around 300 ft. in order to allow for the remaining third to be used as a deck park. This limitation also left the mechanics' maintenance efforts fully exposed to the weather conditions. Landing-on would prove risky, especially when attempting to engage the meagre allotment of four hydraulically operated arrester wires – or the fifth non-retarded wire directly ahead of the barrier! All in all, the duties of flying or servicing the aircraft were to prove a stiff test for the personnel involved.

The final choice of aircraft proved to be positive as regards its performance. The Martlet Mks.I and II (or Wildcat as named by the U.S. Navy) was a custom-built carrier machine, well able to withstand the shock of landing-on. Its narrow-track landing gear could render its ground or deck handling tricky at times, but its sturdy structure could absorb much damage and, flown properly, the fighter could give a good account of itself in combat. (Leroy Grumman's fighter was the first of three major designs destined to enter service with the Fleet Air Arm during World War II; the Wildcat, Hellcat and Avenger, along with the Chance-Vought Corsair, were instrumental in placing the Navy's aviation Branch on an equal footing with their Axis adversaries). No.802 Sqdn. was selected to operate the Martlet aboard AUDACITY and so it was that on 13 September, with six Martlets and eight pilots embarked, the carrier slipped its moorings in the Clyde and sailed south. Its assignment was with the escort Group covering Convoy OG74 bound for Gibraltar.

The Bay of Biscay's weather patterns are unpredictable at any time, and the aircraft were exposed to the corrosive influence of the salt spray that affected internal fittings along with the external surfaces. The numbed fingers of the mechanics created enough problems by daylight while any nocturnal work had to be conducted by shielded torchlight. Added to this was the physical effort required to shuttle aircraft along the bulk of the deck length, depending on whether aircraft were being readied for take-off or expected back from their sorties.

The proximity of the convoy route to both the U-Boat bases and their KG 40 aerial contemporaries sited at Bordeaux-Merignac in south west France placed a constant strain on all

This picture provides a graphic illustration of how the CAM-ship Hurricanes were liberally sprayed with corrosive salt water whenever their vessel encountered conditions such as here. Note how the launch ramp is angled slightly to the right of the merchantman's centerline.

concerned, so the presence of the six fighters undoubtedly proved a welcome tactical and moral boost. The Fw 200 bombers' primary duty was to first find the convoy, then orbit within sighting distance but out of range of the escorts guns, after which a regular stream of course and speed details were relayed to the U-Boat captains. Interception of the enemy 'spotters' was a primary task for the Navy pilots who operated in pairs, but observing the presence of U-Boats and marking their locations for the escorts was also indulged in.

The first U-Boat sighting was made on the 20th but next morning came a more positive activity when a *Kondor* was reported heading in towards the convoy. The two Martlets that were 'scrambled' headed for the tail of the convoy where the rescue vessel WALMER CASTLE was stationed, and was now under attack by the KG 40 aircraft, while searching for survivors from ships sunk during the night. The Martlet Mk.II was formidably armed with six .50 machine guns and the *Kondor* crew were given little opportunity to savour their assault on the rescue vessel that left it wreathed in flames.

Sub-Lt. Fletcher directed a short burst of fire towards the rear fuselage that literally 'sawed' it away and left the four-engine predator to tumble into the sea. The *Kondor*'s original civil airliner role meant that its airframe was nothing like as firm as that of a custom-built bomber; even so, the striking power of the .50 machine-gun was such that it could render even the strongest airframe liable to failure. An added bonus of the .50 was that it combined the hitting power of cannon-caliber weapons, (but whose ammunition capacity was accordingly reduced due to the larger individual shell size), with the ammunition capacity of smaller rifle-calibre guns such as the .303 (but whose hitting power was weak by comparison).

The *Kondor*'s destruction was to be followed by four more KG 40 losses in the course of AUDACITY's short but valuable operational career. Having returned to Britain with Convoy HG74, she again sailed on the Gibraltar run with OG76 on 31 October. The second Condor encounter was a bitter-sweet success, however; No.802 Sqdn's CO, Lt-Cdr. Wintour, having made two separate attacks, pulled up close to the burning Fw

200, but received return fire that killed him. That same day (8 November) Sub-Lts. Brown and Lamb took on another *Kondor*, with Brown delivering a devastating burst of fire into the cockpit from a head-on angle, after the enemy machine had been harried through the cloud layers.

The second return voyage to Britain with HG76 saw the presence of an Escort Group and CO (Capt. 'Johnny' Walker) whose future actions would set the stage for a steady stream of U-boat losses credited to the unit as the Battle of the Atlantic attained and passed its climax in May 1943. AUDACITY's operational strength was halved but the Lamb and Brown 'team' went after two *Kondor* 'shadowers' on 19 December. Brown once again engaged his quarry from head-on with the same lethal result; Lamb made a similar approach on the second *Kondor* after several unsuccessful passes from behind; he also brought down his target but held on so long that his fighter collected a section of aerial wire!

Next day the same two pilots intercepted two U-Boats astern of the convoy, which were shot-up and their presence reported for the escorts to hunt down. As Brown later landed off the final dusk patrol he had no way of knowing the carrier's last action had been completed. AUDACITY now began to zigzag and several escorts created a 'spoof' attack astern with depth charges and 'Snowflake' flares in a bid to throw the U-Boats off the scent. An unfortunate response by some of the merchantmen, who must have assumed the escort 'action' presaged a real enemy assault, was to fire their own 'Snowflake' flares; the result was to highlight not only themselves but also their carrier cover. U-751, lurking in the immediate vicinity, found itself in the prefect position to carry out *Großadmiral* Dönitz's command that AUDACITY's recurring threat to his U-Boats over the past two months be removed. A torpedo impacted with the hull adjacent to the engine room and 'abandon ship' was piped after she settled

A CAM-ship Hurricane is pictured on its launch ramp while its merchantman 'parent' is anchored in the calm waters of a bay or inlet somewhere in western Britain. The aircraft's lofty position is confirmed by the fact that the cockpit is level with the lookout box on the foremast. The two RAF pilots are wearing their basic flight clothes but are probably posing for the picture since neither is equipped with a parachute harness.

The isolated location for each CAM-ship Hurricane is exemplified by this view of NJ:L, whose catapult unit is being attended to by a mixed party of Service and civilian personnel. The ramp's seventy ft length is marginally angled downward.

down by the stern. Some twenty minutes later U-751, having surfaced, delivered two more torpedoes that blew the forward section of the carrier clean off, whereupon the rest of the truncated warship reared up and disappeared in minutes.

AUDACITY's operational existence was relatively short-lived but the way forward in respect of proper air cover for the Allied convoys had been highlighted by the actions of her aircraft complement. Admiral Dönitz had acknowledged this by confirming that the overall effect during all four convoy runs involving AUDACITY had been to force his U-Boats to submerge or withdraw, while the depredations wrought among the *Kondor* 'shadowers' was all too evident.

The 'Jeep' Carrier

In the two years preceding America's entry into World War II, several leading figures in the U.S. Navy, of which William 'Bull' Halsey was a prominent example, began to push the case for a smaller and practical version of the aircraft carrier. These could then leave the main Fleet Carrier complement free to carry out full operational activities should war come; training and aircraft-ferrying duties would be provided by a string of auxiliary carriers. As regards the construction of such vessels, these would not have to consume shipyard time and effort in being built from scratch; instead they would be based on conversions of merchant vessels already in existence.

In January 1941, two merchant vessels MORMACMAIL and MORMACLAND were selected for conversion. Within three months of their Naval acquisition – a period demanded

by President Roosevelt in place of the originally quoted eighteen months – the former-named vessel emerged from Newport News Naval Yard as USS LONG ISLAND (AVG-1). The other merchantmen was converted in the latter part of 1941, with the intention of being supplied to the Royal Navy; four more vessels from the same shipping Company were also assigned for conversion and dispatch along with what was commissioned during November as HMS ARCHER (BAVG-1).

The two 'utility' carriers were to prove the forerunners of a series of 'Classes' extending to nine in number – seven U.S. and two British -, with all but five (which included AUDACITY) constructed in America. In addition, nineteen British oil tankers and grain-carriers would be converted to auxiliary carrier status during 1943. The AVG abbreviation stood for 'auxiliary/heavier than air/aircraft carrier' respectively while the prefix B stood for 'British'. However, from August 1942, a revised ACV ('Auxiliary/Aircraft Carrier) title was issued, while in July 1943 a final revised CVE title standing for 'carrier/heavier than air/escort' was applied to all U.S.-produced vessels.

The new Royal Navy carrier featured a 410 ft. long flight deck with a hydraulic catapult track on the port side, and a quarter-length hangar situated at the rear of the hull and serviced by a single lift. A small navigation/air control platform on the forward starboard side formed a stark contrast with the prominent 'island' structures applied to the three Royal Navy vessels forming the 'Avenger' Class. In addition the 'Avengers' featured hangars extending more than half the length of the 410 ft. flight deck, which was also served by two lifts. All three were commissioned between March and July 1942

The operational career of ARCHER was destined to be dogged with problems before her final laying-up from active operations in late 1943. During working-up trails, problems arose with the carrier's engines, gyrocompass and steering gear; this list of failures culminated in a collision with another vessel. Entry into operational service did ultimately take place during 1942. Records indicate that ARCHER completed runs to Sierra Leone and South Africa in this period followed by participation in Operation 'Torch' in November.

Massacre off the American Coast

The emphasis of the Battle of the Atlantic during the first half of 1942 basically shifted away from the broad reaches of the ocean to the eastern coastline of the United States. The U-Boats were dispatched to the region where the almost total lack of escort cover, at least up to April or May, provided the Germans with another 'Happy Time'. The Allied Navies were stretched to the limit in escort provision and American priority was almost wholly granted to the trans-Pacific and trans-Atlantic protection not only of cargo vessels but also of troop transports as men and materials were quickly built up both in Britain and Australia.

The absence of proper or even any form of 'blackout' along much of the American coastline undoubtedly added to the ease with which the U-Boats ran up a stunning figure of 609 vessels constituting over three million tons across this and the main North Atlantic zones, and including a sizeable number of oil tankers. (The fact that Allied shipyards were to more than make up this deficiency in the fullness of time, while the emphasis on loading tankers in the Gulf of Mexico seaports changed to

piping the precious fluid across country to loading terminals in the north east, was little consolation to the many seamen who lost their lives in the process).

Atlantic Fortunes in 1942

In the main Atlantic stretch, new tactics and equipment were coming into use during 1942. High-frequency/direction-finding sets (nicknamed 'Huff/Duff') were fitted to the escorts and provided an efficient means of picking up enemy radio signals onto which to 'home'. An improved ASDIC FH3 set was introduced in March. A revised attack method was also introduced by 'Johnny' Walker. One escort would hold back from making a depth-charge run; instead its ASDIC would be used to hold 'contact' with the U-Boat, while its fellow-escorts would sustain the assaults under radio direction as they ran ahead of their 'controller' with their ASDIC sets 'off'. Saturation attacks in place of individual attack-runs could now be indulged in with the attacking warships releasing a beam and stern-delivered pattern over a much greater area. The explosive content of depth charges were also radically improved through the development of RDX or Torpex in place of TNT, while a shallow-setting hydrostatic-pistol had also been brought into operational use by Coastal Command.

The advent of the revised hydrostatic-pistol was equally vital in the destruction of U-Boats. Up to its introduction the depth charges dropped by air had been set to explode at between 100 ft. and 150 ft. below the surface on the assumption this would be the vertical position of the U-Boat when the weapons detonated. Ironically, any vessels caught on or just below the surface, could easily resist the concussive effect upon its otherwise vulnerable pressure hull. Conversely, the precise position of an already submerged vessel in relation to the wake left by its final submersion was difficult to confirm;

A Fulmar has just engaged an arrester-wire with its landing hook and is in the correct flight attitude to ensure a smooth contact with the flight deck. The codes shown here were applied to No.807 Sqdn., which was embarked initially on FURIOUS and then ARK ROYAL between March and November 1941.

Prior to the end of 1939, a series of 700 numbered Flights operated seaplane designs for 'spotting' and reconnaissance duties on board Capital warships and cruisers. From 21 January 1940, these units were amalgamated into one Sqdn. (No.700) and the aircraft allocated to various warships. This Walrus is being launched off a battleship for what would seem to be a short flight to an airfield, to judge by the lowered landing gear.

therefore, even if the U-Boat was within the depth spread of the fuse detonation, there was no guarantee that the depth-charge would be laterally close enough for the pressure hull to suffer fatal or even adverse damage. (Prior to the new fuse system appearing, Coastal Command had adapted their settings to 50 ft. as utilised by the Royal Navy escorts for their anti-submarine activities).

Coastal Command's aircraft were operating ASV Mk.II radar, while the first 'Leigh Light' sets (Named after their inventor S/Ldr. Humphrey de Verde Leigh) were on hand from the mid-year period. The searchlight equipment was mounted either in a retractable 'dustbin' under the rear fuselage of Wellingtons or under the starboard-outer wing on Liberators and projected an intense beam up to 5,000 yds. that gave a clear focus of the vessel under attack without adversely affecting the pilot's night vision. The combination of the Light and the revised depth-charge pistol now enabled the RAF crews to close in on their prey and catch them out. The loss of radar 'contact' previously experienced during the final run-up had been countered thanks to the Leigh Light's appearance in mid-year but the advantage was short-lived.

The capture of a Hudson equipped with ASV Mk.II some months before enabled the German to produce a search receiver that picked out the approaching aircraft well before its crew could be overhead. Known as 'Metox', and becoming available soon after the 'Leigh Light's' operational debut, the cruciform-pattern aerial was not a permanent feature on the conning tower but was clipped in position when the U-Boat was running on the surface and detached prior to normal diving action. (The equipment was nicknamed the '*Biscayakreuz*' or Biscay Cross by the submariners). However, the electronic 'see-saw' battle between aircraft and submarines would take another and decisive twist back in the Allies favor as 1943 opened.

Fleet Air Arm involvement in the Battle during 1942 was still marginal and almost wholly confined to the Fleet carriers, with the makeshift provision of CAM-ships involving only RAF pilots. However, only VICTORIOUS was based in Home Waters for any length of time during the year and stationed at Scapa Flow as part of the Force tasked with combating German capital warship moves to break out into the Atlantic or threaten the convoy route to Russia. Consequently, the deadly sea-borne contest was primarily still being fought out between the *Kriegsmarine* and the Allied surface Navies and their Air Force contemporaries. But full Fleet Air Arm involvement would occur in gathering measure as 1943 was entered and the flow of escort and CAM carriers reached full strength.

CHAPTER FIVE

PART ONE
'Mare Nostrum'

The numerous chronicles dealing with World War II in the Mediterranean have generally not been very flattering to the Italian Armed Forces. Acid comments on that Nation's fighting ability on land such as: "What is the Italian's Army's favourite command in battle; "About turn and advance!" – are regularly bandied about. Similar aspersions are cast up as regards the Italian Navy and Regia Aeronautica's fighting ability. Perhaps it is just as well that the technical and logistical apparatus on hand when Mussolini declared War on the Anglo-French Allies (10 June 1940) was never to be put to its full efficient use – otherwise the often parlous military situation facing Britain in this perceived vital area of military operations between 1940 and 1942 could well have proved an insuperable barrier to surmount, even without German support for its Axis partner.

On 9 June 1940, the Allied Naval control within the Mediterranean was jointly vested in the Royal and French Navies. The latter Force was a formidable one, based at ports in southern France as well as at Oran, Casablanca, Algiers and Dakar in northwest Africa, and the possibility of an effective challenge to the combined Fleets from the Italians was basically discounted. This position rapidly deteriorated within two weeks of Italy's entry into the Conflict when the French Government capitulated to the Axis Powers. Now the Royal Navy was faced with taking on an adversary whose Capital ship complement was of immeasurably greater strength and quality than its own. Nor was the position any better for the RAF or British Army stationed more than 2,000 miles from Gibraltar in Egypt, whose supply route was endangered by enemy bases sited on either side of the central and eastern stretches of the Mediterranean. Indeed, the occupation, or even subjugation by blockade, of the key island of Malta would certainly close off this supply route entirely, and greatly extend supply-times through the dispatch of vessels round the entire length of Africa and into the Red Sea.

After conflict commenced in the Mediterranean, the Fleet Air Arm's involvement extended to two carriers. ARK ROYAL, with twenty-four Skuas and thirty-six Swordfish was based at Gibraltar; along with the battle-cruiser HOOD, the battleships RESOLUTION and VALIANT and the cruiser SHEFFIELD, she formed the nucleus of 'Force H'. (The three named capital ships were later re-assigned and the battle-cruiser RENOWN took over). To the east, EAGLE with a smaller Force of eighteen Swordfish and three Sea Gladiators was operating out of Alexandria in Egypt. Individual Walrus and Swordfish aircraft were also on hand as part of the Navy's catapult strength based on various other warships such as the battleships and cruisers Also on hand in southern France was No.767 Sqdn., whose Swordfish attacked Genoa in mid-June before re-deploying to Malta where it was re-numbered No.830 Sqdn.

The ARK was the first to see full action in the course of what was to prove one of the most melancholy but necessary counter-strokes of World War II (at least in Britain's opinion). The possibility of the French warships berthed in African ports being commandeered by the Axis could not be discounted, despite the reassurances given by the Vichy politicians in control of the geographic 'rump' of their stricken country.

The negotiations with Admiral Gensoul, unlike those with his contemporary Admiral Godfroy in charge of French units at Alexandria, produced no positive reaction to the offer-terms – either join Britain in the Conflict or sail to British or French Caribbean bases for de-militarising – by the time Admiral Somerville, accompanied by other 'heavy' warships, anchored off Oran in HOOD on 3 July. The resultant bombardment blew up one French battleship and badly damaged other warships, although the battleship STRASBOURG got clear and steamed north to Toulon. ARK's aircraft participated in torpedo and bombing attacks over the ensuing three days that saw one serious hit on DUNKERQUE, but reduced Swordfish and Skua numbers by three and two respectively.

Another French battleship RICHELIEU had been 'shadowed' by HERMES while steaming south towards and into Dakar in Senegal. No.814 Sqdn. took off from HERMES and the six Swordfish involved managed just one hit, that fortuitously smashed the warship's steering gear and one propeller; a full year passed before RICHELIEU was back in full commission.

Dakar

Towards the end of September an Anglo-French expedition was dispatched to Dakar with a view to persuading the occupants to come over to the Allied side, peacefully or otherwise. Unlike Oran, the defenders resisted forcibly over a four-day period, with RICHELIEU's heavy guns damaging one of the two battleships present as well as a cruiser and two destroyers; the other capital ship RESOLUTION was also torpedoed. On the 24th six Swordfish of No.820 Sqdn. lifted off ARK ROYAL, laden with 250 lb. semi-armor piercing (SAP) bombs and briefed to attack RICHELIEU. The aircraft

were making their attack-runs, when several Curtiss Hawk fighters latched onto the small formation and took out at least two of the three aircraft failing to return. The Skuas of No.800 Sqdn. were badly out-classed by their French opponents and were barely able to survive, let alone provide protection for the Swordfish. All in all, air operations over Dakar were a basic failure in terms of the small number and indifferent to poor combat capability of the Fleet Air Arm machines – hardly a sound augury for positive future operations against the Axis Powers in the Mediterranean or elsewhere. (The planned landing by an Anglo-French Force lapsed into almost instant farce and swift failure).

Facing-Up

The Italian Fleet was by 1940 a formidable Force at least as regards its equipment. The capital ship element constituted six in number, including the modern, fifteen-inch armed LITTORIO and VITORIO VENETO. The numbers of Italian cruisers, destroyers and other support warships were well ahead of anything the Royal Navy could muster in the Theater of Operations. The one naval element absent, and never to be corrected, was the existence of aircraft carriers. However, the Italian Air Force possessed a large number of modern bomber and fighter designs compared to either the Royal Navy or the

This Fulmar is positioned at the prefect three-point angle for the arrester-hook to engage the deck wire and bring the aircraft to a safe halt on board ARK ROYAL. The three deck handlers on the left will then run forward and disengage the hook. Note the small vertical wire-guide supports that lie flush with the deck when the arrester system is not in use. The aircraft belongs to either No.807 or 808 Sqdn.

RAF, and were based at airfields on the Italian mainland or on Sicily that were within striking distance of the main sea routes.

In contrast the Royal Navy currently presided over a greatly dispersed and motley range of warships. ARK ROYAL at Gibraltar and EAGLE at Alexandria provided the carrier strength. There were capital ships on hand but none were of truly modern construction or performance compared to their Italian counterparts. Cruiser numbers were mainly of the 'light' classification with six-inch main armament. The overall situation for the British Forces appeared gloomy and unlikely to be swung in their favour for the foreseeable future, if at all.

Calling the Enemy's Bluff

The initial challenge to Mussolini's boast about the Mediterranean being 'Mare Nostrum' (Our Sea) was quickly raised by the Fleet based at Alexandria. By late June, bombardments along the Libyan coast especially at Bardia had been completed. Then, the first Fleet incursion deep into the Mediterranean in early July progressed as far as Calabria, situated on the 'Toe' of Italy and southwest of the key naval port of Taranto. Cunningham's Force comprised WARSPITE and escort, with five cruisers ranging ahead and EAGLE with the battleships MALAYA and ROYAL SOVEREIGN steaming behind. EAGLE was bearing the Swordfish from Nos.813 and 824 Sqdns., who would play a part in the Operation, which had the primary role of covering convoys sailing between Malta and Alexandria.

On 8 July units of the Italian Fleet were confirmed steaming south, and then east. A possible encounter with his adversary caused Cunningham to cancel the convoy departure and move his Fleet to intercept the Italian warships during their return to Taranto. This same day, and for the succeeding three days, the British units were subjected to a regular stream of high-level bombing runs by twin-engine SM79s. The result was something of a technical 'draw' in that only one bomb struck a cruiser.

It was perhaps just as well that EAGLE's vulnerable flight deck in particular remained unscathed, since bomb strikes thereon may well have resulted in an internal explosion or explosions that would surely have sealed her fate. On the other

The crew of a Skua are standing by the rear cockpit of their aircraft as a seaman watches one crewmember adjusting the helmet of his colleague. The rear canopy is folded down for the TAG to access his position and would also be so positioned when firing the single .303 Lewis machine gun that can be seen poking out of the recess in the fuselage.

A Fulmar Mk.I is about to cross over the lowered safety barrier on ARK ROYAL while its starboard wing passes over the rear lift. The presence of Skuas appears to date this picture to no later than April 1941 when the final examples of the Blackburn design flown by No.800 Sqdn. were disembarked.

hand the much-vaunted ability of the ship-borne AA firepower to deter, if not shoot down, its aerial opponents was found to be badly astray. The fact that the bombers had to hold a steady course during the bomb-run, which was made at a moderate 10,000 ft. altitude, did not bode well for future AA gunnery success against this form of assault at least.

Next day, the two Swordfish Sqdns. were sent out, with No.813 Sqdn. serving in a reconnaissance role over the enemy warships. Meanwhile No.824 Sqdn. was dispatched on two separate occasions against the Italian units in the hope of at least crippling one or more of the capital ships to the extent that Admiral Cunningham's battleships could close in and complete their destruction. The overall pedestrian performance of the 'Stringbags' meant that even when the warships were sighted, it was nearly thirty minutes later before the aircraft were in attack positions.

Each sub-flight had split off with the intention of approaching from different angles onto the four heavy cruisers and their destroyer escorts, descending from a medium altitude to just above the waves and closing in to around 1,000 yds.

before releasing their torpedoes. The enemy AA fire was intense but caused no casualties among the attacking force, although the water spouts cast up by the warships heavy armament was very off-putting. On the other hand, the claims for at least one solid strike proved to be equally without foundation as the vessels evaded successfully on both occasions.

During the afternoon the main cruiser force came in sight of, and opened fire on, the enemy. WARSPITE soon joined in, and her guns actually damaged the battleship CIULIO CESARE. She and her companion capital ship maintained a course for Taranto, leaving the escort to lay a smoke screen and hinder the pursuing warships. Soon after the action was broken off since the British force was by then dangerously close to the Italian mainland and inviting even more aerial assaults. The day's activities on the 10th included an assault by No.813 Swordfish on units in the Sicilian port of Augusta that resulted in one destroyer squarely torpedoed and a tanker damaged. This initial encounter with units of the Italian Fleet although proving basically inconclusive had provided the first indication of enemy reluctance to engage in wholesale combat that would color the entire War at Sea in this critical Theater of Operations.

The handful of Sea Gladiator forming EAGLE's fighter defence did manage to intercept several of the raids in the course of this and the ensuing four days, and claims for five SM79 and SM81 'kills' were confirmed. Cdr. Keighley-Peach claimed one of these on the 11th; the five-strong formation was dived upon, with the chosen victim sustaining damage from three separate firing passes before bursting into flames and spinning into the Mediterranean. Next day, the same pilot took down two more SM79s using the same method of attack against two separate bomber formations. Finally, the other Section pilot, Lt. Keith, latched onto the tail of a bomber and set it on fire, after which it fell to its watery destruction.

Lt. Massy scored another 'kill' on the 29th during a subsequent convoy escort by EAGLE; his repeated assaults on one of the six SM79s finally set it on fire and it was lost along with all but one of its crew. Following a bombardment operation off Bardia on 17 August, the three Sea Gladiators from EAGLE were operating from Sidi Barrani airfield; Keighley-Peach left an SM79 damaged and fading into the

clouds, while Lts. Young and Keith brought down a second SM79 out of the four Italian bombers lost this day. Finally, on the 31st. Keighley-Peach reached 'Ace' status when, after taking off from EAGLE, he caught a reconnaissance Cant Z506B's crew totally off guard. However, as with the Skua, so the sea-borne Gloster biplane's days of glory, fully deserved as they might be, were coming to an end as they were replaced on naval operations by more modern designs.

Within a week of the 'Battle' of Mers-el-Kebir, 'Force H' was carrying out a diversionary action off Sardinia in support of the Mediterranean Fleet's convoy-support and Calabrian operations. The warships were picked up by reconnaissance aircraft and submitted to several concentrated bombing runs by SM79 formations. The Skuas of No.800 Sqdn. engaged the bombers throughout the 9th. During one of the final attacks, four crews had received sufficient warning of the incoming formation to take off and gain the necessary height advantage. Petty Officer (PO) Theobald could not bring his guns to bear but his gunner, Naval Airman (NA) de Fries had better success as the Skua found itself flying in line with the Lead SM79. A full pan of ammunition from his Lewis machine gun resulted in the bomber nosing downwards with several crew baling

A line of Martlets Mk.1 from No.805 Sqdn. are photographed in the Western Desert during 1941. The Sqdn. reformed in Egypt during January with Fulmars and Buffaloes, but converted onto the Martlet in June. This unit subsequently served in North Africa within three separate RAF Wings. Note how the colors in the fuselage roundel are reversed in shade on aircraft 'X', and the revised position of the fuselage roundel on the neighbouring fighter.

Two Martlets Mk.I from No.805 Sqdn. are well into their take-off run as they raise a thick sand-trail from the North African surface. The camouflage scheme on these early Grumman variants was Sand on the top surfaces and Azure Blue below. Both aircraft are fitted with the larger pattern tail wheel that enabled the pilot to gain more prompt response from the rudder.

out, before it went into the sea. Earlier in the day, another Section of Skuas had caught and dispatched a 'snooping' Cant Z506 B floatplane. Although barely adequate in its fighter role against most Axis opposition, Blackburn's design was enjoying a measure of success. However, the arrival of the Fairey Fulmar would soon relegate the Skua to the backwaters of operations.

'Force H' was again involved in making attacks against Sardinian airfields at the beginning of August, as part of a diversion for the carrier ARGUS and her successful attempt to fly off the first batch of Hurricanes for Malta. Twelve Swordfish took off in the early hours of the 2nd, of which one crashed fatally on take off and a second failed to return from what was a thorough plastering of Elmas. Meanwhile the Skuas were playing their part in warding off SM79 assaults, with one shot down on the 1st along with a second credited to AA fire, while a Cant Z506 seaplane was also downed by a Skua the next day. Although basically keen to carry out offensive operations, Admiral Somerville was none too keen to 'trail his coat' close off the enemy coastline, and was quietly satisfied to return to Gibraltar on the 4th.

ILLUSTRIOUS

The first of the ILLUSTRIOUS Class of Fleet Carriers had been commissioned on 25 May 1940 and by the end of August had been dispatched to operate out of Alexandria thereby bringing the Fleet Air Arm's vessel complement up to three in this Theater of Operations. The new carrier embodied the extra quality of armoured enhancement compared to ARK ROYAL, and certainly EAGLE; conversely, this advancement was made at the sacrifice of aircraft stowage capacity – down to thirty-six compared to the ARK's figure of sixty. The new carrier also incorporated a vital technical piece of equipment in the form of RDF radar. Up to this point radar coverage had been provided either by the battleship VALIANT or the cruisers SHEFFIELD, CALCUTTA and COVENTRY, an arrangement that was far from satisfactory in making a prompt response to encroaching enemy aircraft movements.

On board were the Swordfish of Nos.815 and 819 Sqdns. along with an important and desperately required addition to FAA fighter strength. This was the Fairey Fulmar of which fifteen were on hand with No.806 Sqdn. The Fulmar was a

A Fulmar Mk.II, as confirmed by the air intakes ahead of the wing-roots, and belonging to No.808 Sqdn., heads down ARK ROYAL's flight deck. The metal strip above and behind the engine exhaust stubs is intended to shield the pilot's sight during night operations. This Sqdn. had barely embarked on the ARK before she was sunk in November 1941.

single-engine monoplane that owed some of its design layout to the Battle light bomber, although it was actually developed from the P4/34 light bomber. It had been ordered under Specification O.8/38 and weighed in at 9,800 lbs. all-up – 2,000 lbs. greater than the Sea Hurricane, a design the Admiralty had regarded as unsuitable for carrier operations until the GLORIOUS incident!

Eight .303 machine-guns provided a sound degree of firepower but the perceived need to add a second crewmember acting as Observer intruded upon basic fighter performance factors, especially maximum speed, that was limited to around 280 mph., while climb-rate at 1,200 ft. per minute was barely half that of its major Allied contemporaries or Axis adversaries. Given these limitations, the new aircraft was nonetheless destined to provide a sterling service in the Mediterranean over the ensuing two years that would result in a steady number of 'kills' being credited crews. Certainly, the Fulmar's arrival almost immediately relegated the manoeuvrable but out-dated Sea Gladiator to the pages of naval aerial combat history.

The passage of ILLUSTRIOUS through the Mediterranean coincided with the latest design to join the ranks of the Regia Aeronautica, a design whose malign influence was to affect the carrier's very existence in the months ahead – the Ju 87B. The fifteen aircraft assembled at Comiso in Sicily were available for operations, of which an element sighted the carrier and its escorts west of Malta on 2 September but did not attack, presumably having expended their bombs on alternative targets. The Cant Z501 floatplane that radioed-in the Fleet's existence before it was shot down was soon followed by SM79 formations, two of which attacked without effect, while their crews were surprised to find their advance barred by the Fulmars of No.806 Sqdn. At least three of the bombers were shot down – two by Lt. Barnes and one by the ships' AA gunners – and one heavily damaged during the course of the day's action' further claims for three more were submitted. Joining in the action were thirteen Ju 87Bs, with the first five-strong group getting through while no Fulmars were airborne; Their attacks were apparently directed against the overall Fleet formation, since strikes were claimed upon several vessels, none of which proved true; one hit was recorded against ILLUSTRIOUS, but with the observation that the bomb did not actually explode!

Bomba Action

Following the Oran action, three of No.813 Sqdn.'s Swordfish were disembarked from HERMES and flown to Dekheila, and then to the Desert Air Force HQ further west. From here the crews were to interdict Italian naval vessels operating off the Libyan coastline. A base at Bomba between Tobruk and Benghazi was reconnoitred on 21-22 August, in which was

The Lieutenant and Sub-Lieutenant posing on the wing leading edge of their Fulmar Mk.I are both members of the Royal Naval Volunteer Reserve, better known as the 'Wavy Navy' from the curled braid of their rank insignia. Flying boots and Mae Wests are worn over their uniforms. The Fulmar's large radiator was vulnerable to return fire from enemy aircraft gunners, should the pilot approach from behind his adversary.

located a submarine and a depot ship, and the Swordfish duly took off from their forward airfield at Sidi Barrani, with Capt. Patch (RM) leading. The low approach to the harbor bay revealed the shape of the submarine, which was commencing a test with its load of long-range manned torpedoes, against which Patch successfully delivered his 'tinfish'. (The manned torpedoes were intended to be transported to the immediate target area – in this instance the main Fleet anchorage at Alexandria – after which their crews would steer them into the attack zone, and back to the 'parent' submarine). So it was that Capt. Patch knocked out both forms of submersible threat to the Royal Navy in one move!

The remaining pair of crews continued on into the bay where they found the depot ship with a torpedo boat alongside and in a stationary attitude. The FAA pilots' manoeuvered to attack either flank and got away their torpedoes in the face of steady but ineffective AA fire. Fires were started on the destroyer as a result of the submarine's bursting into flames, while the depot ship also erupted in flames. The climax came shortly after as the aircraft were withdrawing; a massive explosion occurred on the depot ship that enveloped both warships, although the torpedo boat actually survived! Photographic confirmation of the scale of destruction was made next day.

Ranging the Mediterranean

During the months of September and October, the enemy was assailed across the broad spectrum of the Mediterranean, although the emphasis in terms of air operations was wholly from the eastern sector during the latter month. The Swordfish units on EAGLE suffered heavy losses when on 4 September thirteen crews of Nos.815 and 824 Sqdns. were ranged and launched against an airfield on the island of Rhodes. The formation had been delayed in taking off and ran into a collection of CR32 and CR42 fighters, suffering the loss of four crews to direct combat assaults, while a fifth was force-landed on Scarpanto airfield. Fulmar sorties were flown off ILLUSTRIOUS the same day, although the fighters were involved in challenging enemy efforts to attack the Fleet, in the course of which at least two bombers were shot down and several more suffered varying degrees of damage. ILLUSTRIOUS strike aircraft from Nos.815 and 819 Sqdns. hit a second airfield on Rhodes, destroying or damaging upwards of ten aircraft along with sizeable fuel supplies, all for no loss.

Better fortune attended the Swordfish crews from ILLUSTRIOUS on the 17th when a combined bombing and mine-laying sortie was made against the forward supply port of Benghazi. Two destroyers and four merchantmen were sunk in the process, and the resultant closing of all landing facilities for several days forced the Italians to divert their efforts much further west to Tripoli, so causing a noticeable back-log in getting supplies up to the front-lines. Convoy-support occupied

the eastern-based carriers for the remainder of September and throughout October, with the Swordfish crews attacking land targets such as the seaplane base at Leros, while the Fulmars protected the Fleet.

The Fulmar crews continued to prove their aircrafts' superior performance factors – at least in relation to the Sea Gladiator and Skua – by foiling most of the enemy bomber incursions as well as their reconnaissance aircraft. On 12 October, for example, Sub-Lts Sewell and Roberts forced a Cant Z501 'shadower' to land on the sea, where it was thoroughly strafed. Later on, Lt/Cdr. Evans heading a three-plane Section sent one SM79 down in flames while a second bomber-type was forced into 'ditching'. Before the day ended two further SM79s failed to return to Sicily, while a third crew from the same formation collided with high ground. (A series of near misses on EAGLE left her hull damaged, a situation that played a major part in the elderly carrier's exclusion from the forthcoming Taranto operation).

In the western Mediterranean, ARK ROYAL joined in with diversionary attacks on Sardinian airfield by way of ensuring the safe passage of ILLUSTRIOUS to Alexandria. The late-month's disastrous reverse at Dakar, during which the ARK lost nine aircraft, saw the carrier returning to Britain for re-

The overhang of a carrier's flight deck is caught in this picture of a Fulmar Mk.II on final landing approach and with its hook deployed. In the distance can be seen the outline of a Swordfish.

The Walrus's primary duty with the FAA was to operate in the 'spotting' role for naval gunnery. The design was normally embarked on board battleships and cruisers, some were distributed among the group of Armed Merchant Cruisers (AMC) for reconnaissance purposes. The SPOTTER of SPARTIVENTO on this example embarked on the cruiser SHEFFIELD refers to its part in the Naval action in the Mediterranean on 29 November 1940.

fitting; in addition, No.803 Sqdn. disembarked, and its Skuas were replaced by the Fulmars of No.808 Sqdn. after which the carrier returned to Gibraltar.

The Royal Navy's continuing physical and psychological hold over its Italian adversary seemed to be almost unchallengeable. But ever in the minds of the Navy's High Command were the continuing existence of the Italian capital ship force and the threat they presented to the Royal Navy and by extension to the survival of Britain's War effort in the Mediterranean, should proper use be made of these warships.

Taranto – Portent for Pearl Harbor, or Lessons Unlearnt

The Italian Fleet's main base at Taranto comprised two water stretches, the Mar Grande and Mar Piccolo, with a narrow strip of land between. The Mar Grande, the major element of Taranto, was formed of a westward-facing concave bay, with a small island mass (San Pietro) laying directly in the center and about a mile out; A submerged breakwater linked the island with a miniscule island to the southeast (Isoletto San Paulo)

while a second such breakwater to the north of San Pietro curved round clockwise to connect with the mainland. Two surface breakwaters were located on the southwestern side of the bay, the western one of which provided shipping access between its northern tip and the Isoletto San Paulo. Barrage balloons and AA gun sites – both moored in the bay and based ashore – festooned the entire area, while anti-torpedo nets were strung across the inner (eastern) area of the bay where the warships were anchored. Finally, powerful searchlight batteries were on hand to illuminate the area and assist the AA gunners in picking out their targets. All in all, the chances of any aerial attackers gaining access to their targets, let alone delivering punishing strikes, appeared to be minimal.

The Royal Navy, acting upon its historic premise that 'the impossible takes a little longer' took on the daunting task of challenging the Italian Fleet's sense of total security in a fashion that would ironically send the right or wrong tactical message to two other major Navies of World War II – depending on whether one was Japanese or American! The available strike force would of necessity involve the venerable Swordfish from

ILLUSTRIOUS and EAGLE. Fairey's biplane, affectionately known as the 'Stringbag', would appear to be frighteningly vulnerable to the multifarious and formidable defensive system facing its crews at Taranto. The relatively flimsy airframe construction, allied to its low speed, rendered it liable to instant destruction in such circumstances.

The original date for the assault was set for 21 October – the Battle of Trafalgar – but this portentous occasion had to be passed up when a hangar fire in ILLUSTRIOUS delayed proceedings until 11 November. This latter date representing Britain's Armistice Day from World War I proved to be an ironic choice, since no sense of peaceful intention pervaded the deck of ILLUSTRIOUS as the dusk settled on her surroundings that evening! On board were five Swordfish from EAGLE, transferred there due to their carrier's withdrawal from what was named Operation 'Judgment'; structural damage from bombing 'near-misses' had adversely affected the veteran carrier's operational ability.

On 8 November ILLUSTRIOUS stood out from Alexandria along with its fellow-warships, whose brief was to support the safe transit of Malta-bound convoy MB8. On board the carrier were a Section of Sea Gladiators from EAGLE, and it was two of these fighters that achieved the first 'kill' in the course of this latest operation. Sub-Lts. Sewell and Nicolls switched over from their Fulmars to engage and dispatch a Cant Z501 'shadower'. Next day, Sub-Lt. Orr – a future 'Ace' along with Sewell – closed in on another Cant Z501 and brought it down. Then, with the convoy safely in port, ILLUSTRIOUS was positioned for Taranto. During the 10th, yet another 'shadowing' Cant Z501 felt the fatal impact of Fulmar machine guns, fired by Lts. Sewell and Barnes. A similar thorough effort to 'cleanse' the air around the Fleet of all 'shadowers' continued over the vital twenty-four hours surrounding the launch and recovery of the attacking Swordfish. In this time, four separate enemy aircraft were either driven off or downed, of which two were later listed in Italian records as lost.

To the west ARK ROYAL had sailed on the 8th. to make another diversionary sortie to Cagliari in Sardinia. This same day, No.808 Sqdn. achieved its first 'kill' on Fulmars, when Lt. Tillard brought down an SM79. Further success attended next days operations, when Tillard shot down a Cant Z506B and was later credited with a SM79 out of a large formation. The Skuas of No.800 Sqdn. were also hotly involved in the combat and although no confirmed 'kills' were registered, most of the bombers were damaged and crewmembers killed or wounded.

A total of twenty-one aircraft were ranged for the operation that included sixteen from Nos.815 and 819 Sqdns. with the remainder drawn from Nos.813 and 824 Sqdns. transferred over from EAGLE. More would have been available had not water contamination of their fuel tanks rendered three Swordfish useless. Not all were equipped with torpedoes, since the area would have to be illuminated. This latter duty was allotted to three aircraft in each wave that were also carrying bombs with which to attack units of cruisers and destroyers berthed in the Mar Piccolo; the 250 lb. semi-armor piercing bombs allotted for this purpose were expected to have a better chance of penetrating the thinner skins of the cruisers, destroyers and other support warships in contrast to their use against the capital ships.

The overall Force was split into two waves, of which six out of twelve in the first, and five out of nine in the second, wave were bearing torpedoes; the remaining ten aircraft were loaded with bombs. The place of the Telegraphist/Air Gunner (TAG) in each aircraft was taken up by a long-range fuel tank; this was deemed to be of more practical value than the single machine gun normally positioned in the rear cockpit. And so it was that twenty-one flimsy biplanes whose performance seemed more suited to the previous World Conflict prepared to tackle an apparently impregnable naval 'Fortress', with the odds stacked firmly in favor of the latter

The weather was good and the first wave was launched at 2040 hours, some 170 miles distant from Taranto. The mixed Force of torpedo and flare-carrying aircraft climbed to 8,000 ft. The plan was for the flare-carriers to release their loads over the southeastern area of the base in order to illuminate the capital ships and so provide the necessary visual reference for the attackers, whose approach would be from the west. The early arrival of one Swordfish who had become separated from the formation and had proceeded ahead on his own was later stated as the reason why the Italian defences were already alerted and beginning to respond before the main assault had even commenced.

The theoretical superiority of the defensive system held one or two practical obstacles. First, the AA guns, although directed upwards at first, would then have had to assume a more horizontal approach, especially against torpedo bombers, with the resultant danger of counter-strikes among the relatively close-moored warships In fact the Italian authorities had previously confirmed that barrage fire from the warships would not be indulged in should the shore-based batteries already be in action – a scenario that minimised but could not entirely exclude 'friendly fire' incidents should the gunfire be directed at low-flying aircraft. Second, the sheer mass of searchlights situated along the length and breadth of the bay could create a counter-illumination effect that could easily blind the AA gunners attempting to peer into their beams. The official intention was for two searchlights on each warship to operate in concert with shore batteries located in the same harbour zone. It is arguable that the presence of barrage balloon cables was as great a, if not greater, lethal threat to the Swordfish crews as the AA fire! Be that as it may, the courage of the Fleet Air Arm crews cannot be under-stated.

L/Cdr.Williamson the Force Leader was first to penetrate the Mar Piccolo along with two other Sqdn. crews. Heading in towards the battleship CONTE DI CAVOUR, the Lead Swordfish released its 'tinfish' that impacted with the warship; any sense of triumph was quickly dispelled when the aircraft hit the water and crashed, fortunately without killing the two airmen. Had they known it, the strike had fatally crippled their target, whereas the other two Swordfish torpedoes had no similar success. The other Sub-flight of Swordfish approached over the northern edge of the Mar Piccolo and descended upon their targets. LITTORIO suffered two strikes in quick succession that put her out of commission for many months. All five surviving torpedo Swordfish succeeded in threading their precarious path through the AA fire and balloon barrages and back to ILLUSTRIOUS.

The bombers did not generally match the torpedo-bombers' success; the former-mentioned crews having released

their flares, then attacked ships and oil tank installations in or around the Mar Piccolo. No hits were confirmed on either; one of EAGLE's crews did strike a destroyer but the 250 lb. bomb failed to detonate. On the other hand, Sub-Lt. Sarra, an EAGLE-based pilot, released his load over a warehouse that simply blew up.

The second attack wave had been launched one hour later, and naturally arrived over a fully alert, if somewhat confused, defensive zone. The three flare-operators did their basic duty before attempting to add to the destruction over the Mar Piccolo. Only eight aircraft were on hand since one Swordfish had suffered fuel loss and was forced to land back on board. The torpedo-carriers closed in on Taranto across the northern rim of the bay and set about picking out targets. LITTORIO became the focus for at least three crews, but Lt. Bayly's aircraft was seen to veer across its companions' flight-path and smash into the water; both airmen were to become the sole fatalities this night. Lt. Torrens-Spence (No.819 Sqdn.) planted his torpedo on LITTORIO almost in the same location as one of the first-wave attackers, thereby adding to the already stricken battleship's woes.

An officer and two Petty Officers are manoeuvering a bomb-loader unit that bears a 500 lb. bomb for mounting onto the flexible 'crutch' frame under this Skua's fuselage. The frame is designed to be lowered just before bomb release. The loading procedure is watched by three other personnel including an RAF NCO (right).

A Swordfish from this wave miraculously survived impact with a barrage balloon cable that ironically had been set free from its mooring! One of the last crews led by Lt. Clifford that penetrated the harbor managed to plant their torpedo squarely into the hull of a third battleship (CAIO DUILIO). The airmen experienced two operational factors that surely raised their chances of survival during the attack. One was the complete absence of searchlights; the second related to the overall angle of the gunfire that proved to be high enough for the torpedo-bomber elements to slip into and out of Taranto with virtual immunity!

Back on ILLUSTRIOUS, the mood among the aviators was primarily one of disappointment, allied with apprehension at the distinct prospect of having to repeat the sortie, according to Admiral Cunningham's frame of mind. Fortunately, the weather conditions intruded upon the situation, and it was not until the post-raid RAF reconnaissance photographs became available that the true scale of success emerged. Of the three stricken battleships, CONTE DI CAVOUR was down by the stern and was to prove the worst afflicted, since the scale of damage merited her permanent withdrawal from active duty. CAIO DUILIO, having been beached, was repaired over a period of seven months. The tensile qualities of the more modern LITTORIO were proven, despite having suffered a seeming trio of strikes that settled her by the head, because she was back in commission by March 1941.

The aerial successors to Drake's 'bearding' of the Spanish Fleet in Calais, and Nelson's destruction of the French/Spanish Fleet at Trafalgar, had further added to that glorious Naval tradition. Even more important than the physical damage inflicted upon the Italian Navy was the psychological 'damage' inflicted upon its High Command. How could their seamen challenge, let alone, defeat the Royal Navy at sea, when a marginal Force of antiquated biplanes could inflict such heavy punishment among its warships and sailors in a reputedly secure anchorage? More ominously for the 'Battleship Brigade' around the World was the proof that the surface warship was facing a fight at odds against the aeroplane. Over the next thirteen months the Anglo-American Navies in particular were to learn this change in operational emphasis in a most painful fashion in the South China Sea and at Pearl Harbour respectively.

1941 – On the Back Foot

Counter-Blow

For the remainder of 1940 the Royal Navy paced through the Italian's 'backyard' with almost total immunity. Late in November another potential sea action between Italian and

Belts of .303 ammunition for some of the eight machine guns on a Fulmar are being fed into the gun bays. Note how the rear-inner wing section is folded forward. The relatively cramped hangar conditions are exemplified by the close proximity of an Albacore from No.817 Sqdn. whose wings are also folded.

British capital ships loomed up in the western Mediterranean off Cap Spartivento in Sardinia. A convoy escorted by Force H ran across an enemy Force including VITTORIO VENETO and CUILIO CESARE. Although only the battleship RENOWN was on hand, the Italians still withdrew to the northeast. Two torpedo strikes by ARK ROYAL's Swordfish were launched during the engagement – the first against the battleships, the second against their cruiser support Sqdn. – but with no hits recorded. The Skuas of No.803 also bombed the latter-named units, with equal lack of success. Late in the day, Italian high-level bombers counter-attacked in the face of spirited opposition from the Fulmars of No.808 Sqdn. as well as the ARK's Skuas that cost the Regia Aeronautica several aircraft for no result.

The theoretical surface superiority of the Italian Navy had once again been more than cancelled out by the presence of the Fleet Air Arm, while its own aerial threat had conversely proved virtually useless. In this latter failure can be seen the seeds of a complacency regarding aerial effect against its own warships – a complacency that should have been dispelled by the recent events at Taranto created by the Royal Navy's own airborne assault Force. (On the other hand, that attack had been delivered against a static Force, as opposed to a highly mobile Force steaming in the open stretches of the sea, with a correspondingly higher degree of immunity from bombs and even torpedoes).

The British Army's Offensive to drive the Italians out of Egypt began on 9 December. The Navy supported the soldiers by bombarding coastal positions, through use of its capital ship heavy weapons; Swordfish from EAGLE joined in the Land action with their crews carrying out dive-bombing sorties. However, Nemesis was waiting just around the corner as the

The after-lift on ARK ROYAL supports a Swordfish whose engine is already warming up as the deck handlers prepare to unfold the starboard wing. The other two 'Stringbags' are fully prepared for take off, while four Skuas on the after flight deck are similarly prepared for launch.

year closed and Adolf Hitler began to bolster his failed Ally's attempts to carry out a land Invasion of Greece as well as an equal failure to challenge the Royal Navy at sea, and Wavell's Army on land.

The *Luftwaffe* in the form of *Fliegerkorps* X commanded by *General* Geisler, had transferred wholesale into Sicily during December. Included among *Korps* strength were the Ju 87s of I./St.G (*Stukageschwader*) 1 led by *Hauptmann* Hozzel and II/St.G 2 commanded by *Major* Enneccerus. Both units were well trained in the art of anti-shipping attacks, while the '*Stuka*' was rightly respected, if not feared, as a precision bomb-aiming machine, of which more than 50 were on hand.

Admiral Cunningham once again stood out to sea on 7 January in order to cover convoy movements and, with that primary duty completed, to then seek out enemy shipping close to the Italian coastline. He appeared confident that little or no damage was likely to occur to any of his warships that included the carrier ILLUSTRIOUS, especially when given the armoured nature of this vessel's structure. By 10 January the Fleet was steaming off the Island of Pantellaria in the Narrows between Tunisia and western Sicily, having taken over convoy

escort duties from Force H, and with ILLUSTRIOUS positioned between the battleships WARSPITE and VALIANT. To the north, and well within attack range from their airfield at Trapani in northwest Sicily, the crews of the two *Stuka Gruppen* were preparing for operations against the Royal Navy.

The fighter resources on hand to fend off attackers was slim enough at any time, even when the units concerned were up to full serviceable aircraft strength. On 10 January No.806 Sqdn. appears to have had just twelve Fulmars qualifying for this category. This was an ominous portent for the chances of beating off the impending aerial assault. During the late morning, several SM79s made attack runs at low altitude, the effect of which was to draw the Combat Air Patrol fighters down and off in extended tail-chases that neither brought down any of the retiring enemy aircraft nor left the Fleet with any form of high cover – not that the total number of Fulmars could have done more than blunt the effect of the looming *Luftwaffe* assault had all been in place at the time!

Prior to the attack, two experienced Swordfish pilots from No.819 Sqdn. Lts. Charles Lamb (who had survived the sinking of COURAGEOUS in 1939) and Michael Torrens-Spence (A fellow member of the Taranto assault Force) were discussing the general situation before Lamb took off on his anti-submarine patrol. The latter had been privy to Intelligence reports regarding the *Luftwaffe*'s presence and grimly suggested that the Germans would soon create a Hell over the Fleet compared to all previous experiences borne by Italian equivalent efforts. His forecast was accurate within a matter of hours, as Lt. Lamb ended his patrol and prepared to land, only to be shocked as all shipboard guns opened up and a German aircraft swept by. The battle for survival was on!

Four Fulmars already ranged on the deck 'scrambled' into the air just as the *Luftwaffe* formation arrived overhead, before breaking up into disciplined sub-formations and tipping over into their coordinated dives. One group of ten *Stukas* engaged the two battleships by way of drawing off their supporting AA fire for ILLUSTRIOUS, and the remaining thirty-three concentrated on the carrier. Sub-formations consisting of two *Ketten* (vee-formations) attacked from astern and fine on either beam; the AA gunners' fire was accordingly diluted as they strove to bring their weapons to bear.

Two further fighters had been brought up from the hangar but just one got clear before the deadly accuracy of the first wave began to make itself felt. While several bombs burst close to the carrier's hull, the litany of destruction began. One bomb struck one 'pompom' gun mount before detonating in the sea. Almost at once, the forward flight deck on the port side absorbed a strike that started fires below. A second gun mount ahead of the superstructure was literally torn off and cast into the sea. So far, the scale of damage was seemingly sustainable – that is, until one of the 500 kg. weapons smashed into the aft hangar through the lowered lift-well, having already demolished the single ranged Fulmar and obliterated its unfortunate crew. The carnage was terrible, aided by the disintegration of the fire screens that scattered huge metal shards everywhere, causing frightful degrees of mutilation. Damage sustained by the gun mounts around this section of the carrier that rendered most out of action was later associated with this particular bomb strike as well as a second that exploded ammunition and aviation fuel. With little or no AA fire to oppose their approach, the remaining *Stukas* secured a sixth strike that further punched through the flight deck aft, knocked out the steering gear and sent the carrier into an uncontrollable series of manoeuvres for some time. Many of the aircrew that had participated in the Taranto operation were killed or fatally injured when the wardroom they were in was shredded thanks to the impact of this final bomb.

The handful of Fulmars that had managed to get airborne found themselves embroiled in a maelstrom of wildly gyrating Ju 87s, but did their level best to at least bring their guns to bear. With the bombers heading in at around 10,000 ft. and virtually overhead as the fighters took off, combined with the sedate climb-rate for the Fulmar of some 1,200 ft. a minute, there had been no prospect at all of the FAA crews gaining the necessary height advantage before the assaults commenced. Indeed the *Luftwaffe* rear gunners handed out punishment along with their pilots' use of the Ju 87 fixed wing guns, as the dive-bombers swarmed around their prey. One Fulmar flown by Sub-Lt. Lowe was later credited with a 'kill' but barely had time to savour the victory before being taken down from behind by another Ju 87, with both crewmembers being killed. The other four crews, having expended their ammunition, headed for Malta and landed at Hal Far, where they were refuelled and rearmed, ready for the inevitable call for support from ILLUSTRIOUS as further air attacks developed.

The entire *Luftwaffe* assault was completed within less than ten minutes. The basic result of the action, to use a soccer analogy, could be regarded as a technical 'draw', but with one 'team' (the *Luftwaffe*) pressing the other 'team' (The Royal Navy) back into its own penalty area. The value of the 'armored box' concept applied to this modern Class of carrier had at least kept the warship afloat; on the other hand, ILLUSTRIOUS was now effectively rendered useless in her primary function until such time as she could be repaired – and that was assuming her continued survival while still within range of further *Luftwaffe* attacks. The 'Achilles Heel' formed of her un-armored lifts had been fully exposed, as was the inability of her flight deck, even with full armor provision, to withstand the striking power of a 500 kg. bomb. Over the ensuing two years two of the sister-ships to ILLUSTRIOUS would find themselves in a similar situation of heavily qualified survival.

Having regained a measure of control over his errant warship, Capt. Boyd then steered his crippled charge towards Grand Harbor in Malta. The *Luftwaffe* had obviously not finished with ILLUSTRIOUS and resumed their efforts to sink her during the late afternoon. The carrier's much closer proximity to Malta enabled a more concerted and controlled fighter defence to be put up against the attackers. In the case of the Fulmars, they appeared over their carrier as the attackers were completing their dives and a protracted tail-chase ensued north towards Sicily. A final torpedo attack by SM79s in the evening proved fruitless and the smoke-shrouded carrier, some of her internal fires not yet fully extinguished, finally berthed in Grand Harbor. Both ship and crew's immediate ordeal was over, but another thirteen days would elapse before ILLUSTRIOUS would slip out eastwards in the night towards Alexandria and ultimately an American repair yard. In the course of the day's action, just three Ju 87s were confirmed as shot down, a marginal cost in knocking a major Royal Navy warship out of action.

Although there were three days within this overall period on which major air assaults were conducted on Grand Harbor, it was only on the 13th that Axis reconnaissance aircraft confirmed the presence there of the carrier. In that short time-span, the Island's AA defences had been concentrated around Valetta, to bolster the small number of RAF and FAA fighters available. The 'Box' barrage thrown up by the fast-firing Bofors and the more-steady fire-rate of the batteries equipped with 5.25-inch guns, was to prove a firm deterrent to the dive-bombers in particular.

Even so, the presence of more than sixty Ju 87s and Ju 88s on the 16th ensured that some of their ordnance would impact close to, or on two occasions upon, their target. Three days later, the latest major effort to destroy ILLUSTRIOUS involved at least two waves of either Ju 87 or Ju 88 formations, along with a handful of He 111s. The British fighters continued to peck at their adversaries, who did not secure a single direct hit although structural damage was caused through the concussive effect of near misses. Five enemy bombers were added to the growing tally of 'kills' this day, of which one was claimed by Lt. Henley. However, his Fulmar was fatally crippled during the same action and he was forced to 'ditch' offshore

Lessons

Another salutary lesson for the Royal Navy arising from the 10 January action lay in the AA weapon provision. The eight high-angle twin-gun mounts were neither too accurate nor able to throw up a great pattern of shells against aircraft, while the 'pom-pom' batteries were even more inaccurate despite their multiple-barrel layout and fast rate of fire. All in all, the Fleet Carriers were dangerously short of striking power in this vital field, as indeed were the vast majority of the Nation's warships – even those specially commissioned to act in the AA role. It would take the wholesale introduction of the Oerlikon and Bofors Companies' AA designs to even begin tilting the defensive balance back in the Royal Navy's favor.

The generally mediocre to abysmal standard of Naval AA gunnery was reportedly demonstrated in the late 1930s by an incident involving a 'Queen Bee', an adapted Tiger Moth primary trainer, un-manned aircraft under radio control, that was featured in a demonstration to Press newspaper and film representatives. The demonstration was laid on with a view to highlighting the deadly accuracy of the Navy's weaponry in this field. However, the 'Queen Bee' appeared totally unwilling to oblige as she proceeded to fly unscathed through the 'wall' of fire directed at her pedestrian progress. In desperation, one of the Senior Staff muttered to the aircraft controller; "dial S for Spin!" The requisite action resulted in the aircraft tumbling out of the sky – a scene that one newsreel commentator was

alleged to have commented upon with more vigour than honesty; "No aircraft can withstand the withering blast delivered by the Navy's gunners!"

FORMIDABLE

The second of the four original ILLUSTRIOUS Class carriers had been commissioned in November 1940, FORMIDABLE was also assigned to the Mediterranean Fleet in place of her battered sister-ship and arrived at Alexandria on 10 March 1941. On board were the by-now familiar Fulmars, in this case provided to No. 803 Sqdn. The carrier's strike-force aircraft by comparison consisted of yet another new design to appear over the Mediterranean at least; this was the Fairey Albacore that was a perceived replacement for the venerable Swordfish. Nos. 826 and 829 Sqdn. – the former unit having been the first to fly the Albacore on operations over Home Waters fully twelve months before – had been assigned to FORMIDABLE.

The Albacore had been built to Specification S.41/36 and featured several improvements over the Swordfish, including all-metal monocoque fuselage skin, sleeve-valve engine with a variable-pitch propeller, flaps that also served as dive brakes and – most significant in view of the need for crew comfort – a fully enclosed cockpit. On the other hand the drag penalty imposed by the heavier airframe and the retention of a fixed landing gear resulted in a disappointing increase in overall speed and climb-rate, although range and maximum service ceiling was virtually doubled. And so it was to be that the Albacore's front-line service career would only last until 1942-1943, whereas its supposed 'predecessor' the 'Stringbag' would soldier on until the end of World War II!

Matapan

The decision to divert a sizeable proportion of Wavell's victorious Army northward across the Mediterranean to Greece was to ultimately result in a 'no-win' situation both as regards that gallant country's attempts to stem the Axis tide of conquest even with Britain's assistance, and Gen Wavell's inevitably weakened Force's inability to withstand the onrush of Rommel's *Afrikakorps* when this took place towards the end of March.

British convoy movements to Greece commenced at the beginning of March, and towards the month-end the threat of Italian naval challenges to such movements began to take shape according to Intelligence service monitoring of the enemy's radio traffic. Admiral Iachino's original brief was to sail up into the Aegean Sea to interdict British convoy traffic to Greece. However, his fear of being trapped by Cunningham's Fleet in this rather restricted region led him to alter course to south east of Crete in the hope of picking off the convoy traffic in more open waters. Iachino's caution was all the more

On 13 November 1941 ARK ROYAL was returning to Gibraltar from her latest operational sortie when she unknowingly ran across the path of U-81. The *Kriegsmarine* submarine probably fired off more than one torpedo but the one recorded strike was enough to fatally cripple the carrier. At this point a destroyer is manoeuvering alongside the stricken warship.

puzzling since he had accepted the 'false trail' laid on by Cunningham that fooled Italian reconnaissance aircraft into reporting the Mediterranean Fleet to be berthed with awnings stretched over the battleships' quarterdecks as if preparing for social events!

Admiral Cunningham's deception had worked, in addition to which all convoy movements had either been halted or, in the case of the one heading for Greece, ordered to turn back. Vice-Admiral Pridham-Whipple was duly ordered to concentrate his cruiser/destroyer Force south of Crete on 28 March, and after darkness fell that night, Cunningham sallied forth from Alexandria with his main Fleet that included the newly-arrived FORMIDABLE. RAF patrol aircraft had reported a small cruiser force steaming west of Crete the previous day, and aircraft from FORMIDABLE confirmed this fact early next day.

The planned rendezvous with Cunningham was still several hours away when Pridham-Whipple's warship contingent made contact with the Italian cruisers – and then with what was recorded as 'two battleships'. Sandwiched between the two arms of the Italian Navy whose warships outpaced his, the Vice-Admiral had no choice but to steam full ahead and hope that he would close with Cunningham's main Force before his flimsy warships came within range of the enemy's heavy guns. In the event it was the Albacores flying off FORMIDABLE that almost certainly proved to be the salvation of the hard-pressed light Force, since Iachino had already expended nearly one hundred fifteen-inch rounds against his opponents, fortunately without effect. What turned out to be not two battleships but VITTORIO VENETO on her own was attacked by six Albacores of No.826 Sqdn., but despite making runs from both flanks of their target, none of

ARK ROYAL has canted over to starboard following the single torpedo strike by U-81 on 13 November 1941. Five Swordfish cling precariously to the flight deck. Although the carrier was temporarily stabilised, a flow of water into her boiler uptakes sealed her fate the day following her being struck.

VICTORIOUS first embarked Sea Hurricanes in June 1942 when No.885 Sqdn. arrived with Mk.Ibs. The original photo caption states this aircraft is about to land on. It is more likely that the pilot is over-shooting when given his height, position along the deck length and the absence of a raised safety barrier.

the torpedoes struck home. However, Admiral Iachino was seemingly not prepared to accept further aerial challenges and reversed course to the northwest.

A second strike against the retreating Italian warships was launched just after noon in the hope of either sinking or crippling the capital ship so that she could be engaged on the surface in the latter instance. The five aircraft included two Swordfish of No.829 Sqdn. led by Lt-Cdr. Dalyell-Stead. As the formation closed with their target, the Italian AA gunners' attention was diverted by the presence of RAF Blenheims operating from Greece. The Lead Albacore gained its dropping position and was turning away when it was smashed out of the sky and its crew killed. Observers on the other aircraft saw how the released torpedo struck the battleship around that ever-vulnerable point on any vessel, the propeller shafts.

The rear compartments were flooded as VITTORIO VENETO staggered to a halt, listing to port and down by the

stern. At this stage hopes ran high for a surface engagement but the damage-repair parties unfortunately proved their value by quickly getting the battleship underway and at increasing speed. Meanwhile the returning aircraft were fortunate to find their floating 'airfield' still intact. During their absence a two-pronged assault by individual SM79 torpedo-bombers had seen the carrier surviving only through frantic manoeuvering.

A third strike was launched in the late afternoon comprising six Albacores and two Swordfish, with a further two Swordfish of No.815 Sqdn. currently detached to Maleme on Crete; one of the pilots was Lt. Torrens-Spence, who had participated in the Taranto operation, and whose torpedo was to play a vital part in the ensuing night's surface action. The Italian warships were by now steaming in a compact formation, and their AA defences threw up a seemingly impenetrable wall of fire. However, the attacking crews approached from various angles and split the overall defensive effort.

The cruiser POLA was positioned in the middle of the starboard column and sustained a single strike that brought her to a halt, the weapon in question being credited to the Torrens-Spence Swordfish. The potential loss of one warship would not normally have been a critical factor in any action, but this was not the case here. Admiral Iachino was under the misapprehension – not dispelled by his own air reconnaissance confirming the close proximity of the enemy main Force, as well as the presence of the Swordfish floatplane 'spotter' from WARSPITE – that Cunningham's Fleet was much further away. This factor persuaded him there was little risk in detaching the cruisers FIUME and ZARA along with two destroyers to assist the cripple.

Cunningham's battleships were steaming in the dark as midnight was approaching when radar 'contact' was made with the unsuspecting Italian warships attending to POLA; they in turn were bereft of any notion of the impending danger since none were similarly equipped with such surveillance sets. So it was that when a bank of searchlights illuminated the hapless Italians their trio of warships was deluged by a rain of heavy shells that literally threw gun turrets and other large fittings into the air. The murderous barrage ironically left just POLA afloat and she was despatched by torpedo in the morning.

Grecian Interlude and 'Ghost' Squadrons

Following the loss of their carrier, Nos.815 and 819 Sqdns. personnel were concentrated within the ranks of the former unit and No.819 Sqdn. was disbanded. The expanded Sqdn. was initially based at Dekheila in North Africa and participated in the campaign that was currently driving the Italian Army back into Libya. An advance party of aircraft and personnel was detached to Crete in January and in mid-February, the remainder of the Swordfish also moved to the island, from where the crews were tasked with protecting British troop and equipment convoys heading for Greece. This activity having been largely completed by early March, a further transfer to Eleusis in Greece was carried out.

The RAF presence in Greece was already several months old at this time, and from 9 February bombers and fighters were operating from a forward airfield called Paramythia deep in the mountains of western Greece and close to the Adriatic coast. The extended valley containing the airfield was at an altitude of 3000 ft. but the surrounding mountains topped 6000 ft. The airfield's existence was seemingly unknown to the enemy, and the Swordfish crews forming the detachment sent to operate from the hill-shrouded airfield were instructed not to complete their hazardous flight to there should they be spotted by Italian aircraft but to return to Eleusis.

Their primary duty was to attack shipping in the Albanian ports of Valona and Durazzo. However, there was a basic logistical limitation due to the airfield's geographic isolation. The lack of proper road access meant that ordnance and fuel reserves were always very restricted. Consequently the Swordfish making each sortie would then have to stage back to Eleusis in order to pick up further stocks of torpedoes.

During the main moon periods of March and April the Swordfish crews wended their way through the high terrain and descended upon their targets, then made the equally difficult return leg to Paramythia. The greatly varied and unpredictable barometric pressures encountered in the region meant that pilots had to be very careful, especially when descending to their final attack runs over the sea. Even so, Lt. Lamb while making did make temporary contact with the water during the first sortie on 13 March, and was fortunate to survive the experience! One freighter was sunk but the CO, Lt-Cdr. Jago did not return although all three airmen survived as POWs. Blenheims from No.211 Sqdn. who acted in a diversionary role joined the FAA crews. Lt. Lamb demonstrated both his flying skill and the maneuverability of the Swordfish next day. He was on the return leg from Eleusis and off Corfu when two CR42 biplane fighters attacked. Two passes were made but on each occasion Lamb literally stood his aircraft on its tail; on the second pass the over-concentration of the enemy pilots on their prey saw them collide fatally!

Between 13 March and mid-April, the 'Stringbags' maintained the pressure on enemy shipping and were credited with several vessels sunk or damaged. Germany had invaded Yugoslavia and Greece on 6 April. By mid-month the RAF bomber strength had been virtually reduced to nil through operational attrition, and the FAA crews were ordered out following the latest bombing attack on the 17th. (It took the Italians six weeks to discover the mystery airfield but after succeeding on 22 March, their aircraft then conducted regular attacks). However, a final attack that evening led by the Sqdn.'s new CO, Lt. Torrens-Spence, exacted a final retribution by sinking two freighters at Valona although one crew was shot down and captured. The saga of the 'Ghost' airfields and its occupants had been brought to its inevitable conclusion. The Swordfish then staged through Eleusis to Maleme on Crete.

Dark Days off Crete

The severe pounding handed out to ILLUSTRIOUS by the *Luftwaffe* dive bombers in January 1941 was a clear warning to the Royal Navy that air power was now taking over from the capital ship as the most potent form of attack in both tactical and strategic form. The absence of air cover over its surface warships – or indeed over any of the Navies involved during World War II – was destined to bring about sustained punishment and losses whenever this scenario arose. By the end of April, the Land Campaign in Greece had terminated in a scrambled evacuation of Britain's service personnel from that country, now under full Axis control. The evacuated soldiers and airmen found themselves but sixty miles off the southern tip of Greece, on the island of Crete, a location that was within striking distance of the *Luftwaffe* and Germany's elite *Fallschirmjäger* (Parachute) Army. Sure enough, the final days of May witnessed the launching of an Invasion force to take over the island.

FORMIDABLE's aircraft had been trying to blunt the worst of the German effort by attacking various installations, including airfields on Scarpanto, an island east of Crete. Her aircraft complement consisted of just half her normal maximum figure, at fifteen Swordfish and twelve Fulmar fighters. The exposure to air attack in these circumstances was always high, and duly arose on 25 May. The same unit (II./St.G 2) that had been engaged in the attack on ILLUSTRIOUS appeared overhead to challenge FORMIDABLE's progress. The minimal Fulmar patrol of two was unable to do more than disturb an element of the Ju 87 formation that duly went about its business in deadly accuracy.

Despite the best efforts of the helmsman, at least two bombs impacted with the rear and forward flight deck, with the latter strike penetrating the armoured deck and exploding inside to cause serious damage and fires that were fortunately brought swiftly under control. Although the scale of damage was nothing like as severe as that borne by ILLUSTRIOUS it was more than sufficient to place the carrier out of effective action as a flying platform, while the 'mining' effect of near misses also adversely affected the hull structure and caused speed to be noticeably reduced. The Navy's complement of four modern Fleet carriers had now been effectively reduced to two, with ARK ROYAL and VICTORIOUS being the fortunate exceptions. FORMIDABLE was destined to join ILLUSTRIOUS in the American repair dockyard at Norfolk for many months ahead.

The long-term loss of FORMIDABLE as an aerial fighting platform did not largely apply to her Sqdns. The aircraft, aircrew and support personnel, were disembarked at Alexandria for what transpired as a regular spell of operational 'shore duty' in support of the British and Commonwealth forces. Nos.803 and 806 Sqdns. took on RAF Hurricanes and No.826 Sqdn. continued land-based operations from North Africa and Malta with its Albacores until disbandment in October 1943. The exception was No.829 Sqdn.'s Swordfish and Albacores who, although taking part in the Syrian Campaign, saw its the Swordfish element again embarked on FORMIDABLE to provide anti-submarines patrols before her departure for the United States. The remaining Sqdns. became a part of No.201 Naval Cooperation Group within the Middle East Air Force (MEAF) and were soon in action.

'Tiger'

Just two to three weeks prior to her being crippled, FORMIDABLE, along with ARK ROYAL, had played its part in covering the vital 'Tiger' convoy. This was a special force whose merchantmen were laden with scores of tanks and aircraft for the British forces in North Africa. The need to get these supplies through as quickly as possible impelled the Government to direct its ships through the greatly reduced Mediterranean route compared to that around Africa. ARK's available Fulmar numbers was limited to just twelve shared between Nos.807 and 808 Sqdns. These were first into sustained action on 8 May when hard-fought air battles with SM79s escorted by CR42s, as well as Ju 87s and Bf 110s, resulted in a number of Axis casualties at the cost of two Fulmars and one crew lost and a third fighter 'written off'.

The following day, both carriers' aircraft were involved as the Mediterranean Fleet was then south of Malta. However, the indifferent weather conditions worked in the convoy's favor as it was not picked up. A 'shadower' had gained visual sight

Although this picture is taken at Scapa Flow in Scotland, its content has a direct link to Malta. The lone Fulmar is facing a row of U.S. Navy Devastator glide-bombers and a single F4F Wildcat. The latter had been disembarked from USS WASP. Their places were taken by Spitfires Mk.V destined to be flown off to the beleaguered Island by the U.S. Navy carrier during Spring, 1942.

and managed to stagger back to Sicily after being shot up by Fulmars of No.806 Sqdn. but it was the following night (10th) before the next attack came in. This consisted of torpedo-bombers attempting to utilise the moonlight condition, but failing in their endeavours. Four of the five merchantmen were still afloat by the 11th when the final Axis air assault came in. Nine Ju 88s of LG 1 were challenged by two Fulmars of FORMIDABLE's No.806 Sqdn. The single enemy loss was achieved in a tragic manner because Lt. Sparkes collided with his target, causing both crews to be killed in the collision. However, the safe delivery of 283 out of 330 tanks and forty-three out of fifty-three Hurricanes had been basically achieved, and the convoy steamed into Alexandria two days later.

Crisis: 'Behind the Lines' – Iraq

By late April 1941 the overall military situation in the Mediterranean was still in a critical form for the British. Greece had just fallen and the island of Crete was the next likely Axis target. The weakened forces in North Africa were similarly being put on the back foot by the *Afrikakorps*. It was now that a third more subtle, but equally dangerous, threat to Britain's military security in the Middle East began to arise in Iraq. Originally a British mandated territory arising out of Turkey's defeat in 1918, Iraq had gained independence in 1927 but agreed under Treaty terms to allow British bases to be established and permit troop movements through its land. Rashid Ali, a pro-Axis politician, had recently seized power and this act raised the distinct possibility of German/Italian military incursions. A military 'face-off' between the two countries finally led to authorisation from London for the occupants of the main airfield at Habbaniyah to forcibly remove the Iraqi forces surrounding the area, and the Campaign began on 2 May.

No.814 Sqdn., normally embarked on HERMES but now assigned to this land-based duty, furnished part of the air support based at the other RAF airfield, Shaibah. However, the first sortie flown was a passive one in that the six aircraft flew over Basra in a 'show of strength'. Over the next two weeks, operations took on a positive angle when a bridge over the Euphrates, and barracks at Nazari were among the selected targets. One Swordfish was damaged by AA fire and force-landed on the 15th; Lt. Dundas, witnessing the incident, quickly landed and picked up the crew as Iraqi soldiers closed in and fired, damaging but not fatally crippling the rescue Swordfish.

Luftwaffe reinforcements in the form of He 111s of 4./ KG 4 and Bf 110s of 6./ZG 76 had arrived by mid-month, but their effect on the overall Campaign's conduct was surprisingly small and short-lived, although separate attacks on Habbaniyah by each unit did inflict notable losses among the RAF aircraft. By the 30th the main British land force was at the gates of

A Seafire's momentum has taken it over the forward edge of an escort carrier's already short flight deck and down onto the foredeck. The pilot is commencing his exit from the cockpit, which is suspended nearly fifteen feet above the foredeck surface, and risks injury should he slip forward.

Baghdad, whereupon Rashid Ali fled his post and the city mayor negotiated a truce.

Crisis: 'Behind the Lines' – Syria

Just as Iraq had been placed under British mandate following the end of World War I so two other former Turkish-controlled territories – Syria and Lebanon – had been allocated to France on the same legal basis. Both lands fell under Vichy French administration from June 1940, so creating an ambivalent political state of relations with Britain. By May 1941, to the suspicion of subversive activities by the Axis powers being conducted within Syria, was now added the very real threat of a military incursion, spearheaded by an airborne Invasion conducted from Greece. The disastrous 'Pyrrhic victory' of the *Fallschirmjäger* over Crete was yet to be confirmed by Hitler, so this potentially grave scenario was still relevant when the British government finally imposed on Gen. Wavell to order a ground advance into Syria. This was despite his (Wavell's) reservations about drawing forces away from his projected build-up for Operation 'Battleaxe' that was intended as a counter-offensive against Rommel.

Prior to the Operation's launch on 8 June, the RAF had conducted photo-reconnaissance sorties as well as the occasional strafing attack on Lebanese targets while flying out of Palestine. In fact the air support for Operation 'Exporter' was to come from units based all over the region, from Iraq to Egypt, Transjordan, Palestine and Cyprus. Once again the FAA were called on to operate. On hand were the four Sqdns. not long disembarked from the heavily damaged FORMIDABLE – Nos.803 and 806 (Fulmars) located in Palestine and Egypt, 826 (Swordfish), and 829 (Albacores) stationed in Cyprus; also on the island were the Swordfish from No.815 Sqdn.

The invading British and Commonwealth Force crossed into southern Lebanon and Syria along their borders with Palestine, and so it was the Sqdns. based there that first engaged the Vichy French Air Force, among whose numbers were the D520s of GCIII/6. The Fulmars of No.803 Sqdn. were given a patrolling brief above Royal Navy cruisers operating off the Lebanese coast, and it was the FAA crews' misfortune to come up against a six-strong GCIII/6 formation during the 8th. Although the Fulmars were in equal numbers, it was the sole positive feature of the ensuing combat. The Vichy French pilots held a clear edge in manoeuvrability and speed as well as possessing cannon armament. Three Fulmars were shot down, with only one of the crews surviving, and a fourth was severely shot up and fortunate to regain its airfield at Lydda, where it was 'written off'. All this carnage was not in any way balanced up since all six D520s remained unscathed.

No.829 Sqdn.'s Albacores transferred to Lydda on the 10th while No.815 Sqdn., remaining on Cyprus for the duration of 'Exporter', recorded a night sortie against a seaport two days later. The Vichy French military strength was not only equal if not marginally superior to their adversary, but the degree of resistance was to prove much more protracted and intense than that experienced in Iraq. (This could be partially explained by the 'fact' that far from inviting Axis involvement, the French authorities had previously ordered all existing German and Italian personnel out of Syria, and therefore regarded the British intervention as unjustified and an 'act of war').

Vichy French reinforcements of aircraft and warships were steadily indulged in as the Campaign progressed, with the latter element involving three destroyers dispatched from Toulon. These were skirting Cyprus when 'spotted' by an RAF Sunderland on the 15th. Next day No.815 Sqdn. was sent out and intercepted the flotilla off the Syrian coast. No more than six aircraft were on the unit's strength at any one time, but this mattered naught for the PAUL CHEVALIER, which absorbed the fatal effect of a single well-directed torpedo; AA fire took down one of the attackers, but both airmen were rescued by one of the surviving warships.

By the 21st the main British force based in Iraq was free to commence the eastern part of a vast 'pincers' movement against Syria, but the lack of air cover coupled to an intensive bombing assault by the Vichy French bombers temporarily curbed its forward advance. On the other hand, the steady build-up of RAF strength, particularly in bombers, coupled to a higher casualty rate among its adversary's ranks as June came to a close and July was entered, created a logistical 'haemorrhage' that in turn allowed the British ground forces to continue their slow but inexorable advance on both fronts while relatively free from attack.

The FAA units continued to operate mainly off the Syrian coast on patrol and anti-shipping duties, where a second notable success was scored on 4 July. This time round it was the Albacores of No.829 that were involved as the Vichy French strove ever more desperately to shore up their by now parlous situation with British forces streaming northward and westward into the Syrian heartland. The steamer SAINT-DIDIER was located off the Turkish coast and attacked unsuccessfully by one Albacore. Nothing daunted – and not withstanding that when next located the vessel was deep in Turkish territorial waters off Adalia – further attacks were made, with one torpedo impacting against a jetty! The remaining three 'tin-fish' from this attacking force struck home and the steamer went under.

This was the final major involvement of the Fleet Air Arm in the Syrian Campaign that was concluded on the 14th with the appropriate signing ceremony. The action had contained a strong element of bitterness and sadness in that it had witnessed citizen fighting against citizen, since the assault force had included the Free French. The FAA units now largely transferred to Egypt, where Nos.803 and 806 Sqdn. rapidly, and surely thankfully, exchanged their Fulmars for Mk.1 Hurricanes in July, joining with No.805 Sqdn.'s Martlets to form the Naval Fighter Wing based in Egypt.

Pathfinders

The Fairey Albacore's somewhat short operational career did not feature many highlights before its withdrawal from front-line service, but one shining exception involved Nos.815, 821 and 826 Sqdns. in the desert between mid-1941 and the end of 1942. The first-mentioned Sqdn. was the first Albacore-equipped unit to be based in North Africa, and moved up from Dekheila towards the battle front for operations in August; the Base airfield was Ma'aten Bagush, but the loaded aircraft would fly up to and land on airfields right up at the Front in order to top up their fuel.

The aircraft were flown on nocturnal sorties against small concentrations such as ammunition dumps and armoured or soft-skin vehicle laagers. The aerial navigator's task during World War II was never easy, even with the latter-day

A Seafire Mk.Ib is in the process of being 'struck down' in the forward hangar on FURIOUS as the pilot is climbing out of the cockpit. Note the unusual T-pattern of the lift that permitted the stowage of this and other fixed-wing FAA aircraft such as the Sea Hurricane.

introduction of specialist equipment aids such as GEE, H2S and the like. However, those crews flying over land had at least a measure of guidance from the ground in reasonable weather conditions. Contrast this with the total absence of equivalent reference points on the oceans, as well as the more limited spaces on FAA aircraft into which to insert the above-mentioned equipment, and it can then be realised how the FAA Observer had to be very sound in his overall ability, both for his own and his crew's sake!

And so it proved to be the case that the trackless wastes of the desert were generally to prove no more a test of the individual Observer's navigation skills than the equally open ocean waters. As a result, the *Afrikakorps* was provided with a constant headache as its AA gunners sought to even pick out the slow-flying Albacores, let alone bring their gunfire to bear. The targets were illuminated by flares of which upwards of thirty-two were carried to allow for a sustained period of illumination, after which dive-bombing runs were carried out. The switch, from regular direct operations to acting in a 'Pathfinder' role for the RAF, occurred around September-October. This made good sense, since the mainly Wellington twin-engine bombers involved could drop a greater individual bomb-load; conversely, the continuous precision flare-marking of each target by the FAA crews was of tremendous benefit to their RAF contemporaries, especially if the bomber force had lost time and/or distance concentration for whatever reason.

As the Desert Campaign fluctuated initially in favor of, and then against, the Eighth Army during the winter of 1941-1942, so the FAA Sqdns. transferred their aircraft and support

material in similar fashion. The retention of torpedoes as part of the ordnance quota was to prove a sound decision when No.826 Sqdn. was alerted to attack a large enemy convoy that contained a troopship. Five crews took off from Berka, Benghazi on 23 January 1942 and duly delivered their 'tinfish', one of which fatally crippled the troopship; one Albacore flown by the Sqdn. CO (Lt-Cdr. Corbett) was shot down and the crew made POWs.

The third Albacore-equipped unit, No.815, arrived from Britain in late 1940 but only converted onto the Albacore in March 1942. By now, the range of targets involved the marking of harbors through which the Axis Powers were directing their supplies, as well as enemy airfields. More active duties were not ignored, and a steady number of mine-laying sorties as well as torpedo attacks against shipping were also indulged in, particularly during the final period of retreat to El Alamein. During the Eighth Army's period of regeneration leading up to the culminating and decisive Battle on 23 October, the Albacores regularly marked out positions for the RAF, so contributing to the disruptive effect on further enemy ground advances created by the constant bombing.

Force H

The sole operational carrier now in Mediterranean waters was the immortal ARK ROYAL although the faithful 'supply' carrier ARGUS was also regularly functioning in its equally vital role as a provider of fighters for Malta. Dr. Goebbel's recurrent cry, "Where is ARK ROYAL, Mr. Churchill?" was still being thrown back in his face, as the carrier and its aircraft continued to inflict punishment upon the Axis forces. Since the beginning of 1941 the ARK had participated in several Force H actions, spanning the length and breadth of the western Mediterranean.

These included the bombardment of Genoa, when 'spotting' for the battleships' guns had been supplemented by minelaying and bombing sorties to that city as well as La Spezia and Pisa. Between April and June she shared the 'ferrying' duty with ARGUS when Hurricanes were dispatched from her deck on seven occasions. During this period the last operational Skua-equipped Sqdn. No.800 was displaced by the Fulmars of No.807 Sqdn. An interesting aspect of ARK's service during mid-1941 was the embarking of two Sea Hurricanes for trials during July. The Hawker fighter's overall performance at low level was deemed inferior to that of the Fulmar, while the inability to 'strike' them below decks created a problem on deck. However, the Sea Hurricane would have its day in Fleet Air Arm service in the months ahead, with operations in the Mediterranean proving the fighter's value to the Navy.

Loss of ARK ROYAL

From her first 'near-miss' experience in the North Sea over two years previous the Navy's first custom-built modern Fleet carrier had justified her reputation as a survivor from the regular efforts of the Axis aircrews to secure her demise. There are numerous photographs taken that show the huge water fountains thrown up by sticks of bombs released in particular by the Italian high-level bombers, through which the ARK ROYAL steamed majestically onwards. Her seeming invulnerability to damage of any form bestowed on her a truly legendary status within the Royal Navy. Consequently, on 13 November, as the carrier was approaching Gibraltar following the latest delivery of RAF fighters to Malta, there was naturally no indication of impending doom among the ship's personnel who were anticipating another dockside spell on the Rock before their next sortie.

The *Kriegsmarine* had been steadily infiltrating numbers of U-Boats into the Mediterranean to bolster their Italian Ally's somewhat shaky performance at sea. On 13 November, U-81 was operating in the extreme western Mediterranean when her captain sighted the ARK. A careful stalking approach culminated in the successful discharge of a single torpedo against the carrier's starboard side although it was likely that more than one weapon had been fired. In the event, the strike was to ultimately prove fatal.

ARK ROYAL took up a steady list as all power failed and water began to penetrate her innards. The absence of diesel generators with which to combat the loss of her steam-driven generators seemed to have confirmed her immediate loss. However, electric cables from the destroyer LEGION were passed on board and connected up, so allowing the seawater to be pumped out and the vessel thereby marginally stabilised. Steam was again raised and the carrier began a laboriously slow progress towards Gibraltar.

Sadly, this reprieve was only temporary, because the water pressure on the ship's funnel uptake passing under the hangar deck proved too great. The resultant flooding pushed her over the maximum angle-degree beyond which recovery was impossible, apart from which the ability to operate her engines was now totally compromised. As daylight came in on the 14th and Gibraltar was appearing faintly in the distance, the ARK gracefully slid over and under the calm Mediterranean waters, and a true British Naval legend had gone.

Worsening Trend

ARK ROYAL's loss seemed to spell the beginning of a two-month period of severe depredation among the Royal Navy's Mediterranean force. On 25 November during a sortie by the Mediterranean Fleet the battleship BARHAM absorbed a torpedo spread from U-331 (*Kapitänleutnant* Tiesenhausen). The World War I capital ship rolled rapidly over to port before her after magazine exploded in a fearsome blast that killed over two-thirds of her crew. (The incident was recorded in all its frightful impressiveness by a film cameraman on one of the escorts).

On 19 December, two more capital ships QUEEN ELIZABETH and RESOLUTION, both contemporaries of BARHAM, were heavily damaged at their Alexandria berths by Italian frogmen using delay-action mines. Several cruisers sunk or damaged during the same period had also supplemented these losses. The Royal Navy's grasp on maritime matters had been seriously loosened, both in terms of surface and aerial strength. This disability would in turn be reflected in the immediate future by the relative immunity from attack for the various supply convoys ferrying men and material over to the *Afrikakorps*.

1942 –Year of Decision

The beginning of 1942 witnessed the existence of a truly global conflict following the involvement of America and the Japanese Empire from 7 December onwards. For the bulk of the year the three Axis powers would be largely in the military 'driving seat' as the Japanese seized vast swathes of territory across the Far East, the Germans swept back across Soviet territory and the *Afrikakorps* and its Italian contemporary dispatched the British Eighth Army back deep into Egypt.

The Royal Navy's fortunes had taken a further turn for the worse off Malaya on 10 December, when the modern battleship PRINCE OF WALES and the elderly battle cruiser REPULSE had succumbed to a devastating bomb and torpedo assault by Japanese 'Betty' and 'Nell' twin-engine bombers. The twilight was fast closing in on the career of the battleship providing the core of naval operations as demonstrated in this action. The absence through structural damage of the carrier INDOMITABLE as a planned element of what was code-named 'Force Z', as well as the immediate absence on the day of fighter cover by the RAF, probably contributed to this latest disaster for the Royal Navy. However, this factor only further emphasised the vulnerability of large surface warships when forced to operate on their own. Air power was here to stay, whether on land or at sea!

The last time EAGLE had operated in the Mediterranean she had been based in Alexandria. Now the veteran carrier was back, but this time was based at Gibraltar. The urgent need for a refit had been basically satisfied in December and

January, but not in respect of her boilers, which were worn out and now only permitted her to attain a maximum speed of around twenty knots, to present a critical deficiency as regarded the launching of aircraft. Her defensive armament was stepped up by twelve 20mm Oerliken cannon, while Type 290 sea/air warning and Type 285 gunnery fire control radar equipment was introduced. By mid-February the carrier was ready to depart the Mersey and take up her revised operational station where she joined the battleship MALAYA and the cruiser HERMIONE to complete a revised, and arguably reduced-strength, Force H.

The ever more urgent need to sustain Malta as a fighting bastion was to involve both EAGLE and the even more venerable ARGUS in a regular 'ferrying' role. Up to now the Air Ministry in its wisdom had reinforced the island's aerial

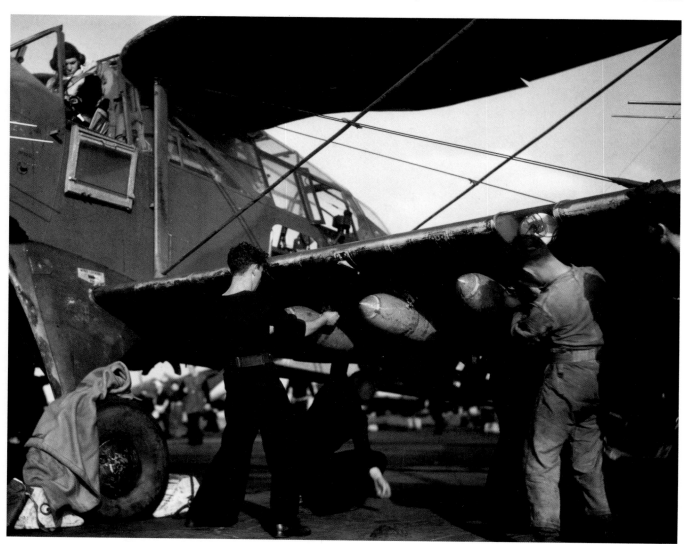

An Albacore pilot from No.820 Sqdn. sits in the cockpit while armorers put the finishing adjustments to the three 250 lb. bombs mounted under the port wing. The black fuselage and wing undersides were sprayed in this manner for the purpose of conducting night bombing and torpedo operations over North Africa and the Mediterranean Sea.

432 Sqdn. operated on the Albacore between April 1941 and December 1941 and embarked on VICTORIOUS. After service in the North Atlantic and Operation 'Pedestal', VICTORIOUS also participated in Operation 'Torch'. The solid outline of the Albacore is well defined in this picture, along with the curved camouflage separation line on the fuselage.

defence with Hurricanes, but the Hawker design was by now being badly out-performed by the Bf 109F that was the *Luftwaffe's* standard fighter in the Theater. The belated decision to switch over to the Spitfire Mk.V was now taken but the first batch of these machines' due for late February delivery had to be temporarily postponed due to the discovery of problems with the supplementary fuel tanks, and it was 6 March before EAGLE again stood out to sea. This time round, all fifteen of the RAF pilots lifted off the carrier's deck and completed their hazardous flight under navigational guidance from several Blenheims. More Spitfires were dispatched during a second March sortie but then boiler problems forced EAGLE into a month-long dry-dock spell, during which time the USS WASP completed the first of two successive monthly 'delivery' runs involving over 100 Spitfires.

Back on station EAGLE continued the fighter delivery process along with ARGUS as the summer approached; in addition to the RAF's requirements, a number of Albacores for the Navy's operations out of Malta were also dispatched during the May run; ironically all six biplanes involved were forced to land back due to engine problems! During the operation, a series of concentrated torpedo attacks was made by some six SM79s in the moonlight conditions. Intelligent manoeuvring ensured that none of the weapons struck home although one passed on an uncomfortably close parallel course to the carrier!

HMS EAGLE

The four Sea Hurricanes Ib on board were fitted with IFF and four-channel TR1196 in place of the single-channel TR9 sets, and whip aerials replaced the original 'mast' structure. On 12 June Lt. Crosley and another pilot were launched to intercept a 'bogey' but the other pilot's engine 'blew up' as the 'bogey' was sighted and the throttles opened. Crosley turned as the enemy aircraft was abeam and endeavoured to close to firing range from the port quarter. He was still well out of range when directly behind – and therefore an easy non-deflection shot for the gunners on what was now identified as an Z1007 tri-motor bomber. However, his luck held as he closed in and unleashed a burst of fire into the bomber's underside. The result was that the left wing of the Z1007 caught fire and the pilot sought what turned out to be a successful 'ditching' action; the seven-man crew were even more fortunate in being picked up by an RN destroyer.

Next day Crosley and the same fellow-pilot were again dispatched to intercept a 'bogey' and this aircraft was finally sighted while flying south towards Africa.; it was identified as a Ju 88 flying some 2,000 ft. higher. The other pilot attacked first while Crosley climbed before making his approach. Again, he was still out of range when in the desired deflection angle of thirty degrees, so a tail-chase ensued. A full twelve-second burst of fire realised smoke from the left engine but the Ju 88 kept flying; it disappeared off EAGLE's ADR screen but no visual sighting of a crash or 'ditching' was made by either Sea Hurricane pilot. (The Crosley experience on both occasions demonstrated a recurring problem, namely that of estimating range – a factor of anything up to 1:2 in terms of estimated/ real range was regularly experienced by many fighter pilots in combat).

Operation 'Torch'

The Anglo-American plan to invade northwest Africa was reluctantly agreed to by the American Government, whose original albeit hopelessly idealistic suggestion was for a more direct assault of *Festung Europa* through central Europe. Any such prospect for success was literally killed off by the British 'Reconnaissance in Force' launched upon the Channel port of Dieppe in mid-August that was thoroughly repulsed and in Churchill's words 'yielded bloody evidence of the strength of the Atlantic Wall'.

The sole airfield in Allied hands in the run-up to 'Torch' was the limited facility provided by Gibraltar. So it was that the air cover to be provided along an extended Front of some two hundred or so miles was destined to be shared between the RAF, the USAAF and both Nations' carrier forces. The Royal Navy's strength in this field was still rather stretched, but the Fleet carriers FORMIDABLE and VICTORIOUS along with FURIOUS joined Force H and were assigned to provide a covering force standing out to sea from the main landing points at Oran and Algiers that involved British forces; the third landing at Casablanca was a wholly American affair. The escort carriers BITER and DASHER would provide close support at Oran, while FURIOUS was to be detached from the covering force to add to their efforts. Further east at Algiers ARGUS and AVENGER would be on hand.

The Fleet carriers and FURIOUS had between them thirty-six Seafires, thirty-six Martlets, seven Fulmars as well as over thirty Albacores. Twenty-seven Sea Hurricanes were on hand to support the Oran attackers while equal numbers of Seafires and Hurricanes (eighteen) were to over-fly Algiers. The air cover was expected to last only as long as it took the Allied ground troops to seize airfields in the vicinity, into which the RAF and USAAF reinforcements could then be flown. This applied particularly at Oran with its two major locations of La Senia and Tafaroui. Algiers also possessed a large airfield at Blida well to the southwest of the city.

The Seafire Arrives

The Seafires Mk.1B of No.801 and Mk.IIC of 807 Sqdns. on FURIOUS represented the first of Supermarine's superlative fighting machine to enter service with the Fleet Air Arm. The Mk.IIC was also on hand with Nos.885 Sqdn. (FORMIDABLE), 884 Sqdn. (VICTORIOUS), and 880 Sqdn.

(ARGUS) It at last seemed, as the fourth year of World War II was entered, that the Admiralty was in possession of a fighter design that could match its Axis adversaries in most if not all respects. The Mk.1B was actually a 'navalised' version of the RAF's Mk.VB, albeit in one respect only, namely the fitting of an arrester-hook; overall performance was adequate for 1942 but somewhat limited by its Merlin 45 or 46 power-plants producing up to 1,470 hp, and the aerodynamic hindrance of a tropical filter under the nose.

The Mk.IIC was similarly powered but featured the producer's revised 'C' type wing as fitted to the RAF's Mk. VC and a strengthened rear fuselage into which were fitted catapult spools. Two sub-versions were built, the FIIC and LIIC with the latter variant powered by a Merlin 32 producing 1,640 hp, a four bladed propeller compared to the three-bladed unit on the Mks.1B and FIIC, and intended for low-level operations. Armament on all three variants consisted of two 20mm cannon and four .303 machine guns, even though the 'C' type wing could accommodate four cannon; on the other hand the Mk. IIC had provision for the carriage of bombs under the center fuselage or wings up to a maximum weight of 250 lbs.

These early variants suffered the same stowage limitation as the Sea Hurricane in that the wings were fixed, a situation that would only be remedied when a manually folding facility was introduced on the Seafire Mk.III. The new FAA fighter's ability to face its adversaries on equal terms promised a bright future for the Seafire; however, the practical experiences for the Supermarine fighter between now and VJ-Day while operating off the harsher 'base' offered by carrier decks compared to airfields would result in mixed fortunes for both the pilots and their machines!

One potential disadvantage for Seafire pilots forced to bale out lay in the compact nature of the cockpit area. The space was a tight fit for anybody of more than medium build, let alone the occupant who was generally enclosed in a bulky flight suit, whose girth was further extended by the wearing of a parachute harness and a seat-type parachute pack. The profusion of levers and knobs could be a further hindrance to anybody attempting to bale out, since these could easily snag the pilot's clothing.

The experiences of the Allied aviators at Algiers was to prove the more easier-paced of the separate actions, with sorties being conducted against coastal defences and airfields during the course of the day's action. In the case of the FAA the initial fighter patrol of four Martlets of No.882 Sqdn. after shooting up Blida were relived by a second Section led by Lt. Nation. The Leader's attention was soon drawn to signs of possible surrender rather than resistance from the airfield. Following radio discussions with VICTORIOUS and Admiral Lyster, clearance was granted for one fighter – naturally that of Lt. Nation! – to land and establish the full facts. Upon drawing up to a hangar and being conducted to a French senior officer, this individual confirmed the airfield's surrender to the Allies in writing; a few hours later an American Ranger party arrived to take over Blida. General resistance at Algiers followed this pattern in that the Allies were in complete control by nightfall.

At Oran the entire ground force was composed of American troops, in the hope that the Vichy French would not adopt the same hostile stance in the event of British personnel's presence – the bitter memories of the Royal Naval action in July 1940 had been seen as a reason for much sterner French resistance in this instance. Resistance was in fact met both on the ground and in the air from the commencement of the Invasion. Air operations began at dawn, with specific FAA strikes directed at Senia and Tafaroui. No.822 Sqdn.'s Albacores carried out a thorough plastering of the airfield's hangars at the former location and destroyed upwards of fifty Vichy aircraft in the process. On hand as escort were Sea Hurricanes from FURIOUS's two fighter Sqdns., which proved very timely although not entirely beneficial to the slow-flying Albacores.

Just as the latter were tipping over into their dives, a number of D520C fighters made their appearance and quickly knocked three of these attackers out of the sky; a fourth fell to well-directed AA fire. This sharp reverse was at least logistically balanced out by the FAA escorts who downed fully five of the stubby but aerodynamically pleasant French fighters, whose general performance was certainly on a par with its FAA contemporary, even if the four 20mm cannon armament on the Sea Hurricane out-matched the single cannon and four machine gun complement of the D520C. The action over, the surviving aircraft headed back to their carrier but only No.800 Sqdn. fully succeeded in their effort. No.804 Sqdn. also got down but in vastly inferior conditions, all six pilots having been forced to crash-land ashore after becoming lost in the poor visibility!

FAA action at Tafaroui was more limited when the Seafires off FURIOUS strafed the airfield and destroyed a handful of machines. Elsewhere, the Seafires of No.807 Sqdn. also indulged in shooting up Vichy French aircraft, while one of their number enjoyed a more personal success when the Sqdn. was engaged by D520Cs. This time round, the French pilots were rather on the back foot in their fighters' performance

The U.S. Navy carrier RANGER was part of the American Force deployed for Operation 'Torch'. One of its Wildcats is pictured ready to be launched. The huge yellow surround to the fuselage marking was also applied to FAA aircraft participating in the Landings. In addition a star design was superimposed over the British roundel colors, to reportedly create the illusion among the Vichy French defenders that the Landings were wholly American in nature.

The Albacore never enjoyed the public fame accorded to its contemporaries such as the Swordfish and Seafire, but it served the FAA in good measure, especially in the Mediterranean up to summer, 1943. This aircraft from No.826 Sqdn. is photographed sometime before the unit codes changed to S4. It bears the black under surfaces for nocturnal operations, against which the 4K codes are outlined in white

compared to the Seafires, and Sub-Lt. Baldwin proved the point when he brought down one of the defenders. The Albacore Sqdns. were taking on a variety of targets among which were two separate enemy naval fortresses whose guns were harassing attacking destroyers and ground forces respectively. The attacks by Nos.820 and 832 Sqdns. resulted in the majority of their 250 lb. bombs striking home and resulted in closing down the bombardments.

Whereas the Algiers landings were completed satisfactorily within twenty-four hours, the action at Oran extended into the 10th. The main airfields were secured and in Allied use by the 9th; tactical reconnaissance sorties were flown both by Seafires and the Fulmars of No.809 Sqdn. who had been trained for this specific function. By the 10th the Vichy French authorities could be in no doubt as to the final outcome of the Operation, and negotiations on this day brought 'Torch' to its conclusion – a conclusion that had witnessed a thankfully reduced scale of Allied casualties campared to what might have been inflicted had the opposition been pitched on a more determined scale.

The degree of intervention by the *Luftwaffe* had been surprisingly small so far but a twilight sortie by Ju 88s nearly demonstrated the continuing vulnerability of the carrier to air attack. ARGUS was steaming close inshore near Algiers and had not long launched three of her No.880 Sqdn. Seafires on a Combat Air Patrol (CAP) when the enemy formation was sighted. The superior altitude of the attackers meant that they were able to swoop down on the veteran carrier free of attention from the Seafires, while those fighters ranged on the deck with their pilots at 'cockpit readiness' status could not launch due to their warship being well out of the head-on wind direction.

The odds of ARGUS escaping a heavy battering let alone surviving appeared minimal in these circumstances, but a combination of sound manoeuvering linked with indifferent to poor bombing tactics saved the day. Just one bomb struck the aft section of the deck and excised the tail of a Seafire but otherwise left the carrier in sound order. Several other bombs impacted close to the hull but again left ARGUS intact. (There is no doubt that the carrier would have gone the same way as HERMES since she did not possess an armoured deck, and even this provision would have been no absolute guarantee of survival in the event of sufficient numbers of heavy-caliber bombs striking home).

Tragic 'Torch' Postscript

The presence within 'Torch' of three escort carriers not only held the promise of an expanding FAA force just for the purpose of conducting offensive operations of this nature; the steady introduction of the escort carrier to overall naval operations meant that the security of the convoy routes would be enhanced by the regular presence of these warships as they came into service in ever-increasing numbers.

The delay in service-entry of more escort carriers was primarily due to the Admiralty's insistence that the American-built vessels should be brought up to stricter standards as regards fire protection provision. However, a structural 'Achilles heel' of all these vessels lay in the fact that their commercial service hulls were of necessity un-armored, and moreover were of welded design compared to the sturdier (although not invulnerable) riveted pattern. All three escort carriers had been detached from the Northwest African Operation by the 12th and assigned to a support role for convoys sailing back to Britain. BITER and DASHER accomplished their voyages by the 19th and AVENGER commenced her homeward run on the 14th along with ARGUS.

The Sea Hurricane pilots of Nos.802 and 883 Sqdns. with their support crews had played their part in ensuring a swift and positive conclusion to 'Torch' and were doubtless anticipating some form of rest and recreation on return to Britain. However, this promise was to be tragically denied as convoy MKF1 steamed northward through the stygian darkness during the early hours of the 15th. U-Boats were in contact and an attack developed that saw one merchantman struck by

a torpedo. AVENGER was positioned within the port-inner column of the convoy and almost immediately was reportedly struck squarely by a second torpedo in the region of where her magazine and oil fuel tanks on the port side were located. Eyewitnesses in the vessel immediately astern of the carrier saw an explosion, followed almost immediately by a second more violent blast that broke the warship in two and enveloped the structure in flames. In less than two minutes the truncated remains had disappeared under the waves, leaving scattered pools of burning aviation fuel and pitifully few survivors – less than twenty out of a crew complement of around 550. (This cataclysmic incident subsequently witnessed the disbandment of both Sea Hurricane Sqdns. In No.802's case, the incident was the culmination of a tragic record of involvement in carrier losses; the previous two incidents had occurred when the unit was embarked first on GLORIOUS in June 1940 and then on AUDACITY the previous December to this final disaster).

Part Two
Malta

"Waking or sleeping, Malta is always in my thoughts." – *Admiral Lord Nelson*

Nelson's remark about Malta was made many decades ahead of World War II, but the island's importance to the Allied cause was to fully reflect the Royal Naval hero's words. Set almost directly in the middle of the Mediterranean and almost enclosed by Axis territory to the north (The southern Italian mainland, and the island of Sicily) and Vichy territory to the west (Tunisia), the military and civilian population were destined to endure over two years of being besieged by air, while the convoys upon which their survival depended were forced to traverse hundreds of miles from either Gibraltar or Alexandria. Each sailing was conducted in the face of determined opposition from the Axis Air Forces, and – to a surprising but thankfully reduced degree – from the Italian Navy, bolstered from late 1941 onward by *Kriegsmarine* U-Boats.

However, the British military's pre-war assessment of Malta's value as a major naval base in the Mediterranean was basically regarded as virtually nil, since its defence in the face of a hostile Italian Nation was felt to be unsustainable. Instead, it was to be treated as a staging post, a move reflecting at least a partial change of mind by the Committee of Imperial Defence.

Three airfields were built but no flying units were allotted. The lack of provision for submarine pens could be regarded as another indicator of the island's irreversible vulnerability should a Conflict break out. On the other hand a single radar set was delivered in early 1939, and provision was made for AA defences on a small scale.

The initial air defence of Malta rested upon a single-figure number of Gloster Sea Gladiator biplanes, but these were supplemented by Hurricanes during the latter part of June 1940. Also arriving on the Island were the Swordfish of No.830 Sqdn. that had formerly been based in southern France as one of two FAA training units. The new Sqdn.'s strength was added to in September when it absorbed the Swordfish of 3 Anti-aircraft Cooperation Unit (AACU), with this extra element being utilised for Air-Sea Rescue (ASR) duties.

ARGUS – The Vital Supply Lynch Pin
The first batch of Hurricanes to arrive in Malta had made a protracted overland flight across France and the Mediterranean during the final stage of France's collapse. One alternative means of further 'deliveries' was to ship crated aircraft out to West Africa, where they would be assembled and flown up to

Spitfires Mk.V are spotted on the deck of EAGLE along with two Sea Hurricanes Mk.Ib seen on the extreme left. The Spitfires were intended for the Island of Malta, and this 'delivery' was one of a number made both by EAGLE and ARGUS (seen in the background) during the first half of 1942. The USS WASP also made two runs during the same period.

Egypt, thence to Malta. A speedier and more direct delivery method lay in the use of an aircraft carrier, in this instance ARGUS. The first batch of twelve fighters along with two Skuas – the latter intended to act as navigation 'guides' – were duly placed on board. A majority of the RAF pilots were pre-war carrier-based personnel who had elected to remain with their Service following the Navy's regaining of its own Air Arm.

On 23 July. ARGUS slipped her moorings in Greenock, and eight days later was ready to depart from Gibraltar in the company of Force H. A precipitate decision to launch the formation on 1 August was cancelled, thanks to the pilot's (correct) protests that the distance to be flown at the current range from Malta was too great. Next day, with Italian bombers having picked up the warships, the Hurricanes were dispatched and made a safe landfall, apart from one fighter that crashed on landing at Luqa.

It was to be a further 3 1/2 months before Malta's modest stock of modern fighters that had in the interim been steadily whittled down would be replenished, and ARGUS was the chosen vehicle for delivery. Once again twelve Hurricanes were to fly-off and head for the Island under the initial navigational guidance of two Skuas. However, where the previous delivery effort had proved a virtual success, this time round the result was to be stark tragedy. The first sub-flight of seven aircraft took off on the 400-mile flight but spent precious time in forming up and setting course. Flying at a lower altitude than

that normally ensuring the Hurricane's best cruising speed performance the formation also experienced a wind veering from a rear angle to one virtually head-on. Rendezvous with a Sunderland acting as the second-stage navigator was made over Galite Island near the northeast coastline of Tunisia but when still some distance short of Malta, one Hurricane ran out of fuel. The pilot baled out and was fortunate to be picked up by the flying boat, which then hastily resumed its primary navigation duty. Then, a second pilot suffering fuel failure also baled out but was not subsequently found. The remaining four Hurricanes were flying on fumes when they finally alighted at Luqa. A worse experience awaited the other sub-flight. Thanks to a combination of failure to rendezvous over Galite Island, and subsequent navigational problems experienced by the Skua 'guide', not one of the six Hurricanes got through while all six pilots were lost in the sea. The Skua pilot ended up crash-landing on Sicily! Thus, the Hurricane numbers on the beleaguered island had not been increased at all; arguably worse, was the loss of several experienced fighter pilots among those killed.

The Best Form of Defence

Malta's location between Southern Italy, Sicily and North Africa was of prime importance if the Axis supply routes by sea were to be effectively interdicted. Sorties mounted by the Wellington bombers from No.148 Sqdn. dispatched to Malta at the beginning of November supplemented the Swordfish of

EAGLE's rear flight deck as seen from an accompanying escort vessel during a ferrying sortie to Malta; the Spitfires Mk.V parked at the rear of the group appear to be in imminent danger of sliding back off the deck's 'round-down' and into the Mediterranean! The picture angle picks out the bulky 'island' superstructure and the equally large mainmast.

No.830 Sqdn. whose crews were by then operational veterans. Sorties in July had met with little tangible result but with several aircraft shot down during a sortie to Augusta harbor, Sicily, while some of the surviving aircraft were damaged during bombing raids.

Before the year-end, attacks involving the dropping of bombs and laying of mines had been delivered against a range of Italian ports and on 9 January ARK ROYAL flew off six Swordfish of No.812X Sqdn. who were duly incorporated into No.830's ranks. The value of submarines was not lost on the Admiralty and the first two members of what was titled the 10th Submarine Flotilla arrived during December 1940. By February four submarines were 'on station', although the rate of sinkings during this initial operational period, especially among the Axis merchantmen, was disappointingly low. Matters were to improve as the year advanced however.

Fulmar Swansong

The 'orphaned' pilots of No.806 Sqdn. and their Fulmars were not immediately transferred out of Malta following the loss of their parent carrier ILLUSTRIOUS; instead both were utilised for use in the Island's defence. However, the Fulmars' performance was such that they were not used to directly oppose Axis raiders but were expected to pick up and dispatch any 'stragglers'. By the end of February, the presence of 7./JG 26 along with its Bf 109Es and battle-experienced pilots based on Sicily was proving a mortal threat to the RAF Hurricanes; any encounter between the enemy fighters and the Fulmars was likely to be even more fraught with danger for the trio of machines still on hand. On 2 March Lt. Barnes led the other two Fulmars aloft in response to a low-approaching formation.

The Navy fighters were slowly circling when ground observers at Hal Far saw a small swarm of what swiftly evolved as Bf 109s swooping in upon the Fulmars and raining fire upon all three before disappearing as quickly as they came. Amazingly, although Lt. Barnes's aircraft at least was thoroughly shot up, all three pilots remained virtually un-injured and promptly dropped back safely onto the airfield. The sturdy structural qualities of the Fairey design had passed the test on this occasion, although this might not have proved the case had the Bf 109s stayed around to further engage their opponents. From this point onwards, the Fulmar was dispensed with as regards the Island's defence. (It is all the more tragic to record that Barnes was fatally shot that same evening when the car he was travelling in was challenged by a Maltese soldier on sentry duty).

A Stitch in Time

The specific value of ARK ROYAL to the series of convoys pushed through to Malta during 1941 was unquestioned. Convoy 'Excess' had gone through during January, although two of the merchantmen sailing with Force H were actually bound for Greece, while two more merchantmen made the reverse voyage from Alexandria to Malta. In fact the vast bulk of the island's supply reinforcement during its first year of siege was delivered from the eastern Mediterranean location; it was not until the middle of 1941 that further reinforcements arrived from the west, when convoy 'Substance' sailed during July.

This latest venture consisted of six merchantmen and a troopship that departed Gibraltar on the 21st. Over the ensuing period up to the 24th Force H accompanied the convoy. On the penultimate day's operation, seven Fulmars of No.808 Sqdn. were launched and linked up with the four other fighters on patrol. The combined force engaged a mixed formation of SM79s and Z1007s carrying bombs and torpedoes. The resultant combat produced mixed results, because even though one bomber was shot down and several others claimed as 'kills', no less than three of the Fulmars were forced to 'ditch' after receiving engine damage. Another SM79 was shot down by AA fire but did deliver a damaging albeit not fatal strike against the cruiser MANCHESTER.

A Fulmar shot down one further SM79 during a second sortie later the same day, while a second torpedo-bomber 'ditched' off Sicily on its return. The final series of sorties on the 25th bore mixed fruits for both No.807 and 808 Sqdns. Two Fulmars intercepted a Z506B floatplane; this was downed by two of the four fighters, but not before return fire had fatally crippled Sub-Lt. Grant's aircraft, that crashed along with its crew. Two more crews were shot down, one fatally, in a separate action against an SM79 formation. Of the twenty-

four Fulmars embarked no less than half had been lost in action or otherwise 'written off', but the convoy had sailed through unscathed.

'Halberd'

The second major eastbound convoy to sail to Malta during 1941 was code-named 'Halberd', and was dispatched during September. By this stage of World War II Hitler was fully pre-occupied by the Russian Campaign and so the main resistance to the convoy's progress was laid at the door of the Italians. It was intended that the main Italian Fleet would be added to the assaults mounted by the Regia Aeronautica; once again the presence of the battleships RODNEY and PRINCE OF WALES, as well as the specific threat posed by ARK ROYAL's aircraft persuaded Admiral Iachino to retain his major warships at their anchorages.

As regards the Italian air attacks, these met with a measure of success during the main air action involving Force H on the 23rd when a combined force of high-level SM79s attacked.

INDOMITABLE's flight deck hosts an interesting collection of aircraft. The Sea Hurricanes Mk.Ib of Nos.800 and 880 Sqdns. – the former unit identified by single code letters and yellow cowling bands – occupy the central area. Four Martlets Mk.II are further back while four Albacores are at the extreme rear. Picture was taken at Freetown in West Africa prior to the carrier's participation in Operation 'Pedestal'.

None of the bombers enjoyed success but the cruiser MANCHESTER and the destroyer FEARLESS were both torpedoed, with fatal results for the latter warship. A second force of BR20 bombers also failed in their endeavours, while the Fulmar fighters were later credited with two SM79s along with a further two for the AA gunners; unhappily, the gunners also gained 'credit' for three Fulmars, although all six airmen concerned survived to be picked up!

The four-day voyage made by the nine merchantmen and their heavy surface escort continued to be strongly contested following Force H's detachment, but none of the cargo ships failed to get through. A course change to steer north of the island of Pantellaria instead of to its south probably threw the Italians off track for some time although torpedo-boat attacks were then made in the early hours of the 24th in the course of which one merchantman was struck but managed despite severe damage to gain Grand Harbor later the same day. Indeed, there was to be just two losses from among the fifty-seven merchantmen making the run to Malta up to this stage of 1941!

It was as well that this positive situation had occurred because the garrison and population of the island would find themselves facing physical and material starvation over the ensuing year to eighteen months as the Axis Powers began to turn the current tide of convoy success into one of frustration and large-scale failure for the Allies. As a portent to these hard times, the sailing of four merchantmen making solo efforts during October and November failed miserably, with three of the vessels sunk during the outward run and a fourth dispatched on the way back to Gibraltar.

On the Offensive

The overwhelming commitment of the *Luftwaffe* to Operation BARBAROSSA from June 1941 was an undoubted factor in easing some of the direct pressure on Malta. This in turn encouraged the Admiralty to retain what was now termed the 10th Submarine Flotilla during September; the absence of submarine pens as a primary protective measure for the underwater predators was regarded as being equalised by the stepping down of the air assaults and the relative freedom from loss or damage likely to be borne by the submarines. The September record for the U-Class vessels along with the Malta-based aircraft, included no less than three large passenger liners that were vital to the transport of personnel to North Africa, and had actually made successful runs just weeks prior to their loss.

A further measure for interdicting Axis convoy traffic to North Africa was initiated during October when Force K, consisting of two light cruisers and two destroyers arrived to take over from the original Malta Strike Force of four destroyers first deployed in April, thereby supplementing the current efforts of both the FAA and RAF aircrew as well as the submarines. The three-fold form of assault soon began to pay off, with one action in particular standing out. This occurred on the night of 9/10 November when Force K

A No.800 Sqdn. Sea Hurricane has already lifted into level flight scant seconds after commencing its take-off run. The unit codes are applied to the wing leading edges and fuselage, and the black spinner's color contrasts with the yellow cowling bands. A Swordfish and Albacore are also warming up.

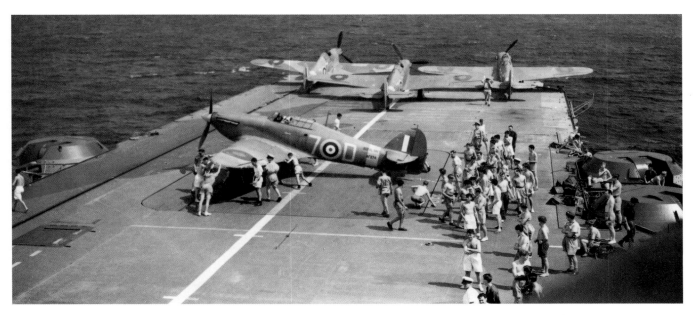

The forward lift on INDOMITABLE was able to accommodate fixed-wing FAA aircraft such as this Sea Hurricane from No.880 Sqdn. The carrier's three predecessors in the Illustrious Class – ILLUSTRIOUS, VICTORIOUS and FORMIDABLE – featured lifts with dimensions too small to provide a similar service.

intercepted and sank all seven merchantmen within a strongly escorted convoy. Around this time the Force's strength was doubled and further inroads were made on Axis shipping; this included the sinking of two Italian cruisers laden with fuel for Rommel's Army by a separate destroyer force off Cap Bon in mid-December, as well as several supply vessels that included a tanker. (The use of naval vessels as auxiliary tankers clearly indicated the desperate need for Axis re-supply using any measures possible).

The Tide Turns Again

The detachment of *Luftwaffe* units from the Russian Front to Sicily during December was in direct response to the depredations wrought upon the shipping by the British forces. However, by grim coincidence the task for the German aircrew was made easier by what happened on 19 December. A day before, Force K had rendezvoused with HMS BRECONSHIRE and its covering force of Admiral Vian's escort screen. Then, after berthing in Grand Harbor and replenishing all necessary fuel and ammunition stocks, the Force had sailed in response to an air reconnaissance report of a Tripoli-bound convoy.

Its course was unknowingly made into a recently laid minefield and the cruiser AURORA, one of Force K's original complement, suffered heavy damage to her steering equipment that saw her limp back to Malta. The destroyer KANDAHAR had her stern blown off and was left to drift helplessly until the following day when she was deliberately sunk. The worst experience was suffered by the cruiser NEPTUNE, which struck no less than four mines over a period of three to four

hours and went down with the vast majority of her crew; the pitifully few survivors drifted for several days on a single Carley raft, but just one among this number survived to be picked up by a roving Italian patrol boat.

1942 – the Cruellest Months

As 1942 entered its early stage the overall military situation for the 'Big Three' of the Allied coalition and their supporting group of nations was generally heading for its lowest ever point in World War II. British and American forces in the Pacific and Far East were being overwhelmed by the Japanese, while the German U-Boats were temporarily reaping a grim harvest off the shores of the United States, although the main Battle of the Atlantic was in a rather more stabilised state, at least up to the mid point of 1942. The Russian counter-offensive launched in December 1941 that had thrown the *Wehrmacht* well back from the gates of Moscow had itself begun to run out of steam. Finally, in North Africa the Eighth Army's advance to the area around Benghazi had been swiftly and peremptorily reversed by the *Afrikakorps*, with the current frontlines centered around Gazala.

Malta and its defenders were still regarded as a primary 'thorn in the side' of the Axis Armies and their sea-borne supply routes, as had been proven during the latter half of 1941, but this position was now to change noticeably over the ensuing months. In spite of the critical position of his forces in Russia, Hitler had sanctioned the withdrawal of sizeable numbers of *Luftwaffe* bomber and fighters from the Eastern Front to Sicily. Although the *Führer*'s attitude towards Mediterranean operations was at best ambivalent and at worst dismissive of their influence on Germany's conduct of the war, his sanctioning of the fore-mentioned transfers appeared to indicate his irritation at the negative effect Malta's sea and air assault forces had been bringing to bear on the North African Campaign.

The main element of *Fliegerkorps* II's re-deployed strength comprised six *Gruppen* of Ju 88s and two of Ju 87s, which were supported by four *Gruppen* of Bf 109Fs and the Bf 110s of III./ZG 26 – around 400 aircraft in all. Also on hand in Sicily were some 210 aircraft of the Regia Aeronautica, with a similar total of machines based on Sardinia; the latter force's function was to interdict the convoy route from Gibraltar. The *Luftwaffe* authorities were confident that the island could be neutralised if not totally knocked out as a major military base, even without the ultimate sanction of invasion and occupation. And so Malta's crucifixion was now on hand, although its full implementation would be delayed until around March, due to several factors. These included the diversion of some units to help stem the British current advance into Cyrenaica (Operation 'Crusader'), and adverse winter weather conditions as the year opened.

The scale of aerial assault on Malta between February and April 1942 witnessed an ever-growing pace of intensity as the Axis aircraft pressed home their numerical and logistical advantage against the defending fighters. The RAF's strength had been increased in number and quality by the injection of the initial Spitfire 'deliveries' during March and April but a steady rate of attrition caused by losses in combat and destruction on the ground through strafing and bombing had again reduced the overall figure of serviceable fighters to a parlous level.

The three main airfields had absorbed over half the estimated 3100 tons of bombs dropped in February and March and around one-third of the April figure. However, the overall figure for this month reached a horrendous level of nearly 7,000 tons that was never to be remotely approached in the course of the entire period of siege. Bombs rained down on Grand Harbor to take a steady toll in damaged and sunken shipping, while other military targets (including AA gun-sites) were given almost equally harsh treatment. The one horror spared the civilian population in particular was the absence of fire thanks to the stone building structures. What nobody on Malta could be spared was the ever-decreasing food supplies during this stage of the siege and the inevitable enervating effect arising from continuous hunger.

In the meantime, the RAF and FAA crews were doing their utmost to continue the block on Axis sea-borne supplies in the face of ever-increasing *Luftwaffe* assaults upon their airfields. Nos.828 and 830 Sqdns. with their Albacores and

Swordfish were operating alongside RAF Wellingtons and Blenheims in hunting down convoys, and attacking these with torpedoes; reconnaissance sorties by Marylands of No.60 Sqdn. were the reported source for discovery of the enemy shipping columns, but this unit's crews' successes were dictated by the intelligence gathered back at Bletchley Park through 'Ultra' – a 'fact' that naturally could not be made public to either friend or foe! – rather than by their own navigational and surveillance abilities, good as these undoubtedly might have been.

The availability of ASV equipment fitted to some of the Wellingtons permitted these aircrafts' use in guiding their FAA contemporaries to the scene of a convoy, as occurred on 29 January, when a Mk.VIII 'Wimpy' of the Special Duties Flight led four Swordfish in upon shipping steaming north of Tripoli. Although several torpedo 'strikes' were claimed at the cost of one aircraft, only one merchantman was subsequently observed sagging by the stern, and eventually confirmed as entering port; however, the same vessel reportedly never resumed operating as a supply source, and so was effectively deleted from Axis service as surely as if she had been sunk!

Some of the FAA aircraft also featured ASV equipment, and a Swordfish so fitted played a part in the locating and continued monitoring of an important convoy that included the troopship VICTORIA, which was bearing urgently needed reinforcements for Rommel. The total availability of all forms of the island's strike aircraft on 23 January however was no more than thirty; further aircraft resources were stationed around Benghazi as well, including No.826 Sqdn.'s Albacores. Beauforts from the latter force made the first direct assault, with one torpedo striking but not fatally damaging the troopship. Shortly after, the Albacores of No.826 Sqdn. made their runs in the face of steady AA fire and passes made by two Ju 88C fighters. The aircraft bearing the Sqdn. CO, Lt-Cdr. Corbett succumbed to the shipboard gunners after torpedo-release, but one of the other crews placed their weapon squarely against the VICTORIA's hull; this time round there was no reprieve and the vessel soon slipped gently under the waves.

Malta's contribution to the action consisted of Wellingtons, Swordfish and Albacores. The single ASV 'Stringbag' with Lt-Cdr Hopkins (830 Sqdn. CO) on board had preceded the first of two FAA strike forces in order to take over convoy surveillance duties. However, a combination of engine problems and abysmal weather conditions split up the force and no attack ensued. Later in the day, the ASV aircraft again set out ahead of the second strike force; this time round, only three of the five armed aircraft made contact with the convoy, but no positive results were enjoyed. Each sortie had occupied more than six hours duration which when given the adverse weather conditions and open cockpit facilities, spoke volumes about the fortitude of the crews concerned!

The sinking of Axis vessels occasionally assumed a tragic aspect that was all the more poignant because the perpetrators and victims were from the same nation. On what was ever regarded as an unlucky date – namely, Friday the 13th February – a two-vessel convoy was steaming a westerly course off Tunisia when Albacores of No.828 Sqdn. came in through AA fire and a smoke screen laid by the two escorts; only one crew got its torpedo got through to cripple but not sink the ARIOSTO. Several hours later the submarine P38 administered the 'coup de grace' and over 400 personnel failed to survive the sinking. Included among these unfortunates was a proportion from a contingent of British and Commonwealth POWs on their way to camps in Italy.

The proximity of Sicily to Malta and the resultant regular presence of Bf 109s over and around the island created constant problems for any British aircraft, in particular for designs such as the Swordfish and Albacore. On 18 January for example an Albacore on anti-submarine duties was 'bounced' and shot down by a Bf 109F although both airmen survived to be picked up later. Then, two 'Stringbag' replacements arriving from North Africa for assignment to No.830 Sqdn. were similarly assailed while on landing approach to Hal Far. With the single rear-firing guns displaced by luggage in the gunners' compartments, it was left to the pilots to take desperate evasive action that along with supporting AA fire and the quick appearance of Hurricanes left the airmen intact, although one aircraft was badly shot up.

Invasion?

The prospects for an invasion of Malta took a turn for the worse around April and May when, following discussions with Mussolini and senior figures within the German High Command, Hitler tentatively agreed that action might be necessary. On the other hand, priority for this move was only accorded a secondary status to that of advancing the *Afrikakorps* into Egypt and re-capturing Tobruk in the process. The ever-improving supply position across the sea-lanes to North Africa was allowing the Axis forces to build up their resources for the intended drive eastwards. Of course, should Rommel's troops succeed in pushing all the way to Cairo and beyond, then the relevance of Malta to the overall Mediterranean situation could become a redundant factor, and invasion no longer a consideration. Reconnaissance flights over Sicily had revealed huge cleared areas that could indicate their use for glider launching, which were adjacent to rail links containing sidings, thereby heightening the fears of an impending invasion.

Malta Convoy Fortunes in 1942

The overall supply situation on Malta was by the early summer of 1942 in a parlous state, and the need to force through the necessary convoys from either end of the Mediterranean was of paramount importance. The convoy sent westward from Alexandria in March had suffered severely. One merchantman was lost en route, a second (HMS BRECONSHIRE, a

A Sea Hurricane Mk.Ib of No.800 Sqdn. with its black spinner and yellow noseband, and wheel blocks lying on the nearside wing, is manoeuvered into position on the deck of INDOMITABLE. A second Sea Hurricane from No.880 Sqdn. is parked on the forward deck. Aircraft carrier in front of INDOMITABLE is VICTORIOUS, and sandwiched in between is a cruiser from the Escort force.

This photograph is taken on VICTORIOUS, looking back on INDOMITABLE from which an Albacore from either No.817 or 832 Sqdn. has just been launched. The Sea Hurricane of No.885 Sqdn. in the foreground displays the yellow 'friendly' identification stripes on the wing leading edges and on the vertical fin that were applied to all the FAA fighters involved in Operation 'Pedestal'

converted Holt fast liner that had already made several runs to Malta) had to be beached on the island's coast and the other two, although safely berthed, were then bombed before being properly unloaded. Less than 20% of the total cargo content was delivered, although the exposed bilges on BRECONSHIRE did permit the subsequent siphoning-off of some of her fuel oil cargo. In addition, the incessant bombing of Malta during March and into April proved so severe that the decision to withdraw the 10th Submarine Flotilla was reluctantly taken. So it was that Operation 'Harpoon' was initiated during June, involving six merchantmen departing Gibraltar, escorted by four cruisers, sixteen destroyers and the fast minelayer MANXMAN, as well as MALAYA and ARGUS. A simultaneous convoy exercise ('Vigorous') was to be launched from the east with no less than eleven more merchantmen being included.

As regards 'Harpoon', the continuing presence of Axis Air Force units on Sicily and Sardinia did not bode well for the action's success. An increased fighter complement of

sixteen Sea Hurricanes aboard EAGLE and six Fulmars shared with ARGUS was to prove no more than an adequate force with which to take on the enemy aircraft. Apart from this, both carriers' slow maximum speed, allied to the inconvenient wind angle that necessitated turning away from the convoy's course, heightened the problems of launching and recovering aircraft. Although by early May the bulk of the *Luftwaffe* units had again been drawn off to support the projected *Wehrmacht* Offensive in Russia – less than fifty bombers and fighters being retained in Sicily – the Regia Aeronautica could field some 170 level and dive-bombers, while its fighter content included CR42 biplanes that were to double up as light bombers.

The continued dependence upon the Fulmar and to a lesser extent the Sea Hurricane 1B as the FAA's main fighter element was by now casting up serious problems for the pilots and crews. Among the Regia Aeronautica's equivalent force were two or three designs with superior performance qualities. The MC200 was roughly equal in manoeuverability, speed and climb rate to the Sea Hurricane, while the Macchi MC202 and the Reggiane Re2001 were both away ahead in respect of these vital issues – and out of sight compared to the Fulmar! While the eight .303 machine-gun batteries in both FAA aircraft was double the four-gun capacity of the Italian fighters, the latter included .50 caliber weapons with greater striking power. Also on hand in varying numbers was the *Luftwaffe*'s Bf 109F that was arguably the best fighter available in the Mediterranean, at least until the advent of the first Spitfires based on Malta.

The period between the convoy's departure from Gibraltar (12th) and the point where all but the destroyer escorts turned back at the Sicilian Narrows (14th) witnessed just a single loss, with the FAA fighters inflicting a steady toll on the attacking aircraft, before matters turned sour. The initial contact with the convoy was made by a Ju88D of 1 (F)/122 that was quickly homed in upon by two Sea Hurricanes of No. 801 Sqdn; their gunfire appeared to strike home with sufficient effect to cause a crash-landing in Algerian territory. A succession of 'shadowers' appeared during the afternoon, all of which were chased away but not engaged, with one unlucky exception. Sub-Lt. Crosley flying with No.813F Sqdn. closed in upon what was a Z1007. After some five minutes the range was closed to a point where Crosley directed an accurate burst of fire into the bomber's undersides and port wing; fire erupted around the port engine and the Italian pilot was compelled to attempt a 'ditching' which left all six airmen alive.

Next morning Sub-Lt. Crosley was again involved in combat with a 'shadower', being another Ju 88D from 1 (F)/122. Crosley and his Leader (Lt. King-Joyce) approached from above and to port and their prolonged bursts of fire left the aircraft staggering along at minimum speed; its final demise was not witnessed but the German unit recorded an aircraft loss in virtually the same location as recorded by the two assailants.

Air attacks began in the late morning of the 14th with an unusual but potentially troublesome combination of two SM79s and eight CR42s, also bearing bombs. The two tri-motors were flying ahead of the biplanes, and one of the former machines was set upon by another pair of Sea Hurricanes from No.801 Sqdn, and dispatched in flames into the sea. Meanwhile the CR42 force got through to dive-bomb several of the major warships albeit with no effect. The nimble Fiat fighters enjoyed a maximum speed figure that would normally have proved too much for any engaging Fulmar, but two of the attacking pilots could not have been paying full attention as they cleared away over the bows of ARGUS. Two Fulmars of No.807 Sqdn. – one being flown by Sub-Lt. Peter Twiss, destined to become a chief Test Pilot with the Fairey Company after World War II – swooped down and opened fire. Both pilots baled out of their stricken aircraft although Twiss had to partially lower his flaps in order to hold in position with the second CR42 as

It is the morning of 11 August and the 'Pedestal' convoy is teaming towards Malta in perfect weather conditions. The veteran carrier EAGLE in the distance, is photographed through the wing bracing wires of an Albacore on one of the other two Fleet carriers, and has just launched a Sea Hurricane. This is believed to be one of the last photographs taken of the carrier prior to her loss.

it began to turn before delivering an accurate and lethal burst of fire

A cleverly executed two-wave torpedo assault by thirty-three SM79s and SM81s along with high-level bombing by a small force of four Cant Z1007s then ensued around late morning. On hand as escorts were twenty-eight MC200 and CR42s, while a supplementary force of ten Z1007 bombers were tailing these formations by some thirty minutes. So far the 'kill'/loss situation had been totally in the FAA's favor but the impending action would change that happy scenario. First, Lt Hall's Fulmar was damaged by an SM79's return fire, after which the fighter was harried by CR42s as its pilot attempted to head for ARGUS; Hall was in the process of 'ditching' when the aircraft absorbed further hits – from a destroyer AA batteries! – and crashed, leaving just the Observer Sub-Lt. Urry alive. Then, radio contact was lost with Sub-Lt. Palmer's Fulmar and aircraft and crew were later declared MIA.

Although the FAA fighters were far too few in number to ward off more than a proportion of the attackers, and were further hindered by having to take on the Italian escort fighters, all of the bombs and a majority of the torpedoes released failed to find their mark. Three of the latter weapon-type did get through however; the cruiser LIVERPOOL received serious damage to its engine room from one torpedo strike, while a further two torpedoes took out the cargo vessel TANIMBAR. Following the conclusion of this prolonged and frenetic combat, three bombers were claimed shot down by the ships' gunners to add to the pair already claimed by Lt. Hall and Sub-Lt. Palmer, while further claims were submitted for several more SM79s, SM84s, MC200s and CR42s. Total Italian losses were two SM79s and no less than six SM81s, a discouraging result in the face of the limited scale of success, even if one of the vital merchantmen had been culled from the convoy.

'Shadowers' continued to dog the heels of the convoys up to the early evening when the next and final day's mass action took place. This time around, the attacking force came out of Sicily as opposed to Sardinia. First on the scene were the Ju 88s of *KueFlGr* 606 that concentrated on dive-bombing ARGUS; none of the bombs struck home although several impacted uncomfortably close by. In turn, two of the *Luftwaffe* aircraft were brought down, but another Fulmar operating off ARGUS went missing. This initial assault was followed up by a mix of Ju 87B and Ju 87R variants manned by Italian crews and escorted by Macchi C.202s, formidable fighters for even the Sea Hurricane to take on; backing these up was a formation of SM79 torpedo-bombers.

Once again, there were no recorded strikes against the convoy, although ARGUS had to take sharp evasive action in the face of no less than three closely spaced torpedoes. The handful of No.813F fighters for their part, found themselves hard-pressed to survive the attentions of the MC200 and Re2001 escort force that out-numbered the FAA pilots by over five-to-one, while also attending to the main attacking force. Sub-Lt. Bullivant was forced to bale out from his blazing Sea Hurricane, while two of the sub-force engaged by the enemy fighters was badly shot-up; one of these was subsequently jettisoned over EAGLE's side after Sub-Lt. Spedding crashed on landing. Finally, the AA gunners recorded another 'own goal', when Sub-Lt. Rankin's ARGUS-based Fulmar was forced into a 'ditching' from which the crew emerged unscathed after the fighter was fatally crippled!

As regards enemy casualties, just one Re2001 was actually shot down, while two of the SM79s were destroyed, one in action and one involved in a crash-landing on Sicily. Although the Ju 87 force managed an un-impeded assault against the convoy, none of the claims for damaged vessels proved correct. Ironically, though free from fighter attack, these aircraft were to end up in equal danger from having to operate at the extreme limit of their range; several among their number barely regained their airfield before running out of fuel, while a single example was forced to 'ditch' just short of the island due to fuel starvation.

Next morning, an Italian naval force of two cruisers and four destroyers initiated their challenge to which the destroyers spiritedly reacted, but the latter's absence from the immediate vicinity of the convoy permitted enemy aircraft to deliver their attacks with little interference from AA fire. All too soon, the convoy strength was reduced to just two, whose cargo content of around 15,000 tons was extremely welcome but was nevertheless away below the level required for the island's continuance as a viable defensive outpost.

The bright hopes for the 'Vigorous' portion of the relief force were to be totally expunged however. Two vessels had already been lost by the 14th when the looming threat posed by Italian capital ships was confirmed. A series of orders for withdrawal and then a reversal of course for Malta were issued to Admiral Vian by the C-in-C Mediterranean Fleet With AA ammunition running low, Vian, having finally been allowed by Admiral Harwood to act on his own initiative, decided to cancel the entire operation. The loss of one cruiser and three lighter escorts in addition to the two merchantmen had brought not one measure of possible relief to the sorely tried occupants of Malta. (The unfortunate and contradictory set of 'directions' from Admiral Harwood in Alexandria was to set a precedent for an even greater 'Central control' disaster barely three weeks later in the Arctic when convoy PQ17 was needlessly and expensively dispersed on orders from the Admiralty).

'Pedestal'

While the fast minelayer WELSHMAN and submarines continued to run in what amounted to extremely limited amounts of supplies to the hard-pressed service personnel in the form of fuel, ammunition and spare parts, the Admiralty pondered its next measure to push through to the island. The extended sea route from the east and the overall domination exercised by the Axis Air Forces based in this section of North Africa were likely reasons why the latest Plan was totally concentrated on a Gibraltar-based action.

No less than fourteen merchantmen with a fast-steaming performance were collected for the voyage, and sailed from their Scottish assembly-point on the 1st. The escort force was even more impressive with the battleships RODNEY and NELSON forming the immediate defensive core, as regards both AA fire provision and a counter-measure to the appearance of their Italian contemporaries. Twenty-six destroyers and seven cruisers were also on hand, with three of the latter assigned as direct protection for three of the four aircraft carriers also taking part in the operation. (The fourth was FURIOUS whose function was the 'passive' one of delivering the latest Spitfire batch to Malta).

INDOMITABLE, VICTORIOUS and EAGLE were to provide the air cover as far as the approaches to Malta, when the RAF would take over. Twelve FAA Sqdns. were represented on board the three carriers, eight of which comprised the fighter force totalling forty-six Sea Hurricanes (with four more in disassembled form on EAGLE), eighteen Fulmars and ten Martlet IIs. The Sea Hurricanes fixed wings and consequent inability to be 'struck down' into, and 'ranged' from, the hangars of VICTORIOUS – a disability not shared by the other two carriers, the dimensions of whose lifts were adequate for this function – meant that they would of necessity be first into action. On the other hand the decidedly limited performance (by 1942) of the Fulmar, allied to the small number of Martlets with a Hurricane-matching performance, were probable factors dictating the priority of launch in favor of the Hawker fighter, especially since these fighters were to form the top layer of the defensive 'screen' around 20,000 ft. The Martlets would assume a medium altitude role, while the Fulmars and Sea Hurricanes on VICTORIOUS would be assigned the low-level position. In addition a total of thirty-six Albacores were on hand to provide anti-submarine cover.

The odds facing the Royal Naval aviators even at maximum operational strength were daunting. Upwards of 650 Axis aircraft were available to challenge the convoy's progress, a fair proportion of which were high performance machines such as the Ju 88, Bf 109 and the Italian fighter designs, the Macchi MC202 and Reggiane Re2001. The remainder consisted of the reliable SM79 along with its SM84 contemporary, the CR42 fighter biplane and finally the nemesis of many an Allied convoy, the Ju 87. Air support from Malta would not be available until the 13th when the vessels would be entering the Narrows between Sicily and Tunisia, and the island's Beaufighters could range out this far; Spitfire cover would have to wait until the ships were nearer at hand.

Several days before 'Pedestal' was initiated, the three carriers exercised together in a bid to iron out the problems likely to arise in joint operations of what was a newly-formed sub-force, while attempting to maintain a comprehensive convoy cover at both low, medium and high levels; the latter duties, as well as the maintenance of a Combat Air Patrol over their own warships, were assigned to INDOMITABLE and EAGLE but events at the very beginning of Axis incursions would see this defensive aspect limited almost wholly to the fighters based on the former-named vessel. The provision of radar equipment was vital to the Operation in order to 'scramble' the maximum number of fighters in time to properly engage the incoming enemy formations. The Type 79B sets on VICTORIOUS were judged to posses a superior height-finding capability compared to the Type 281 equivalent mounted on INDOMITABLE and the cruiser SIRIUS The latter two warships were therefore assigned to operate their equipment in an 'all-round' search role. VHF radio/telephony sets were installed in both ships and fighters along with Identification Friend or Foe (IFF).

The latter facility was intended to minimise the chance of, even if it could not guarantee total immunity from, AA fire downing one's own aircraft. An added refinement was for any returning formation to circle at a safe visual distance for both lookouts and radar operators to establish its 'friendly' status. Should a fighter pursue an opponent in over the convoy then yellow stripes on the wing leading edges, forward engine cowling and the fin were (hopefully) intended to provide a timely warning to the ships' gunners – all very well in theory

On 11 August the 'Pedestal' escort Force suffered a severe loss when EAGLE was struck by no less than four torpedoes from U-73 and sank within eight minutes, becoming the last FAA Fleet carrier to suffer this fate. With her went nearly all of her Hurricanes, so reducing the overall defensive strength by nearly 25%.

but hard if not impossible to act upon in the heat of an air/sea battle such as was sure to develop as the mighty force steamed 'in harms way' towards its goal.

The convoy commenced its perilous voyage on 9-10 August and over the next two to three days held course in close and parallel to the Algerian and Tunisian coast as far as Cap Bon This action in itself, although maintaining a position as far distant as possible from Axis airfields in Sardinia and Sicily, was from the start no guarantee of freedom from discovery. The country's Vichy authorities and its aircraft crews in particular were ambivalent in their overall attitude towards the conduct of the Conflict – an attitude that could extend towards making 'accidental' observations over the radio of Allied shipping movements – although rarely if ever providing the reverse service! In the event, the convoy's existence to the enemy was confirmed by air reconnaissance early on the 11th (It should also be mentioned that Axis agents in Spanish Morocco could easily monitor the progress of vessels out of Gibraltar, while the Spanish fishing fleets were probably another source of 'accidental' disclosures, given the neutral but Fascist control of their country!)

During 1933, the German light cruiser KÖLN had been anchored next to EAGLE in the Chinese port of Tsingtau. A social visit to the Royal Navy carrier had involved a group of naval cadets, one of which was Helmut Rosenbaum. The then adolescent *Kriegsmarine* sailor was by August 1942 the commander of U-73 based at La Spezia in northern Italy. His warship had departed the base several days previous and by the morning of the 11th was in the immediate vicinity of the massive convoy. The daunting presence of the close escort 'screen' did not deflect Rosenbaum from carrying out an extended stalking manouever that finally brought his U-Boat within easy striking range of his former 'host', EAGLE. (Rosenbaum's task was probably made easier by the variation in density and salinity of the western Mediterranean depths that adversely affected the escort vessels' Asdic sets, but he still required the skill to maintain minimum periscope sight while avoiding visual detection during his protracted bid to penetrate the escort screen unseen).

A spread of four torpedoes was fired from close range that, even had they been observed, could never have been avoided by a change of course. The mass impact of the weapons ensured that there was no prospect of survival for the veteran carrier, even at her reduced speed of thirteen knots. The wholesale puncturing of her port side, allied to her forward motion, saw the vessel slew over at an increasing and irrecoverable angle. Within a matter of minutes, eight in all, the warship was bottom up before subsiding gently below the smooth Mediterranean surface. In this brief period of natural confusion and chaos, no less than 931 officers and seamen out of the 1,160 on board managed to scramble into the thankfully calm waters, to be later picked up by two destroyers and a rescue tug. No less than sixteen Sea Hurricanes had been ruthlessly deleted from 'Pedestal's vital air cover in a single stroke. All that was left was the Flight of four other fighters from No.813 Sqdn. that was aloft on a patrol at the time of the fatal incident. All four pilots, undoubtedly shaken by being so peremptorily 'orphaned', landed on one or other of the

surviving Fleet carriers. Sub-Lt. Hutton, having selected INDOMITABLE for his 'roost' was forced to find a new home on VICTORIOUS next day, thanks to further damage inflicted on the first-named warship! Sub-Lt Hankey joined him on board VICTORIOUS, but sadly neither airman would survive the overall action.

EAGLE's loss seemed an ominous portent for 'Pedestal's' ultimate success, since the main action had not then even been joined. In fact it was the same evening before the first aerial challenge was launched. Prior to this action a single Ju 88 of 2(F)/122 was brought down by a Section from No.880 Sqdn. although accurate return fire forced Lt. Forrest to 'ditch' A thirty-strong formation of Ju 88s and six He 111s were met by fighters either in the air or launched after being at 'cockpit readiness' on the carrier decks. The AA gunners joined in the action, which resulted in no ship losses but cost the enemy a single Ju 88. However, the gunners continued to fire at all and sundry in the deepening gloom even after the action was over and the FAA pilots were attempting to land on in the face of rapidly diminishing fuel reserves. Lt. Popham an 885 Sqdn. pilot was fortunate to land intact on VICTORIOUS – even although he was being 'waved off' by the carrier's DLCO since the warship was manoeuvering vigorously at the time – and

A Martlet Mk.II is in the process of being recovered on board INDOMITABLE. The fighter has probably suffered sufficient damage or malfunction to its tail wheel for a steerable trolley to be placed under the rear fuselage, although trolleys were also used when directing an aircraft into a specific position on deck or onto a lift. Although just ten Martlets from No.806 Sqdn. were available for 'Pedestal' their pilots were credited with a good proportion of the Axis aircraft claimed as 'kills' during the Operation.

INDOMITABLE appears to be dead in the water after absorbing at least two direct hits from bombs delivered by Ju 87 dive-bombers. In spite of both lifts have been penetrated or badly damaged, the Fleet carrier managed to return to Gibraltar but was then out of commission for several months. The incident occurred just before the Main Force of escorts was due to turn back.

his fighter went up on flames after touching down and colliding with another parked aircraft!

Capt. Troubridge on INDOMITABLE accepted the risk of U-Boat attack by maintaining a straight course and illuminating his deck lights in order to guarantee the safe landing-on of his fighters. Lt-Cdr Judd, CO of No. 880 Sqdn. was so incensed by the indiscriminate AA fire emanating even from his own carrier INDOMITABLE that, upon landing, he physically and verbally abused the officer in charge of a specific pom-pom Section. Judd's ire was particularly roused by the continued firing of the battery, even when he had approached at minimum speed and with his wheels lowered. At least two more fighters, a Sea Hurricane of No.880 Sqdn. and a Fulmar of No.809 Sqdn. were 'written off' through collision damage when landing-on INDOMITABLE; ten other aircraft, including four 'strays' touched down safely. During the final hours of the 11th, a small degree of relief from future air assaults on the convoy had been achieved by Malta-based Beufighters of No.248 Sqdn. The nine crews involved attacked two major airfields on Sardinia to leave six SM79s destroyed and several more damaged.

'The Glorious Twelfth!'
The full action for the FAA fighters occurred next day, when they were met by a series of challenges that were basically thwarted. The standard threat came from both the level and dive-bombers, as well as torpedo-bombers. To these standard forms of aerial assault were added one or two exotic variations, one of which was to involve a radio-controlled SM79 loaded with explosives!

The procession of 'shadowers' began early on the 12th when a Ju 88D of 1(F)/122 picked out the convoy about 200 miles west of Cap Bon. At this time twelve FAA fighters were up and on patrol with all other available serviceable aircraft at 'readiness'. Two of the 'shadowers', both Z1007s, were unfortunate to be intercepted, of which one was downed by No.884 Sqdn. Fulmars. What turned out to be the first of four concerted air assaults was first recorded on radar screens around 0900, flying at 18,000 ft. The twenty-four Ju 88s concerned all came from the ranks of LG 1 but the range at which they were detected permitted ample time for Sea Hurricanes of Nos.800, 880 and 885 Sqdns. to be launched and gain the necessary altitude for timely interception. In fact the radar operators' work this day was to pay particular dividends in getting the fighters into good position for the bulk of interceptions; on this initial occasion twelve out of nineteen Sea Hurricanes were on hand to challenge the bombers' progress well short of their target. .

The two Sections of No.800 Sqdn. opened proceedings and ripped through the formation, later claiming at least four Ju 88s dispatched into the sea and several more slumping away in various states of distress, all for the loss of one of their number – Lt. Roberts, who succeeded in 'ditching'. No.880 Sqdn.'s contribution to the action further added at least two more Ju88 to the tally of claimed 'kills'. Among this unit's number was a pilot who had already made his name with the RAF during the Battle of Britain. Blue Section was being led by Lt. 'Dickie' Cork who had flown in Douglas Bader's No.242 Flight of the 'Duxford Wing'; his involvement in the joint destruction of the first Ju 88 was only the start of a notable

"If Blood be the Price of Admiralty, Lord God we have paid in full." This dramatic picture of the oil tanker OHIO entering Grand Harbor provides a prime example of the foregoing phrase. In order to ensure her safe if extremely fortuitous arrival in Malta with her vital cargo along with four other merchantmen out of the fourteen 'Pedestal' vessels, the Royal Navy had lost one aircraft carrier with a second heavily damaged, as well as several other escorts sunk or damaged.

tally of victories this day. His first solo 'kill' was achieved shortly afterwards when a Ju 88 seen straggling southwards was summarily dispatched.

The Sqdn.'s other Section was led By Lt-Cdr Judd, but this No.880 sub-unit along with the three fighters from VICTORIOUS were seemingly launched too late to be engaged in the main action. Each made up for this deficiency in some way, however. Judd's Section caught a Z1007 'shadower', set two engines on fire and forced it into a 'ditching' after a short tail-chase back towards Sardinia. The three other Sea Hurricanes (two from No.885 Sqdn. and a No.801 Sqdn. 'survivor' from EAGLE) intercepted the enemy formation as the survivors broke away for Sicily. Sadly, only two returned to the carrier; Sub-Lt Hankey, the former EAGLE pilot was later declared MIA through unknown causes.

The majority of the LG 1 attackers had been thwarted from even commencing their bombing runs, and the AA gunners claimed at least two out of this reduced number. However, the litany of suffering for the *Luftwaffe* crews had not reached its conclusion even as they headed north to Sardinia. A patrol of Italian G50 fighters descended on the Ju 88s apparently in the mistaken belief that they represented a second attack on Sardinian targets by the Malta-based Beaufighters – a classic example of aircraft recognition misidentification, if ever there was one! Before the error had been rectified, one bomber from 5./LG 1 was shot down and

two of its crew killed, to add to the six other I and II *Gruppen* aircraft declared lost off this sortie.

So far, the air battle seemed to be progressing in general favour of the defenders, with the fighters ensuring that minimal contact was made between the Axis attackers and the convoy, while the AA gunners added their contribution towards this positive situation. The second full-scale assault was delivered by the combined efforts of the Regia Aeronautica operating out of Sardinia and the *Luftwaffe* units stationed in Sicily. The German airmen had much further to fly than their Italian contemporaries, in addition to which the Sicily-based Bf 109s could not provide cover unless transferring temporarily to Sardinia and thereby coming within operational range of the convoy, a move initiated by *Hptm.* Heinz Bär leading twenty other pilots of I./JG 77.

During the late morning the first group of ten SM84 bombers took off, armed with what was an advanced type of weapon for 1942, namely the 'Motorbomba FF' that was to be dropped by parachute ahead of the convoy. Driven by a gyroscopically controlled motor and automatically released from their parachutes on impact, they would then describe a circling motion through the water. After travelling a set distant a self-destruct mechanism would kick in, in the event of the target source not having been struck in the meantime. A further thirty-one torpedo-bearing SM79s accompanied by fifteen CR42s bearing 100 kg. bombs, and ten SM84s also equipped with torpedoes then lifted off. Finally, the force's fighter escort of fourteen MC202s took to the air.

The FAA defensive response was once again well in hand with two Fulmars of No.884 Sqdn. first off and climbing up to between 10,000 and 15,000 ft., well above the originally planned patrol band for the Fairey design. They were backed by four Sea Hurricanes of No.800 Sqdn. headed by Lt-Cdr Brabner (No.801 Sqdn. CO) and an equal number of No.806 Sqdn. Martlets led by Lt. Johnson (CO). Next up was Lt-Cdr Bruen (No.800 Sqdn. CO) with one Section. Finally, Nos.809 and 885 Sqdns. launched four Fulmars and four Sea Hurricanes respectively. The odds against the Navy pilots were arguably greater this time round, but the need for the torpedo bombers to ultimately come down to sea-level in order to accomplish their purpose meant that their challengers would surely have a height advantage to be suitably exploited once the nature of the latest attack was revealed, in a fashion that had been denied them by the high-level approach of LG 1.

The 'MotorbombaFF' formation was pounced upon by the original pair of Fulmars as it discharged its weapons and turned for home, but before the SM84's superior speed began to show up, several of the bombers had been peppered by the fighters' gunfire with three claimed as definite 'kills' after being set on fire. No.801's Section was briefly engaged by Italian escorts before reforming and descending upon a mixed formation of SM79s and SM84s; also taking on the enemy formation at this stage was the four Martlets of Lt. Johnson's Section. Then, as the mass of aircraft closed to within range of the convoy, Lt-Cdr Bruen brought his Section into action.

The frenetic series of combats that swiftly occupied this expanse of Mediterranean airspace yielded solid results. At least two SM79s were reported by the Martlet pilots to have crashed, with a further SM79 and SM84 added to the 'definite kill' list. Lt-Cdr Bruen's Section took down a further two SM79s, but suffered the fatal loss of Lt. Lucas who went missing. One of the three remaining 'orphaned' No.801 Sqdn. pilots chalked up an Italian fighter, which was successfully 'bounced' by Sub-Lt. Hutton flying within No.800 Sqdn.'s Section. Elsewhere, the Fulmars of No.809 Sqdn. managed to drive off a *Schwarm* of Ju 88s, downed one Italian bomber and badly damaged another before becoming embroiled with the escort fighters and successfully shaking them off. Their final action involved engaging part of the incoming Ju 88 force before fuel shortage forced their withdrawal.

The wholesale involvement of the FAA fighters with the current flock of Italian aircraft now virtually left the way clear for the rapidly encroaching *Luftwaffe* formation from Sicily. The Ju 88s of KG 54 and KG 77 numbering around forty in total carried out their dive-bombing runs but their crews achieved very little in what were favourable circumstances,

The aftermath of 'Pedestal' is captured in this picture of INDOMITABLE's flight deck. The after lift was struck squarely and almost completely shattered, and a similar fate overtook the forward lift. The scale of damage meant that the carrier spent a lengthy period under repair back in Britain. The Seafires on the deck had not been part of INDOMITABLE's complement during the run to Malta.

even allowing for the shipboard AA fire. One bomb did strike the freighter DEUCALIAN but did not prove fatal, although causing her to fall out of line and seek a separate course to Malta by skirting the Tunisian coast. Otherwise the worst experience for some vessels was that of being straddled.

A handful of the FAA fighters did become involved with the Ju 88 formation, including the Martlet of Lt/Cdr. Johnson. He reportedly closed repeatedly with one bomber that was stated to have been finally brought down; in the process of the engagement, his fighter was damaged and Johnson suffered wounds. On approaching for his landing on INDOMITABLE, the absence of any flap control through damage and the failure of the tail-hook to engage a wire contributed to the aircraft's loss; the fighter toppled over the deck's port side and immediately sank, taking the hapless pilot down with it.

The first of two unusual variations in bombing methods turned up at the end of the conventional assault. This was a radio-controlled 'bomb' in the form of an SM79 that was to

A Martlet pilot attempting a landing on a Fleet carrier is in for a rough time. The fighter's port landing gear has crumpled up under the fuselage, probably due to striking the flight deck 'round-down', while the other strut appears to only be partially deployed. The arrester-hook looks as if it will engage a wire and at least bring the Wildcat to a safe if awkward halt.

The Sea Hurricane Mk.Ib, although out-dated in some respects, served the FAA well up to the end of 1942 when it was withdrawn from Fleet carrier operations. This line of four display the under-sized de Havilland spinner and the eight machine guns that were recognition features of the Hawker variant. Note the anti-dazzle strips ahead of and below the cockpit windshields.

be guided to its target by its inventor flying in an accompanying Z1007. In the event nothing positive came of the experiment. Problems with the guidance system caused the pilot-less machine to head inexorably southward over the convoy and towards the Algerian hinterland, where the 1,000-kg explosive content only succeeded in blowing a huge hole in the side of a mountain.

A more potent albeit very limited threat was initially treated with a mix of curiosity and distain. This took the form of two Reggiane Re2001 fighters that turned up as the fighters were in their carrier landing circuits and which were mistaken for FAA fighters indulging in a 'beat-up' exercise; these released small fragmentation bombs upon VICTORIOUS that did not properly explode, although their blast did inflict several fatal casualties. (Quite why the observers should have thought their airborne contemporaries were making such an inappropriate act at a time of high tension probably confirms the 'confusion' factor generally existing in combat of any form).

The third Axis sortie involved a comparatively small formation of He 111s from 6./KG 26 'Loewen' armed with torpedoes and accompanied by the Bf 110s of 8./ZG 26 'Horst Wessel'. The enemy bombers were flying at minimum altitude and the two Sections of No.880 Sqdn. vectored onto the incoming force were forced to engage in a tail-chase. This factor allowed the *Luftwaffe* gunners coordinate their defensive fire upon the Sea Hurricanes as the latter painfully closed the gap. Lt-Cdr Judd's fighter took the brunt of well-directed fire that resulted in one wing being sawn off, whereby the aircraft plunged into the sea, killing the fiery-tempered pilot in the process.

The escorts set upon Lt. Cork's Section as the four fighters broke away from the fusillade of AA fire now greeting both attackers and defenders. Sub-Lt. Cruikshank was promptly shot down, but Cork evened the score by catching up with one of the two Bf 110s involved in his companion's loss. Cork's cannon armament set fire to one engine as the aircraft zoomed upwards and its pilot was seen to bale out. Elsewhere, a Z1007 'shadower' was challenged by three Fulmars of No.884 Sqdn., but the Section Leader Lt. Churchill did not emerge from the action. Lt. Cork appeared to have joined in the hunt after this aircraft and indeed was credited with its destruction after it came down near the Tunisian coast. The worthy Lieutenant was now within one 'kill' of recording an 'Ace' status in a single day.

It was late afternoon when the radar screens began to show up their latest crop of 'blips' that indicated up to four formations gathering both to the northwest and the southeast. The former collection consisted of two groups of aircraft, bomb-laden CR42s led by two SM79s under Re2001 escort and eight

SM79s covered by MC202s. The other force was split between the Regia Aeronautica and the *Luftwaffe* and was operating out of the island of Pantellaria. A total of nine Italian-manned Ju 87s and fourteen SM79s were to be covered by twenty-eight MC202s, while twenty Ju 87s of I./StG 3 were supported by the Bf 109Fs of 8./JG 53 '*Pik As.*' Should the entire mass of aircraft descent upon the convoy en masse, then the prospects for the FAA fighters to provide even an adequate defensive cover for the convoy were very poor, especially given the steadily reduced numbers of fighters on hand by this stage of the Battle.

As it so happened, the Sardinian-based attackers never did succeed in homing-in upon the convoy. One of the CR42 formation was downed by a Martlet of No.806 Sqdn. that had been vectored in its direction. However, the threat posed by the force coming in from the southeast and seen to be splitting into several groups was still sizeable and was responded to by the dispatch of twenty-one fighters. Before the main action was joined, a single SM79 was intercepted by a mixed Fulmar/Sea Hurricane sub-force.

One of the former aircraft-type belonging to No.809 Sqdn. finished its attack run by breaking upwards instead of downwards, an act that proved fatal as the single heavy machine gun in the bomber's dorsal turret hammered its fire into the fighter. The Fulmar burst into flames and bore Lt. Nihill's crew to their deaths after it sliced out of control into the water. A small consolation was earned when the remaining FAA fighters combined to bring the bomber down off the Tunisian coast. A second Fulmar crew from No.809 Sqdn. was brought down when its Section was 'bounced' by enemy fighters after launch from INDOMITABLE.

The remaining crews' plight was alleviated by the appearance of Lt. Cork's cannon-armed Sea Hurricane that was the sole example on hand during 'Pedestal' along with the other standard-armed fighters in his Section. During the resultant melee Cork latched onto an unfortunate SM79 that had strayed into the area; before his ammunition was expended Cork had set the bomber on fire and achieved an 'Ace' in a day' status. However, Cork's fighter was then thoroughly shot up by Italian fighters while he was indulging in the photographing of the 'ditched' crew; this battle damage included the vulnerable radiator and he was fortunate to regain the deck of VICTORIOUS, where his favorite Sea Hurricane was deemed unworthy of repair and 'ditched' over the side!

As the day was fading into evening, the general shape of the convoy remained almost intact although one freighter had been crippled and forced to leave its ranks. The two remaining carriers were still operating freely but this positive situation was altered in a swift, brutal manner. INDOMITABLE was assailed by twelve of the Ju 87s from I./StG 3 that broke through the fighter screen and dived down through the AA barrage. Once again the decided vulnerability of a carrier's open deck to its continued operational use, albeit not the vessel's basic ability to survive, was demonstrated. Bomb strikes were delivered that pierced the deck and exploded inside the carrier's interior, as well as rendering the flight deck and its two lifts out of action. The warship was temporarily halted in the water, but then regained forward motion. Now the air cover was totally dependent upon the single functional carrier VICTORIOUS. However, the effect of this even more serious limitation on air operations was ironically minimal since the Main force of escorts was literally at the point of withdrawal to Gibraltar!

A Section from No.880 Sqdn. had just left the deck of the crippled carrier when the Stuka assault came in. Two of the FAA pilots (Sub-Lt Ritchie of No.801 Sqdn. leading Lt. Fiddes from No.880 Sqdn.), almost immediately after take-off took on a Ju 87 that had just flattened out after releasing its bomb and brought it down after a short chase. Ritchie then engaged a second Ju 87 that went into the sea under a fusillade of bullets, after which he took on a group of five Ju 87s, one of which was claimed as a 'kill'. By then, the other fighter flown by Lt. Fiddes was floating in the sea, having been brought down by 'friendly fire' as the whirling mass of aircraft embroiled within the convoy zone was of necessity opened up upon by the AA gunners; Fiddes fortunately survived the experience! Four Ju 87s, two each from the Italian and *Luftwaffe* formations and one SM79 were confirmed as MIA, compared to the FAA claims for nine aircraft including two fighters.

As it so happened this proportion of confirmed to claimed Axis losses was to be in general keeping with the respective figures for the entire Operation – around twenty and thirty-nine respectively. Much more important than the inevitable disparity between those statistics was the incontrovertible fact that up to the evening of the 12th all the best efforts of the Axis air and surface forces had only inflicted the barest degree of loss upon the fourteen freighters, whose safe delivery to Malta was at the heart of 'Pedestal'. This fine achievement was attained by a force whose ranks were barely adequate from the very beginning and whose numbers were already seriously whittled down both by the loss of EAGLE and combat operations during the 11th and 12th. The operational cost to the FAA was seven Sea Hurricanes, three Fulmars and a single Martlet lost in combat along with eight pilots and three other aircrew. Two other fighters had been lost in 'ditching' incidents and four battle-damaged aircraft ejected over the side.

Lessons

The relative success of the FAA aircrew during 'Pedestal' owed an immeasurable deal to the endeavours of the personnel

An echelon-right formation of Albacores from No.826 Sqdn. is neatly formed apart from the aircraft at the far end. This unit disembarked from FORMIDABLE in May 1941 when the carrier was badly damaged off Crete. From then until August 1943 the crews operated in support of the British Eighth and First Armies across the entire breadth of the North African Desert.

Opposite
Top: A vertical view of a Sea Hurricane Mk.Ib shows two mechanics and a Petty Officer servicing the gun bays with their distinctive 'diamond' shape. The gun camera is housed in the starboard wing leading edge and has its Plexiglas cover detached. The raised elliptical shape directly behind the propeller spinner is the oil collector ring.

Bottom: The hangar interior on board the veteran carrier ARGUS displays the stark simplicity of its layout. Two mechanics are working (right) by a Petty Officer are working on the Sea Hurricane on the forward edge of the hangar deck. ARGUS was instrumental in delivering large numbers of fighters to Malta up to 1942, and also served in a pilot training role in Home Waters until 1944.

actually manning the carriers. The existence of shipboard radar and sound control of aircraft dispositions by launching appropriate numbers and doing so in time to largely intercept the confusing and potentially overwhelming mass of Axis aircraft played a vital part in this success. Then, too, the mechanics' magnificent efforts in promptly patching up and rendering airworthy a succession of damaged fighters cannot be under estimated; the men's work was moreover carried out in the dirt, dust and sweltering heat created by enclosed armoured hangars whose top deck surfaces in no way warded off the heat of the Mediterranean high summer! Their colleagues up on the decks who were totally exposed to the effect of bombs and ammunition – the latter discharged both

by the Axis aircraft and their own AA gunners on surrounding warships – were equally worthy of mention as they manhandled the aircraft up from and into the hangars, ranged them for take off and dispersed them on landing.

The Operation probably witnessed the last full involvement in numbers of the Fulmar in combat, while the Sea Hurricane was also beginning to show its longevity to some extent. Both designs relied upon the .303 machine gun, a weapon that lacked true penetrating power against the current crop of metal-covered and armor-provisioned military aircraft and whose maximum range was fairly short, forcing the attacker to come well within the field of return gunfire. In the latter instance a tail-chase of an adversary with rear defensive armament also tended to throw up the vulnerability of an oil-cooled engine such as the Merlin. A single strike on the glycol tank was usually enough to run the engine 'dry' of this vital coolant and all power would be lost; this factor probably contributed to the loss of several fighters last seen to be in hot pursuit of bombers. The prominent radiator baths on both types formed another vulnerable area in the event of their being damaged. (The Hispano cannon fitted to Lt. Cork's Sea Hurricane, although featuring a rate of fire barely half that of the 1200 RPM figure for the .303 machine gun, fired explosive shells twice the weight of a .303 bullet. This provided a far greater and lethal 'punch' and probably played a key role in this pilot's successes; had such a weapon been available within the ranks of the Sea Hurricanes then the final tally of destroyed Axis aircraft would surely have been materially increased!).

'The Inglorious Thirteenth!'
The positive nature of the 'Pedestal' venture was sustained up to the point of the departure of the main escort force. As the warships headed westwards their crews were greeted with the sight of an intact group of merchantmen and their lighter escort warships continuing to skirt the northern Tunisian coast and heading towards Cap Bon. They were not to know that this situation was set to drastically deteriorate overnight.

First, the initiative of an Italian U-Boat's Captain belied the overall long-term inefficiency of his fellow-members by taking out the cruiser CAIRO, probably damaging NIGERIA and also the vital oil tanker OHIO with a single spread of torpedoes. Then, with air cover from both the FAA and RAF absent, the final day's air formation struck to sink at least two of the merchantmen. Around the same time a second Italian U-Boat seriously damaged the cruiser KENYA. The somewhat disorganised group of vessels met further trouble early next morning when E-boats ambushed the convoy and sank at least three or four more merchantmen as well as fatally crippling another cruiser MANCHESTER. The convoys' integrity had been badly battered and was further affected when two more merchantmen were sunk, one of which (WAIRAMAMA) disintegrated under the impact of its exploding petrol and ammunition load.

Of the five merchantmen still in position, the OHIO would now appear to be the vessel with the least chance of survival. Not only had she survived a torpedo strike, but also her forward deck absorbed the impact of a shot-down Ju87 that left her volatile cargo mercifully intact. Then, engine failure caused her to stop as the other surviving merchantmen headed towards their destination. The destruction of the now isolated vessel by one form or another appeared imminent, but the ensuing forty-eight hours was to witness a seemingly impossible upturn in the tanker's fortunes.

Between the evening of the 13th and the following day, four merchantmen steamed into Malta. Their cargoes, vital as they were to prove, were no more vital than the aviation fuel in the tanks of OHIO – but she was not there. In fact, the vessel was barely afloat and was at one time abandoned as fatally damaged before Capt. Mason decided to re-board her with a volunteer party. The tanker was proving exceedingly difficult to bring under steerage control, even with the assistance of the destroyers BRAMHAM and PENN.

Slowly, painfully, with towing cables and one of the destroyers lashed to her side, the errant tanker was headed towards the salvation that awaited both her and Malta. The motley formation finally eased its torturous sea passage into Grand Harbor on the 15th and the 13,000 tons of fuel was to prove of incalculable value for the island's air defensive force. However, the arrival of the 'Pedestal' remnants was not to prove the ultimate salvation for Malta. Two more convoys right at the end of 1942 were to prove the final and vital saving factor, although by then the Allied advance across the breadth of North Africa spelt the ultimate doom of the Axis Armies and thereby guaranteed the future survival of the island.

'The Price of Admiralty' had been demonstrated in the most brutal but effective manner during 'Pedestal'. The seven warships sunk or seriously damaged along with their numerous dead and injured crews had 'done their duty' in ensuring the basic survival of the convoy and therefore of the equally vital island landmass. In Admiral Cunningham's words, "it takes three years to build a warship – it takes 300 years to build a tradition." The Royal Navy had once again lived up to that grim but pertinent principle!

Hanging On
Malta's survival was still a matter of grave concern, despite the relative success of 'Pedestal'. Rommel's forces were still firmly placed at the approaches to the Suez Canal, although their logistical position was steadily deteriorating while that of the Eighth Army was conversely building up. The pendulum

A Seafire pilot's approach to his carrier's deck has been made in perfect fashion, with the arrester hook engaging the wire However, the lightweight fighter's tendency to 'float' at this critical point often resulted in a failed 'hook-up' or a violent reaction on engaging a wire when the aircraft was either too tail or nose high; the result all too often was a smashed-up machine, ready for a 'write off'!

of success in North Africa had swung steadily but inexorably in favor of the *Afrikakorps* during the first half of 1942. This had been primarily due to the relative inability of the RAF and the Royal Navy to properly interdict the Axis convoy routes traversing down either side of Malta and pouring resources in through the ports of Tripoli and then, after its swift recapture during January, Benghazi. The constant hammering suffered by Malta had ultimately forced the withdrawal of the vast bulk of the cruisers and submarines while the air resources, both defensive and offensive had been seriously whittled down almost to the point of impotence

As August ended and September began, the overall situation that had been stabilised on land by Rommel's advance stalling out around Alamein from July onward, was about to commence an initially slow but ultimately inexorable slide in the Allies favor. The full availability of aviation fuel brought in by the OHIO meant that a regular programme of anti-shipping strikes could again be indulged in. Conversely, the sound air defences on hand provided the Beaufort and FAA attackers with protection from the full depredations previously brought about by the unfettered Axis bombing assaults. Finally, a submarine Flotilla arrived back in Grand harbor to lend its weight to the impending Offensive.

Turning the Screw

Although the bulk of the convoy traffic sailing during late August and through the course of September was destined to still get through, the losses inflicted upon its ranks, especially that part sailing around Sicily and destined for Tripoli, forced an important operational shift. This involved dispatching convoys from southern Italy eastwards to Greece and Crete, then southeast to Tobruk, which meant that the voyages were materially extended in time. However, even during the latter part of August, the loss of several oil tankers inflicted a fatal blow to the possible success of Rommel's latest offensive around Alam Al Halfa, while the cargo borne on one tanker getting through to Tobruk was found to be useless thanks to contamination! (Fuel also formed a part of the cargo content on standard freighter loads, and the loss of at least three merchantmen in this category as well as four oil tankers during September further added to Rommel's logistical woes).

The bulk of the anti-shipping Offensive was to be conducted by the RAF and the Navy's submarines. However, the few Albacores and Swordfish still on hand in Malta also played a part, as on 26 September. Two Albacores guided by an ASV-equipped Swordfish closed with a small convoy heading east from Italy; the freighter UNIONE absorbed one torpedo strike that was sufficient to force her destroyer escort to take up a tow and divert into a Greek seaport. On 14 October as the Offensive became ever more intense and successful, a similar-strength formation picked up a single-freighter convoy on the approach to Tripoli. The flares released by the Swordfish permitted a clear sight for one Albacore whose torpedo was claimed to have struck home in the face of intense AA fire that riddled but did not bring down the biplane. The freighter was the AMSTERDAM that over the ensuing three days laboured along under tow and finally was beached east of Tripoli. A second attack by two Albacores failed to inflict further damage on the hulk, which was finally dispatched by a submarine.

A mixed RAF/FAA formation headed after yet another convoy off Lampedusa on the evening of 19 October. The single tanker and three freighters were well guarded by a destroyer escort, whose smokescreen added to the already poor

The anti-shipping Campaign against the Axis in the Mediterranean was conducted both from North Africa and also Malta. A torpedo-laden Albacore is photographed on the Island sometime during the winter of 1942-1943. The aircraft codes are indistinct but appear to be the S5A+ sequence used by No.821 Sqdn., which did operate off Malta during the foregoing period of World War II.

visibility. Sub-Lt. Pratt delivered his 'tinfish' against the TITANIA, which did take one strike, and the crippled vessel was sunk next day by a submarine. On return to Malta, the aircraft were hastily re-armed and sent out again in deteriorating weather. Jamming of the ASV equipment allied to heavy cloud and rainsqualls did not prevent the convoy being picked out.

Only three vessels were now on hand, including the tanker PANUCO. This time round she was targeted by Lt Elliott in the ASV Swordfish; the resultant strike did set the tanker on fire and the vessel abandoned but in circumstances recalling the OHIO incident she was re-boarded, the blaze was extinguished and the vessel steered safely into Tripoli, albeit with a degree of cargo loss. By the month-end nearly half of the supplies heading for North Africa were nestling under the Mediterranean or still in the holds of freighters forced to turn back; nearly 60,000 tons had been lost on the series of freighters or tankers recorded as sunk, and whose numbers ran well into double figures.

It was not until the beginning of November, when the prolonged and bloody Battle of El Alamein finally saw the Axis soldiers having to give way and retreat, that the prospect of relief begin to painfully emerge. Operation 'Torch' on 8 November gave added promise that the island's parlous operational and human condition was within measurable sight of permanent salvation. More supplies were still required and the need was fulfilled towards the end of November with convoy 'Stoneage' dispatched from Alexandria. By then, the Eighth Army's advance had ensured that Axis interference from the air would be greatly reduced as airfields all long the coastline were captured or largely rendered out of action. The potential threat still posed by the Italian Navy was recognised by the huge escort of four cruisers and seventeen destroyers for the four freighters. That threat did not materialise and the entire convoy sailed safely into Grand Harbor.

CHAPTER SIX

The Far East Boils Over
1941-1942

1940-1941 Red Sea-Indian Ocean Operations

The relative success of the Royal Navy over its Axis opponents in the Mediterranean between June 1940 and the first half of 1941, was mirrored to a smaller degree in the region of the Red Sea and the Horn of Africa. Mussolini's Invasion of Ethiopia directed from his neighbouring colonies of Eritrea and Somaliland had rebounded by early April in the face of the advancing British and Commonwealth forces. However, the naval units in the port of Massawa in Eritrea still posed a theoretical threat to sea-going traffic along the East Africa coastline and up into the Red Sea, especially when given the narrow confines of the Red Sea. However, the operational inertia displayed by the original assembly of four cruisers, nine destroyers and eight submarines had seemingly mirrored the operational 'paralysis' of the main Italian Fleet over the past months! Now, that sizeable force was reduced to five destroyers and several auxiliary vessels, which were faced by the carrier HERMES and the 'in transit' FORMIDABLE's aircraft backed by cruiser support as the Royal Navy closed in to invest Massawa, which was positioned towards the southern end of the Red Sea.

Nos.813 and 824 Sqdns. from EAGLE were now located at Port Sudan some 200 miles north of Massawa. There, the two units were awaiting the arrival of their carrier, whose transit through the Suez Canal for a counter-offensive against German raiders in the Indian Ocean and South Atlantic trade routes had been delayed by the need to clear the waterway of ships sunk by *Luftwaffe* mines. On 2 April, following an original abortive attempt to sortie three destroyers against British shipping based at Suez, Admiral Bonetti in charge of the area defences authorised the departure of his destroyer flotilla for an assault upon Port Sudan.

When the Italians' plan became known to their adversaries, suitable counter-moves were initiated, with RAF aircraft detailed to reconnoitre for the warships whereabouts, after which the Swordfish crews and other RAF aircraft would attack. Finally, three Navy destroyers at Port Sudan would back up these attacks once they had steered an appropriate interception course. In fact the Swordfish Sqdns. added to the reconnoitring aspect by dispatching seven aircraft, all loaded with 250 lb. bombs, the following morning. An hour after take off, one of the crews confirmed a force of only four destroyers heading towards Port Sudan and well within air-striking distance. A Taranto veteran Lt. Wellham was flying the 'sighting' aircraft E5A, and he duly delivered his ordnance close to one of the by-now frantically manoeuvering warships without any discernable result.

The level-bombing tactic primarily used by the Regia Aeronautica against the Royal Navy had so far achieved little in the way of sunken or damaged warships. The dive-bombing style of the Ju 87 and Ju 88 by contrast had already reaped a steady reward and would continue to do so. The venerable Swordfish's basic brief was to indulge in torpedo or mine-laying operations, both conducted at minimum height. The design's use as a bomber was a secondary factor, not so much because of its bomb load capacity but rather due to its painfully slow speed that rendered it vulnerable to gunfire. In addition, the aircraft was not fitted with a standard bombsight, which made accurate aiming very difficult.

The alternative manner in which to overcome this deficiency was to follow the '*Stuka*' principle of dive-bombing, but here marked differences existed between the 'Stringbag' and Germany's custom-built machines. For a start the *Luftwaffe* aircraft were equipped with a specialised bombsight as well as dive brakes. Furthermore in the case of the Ju 88, the aircraft featured an automatic elevator action that eased the aircraft out of its steep dive upon the point of bomb release. In stark contrast, not only was the Swordfish not designed with dive-

EAGLE was dispatched to the Indian Ocean in early 1941 and operated around the Red Sea zone of operations. From here its aircraft supported the British and Commonwealth Forces' bid to eject the Italians from their occupation of Ethiopia. During this period the Swordfish of Nos.813 and 824 Sqdns. were each credited with the sinking of an Italian destroyer.

bombing in mind, but also its rate of descent was in proportion to its overall performance – that is, very pedestrian!

Notwithstanding all these limitations, the EAGLE crews had decided upon this method of approach to their targets, despite their slow descent in the face of their targets' return AA fire as well as the 'snaking' course being steered. (The individual defensive armament was limited to pairs of 40mm and 13.2mm weapons as well as four 4-inch high-angle guns, and the weight of fire was neither too great nor concentrated, so providing a degree of equalisation with the Swordfish's limited pace of attack).

Bomb aiming was to prove a 'rule of thumb' action, with each pilot having to aim-off between one and one-and-a-half lengths in the hope of striking near or on the target. The majority of the bombs were General purpose (GP) with the remainder Semi-armor-piercing (SAP); the GP weapons were better suited for the purpose of either directly shattering the thin-skinned hulls and superstructures or alternatively of staving-in the lower hull structure through the 'mining' effect of near misses. The ideal approach was at a shallow angle to the warships' course with the bombs dropped in a stick, the intention being to straddle the target. However, this was difficult enough to achieve in level flight, let alone when making a diving approach.

The first handful of individual attacks made by aircraft from the FAA reconnaissance force had resulted in the bomb loads falling well ahead or astern or in one instance fairly close to the warship's side. So far, the evasive tactics combined with the attackers' technical limitations for bombing had paid off for the Italians, but the situation changed dramatically as the first main striking force of seven Swordfish commenced its assault. E4H of No.813 Sqdn. swooped down from around 5,000 ft. upon the third destroyer bringing up the rear of the main echeloned formation. The pilot's deflection calculation was perfect and his salvo of bombs literally blew the hapless

warship out of the water along with its equally hapless crew. No further successes were recorded by the formation although several bombs struck the sea surface close to the warship in question.

Even as the first strike-force was wending its way back to Port Sudan, a second wave was already in the air, consisting of five aircraft and flying in a very loose 'formation' spread across several miles, but in radio contact. This time around, the Swordfish found only two of the three destroyers, which split up upon the aircrafts' approach. E5C of No.824 Sqdn. was first to engage, with its target the destroyer steaming a northeasterly heading. The aircraft faced a minimal amount of AA fire as its pilot measured his degree of aim-off to perfection. Two bombs struck the destroyer amidships and a third impacted in the water close enough to collapse her starboard bow section. Oil fuel was observed gushing out of the stricken vessel, which was also on fire; soon after, she lost way and was last seen motionless, down by the head and with the crew abandoning ship. (The remaining two destroyers were later intercepted after heading towards neutral territory of Saudi Arabia; following a series of unsuccessful bombing runs by RAF aircraft: both were later sunk by the destroyer KINGSTON.).

Force Z – A Pre-Ordained Disaster?

The Royal Navy's presence in what was regarded as the Far Eastern Theater of Operations was limited between 1939 and 1941 due to the requirements of the European theatre of war. The growing hostility of the Japanese Empire to the Western Nations presence in the region spanning the Pacific Ocean into the Indian Ocean was not basically taken seriously. The 'little yellow men's' corporate myopia was seen as one of the salient factors in their being regarded as posing no real threat in military terms, while a British assessment of their ability as aviators was negatively couched, and was partially based on

Two Fulmars Mk.I have been spotted on the central flight deck of ILLUSTRIOUS during the run-up in May 1942 to the Invasion of Vichy France-controlled Madagascar Island off the East African coast. The 17 ft. 10-inch breadth of the Fairey design was sufficient to fit into the rectangular elevator space as seen on the Fleet carrier's rear flight deck. The nearside aircraft displays the wear and tear associated with operations in a salt-water atmosphere.

the 'fact' that they possessed no natural balance due to having been carried on their mothers' backs during early childhood! Such high-handed, not to say bizarre and dangerously ignorant, opinions still held sway in 1941 despite the Japanese Army and Air Force's long-term Campaign against the Chinese. Their equipment was equally regarded as infinitely inferior, and therefore of no value in challenging the United States, the British Empire or the other European Powers in the Far East.

The growing likelihood of a conflict with Japan during the latter months of 1941 saw Churchill adopt a measure that smacked of the age-old 'send a gunboat to quieten the natives' policy – only this time round, the adversary was neither land-bound nor lacking the requisite weaponry with which to strike back. The battleship PRINCE OF WALES, the battle cruiser REPULSE and the Fleet carrier INDOMITABLE were to assemble as Force Z and sail for Singapore. The carrier had only been commissioned in October and was actually located in the West Indies on working-up trials when the project was established. However, the first nail in the Force's coffin occurred when she grounded and so damaged her bow section that a transfer to the Norfolk Navy Yard for a replacement, prefabricated unit was deemed necessary. The work was completed in a remarkably short time, after which the carrier sailed post-haste for its rendezvous with the two capital ships. By 10 December the voyage had progressed as far as Cape Town – and there the Plan was scrapped, thanks to the tragic news emanating from Singapore.

Admiral Tom Phillips the Force Z Commander immediately responded to Japan's entry into World War II on 7 December. Phillips was the epitome of the dedicated 'battleship sailor' and was firmly convinced that his Force could thwart any attempt by the Japanese to carry out a military encroachment on Malaya. The RAF fighters stationed in Malaya could compensate for the current absence of air cover by the FAA. What Phillips and other senior personnel were still ignorant of was the presence of a sizeable air-strike force based in southern Indo-China. This was comprised of modern designed, twin-engine 'Betty' and 'Nell' bombers that could range several hundreds of miles to deliver both bombs and torpedoes. The British warships were sailing into a trap as they eased out of their Singapore berths on the 8th and prepared to challenge the invasion Fleets reported to be heading across the Gulf of Thailand.

By the early morning of the 10th the Force, having abandoned the intention to strike the enemy forces landing at Singora in central Malaya, and on receiving the news that no RAF fighter cover would be available – coupled to the first indications of the Indo-China based bombers being on hand – was steaming back towards Singapore. At the same time, over eighty Japanese bombers and torpedo-bombers were lifting off from airfields at Saigon, having been informed by reconnaissance sources of the battleships' presence. The scene was set for the latest confrontation between Sea and Air Power.

It was towards mid-day when the Japanese aircrews picked up Force Z, as they were (unluckily for the warships) heading back for Saigon, having missed their targets on the outward leg. The AA gunners fought determinedly against the rain of bombs coming out of the high-level aircraft, but their attention

A Fleet carrier is photographed along with three of its Swordfish complement airborne. The aircraft approaching over the stern is probably not landing on since there is a collection of aircraft clustered around the superstructure very close to the safety barrier. In addition, there seems to be a mobile crane whose presence suggests an incident of some kind that may be blocking the flight deck.

A Supermarine Walrus is positioned alongside its parent warship. The airman perched precariously on the upper wing is guiding the ship's crane jib and cable so that it can be hooked onto the wing securing points prior to hoisting the aircraft on board. The slightest slip by the airman will result in fatal contact with the 'pusher' engine's propeller.

was inevitably split by the twin threat posed by the low-flying torpedo bombers, who were fanning out to attack from several angles. Two torpedo strikes on PRINCE OF WALES within minutes of the assault commencing fatally crippled her ability to properly steer thanks to propeller and rudder damage. Further torpedo hits along her hull but below her main armoured belt administered the '*coup de grâce*' and she came to a halt and began to list. (The assumption that the armoured belt had apparently not worked was later ascribed to the warship heeling over in evasive manoeuvres, so exposing the lower hull to the torpedo-impact; the situation was recorded on film by a Post-war diving team, who inspected both wrecks).

Meanwhile REPULSE was also receiving an ultimately terminal battering as her AA defences were similarly overwhelmed and with her hull failing to absorb the striking effect of numerous bombs and at least four torpedoes. The Japanese crews' final sighting was of both warships stationery and listing stance. By 1:00pm the elderly battle cruiser had slipped under the waves, preceding her contemporary in misfortune by just under one hour. A total of 2,081 officers and seamen out of the joint complement of 2,921 were saved by the escorts but neither Admiral Phillips nor Capt. Leach on PRINCE OF WALES were among the former figure.

Prior to World War II, a fellow-member of Phillips on the Joint Services Committee, became so frustrated by the latter's seemingly obtuse attitude towards the superiority of the battleship over aircraft that he burst out with, "Tom, one day you will be standing on a soapbox on the bridge of your battleship (Phillips was in modern parlance 'vertically challenged'!). The bombs and torpedoes will be raining down on your ship – but as it goes under you will be heard to utter; "That was a bloody great mine!" That individual's words had now borne tragic fruit. And who was that man? None other than Sir Arthur Harris, the impending Commander-in-Chief of RAF Bomber Command from February 1942 onwards!

A final comment on the fate of Force Z relates to the absence of the carrier-based fighters and their assumed ability to protect the surface warships. INDOMITABLE had been carrying the Fairey Fulmar for this intended role. Whether this moderately-paced design, that in the event would have been present in limited numbers, could have fended off the large force of bombers successfully will ever be open to question. The proponents of the battleship might well have countered the advocates of air superiority by stating that to date the single instance of a battleship's loss involving aircraft (the BISMARCK) could be ascribed more to good fortune, apart

from which the final action had involved other battleships. In the case of Force Z it had faced a direct challenge from a far greater number of aircraft than had the German warship, apart from which the weather conditions, not to mention the Japanese airmens' battle tactics, had played their part in ensuring success. Air Power had struck another huge and stunning blow at the concept of the battleship's supreme status in combat, and would continue to do so during the ensuing four years of the global Conflict.

On the Back Foot Again

Between December and the beginning of February 1942 the Malayan Campaign progressed to its bloody and fatal conclusion for the British and Commonwealth forces. During this time INDOMITABLE's eastwards movement was cut short on arrival at Columbo on the island of Ceylon (Now Sri Lanka) in late January. On board were fifty RAF Hurricanes that had taken the place of the carrier's Fulmars and Albacores at Aden and were to be flown off to land on Java. A second delivery

Opposite
Top: Out in the India/Ceylon region, a Fairey Fulmar is seen flying low over a fellow-aircraft. Two mechanics are carrying out maintenance work. Both are stripped to the waist against the fierce tropical temperature while the sailor on top of the engine mount wears a sun helmet.

Bottom: A large deck handler group is photographed while manhandling a Fulmar. Coiled-up arrester wire is yet to be re-wound for use. Note the framework on the inside of the flap and the rectangular panel just ahead of the cockpit, which was to prevent the pilot being dazzled by the engine exhaust stubs on night operations.

Below: A graphic view taken from the cockpit of a Fulmar based on Ceylon shows the carrier HERMES in her death throes. She was caught off Ceylon by a force of D3A 'Val' dive-bombers on 9 April 1942 and overwhelmed in a welter of bomb strikes. She had no aircraft embarked at the time but it is doubtful that their presence could have saved her from this sad fate. The photographing fighter was one of a number that arrived over the scene just as the Japanese force was retiring.

with Aden and Ceylon the loading and delivery points was made during February, after which INDOMITABLE joined Admiral Somerville's Eastern Fleet in the Maldives, having re-embarked her Aden-based Sqdns. beforehand.

The five battleships of the Fleet were now supported by three carriers, with VICTORIOUS and the elderly HERMES being the other two. A total of thirty-nine fighters and fifty-seven TSR aircraft were shared between the carriers. Two other Fulmar-equipped Sqdns., Nos.803 and 806 were ashore in Ceylon along with Swordfish of No.788 Sqdn. The Royal Navy's overall prospect of even fending off the impending threat posed by Admiral Nagumo's First Carrier Striking Force whose central core was five of the carriers that had hammered Pearl Harbor, let alone defeating this formidable adversary, appeared to be a total non-starter.

In the case of the respective Air Arms, not only were the Japanese arguably the more seasoned combat veterans, with their flying skills honed through several years combat experience in the China Conflict, that had culminated in the devastating strike on 7 December 1941; their aircraft, whether in the form of the redoubtable A6M Zero fighter or the D3A 'Val' dive bomber and B5N 'Kate' strike aircraft, were truly superior in overall performance to their Fulmar, Sea Hurricane or Albacore opponents. The presence on board FORMIDABLE of twenty Martlets II flown by No.888 Sqdn. was the sole note of operational advance, but even Grumman's portly fighter would be hard pressed to emerge unscathed from a combat with a 'Zero' let alone emerge as the victor. In addition, the total number of enemy aircraft on hand was around double of that provided by the combined FAA/RAF complement in the region. The situation regarding capital ships was no better because all of the Navy's five battleships were markedly inferior in speed and endurance, as well as dating back to World War I or shortly after, compared to the four equivalent Japanese

The Defiant was a tragic failure as a turret-armed day fighter, but numbers of the Boulton-Paul design were converted to target-towing duties. Rear cockpit frames displaced the turrets with the winch operator located inside. A winch mounting is seen on the lower aircraft, which also bears a tropical filter. Both Defiants belong to No.777 Sqdn. initially based in West Africa. The propeller spinners are red and Type CI markings are applied.

warships now steaming as part of Nagumo's force in the Indian Ocean.

The Japanese threat materialised as April was entered but events during the enemy's brief operational spell in the Indian Ocean dictated that the two Fleets were never to come in direct contact, which was just as well in the circumstances! The Japanese scout planes did their utmost to track down the Eastern Fleet but met with no success, whereas the RAF Catalinas utilised for the reverse purpose achieved this objective on the 4th. By then Nagumo had turned his attention towards attacking the key Naval Base at Trincomalee on the following day. During this short interval Somerville had sortied his two Fleet carriers from the Eastern Fleet's Base at Addu

Atoll in the hope of making a nocturnal torpedo assault; the remaining warships of the Fleet that had returned to the Atoll to refuel after failing to make contact over the past day or so stayed in port. (HERMES had been detached to Trincomalee for a re-fit but her days were unknowingly numbered).

Nothing came of the projected FAA attack since contact with Nagumo's force again failed. On the other hand, the attack on the port of Columbo on the 5th met with little surface success other than the wrecking of some port installations. The air battle with RAF Hurricanes yielded better results, with thirteen shot down against seven losses. In addition, one Flight of Swordfish had the misfortune to be intercepted while in transit, and the 'Zeroes' summarily dispatched all six; not even

FORMIDABLE returned to active service in December 1941 following her mauling by the *Luftwaffe* off Crete the previous May. This picture was taken during her 1942 spell of duty in the Indian Ocean. She is launching the Albacores of either 818 or 820 Sqdns. In the background is the veteran battleship WARSPITE.

INDOMITABLE arrived in the Indian Ocean too late to influence events at sea around the Malaya Peninsula in early 1942. However, the carrier was on hand for the capture of Madagascar Island in May. Here an Albacore flies a parallel course to the warship. On deck are four Hurricanes Mk.1b belonging to No.880 Sqdn.: three of the fighters are positioned with their tails over-hanging the deck edge.

the 'Stringbag' could either out-manoeuver or survive the onslaught of gunfire from Japan's supreme fighter at this period of World War II.

Although two Albacores of No.827 Sqdn., one of which went missing while the second survived determined attacks by an intercepting 'Zero', did sight an element of the Japanese carrier force, the resultant efforts to maintain that contact failed over the next two days and Admiral Somerville sailed his force back to Addu Atoll. The final events of the Japanese incursion into the Indian Ocean occurred on the 9th. A second assault on Columbo was thwarted by timely warning of the enemy formation's approach thanks to an RAF Catalina's previous sighting of the Japanese force, that permitted the seaport to again be cleared of shipping. A similar poor scale of destruction by bombing but a superior kill to loss ratio enjoyed by the 'Zeroes' compared to that arising out of the first attack were the twin features of the operation. Better success was only several hours distant however.

HERMES was one of the warships that had cleared out of port but now had the ill luck to be sighted while steaming off Ceylon by the Japanese fliers as they cleared their targets. Her entire establishment of aircraft had been disembarked but their absence was probably still a minor factor in what now ensued. A force of D3A 'Vals' had been re-armed and launched to track down the carrier. The vulnerable warship with her un-armored deck and minimal degree of AA weapons was overwhelmed along with her two escorts by a welter of accurately aimed bombs that sent all three to the bottom; two Fleet Auxiliaries were also destroyed.

The Japanese aircraft were barely through with their task when a handful of RAF Hurricanes and Fulmars of No.803 Sqdn. arrived over the scene of carnage; their pilots only

managed to hasten the departure of the 'Vals' although none were actually shot down. The force of major carriers with which the Royal Navy had entered World War II was now reduced to two, being EAGLE and FURIOUS, of which only the latter named warship was fated to survive the Conflict. The modern ILLUSTRIOUS Class was to enjoy much better fortune in this respect, although three of these (one of which would be adversely affected twice) were all to spend a number of months out of service thanks to heavy damage – all inflicted by aircraft!

Balancing Action at Madagascar (Operation 'Ironclad')

The island of Madagascar situated off the East African coast in line with what was then Portuguese East Africa, lay squarely astride the main trading route to the Suez Canal. The entry of Japan into the War had raised a specific threat to the Allied cause in the region. This arose because the island's current Vichy French occupiers could not be trusted to resist any Japanese demand to allow that Nation's troops to take over, especially when given their previous craven surrender of Indo-China. The port and town of Diago Suarez was positioned on the island's northern tip and plans that had actually been started during January were duly initiated to take it over, if necessary by force.

The absence of British land-based airfields in the region dictated that the Navy's carriers would be called on to provide air cover for the Invasion force. The departure of Nagumo's force back to the Pacific for the impending Coral Sea Operation allowed one of Admiral Somerville's two surviving carriers INDOMITABLE to be dispatched from the Eastern Fleet's revised Base at Bombay for what was termed Operation

'Ironclad'. She was joined by ILLUSTRIOUS, newly re-commissioned following her prolonged repair in Norfolk, VA.

There were nine Sqdns. embarked between the two carriers, and the aircraft involved displayed a range of five different designs, all but one of which (the Martlet) was British in origin. ILLUSTRIOUS bore one Fulmar and twenty Swordfish as well as the twelve Martlets II of Nos.881 with folding wings and 882 Sqdn.'s eight fixed-wing Martlets I. Twelve Fulmars, nine Sea Hurricanes and twenty-four Albacores were based on INDOMITABLE. The involvement of three distinct aircraft types on INDOMITABLE inevitably created a logistical problem with spare parts, and was a situation that was only partially alleviated as the War progressed by the limitation to two distinct aircraft types whenever possible on board the Fleet carriers. By what was now virtually the mid-point of World War II the operational life of the Fulmar as a fighter was fast approaching its close although there was one more major action during August in which the Fairey design would play a part. The Sea Hurricane was also destined to be relegated from front-line FAA service on Fleet carriers by the winter of 1942-1943, although it would continue to operate off escort carriers up to September 1944, albeit in limited numbers.

Although an airfield existed near the Invasion point on the isthmus at whose base Diego Suarez lay, there was to be little or no aerial resistance from there during the course of the short Operation that commenced on 5 May. This important factor was due to the thorough bombing and strafing of the facilities by INDOMITABLE's aircraft that took out the hangars with their content as well as machines dispersed around the airfield. The few aircraft that survived the initial battering were sent up next day to engage the invaders, along with MS406s and Potez 63-11s dispatched from Ivato further south along the island's length and operating out of Anivorano.

The Morane-Saulnier MS406 had enjoyed a brief spell of operational service during the Battle of France and its overall performance and armament of a single 20mm cannon and two 7.5mm machine guns appeared a reasonable match for the Martlet II variant that the French pilots took on. However, the results were one-sided in that No.881 Sqdn. shot four MS406s out of the sky without loss on the 7th. Two Potez 63-11 light attack bombers that were encountered by the Martlet pilots suffered a similar fate.

The French Navy had several surface and submarine warships at Diego Suarez and these were largely destroyed or put out of commission within the first twenty-four hours.

The Sea Hurricanes Mk.Ib of No.880 Sqdn. were first embarked on INDOMITABLE in October 1941. In this picture three fighters are spotted on the forward flight deck and a fourth, having just landed-on is being directed by a deck handler into position. Although the sun appears to be absent the stripped down wear of the sailors indicates the carrier is in a tropical zone such as the Indian Ocean.

Nos.810 and 829 Sqdns. put their Swordfish to swift and lethal effect by sinking a submarine and an Armed Merchant Cruiser (AMC) on the 5th. The sloop D'ENTRECASTEUX was in steaming mode when she was attacked, but was soon badly damaged; this specific action culminated in the warship going aground albeit still seemingly in operational commission. Next day a single Swordfish of No.829 Sqdn. took out a second submarine. Meanwhile the need to curb the harassing gunfire still emanating from the stranded sloop was responded to by the Sea Hurricanes of No.880 Sqdn. – a surprising choice when given the greater striking power of the Albacores or even the Swordfish on hand; however, these aircraft were otherwise engaged in ground support and 'decoy' duties.

In the event the thorough sieving of the sloop's thin hull and superstructure that even the lightweight .303 bullets managed to achieve reportedly left the warship on fire with her guns silenced. (There are separate accounts of the warship's final loss as occurring later on the 5th when a second assault by Swordfish of No.829 achieved this end. However, the Hurricane-based incident is quoted by one of the participating pilots who stated the details in his post-War published book!). Whatever the exact circumstances of the warship's loss, the photographic evidence shows her on an even keel, but sunk submerged to a point just below the deck level.

The Vichy French authorities signalled their unconditional surrender on the 7th. Operation 'Ironclad' however brief in time and operational scale had provided valuable combat experience for the FAA crews, who had flown just over 300 sorties and thereby ensured a swift and safe advance for the British troops. In this manner the frustrations arising out of the previous month's 'stalemate' involving Nagumo's force was cast aside. The operational honing was to prove particularly important for the aircrews and support staff on INDOMITABLE as the plans for the 'Pedestal' convoy gathered pace.

Madagascar's land mass equated in length to that of Britain while its average breadth was some 100 miles, so the process of full occupation was not immediately fulfilled, with the delay extending over six months. In the meantime SAAF and FAA aircraft were based around Diego Suarez, with the latter force involving Fulmars of No.795 Sqdn. and Albacores of No.796 Sqdn. The possibility of Japanese intervention could not be discounted and so the renewed campaign to take over the entire island was commenced on 10 September. ILLUSTRIOUS was

A single Swordfish is tucked discreetly behind the second and third Albacores of No.831 Sqdn. embarked on INDOMITABLE. Two aircrew in the foreground stroll towards their aircraft while the deck handlers prepare to deploy the aircraft wings into position. Note the white outline to the aircraft codes and the Type A1 roundels that date the picture prior to August 1942 when the carrier was severely damaged during Operation 'Pedestal'.

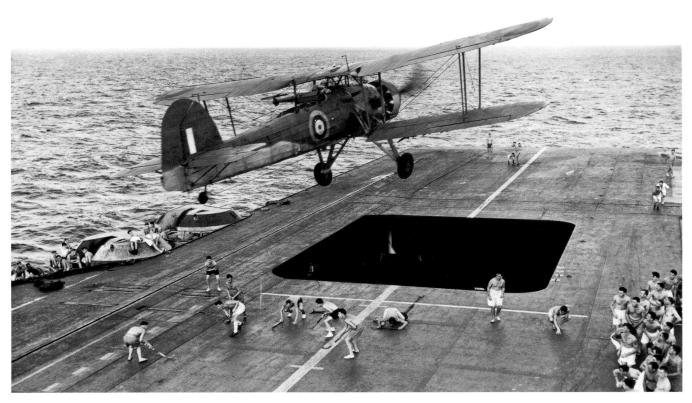

A game of deck hockey on INDOMITABLE is interrupted by A Swordfish Mk.I making a low pass. The aircraft bears a towing winch in the central cockpit area with the tow-wire extending back under the fuselage.

The two nearest Sea Hurricanes Mk.Ib carry the No.880 Sqdn. codes as well as the revised Type C1 national markings introduced around May 1942. The deck weather screens are raised, so the calm sea will probably change to a more disturbed pattern.

Two Martlets Mk.II from No.881 Sqdn. are prepared for take-off from the deck of ILLUSTRIOUS. The Mk.II featured folding wings compared to the fixed wings applied to the Mk.I. Another improvement was the larger tail wheel and strut compared to the much smaller unit fitted to the Mk.I.

The Fleet carrier on which the Fulmar is embarked has left a curving wake behind as it swings into the wind, ready to launch the fighter. The cruiser maintaining its escort station in the background is LONDON.

now the sole carrier on hand in the Indian Ocean on hand to support the operation, since FORMIDABLE had hastily sailed for the Mediterranean to take the place of INDOMITABLE, after she had been put out of commission during the August 'Pedestal' convoy.

The carrier, with her complement of Fulmars, Martlets and Swordfish totalling forty-two aircraft, was used to cover the initial landing at Majunga on the northwest region, after which the ground forces moved inland and southward to secure the key town of Tananarive in the island's center, through which Madagascar's few major roads were linked up. The resistance encountered, whether on the ground or in the air, was generally sparse and disjointed although it was the beginning of November before full occupation was achieved. Of the estimated 230 sorties flown by the land-based Allied aircraft, over half involved the FAA Sqdns, with the Albacores effort including a number of anti-submarine patrols flown out of Majunga.

Turgid Times

The decisive actions on Madagascar were unbeknown to Admiral Somerville to mark the high-water point for the Eastern Fleet as regards the remainder of 1942, and the bulk of 1943. A sortie into the Bay of Bengal by ILLUSTRIOUS and FORMIDABLE during August achieved nothing of substance, and shortly after the latter carrier was withdrawn to European waters to take the place of INDOMITABLE. Japanese naval interest was destined to be almost wholly concentrated within the Pacific for the rest of World War II, although it was not until early 1943 that the U.S. Navy

possessed adequate numbers of carriers in particular to force their opponents to regard that theater of naval operations as of paramount importance.

Equally, the Battle of the Atlantic was still far from won and demanded the maximum concentration of Royal Navy warships. So it was that the transfer of ILLUSTRIOUS back to Home Waters in January 1943 left the Eastern Fleet bereft of FAA air support for the ensuing eight months. On the other hand, future Axis warship intrusions would be largely confined to U-Boats. The main trade routes upon which these would attempt to prey were generally within range of land-based Allied aircraft, and the most likely victims would be freighters traversing the broad expanse of the central Indian Ocean on their own. In truth the Eastern Fleet was to suffer what amounted to 'turgid times' in respect of operational action throughout 1943 – although the seamen would almost certainly have opted for the inevitable spells of boredom that the situation engendered as an acceptable option!

If the overall situation for the Eastern Fleet was stagnant between late 1942 and late 1943 the same could not be said in respect of shore bases. The overall expansion of the Fleet Air Arm at sea was being paralleled by the creation of independent airfields. In the case of the Indian Ocean theatre the FAA had until 1943 tended to be 'tenants' at RAF stations. This trend was initially reversed on 1 September 1942 when Katukurunda (HMS UKASSA) on Ceylon was transferred from the RAF and was intended to house a Repair Yard and Reserve Aircraft Storage facility. Puttalan, also on Ceylon, was commissioned as HMS RAJALIVA on 1 February 1943 and accommodated disembarked Sqdns. as well as storing reserve aircraft. During

A number of FAA Sqdns. in the 700 number sequence were graded as Fleet Requirement Units (FRU). Their duties entailed non-operational functions such as communications, radar calibration, air-to-air or air-to-ground firing, etc. Another function was target-towing, as exemplified by a Miles Martinet; the aircraft undersides are sprayed in yellow and black bands to warn other aircraft to keep clear. The SEAC roundel indicates an aircraft of either 722 or 733 Sqdn., stationed in India or Ceylon respectively.

This side-on view of a Fulmar reveals the generous-sized radiator cover that could create a 'scoop' effect when 'ditching' with the effect of dragging the aircraft under the surface or causing it to somersault. The extended Observer's cockpit was roomy but the canopy provided no means for defensive armament to be installed.

September 1943 Columbo Racecourse (HMS BHERUNDA) was commissioned to house a Fleet Requirements Unit and also facilities for assembling aircraft.

It was no coincidence that these airfields were taken on charge since the island of Ceylon was geographically vital to all Naval operations in the Indian Ocean, given that it housed the large Naval base at Trincomalee – the main land target for Nagumo's carrier aircraft in April 1942. The mainland of India was also in use with Coimbator (HMS GARUDA) coming into service on 1 October 1942 for both the assembly and storage of aircraft. The logistical 'fetters' of the RAF as regards airfield facilities were clearly being cast off, a situation that was long overdue for both Services.

Regeneration

By October 1943 the Battle of the Atlantic was set on its still concentrated but ultimate course towards Allied Victory. At the same time the Axis hold on the Mediterranean was entering a similar stage of progressive failure with the Italian mainland invaded and occupied along its southern reaches. The second 'Attacker' Class of escort carrier to be commissioned was BATTLER and she had recently been part of the force covering the Salerno Landings. Now, the vessel was detached to the Eastern Fleet to operate in a Trade Protection role. The single Sqdn. on board was composed of Swordfish and Seafires Mk.LIIC totalling eighteen aircraft in all, although Wildcats Mk.V would displace the fighter element of six aircraft in mid-1944. BATTLER was to be the first of five escort carriers joining the Eastern Fleet up to August 1944 that would be allocated to the same operational role.

CHAPTER SEVEN

Part One
THE FROZEN HELL
(Russian Convoys)

"Any man or State who fights against Nazidom will have our aid." Winston Churchill expressed this sentiment when he made his broadcast, in the wake of Operation BARBAROSSA, the Nazi Invasion of Soviet Russia on 22 June 1941. The British Prime Minister had long been an inveterate opponent of Communism ever since it was first given National and then International expression from 1917 onwards. Balanced against his natural and heartfelt feelings on the subject of Communism was the absolute necessity to rid the World of the current scourge of National Socialism and its adherents.

The decision to invade Russia had been fundamentally taken by Hitler even before the Battle of Britain had run its full course. The *Führer*'s undoubted view that Britain's exclusion from the Continent in June 1940 would see her marginalized if not finally subdued as a military threat to Nazi domination of western Europe must have been somewhat strengthened by the initial tide of U-Boat success in the North Atlantic, and the military reverses suffered by the British Empire in North Africa, Greece and Crete as 1941 was entered.

The primary risk of entering into a 'twin-Front' Conflict – a situation that was feared by the German military High Command – was countered by Hitler's continuing to assert his opinion that Britain was too taken up with its own survival to assist Russia in any material manner. In any case, the state of the Soviet Armed Forces was assessed as being so poor, especially after the Finnish debacle in 1939-1940, that in Hitler's view, "We have only to kick in the door and the whole rotten structure will come crashing down." The duration of BARBAROSSA was expected to be at an end within a matter of weeks if not months!

Britain's military resources were strained to the utmost at this stage of World War II but Churchill nevertheless ordained

that assistance for the Nation's new-found, if also very surprising, Ally – especially when given the almost two-year span of the August 1939 Nazi-Soviet Pact – would commence as soon as the requisite military hardware and merchant shipping had been assembled.

The first convoy sailing under the prefix PQ was not dispatched until the end of September, although this effort had been preceded in August by the carrier ARGUS and seven merchantmen sailing with a mix of aircraft and ammunition that was unloaded at Archangel. (This port, unlike the other major conduit at Murmansk was only ice-free in the summer). The summer months up in the Arctic Circle produced almost continuous daylight conditions. This negative factor ensured that the voyage duration would extend almost two weeks as the ships skirted the edge of the shrunken Arctic ice-pack in their attempts to stay as far away as possible from the *Luftwaffe* airbases in northern Norway and Finland.

This compared to the ten-day estimate for the equivalent voyage in winter when, due to the southward extension of the ice-pack, the convoys had to be routed between Bear Island and North Cape; the dangerous proximity to the *Luftwaffe* airfields was somewhat equalised by the almost permanent darkness experienced that afforded an enhanced degree of security from air assault. Of course, the presence of much fiercer weather at this stage of the year was the penalty that inevitably balanced out the benefit afforded by the shorter voyage duration

No direct involvement of the Fleet Air Arm in this extreme (in every sense of the word) northern zone of operations was to occur for many months. In fact the first eight convoys sent out during 1941 suffered no losses at all. The lack of German attention was probably linked to their initially supreme confidence that BARBAROSSA would be completed before

A pair of Albacores from No.817 Sqdn. are photographed from another fellow-aircraft in the formation. The Sqdn. was embarked on VICTORIOUS during September 1941 and participated along with No.832 Sqdn. in an abortive torpedo attack against the battleship TIRPITZ on 7 March 1942.

any measure of support from Britain could be on hand to even delay a Russian capitulation, let alone help to stave off final defeat. There again, Hitler and his High Command may have reasoned that Britain was unable to provide any effective degree of logistical support, given its own parlous situation.

Operation 'Crucifixion'

The first sortie conducted by the Navy's aviators saw them called upon to mount an anti-shipping raid against the ports of Kirkenes and Petsamo towards the end of July. This was undertaken at the request of the Soviet Government, who regarded both locations as being vital to the provisioning of the northern German Armies and therefore bound to contain an ample range of suitable targets. The carriers VICTORIOUS and FURIOUS were on hand for the operation; Nos.827 and 828 Sqdns. with their Albacores and No.809 Sqdn.'s Fulmars were embarked on the former vessel, while FURIOUS took equal numbers (nine) of Swordfish and Albacores flown respectively by Nos.812 and 817 Sqdns. as well as the Fulmars of No.800 Sqdn. and four Sea Hurricanes belonging to No.800A Flight. This current 'modern' force of aircraft was expected to be faced by little or no aerial opposition while the Albacores went about their duty under Fulmar protection.

Quite why the *Luftwaffe* fighter strength should either be absent or not immediately available to challenge their Naval opponents was not explained. This anomaly was all the more

apparent, given that the *Wehrmacht* was pushing hard for the area surrounding the port of Murmansk. The close proximity of Murmansk to the Petsamo-Kirkenes region and therefore the likelihood that the *Luftwaffe* would be on hand in a supporting role to the *Wehrmacht* should have been fairly obvious. On the other hand, the need to demonstrate solidarity with the Russians was the likely reason why the sortie went ahead despite the reservations expressed by Admiral Tovey in charge of the Home Fleet as to the viability of the operation. In other words political expediency was to win out over tactical or strategic wisdom!

The passage of what was termed Force P as far as Iceland suffered something of a reverse when the destroyer ACHATES had its bow blown off when it steamed over the edge of a minefield – laid by the British! The outline of the sortie was put to the aircrew at this stage. VICTORIOUS crews would attack Kirkenes while the FURIOUS contingent would assault Petsamo. In the event of the reported mass of shipping not materialising, the alternative targets were to be an iron ore plant and oil storage tanks respectively, so providing at least some degree of potential reward.

On the night of 26-27 July, the Force sailed for its attack rendezvous some eighty miles northeast of Kirkenes, which was reached three days later. Not only were the Navy vessels sailing dangerously close to the northern extremity of Norway, and therefore totally dependent upon their fighters and AA guns for protection, but the hitherto obligingly overcast weather conditions finally cleared to leave them totally exposed to German aerial surveillance. Sure enough, shortly before the order to launch was issued, the slim outline of what was a He 111 loomed up. The cat was now out of the bag, and the attackers were heading into an ambush.

The Albacores of all three Sqdns., and the single Swordfish unit, were launched in mid-afternoon, followed by the Fulmars some twenty minutes later. Also sent aloft were the Sea Hurricanes to act as air cover for the Force. The services of this latter type of aircraft in the direct escort role rather than as a CAP Force might have proved of much greater benefit to the lumbering Albacores in the action about to evolve over the two targets. On the other hand the provision of just four fighters for this important potential duty can now be regarded as less than adequate, regardless of the aerodynamic quality of the aircraft concerned.

The VICTORIOUS-based units were briefed to attack separate sections of Kirkenes. No.827 was to concentrate on shipping straddling the Tower of Kirkenes and in the Langfjord, and No.828 was to focus its attention on Holmengraafjord and moorings east of Renoy Island. The aircraft headed directly into the sun, a situation made more fraught by the minimum altitude being flown, presumably to avoid radar contact being made. A climb to 3,000 ft. as the coast was reached saw the aircraft being engaged by *flak*; all attempts to deceive the gunners by firing Verey flares matching the German Colours of the Day failed and the gunfire intensified. Suddenly, as the Albacores were weaving their way in towards their anticipated targets and the Fulmars orbited overhead, the gunfire ceased. Almost immediately, the sky was being shared with a number of German single and twin-engine fighters (thirteen in all) and up to nine Ju 87s, the latter having apparently just completed

a bombing sortie and about to land when ordered to take on the incoming Force.

The hoped-for 'mass of shipping' was found to consist of a gunnery-training warship and two medium-tonnage merchantmen. These were duly attacked and strikes on the latter vessels that resulted in their catching fire were recorded at the sortie de-briefing session. Whether or not the iron ore plant was ever attacked is an unclear aspect of the operation. What was clear was the extreme vulnerability of the Naval biplanes to the attentions of the *Luftwaffe* fighters. The Fulmar pilots did their level best to draw the enemy fighters away from their charges but no little or no avail. Indeed, it was a surprise that no more than two of the Fulmars were lost in the process. In return, just one of the Bf 110 fighters was recorded as lost according to *Luftwaffe* records.

The Albacore pilots, having delivered their torpedoes and bombs against the disappointingly limited number of targets now attempted to weave their tortuous path back to VICTORIOUS, all the while being harried by the Bf 109s and Bf 110s. The vastly superior speed and firepower of the German aircraft was only matched by the Albacores in terms of manoeuvrability – not much hope of surviving a combat in these circumstances, certainly not with a single machine gun against a battery of machine gun and cannon caliber weapons fitted in both Messerschmitt designs. All too soon, the losses began to mount as crew after crew was culled from the two Sqdns.' ranks.

One surviving Telegraphist/Air Gunner (TAG) recalled the heavy flak barrage greeting the attackers as they came up the fjord, with his instinct being not to fire his Vickers 'K' machine gun, but rather to throw it at the gunners! He recorded the sight of torpedoes scudding through the harbor waters and Albacores skidding in all directions. His Flight of three

The bare and forbidding landscape forming a background to the forward area of VICTORIOUS is part of the Icelandic fjord where the Fleet carrier was anchored during operations in the Barents Sea in the autumn of 1941. Two Fulmars of No.809 Sqdn. share the forward flight deck with a single Albacore from No.817 Sqdn. Also on board were the Albacores of No.832 Sqdn.

Albacores retired at full speed – all of 100 mph according to this eyewitness! – but one wingman was shot down in flames as the mouth of the fjord was reached. The other wingman banked away towards Soviet territory at this point but was soon dispatched by the pursuing Bf 110s.

In the end only nine of the twenty-strong Force of Albacores finally broke free to head for their carrier. One crew from No.827 Sqdn. put in a claim for the Ju 87 that had harried them continuously albeit without landing any hits. For whatever reason the German pilot finally placed his aircraft ahead of his prey – and was promptly fired upon successfully by the Albacore pilot using the single machine gun mounted in the lower starboard wing! (The other loss recorded by the Germans this day was a Ju 87 so the Albacore pilot's claim was well justified).

The nine Albacores of No.817 Sqdn. and nine Swordfish of No.812 Sqdn. experienced even less success when they descended upon Petsamo. Not only was there little or no suitable shipping but the expenditure of their torpedoes against the harbor itself provided equally marginal results in destruction since the jetties were of wooden construction and easily reparable. Those aircraft equipped with bombs did strike at a shipyard and the oil storage tanks but the degree of destruction there was equally poor. On the other hand, despite the appearance of some Bf 109s, just one of the Albacores failed to regain the flight deck of FURIOUS, along with two of the No.800 Sqdn. Fulmars.

All surviving aircraft having been recovered by mid-evening, the Force commenced its prolonged and undoubtedly depressed voyage back to Scapa Flow. Next day, a Do 18 'shadower' was sighted and two of the Sea Hurricanes were quickly launched to intercept. This was duly done and the slow-flying seaplane stood no chance of survival against sixteen machine guns; this aircraft was also fated to become the first confirmed 'kill' by a Sea Hurricane, one of which was flown by Lt-Cdr Judd.

The operation had proved to be an unqualified disaster. No less than twelve Albacores and four Fulmars had been lost along with nine dead and twenty-seven aircrew taken prisoner (In addition, one of the MIA Fulmar crews from No.800 Sqdn. had force-landed on the way in, taken to their dinghy and gained Soviet-occupied territory within two days!). Nothing of significant military gain could be recorded in turn, which was not surprising when given the basic lack of Intelligence information prior to the raid.

The other grim reminder arising from the sortie was the basic vulnerability of both the Albacore and Fulmar when faced with modern aerial opposition. (On the other hand, the most theoretically vulnerable design present on 30 July – the Swordfish of No.812 Sqdn. – had not suffered a single loss,

but this was probably due to the smaller scale of opposition encountered at Petsamo. Nevertheless, the Fairey biplane would be the sole example of these three Fleet Air Arm aircraft still on front-line duties by 1943!).

Norwegian Operations Continue

The decimated Albacore Sqdns. were disembarked from VICTORIOUS and replaced in mid-August by Nos.817 and 832 Sqdns. also operating on the Albacore. The carrier then participated as part of Force M in providing cover as far as Bear Island and the approach to the White Sea for the first-ever convoy to Murmansk. A projected sortie on enemy shipping proceeding north from Tromso to Kirkenes was planned and dispatched on 3 September. However, the clearing cloud cover towards the Norwegian coast, coupled to the likely presence of fighters at Banak, impelled both Sqdn. leaders to obey briefing instructions not to proceed with the sortie under these conditions. Not unnaturally, the events of 30 July were still fresh in the mind of Rear Admiral Wake-Walker!

As it happened, the Force remained operating off the north Norwegian coastal area, and a strike was launched on the 12th against shipping and shore installations around Bodo. One ship was sunk and an aluminium factory at Glomfjord was also struck. The absence of fighters encouraged a second sortie to be planned but this was cancelled when a 'shadower' picked up the Force. On board VICTORIOUS were two Martlets transferred over from ARGUS, and these took to the air and shot down the He 111 after a prolonged tail-chase. Two further Bv 138 'shadowers' appeared, but these heavily armoured floatplanes defied all efforts of the Fulmars to bring them down with their .303 caliber weapons. The greater 'punch' of the .50 caliber machine guns fitted to the Martlets might have achieved success, but these aircraft do not appear to have been dispatched.

One more sortie by VICTORIOUS to the same region was made in mid-October. The first launch on the morning of 9 October was partially thwarted by the heavy seas that damaged five of the thirteen aircraft ranged on the deck, while only three of the remaining serviceable Albacores penetrated what was an adverse weather front to encounter and strike at a single merchantmen. The same afternoon, eight crews in a combined 817/832 Sqdn. effort engaged two merchantmen escorted by flak ships. Their bombs scored several hits, with one vessel's crew taking to the lifeboats.

This action effectively completed all such operations by the carrier for the remainder of 1941; this was due to a change in emphasis from offence to a form of defence – namely, the need to counter the likelihood of the battleship TIRPITZ in particular breaking out into the Atlantic. Consequently VICTORIOUS along with the other Home Fleet warships, was

confined to patrolling the waters between Scapa Flow and Iceland. It was during this time that the carrier temporarily lost the regular battle with Mother Nature. On one patrol, the damage suffered to her bow plates by the storm-tossed North Atlantic was so great that she was forced to undergo a week's refit at Scapa Flow.

The Pace Quickens

As 1942 commenced, the German High Command began to wake up to the continued existence of the Allied convoy route to northern Russia. To the severe reversals suffered by the *Wehrmacht* and SS units engaging the Soviet Armies from early December was now added the need to stem the flow of material entering Russia through the ports of Murmansk and Archangel.

With this pressing issue in mind the Germans began to transfer *Luftwaffe* units to central and northern Norway. The bulk of KG 40's Fw 200s flew into Trondheim-Vaernes from where they could mount surveillance. Elements of KG 26's He 111s, and KG 30's Ju 88s were dispatched up to Bardufoss and Banak respectively, while Kirkenes would also be used for anti-shipping operations. The *Kriegsmarine* added to the potential threat by stationing surface warships along the Norwegian coastline, including several capital ships of which TIRPITZ and SCHARNHORST were to arguably present the gravest danger for both the Atlantic and Arctic convoy routes over the ensuing two to three years. The third and obvious strand of counter-measures involved the deployment of U-Boats. The net was about to be drawn around the merchantmen

Opposite: The first escort carrier to accompany an Arctic convoy was AVENGER. During September twelve Sea Hurricanes Mk.Ib were embarked to provide cover for PQ18 The six fighters on deck are tethered down against the heavy seas that are regularly experienced in these northern latitudes. There is barely enough deck length available for safe take-off.

Above: The deck handlers on board AVENGER are photographed during refuelling operations. The nearest Sea Hurricane's port wing securing ropes or wires are clearly visible. The escort carrier's presence during Convoy PQ18 was instrumental in preventing even more destruction by the *Luftwaffe* torpedo and dive-bombers than the figure of eight merchantmen sunk during this specific run to Russia.

The harsh weather conditions regularly experienced during an Arctic winter are exemplified by this picture. A Swordfish Mk.II is preparing to launch off FENCER in conditions of minimal visibility. Meanwhile the deck handlers are forced to function on a deck liberally covered in snow that would be treacherous to move around on without slipping or sliding – a very dangerous situation when in the vicinity of aircraft propellers and even more so if the carrier was pitching and rolling.

and their currently inadequate Naval support, particularly in respect of aircraft.

Hard Times Ahead

The experiences of the PQ/QP convoy personnel, as 1942 evolved, was to be in ever-starker contrast to their predecessors in 1941. Whereas barely a single loss was recorded between the eleven outward-bound convoys dispatched up to the end of February this positive factor would then give way to a mounting toll in ships and (even more sadly, men) as the German contested their passage to Russia with ever-increasing vigour. The threat from the *Luftwaffe* bombers, and Ju 87 dive-bombers could still only largely be countered by the AA gunners on both the escorts and merchantmen. The availability of aircraft carriers was minimal, with VICTORIOUS the sole Fleet carrier in this Theater of Operations, and her services were primarily required for Home Fleet operations against the ever-present risk of *Kriegsmarine* capital ship sorties into both the Atlantic and Arctic Oceans. And so it was that for the bulk of 1942 convoy air cover fell to the CAM-ships whenever these were on hand.

PQ12 for example sailed on 1 March but an Fw 200, whose report was responded to by TIRPITZ being dispatched from Trondheim, soon picked up the convoy's progress. The Home Fleet contested the battleship's progress and she never got within striking distance. PQ13's experience was far worse, since bad weather badly hindered its progress, and it lost five merchantmen to a combination of aircraft, U-Boats and a destroyer. PQ14 not only lost one merchantmen to a U-Boat assault but also had a large proportion (sixteen) of its surviving complement turn back for Iceland. In PQ15's case, the Navy suffered even more casualties than its charges – five warships compared to three merchantmen. Even though EMPIRE MORN and its Hurricane accompanied PQ15, the fighter

remained in place throughout the voyage for unconfirmed reasons.

The size of the convoys had been steadily increasing, and the dispatch of PQ16 in the latter half of May involved the largest figure to date (thirty-five). One of the convoy's participants was EMPIRE LAWRENCE. Sailing with QP16 at the same time was EMPIRE MORN, and both vessels' Hurricanes would see action. It was the latter-based Hurricane that was first in action. The convoy had been picked up first by a Bv 138, which was subsequently joined, first by an Fw 200 and latterly by two Ju 88s; quite why four aircraft were carrying out this passive action was not clear, but the order to launch was given as the Ju 88s so to speak 'joined the circuit'. The launch was delayed until the enemy aircraft were not in a position to observe the flash of the launch rockets. This situation occurred around 0900 hours with one aircraft in a rain cloud ahead and the others positioned behind the convoy, but presumably at an angle that blanked off the flashes of the discharged rockets. F/O Kendal got clear and banked to port before making a steady climb.

The Fighter Direction Officer (FDO) directed Kendal towards the Bv 138 fine on the port side of the convoy but then a radio malfunction meant that his contact with the Hurricane was hindered although Kendal was receiving the information. The next sight of the fighter was as it closed upon one of the Ju 88s orbiting towards the rear of the convoy's port quarter. The fighter's double burst of gunfire left the bomber emitting smoke from one engine, followed by loss of power in that or the other motor. Shortly afterwards smoke was seen on the sea surface and Kendal's subsequent circling of what was almost certainly the Ju 88's crash site revealed a dinghy close to some wreckage.

What then transpired was pure tragedy. Kendal returned to the convoy and prepared to exit his fighter close to one of the escorts. He was seen to emerge from a patch of cloud, having baled out at around 1,000 ft. but with his parachute only partially deployed until almost at sea level. The destroyer BADSWORTH that picked him up reported he had been seriously injured and died very soon afterwards. The fact that the other three 'shadowers' were not seen again remains as an appropriate but sad epitaph to his action this day.

PQ16's's progress was challenged more lethally by the He 111's and Ju 88s of KG 26 following the inevitable surveillance efforts of an Fw 200. On 27 May I./KG 26 dispatched what was for the unit a relatively meagre Force of eleven He 111's as PQ16 was steaming southeast of Bear Island. The projected assault was planned to coincide with a Ju 87 assault but the torpedo-bombers led by *Hauptmann* Eicke found themselves heading in towards their target alone, the Ju 87 crews having already delivered their bombs. In addition the approach was found not to be from the desired beam position but from a rear angle. Eicke accordingly ordered the formation to split up and each pilot to seek a suitable attack-approach. According to German records, when the attack was completed two bombers were missing.

On EMPIRE LAWRENCE P/O Hay had been prepared for launch, but the RDF information was still not on hand when six Ju 88s swept in from the east and enfiladed the convoy. Some minutes later a five-plane element of what was Eicke's formation was sighted and Hay took off. What was described as a line-astern group of He 111s reportedly swung sharply to port and must have then assumed a line-abreast formation. As he closed in Hay engaged the right-hand bomber, from which pieces flew under the impact of the Hurricane's gunfire. A second pass on a second bomber in the formation produced no discernable effect before Hay's glycol tank was punctured.

The loss of the fluid and the imminent seizure of the engine resulting from this quickly induced Hay to bale out. His dinghy was found to be punctured after he landed in the water, but the destroyer VOLUNTEER – an appropriate-named vessel in view of Hay's similar status! – was swiftly on hand to haul him out of the frigid sea. The warship's Gunnery Officer told Hay that one of the He 111s attacked by him had been seen to fall into the sea. (It is ironic to record that one of the five merchantmen lost during PQ16's voyage was EMPIRE LAWRENCE, but at least she had drawn a small measure of

A Swordfish is photographed in an embarrassing posture, having failed to engage an arrester wire on landing. The deck-handlers are hurrying to the scene to assist the crew out of the cockpit before setting the aircraft back on its tail. Damage has been confined to the buckled propeller. The wing undersides surprisingly bear no attachments for the carriage of ordnance.

revenge before her demise, thanks to her Hurricane and its pilot).

PQ17 – An Avoidable Disaster

The arrival of convoy PQ16 with six/seventh of its merchantmen bearing well over 120,000 tons of supplies must have given the Soviets a feeling that this supply-source would continue to blossom, in spite of a sizeable *Luftwaffe* presence to oppose such activities. However, the meagre air cover afforded by the CAM-ships was set to continue on all the major convoy routes for the bulk of 1942. Hence, when the latest Russian-bound convoy (PQ17) sailed at the end of June, just EMPIRE TIDE was assigned to this duty along with the surface escorts. Rear Admiral Hamilton, at the head of a supporting cruiser Force and in overall command had decreed that the Sea Hurricane be used not against 'shadowers' but an actual bombing or torpedo assault.

Trailing both the convoy and cruiser Force was the Home Fleet with the battleships DUKE OF YORK and the USS WASHINGTON whose brief was to provide a rear cover as far as the approach to Bear Island. At this stage the convoy would be into the second half of its protracted two-week voyage, but would conversely begin to come within range of the *Luftwaffe*.

The Home Fleet contingent included VICTORIOUS but her presence was not intended to provide direct support for the convoy alone. Instead, her Sqdns. of Albacores were on stand-by to challenge any attempt by TIRPITZ, HIPPER or similar heavy warships either to break out into the Atlantic or (presumably) to attack PQ17. By 4 July the convoy was north of Bear Island and still in good close order, although out of its thirty-six original complement of merchantmen, two vessels had 'aborted' the run for various reasons. It was at this point that affairs began to go tragically awry.

The presence of TIRPITZ, ADMIRAL SCHEER and LUETZOW in Altenfjord on the evening of the 4th was Grand Admiral Raeder's latest disposal of his Fleet, but the Admiralty in London had known that. Although at least 400 miles distant from the convoy's approximate location, the strike force's potential ability to disperse and annihilate such a large and slow-steaming adversary seemingly created a panic within the Admiralty hierarchy. Late on the 4th the First Sea Lord, Admiral Dudley Pound, made a fateful decision – the convoy was ordered to scatter and the cruiser force to withdraw westwards!

The scene was set for disaster on a scale resembling the first 'Happy Times' period in late 1940, as the merchantmen fled eastwards singly or in small groups. Bereft of the bulk of surface escort support with which to ward off U-Boat assaults, a number of vessels were fated to fall to the underwater predators over the ensuing five or six days. The situation in respect of protection from air attack proved similarly bleak, and during the same approximate period, a further group of vessels were hunted down and dispatched by Ju 88s and He 111s dropping bombs or torpedoes. The few available escort vessels on hand did in some instances attempt to round up

A Swordfish Mk.III displays the 'pod' mounted between the wheels, which contained the ASV Mk.XI radar equipment fitted as standard on this variant. RATOG pipes protrude behind the landing gear. When fully loaded up, the Mk.III could prove difficult to launch if the wind condition was not favourable.

their charges as far as possible and so provide a measure of protection, but with no great success at preventing the overall degree of punishment.

The Arctic waters between Iceland and Murmansk were littered with the sunken wrecks of twenty-three Allied merchantmen, and the remnants of the once-proud PQ17 convoy (just eleven vessels) torturously limped their way through the German ambuscade into Murmansk towards the end of July. One of these was EMPIRE TIDE, whose aircraft had not been used; while sheltering along the Novaya Zembla coastline, preparations had been made to launch the fighter against an encroaching Ju 88 but the order was cancelled when no attack developed. It was fully twenty days after the 'scatter' order had been issued (24th) before this merchantman was able to anchor in Murmansk The contrast to PQ16 in terms of goods delivered could not be more stark; around 100,000 tons had gone to the bottom of the Arctic wastes, a figure added to by the loss of 430 armoured and 2,350 other vehicles and 210 aircraft.

Admiral Tovey's admonition to Pound prior to his Home Fleet's sailing from Scapa Flow that 'any attempt to scatter the convoy would be sheer bloody murder' now rebounded around the corridors of British Naval power. Compounding the tragedy was the fact that the German warships did not depart Altenfjord until the late morning of the 5th and reversed course several hours later. Sighting reports by a Catalina flying boat and a Royal Navy submarine had been picked by the German B-Dienst Service, upon which information Admiral Raeder ordered a withdrawal back to Altenfjord! Of course, this fact was almost certainly unknown at the time; the bald truth however was that the operational control for the entire action should have been left in the hands of the Senior Naval Staff on the warships.

Even more puzzling was the previous withdrawal of the main Home Fleet elements, whose reputed brief was to take on the German capital ships – why withdraw at a point where the convoy was still within perceived striking range of TIRPITZ and her contemporaries? Admiral Tovey has been quoted as saying that his main Fleet was ever at risk from aircraft and U-Boats should his warships advance towards the northern reaches of Norway in order to take on the German capital ships. Yet the Home Fleet had done precisely this the previous winter when the torpedo bombers on VICTORIOUS had sought out TIRPITZ and that basic risk had been squarely faced.

The political repercussions, particularly between Britain and Soviet Russia, were immediate and bitter. This was hardly surprising, considering that the Russians were being seriously challenged particularly around the Southern sector of the Eastern Front and needed every tank, aircraft and ton of ammunition that had now been denied them through – as Stalin surely viewed matters – his Ally's tactical incompetence if not cowardice. Nor were the Americans too happy about the affair, since a proportion of the sunken vessels had flown the Stars and Stripes. The sense of anger and frustration felt by many of the sailors on the escort vessels at what they sensed would be treated all around the Allied camp as deliberate desertion of their charges was an issue that could not possibly come to light at the time, especially given the dictates of security. Could they have revealed their feelings then, these would surely have echoed Admiral Tovey's pre-operational and bald comment to Pound as outlined in the preceding paragraph!

PQ18 – Resurrection

The pressing need for proper carrier-based air cover to back up the Arctic convoy surface escorts was temporarily suspended for nearly two months in the summer of 1942, due to the parallel suspension of the PQ/QP convoy system. When recommenced in early September, the situation in respect of this vital aspect of security had been altered in a favourable, but limited, manner. On hand as the vessels raised their anchors in Loch Ewe, Scotland on 2 September was the U.S. constructed AVENGER that bore the name of the Class of escort carrier and was the first of fifteen such 'Lend-Lease' warships. The original flight deck length of 410 ft. had been lengthened to 440 ft. as part of the series of modifications by the Admiralty, which were deemed necessary before entering service. Another adaptation was the retention of water in the ballast tanks, which sharply reduced the maximum aviation fuel capacity but was regarded as a necessary measure to increase basic stability.

The provision for two lifts was a definite advance in terms of aircraft movements in flight and their relative disposition on the deck compared to the stark arrangements with AUDACITY. However, one factor weighed against this advance during the PQ18 operation; it was an ironic one, in that the fixed wingspan of the Hawker fighter was too great for them to be accommodated on the lifts in the first place! Moreover, the twelve fighters of Nos.802 and 883 Sqdns. on board AVENGER were of Mk.1b vintage that were armed with .303 machine guns; six were stowed below with their wings detached, due to the limitation of accommodating more than six on the flight deck at one time An even more ironic factor was the existence within the convoy of a batch of Hurricanes Mk.II for delivery to the Soviets. The availability by 1942 of the cannon-armed Hurricane Mk.IIC would have provided the Navy pilots with an immeasurably greater opportunity to shoot down their *Luftwaffe* adversaries compared to what was currently provided.

This Fulmar Mk.IINF/BP791 night fighter of No.784 Sqdn. was assigned to the escort carrier CAMPANIA. On 9 June 1944 the aircraft crash-landed on the carrier's deck but was repaired and re-entered service with No.813 Sqdn. during 1945. The sole external difference with the Fulmar Mk.I are the air intake bulges ahead of the wing roots.

A near miss by an Fw 200's bombs when berthed in Iceland, and a temporary engine breakdown just after sailing for its rendezvous with PQ18, followed by a second such failure a day later must have left the carrier's personnel experiencing a higher degree of apprehension than normal at what might lay ahead. Defensive priority was granted to the destruction or driving away of the *Luftwaffe* 'shadowers'; the intervals in which these aircraft would then (hopefully) be absent would be used to alter the convoy's course as an evasive measure. A major problem in attempting to shoot down the main 'shadowing' aircraft type, the Bv 138 floatplane, lay in the fact that it was heavily armoured and therefore almost impervious to the rifle-caliber fire as possessed by AVENGER's Sea Hurricanes.

The convoy was in the region of Bear Island almost due north of North Cape on 12 September when the initial 'enemy aircraft' alert was sounded and four Hurricanes launched to intercept, but the Bv 138 concerned managed to successfully evade thanks to the low cloud and mist conditions. The three Swordfish of No.825 Sqdn. embarked for this duty over the previous three days had recorded submarine sightings but the absence of depth charges (reportedly due to the aircrafts' inability to lift such weapons into the air in the existing windless conditions) meant that the U-Boats challenge had to be left to the surface escorts. However, the first full aerial and sea-borne assault was delayed until the following day.

The 13th was to prove the crucial day for PQ18 in terms of losses. First, two merchantmen were torpedoed by the

underwater attackers during the morning. As the day progressed, ever more aircraft began to home in upon the convoy. The main *Luftwaffe* opposition was still provided by the torpedo-carrying He 111s of I./KG 26 based at Bardufoss and III./KG26 based at Banak along with the Ju 88s of III./KG 30. The three *Gruppen* between them possessed around 100 aircraft, and a concentrated assault by all three units could reasonably be expected to swamp the air defences of the convoy. *Maj.* Kluemper leading the Bardufoss contingent briefed his twenty-four assembled crews on the morning of the 13th with the emphasis laid on taking out AVENGER.

A combination of dead reckoning navigation and the homing signals from a 'shadower' brought PQ18 within sight, but only after the Force had been compelled to turn eastwards after finding nothing at the original indicated location. The primary target was nowhere to be seen and so Kluemper decided to attack the convoy instead. The He 111s flew alongside and ahead of the starboard flank of the convoy before banking left to commence their attack runs. Also on hand at this time was *Hptm.* Nocken at the head of III./KG 26 as well as III./KG 30's Ju 88s.

The convoy Commodore had ordered a turn to starboard in order for the vessels to 'comb' the torpedo tracks, but his command was somehow not reacted to by the starboard column, whose seven merchantmen remained broadside to their assailants. It was hardly surprising therefore that at least six or more of the mass of torpedoes released found their mark to leave six vessels floundering in various states of terminal distress. A further two vessels with the center column also succumbed to the assault. Nearly one fifth of PQ18's complement had been wiped out at a single stroke – and all without any fighter opposition.

The basic reason for the Sea Hurricanes' absence can be traced to the original briefing, namely to drive away the 'shadowing' aircraft. The order had been adhered to too literally, although the dispersal of the fighters was also stated to have been caused by a prior 'feint' attack on the convoy by Ju 88s that drew several of their number away ahead of the main attack. Whatever the cause for the lack of fighter cover, this meant that resistance was totally in the hands of the Naval and Merchant Service AA gunners. In the event the barrage put up scored a grimly similar number of German casualties to vessels sunk – eight!

AVENGER's original station with the convoy was in trail position to the second starboard column of merchantmen but Captain Colthurst had subsequently taken up a revised position in relation to the convoy. The Hurricanes were still either out of position or had landed back on the carrier's deck for fuel and ammunition replenishment when the second torpedo attack was made an hour later. This time round the aircraft were recorded as He 115 seaplanes from *KuestenFliegerGruppe* (*Kue.Fl.Gp.*) 406 or 906 but the small formation of nine aircraft was forced to jettison its torpedoes prematurely in the face of fierce AA fire that also claimed one of its number.

Next day, the *Luftwaffe* resumed its Offensive, doubtless in the expectation of inflicting further heavy casualties among the convoy's ranks, but with the sinking of AVENGER still a top priority. I./KG 26 took off with almost the same number of aircraft (twenty-two) as on the previous day, but the numbers dispatched by III./KG 26 were much smaller. *Maj.* Kluemper and one other pilot did pick out the carrier – now positioned ahead of the convoy and within a screen of escorts – and deliver what were unsuccessful torpedo-runs. The remainder of the He 111s were not so rewarded, as their attention was all too soon diverted from striking at the carrier to warding off the attentions of the Sea Hurricanes.

The latter were keen not only to wipe out the memory of their lost opportunities on the 13th but also to avenge the death of the No.802 Sqdn. CO, Lt. Taylour, who had been shot down and killed by return fire from a Bv 138. This they proceeded to do with a grim relish and when the air battle was over, the two *Gruppen* mourned the loss of nine aircraft, of which five were credited to the Sea Hurricanes, with others suffering varied degrees of battle damage. Two of the bombers were brought down by their own lethal 'success' when their weapons blew up the American freighter MARY LUCKENBACH that was loaded with ammunition.

One British account of operations on the 14th relates a subsequent attack by twenty-five He 111 torpedo-bombers; this contrasts with the KG 26 history that states the serviceable number of III./KG 26 aircraft (for this must have been the unit involved) was much smaller than that of its fellow *Gruppe*. During this day's various actions, which reportedly included the interception and breaking up by two fighters of a fourteen-strong Ju 88 formation, the AA gunners added no less than three of the Sea Hurricanes to their account as the tangled mass of aircraft weaved around and over the convoy; fortunately, all three pilots were fished alive out of the frozen Arctic waters.

Next day the serviceable number of He 111s assembled between the two KG 26 *Gruppen* totalled just thirteen. Bad weather prevented any operations, and by the 16th the serviceable number had dropped further to just eight. In spite of this severe reduction in He 111s, and the solid cloud layer over the convoy position that inhibited level or dive-bombing sorties by the Ju 88s of III./KG 30, *Hptm.* Hildebrant (2./KG 26) took off in the early afternoon and finally closed with the convoy from a south easterly angle. Although unspecified losses were recorded by the *Luftwaffe*, it was a miracle when flying at a steady speed and delaying torpedo-release until less than 1/2 mile distant from their targets, that any of the He 111s managed to avoid being shot down.

Although the Sea Hurricane pilots took the limelight along with the shipboard AA gunners in thwarting much of the *Luftwaffe* bomber and torpedo-bomber offensive effort, and inflicting most if not all of the forty-one recorded aircraft losses, the three Swordfish had also played their part in PQ18's relative success. The original windless conditions experienced on the 12th must have altered sufficiently for the 'Stringbags' to carry their normal depth charge loads. Their crews, inevitably half-frozen by full exposure to the frigid Arctic air, had more than once sighted a U-Boat and forced each to crash-dive. In addition, the aircraft had guided escort vessels to the U-Boat's location and had been involved in two of the three confirmed sinkings when ONSLOW depth-charged U-589 to destruction and FAULKNER put paid to the career of U-88, both on the 14th.

AVENGER's part in the operation was deemed to be over by the 16th, since the convoy was now within range of Russian-based air cover, and she turned back to accompany QP14's homeward-bound ranks. The *Luftwaffe* was not quite finished with PQ18, since assaults by Ju 88s and He 111s were mounted the following day, the III./KG 30 and III./KG 26 elements having been transferred further east to Petsamo in order to maintain contact. The sole fighter now on immediate hand was the Sea Hurricane borne by the CAM-ship EMPIRE

MORN but an electrical fault within the fighter prevented its launch on the first occasion.

All was in working order when the second wave of torpedo-bombers made their approach. However, the first moments of the sortie were fraught with danger since Burr had to both avoid balloon cables on the merchantmen – and the 'friendly fire' directed at his aircraft during the launch sequence! Although the odds were fifteen to one, F/O Burr managed to cull one from the formation, after making two separate passes. He then utilised the remainder of his patrol by orbiting off the convoy's starboard quarter, awaiting fresh attackers. With his fuel steadily diminishing, the prospects of surviving long enough in the Arctic water before being picked up by an escort were obviously not good enough for the fighter pilot. He therefore decided to head eastwards for Soviet territory and an airfield near Archangel, which he reached around one hour later with approximately 5% remaining fuel capacity.

Part Two
The Arctic Route Secured
1943-1945

Vacuum Situation

PQ18, although producing a positive outcome, was destined to be the last full convoy dispatched to Russia for some three to four months, although a handful of merchantmen were routed independently during this period. The stated reason for this 'vacuum' in Arctic operations was the equally pressing need to counter the on-going U-Boat assaults upon the North Atlantic convoy system, and the consequent diversion of escort vessel strength to this Theater of Operations. Had the PQ/QP convoys continued at this time, it was almost certain they would also have faced a severe limitation on available shipboard air support. This in turn would have been due to the re-assignment of the few aircraft carriers on hand to the impending Operation 'Torch', the Invasion of northwest Africa.

It was mid-January when JW52 (the letters displacing PQ) sailed from Loch Ewe and completed the ten-day voyage without loss, followed in early February by JW53. Enemy air interference was sparse on the first occasion and resulted in two out of four Ju 88s being shot down, while U-Boat interference was kept in check. JW53's progress by contrast met more resistance; the need to sail closer than usual to the North Cape coastline due to the Arctic ice-edge encroaching further south than normal increased the chance of being picked up by Bv 138 'shadowers', which duly occurred four days away from Murmansk. However, the strong surface escort again kept the U-Boats at bay, thanks to the availability of HF/DF equipment that picked out their adversaries.

On the 25th a formation of KG 30 Ju 88s made an appearance but the bulk of the crews indulged in glide-bombing tactics and achieved nothing more than a single nearmiss on one merchantman. Next day witnessed a similar lack of success for another Ju 88 formation. It was as well that both the numbers and bombing skills of the *Luftwaffe* crews were respectively so limited and so poor, because there were no Navy fighters on hand to contest their presence. (DASHER had sailed with JW52 but was forced to turn back after just two days).

The intact arrival of two successive convoys must have been of at least sober satisfaction to the Soviet government. Not so welcome during March was the Anglo-American decision to further postpone the Arctic convoys for what transpired as an even longer period than that created in late 1942. Once again, the primary reason was stated to be the continuing crisis in the North Atlantic, and the attendant need to transfer as many escort vessels as possible to help alleviate if not turn around the situation. Also on the Admiralty Hierarchy's mind was the continuing threat to the convoy system posed by *Kriegsmarine* capital ship strength in Norway, a threat recently heightened by the arrival of SCHARNHORST. In the event, convoys would not traverse the Arctic waters again until the following October. (Russia was to receive an even greater flow of supplies via rail routes up through Persia as well as via Black Sea, and Far Eastern locations. In the course of World War II over 97% of the 17,501,000 tons of Aid dispatched by the Allies got through, of which less than a quarter was delivered via the Arctic).

Back to Business

The renewal of the Russian convoys that was to continue almost un-interrupted for the rest of World War II was initiated

This MAC-ship's full complement of Swordfish are either spotted on the forward flight deck or being brought up from the hangar. The dimensions of the lifts on these conversions of grain-carriers were barely sufficient to allow the 'striking down' or 'ranging' of the 'Stringbags'.

in mid-November 1943 when thirty-two merchantmen, divided into two convoys (JW54A and JW54B) set out for Murmansk and Archangel. By now the sole capital ship on hand able to challenge the convoy movements was SCHARNHORST, since TIRPITZ had been heavily damaged during September by midget submarines and LÜTZOW was back in home waters. A change of Home Fleet command had also taken place in May when Admiral Bruce Fraser succeeded Admiral Tovey. Fraser was a skilled gunnery officer, and moreover seemed to adopt a more aggressive stance in respect of facing up to the enemy capital ships in what was their own nautical 'back yard'. His action in steaming ahead of JW55A as far as the Kola Inlet, (where he was informed through Intelligence of a likely sortie by SCHARNHORST), displayed that aggression, an aggression that paid off just eight days after departing Kola when the German battleship was intercepted and sunk off North Cape on Boxing Day.

The late 1943 convoys all made their passage without Naval air support, despite the commissioning of all eleven of the ATTACKER Class, and fifteen of the twenty-three AMEER Class of escort carrier, by November. The crisis in the North Atlantic had been over since mid-1943 and all was running in the Allies favor. The Mediterranean situation was similarly turned around, so the current absence of carrier support for the Arctic Theater seemed basically indefensible. In fact, it was not until JW57 was dispatched during February 1944 that the escort carrier CHASER was allotted to the convoy. The third built of the ATTACKER Class, CHASER had previously

been the first escort carrier to accommodate the Grumman Avenger during North Atlantic operations; now she was bearing eleven Swordfish and an equal number of Wildcat fighters of No.816 Sqdn.

In the course of this and the subsequent twelve Russian-bound convoys there would be air cover provided by at least one, and in the majority of cases two or three, carriers. This was a stark contrast with the aerial 'famine' that had faced the vast majority of convoy actions up to this stage of World War II.

Whereas the progress of most Arctic convoys to date had faced the combined opposition of aircraft and U-Boats, from now on it was the latter that would constitute the major threat. These predators were to find themselves not only up against a comprehensive 'screen' of surface escorts but also against the carrier-based anti-submarine aircraft. Although the Grumman Avenger was available in sufficient numbers to perform this function, the large majority of the Sqdns. operating on the Arctic run were still flying the well-tried but venerable Swordfish.

JW57 was covered by an impressive array of a single cruiser and no less than thirty-one destroyers and corvettes, while CHASER with her four 'screening' warships would proceed as far as the area around Bear Island. CHASER was one of the escort carriers allocated to the Trade Protection role. The steam heating provision for gun mounts, flying stations and also the catapult equipment was a vital factor for operations in these lethally chilled waters. However, the failure of the system during the outward voyage inevitably led to breakdowns affecting the arrester wires and barrier machinery among other things.

Over the next few days, the Swordfish crews played their part in disrupting the intentions of up to five U-Boats by forcing those intercepted to submerge, although none were actually sunk by the depth charges and rocket projectiles that were discharged. The Wildcats managed to engage at least one Fw 200 'shadower', but one of their number was damaged by return fire, while the performance of the Browning machine guns On the other hand, the carrier's progress through the initially turbulent sea began to adversely affect aircraft serviceability, since even the pedestrian pace of the Swordfish while landing did not prevent a number of the 'Stringbags' suffering heavy damage on making sharp contact with the flight deck. By 28 February, barely half of the Swordfish along with eight Wildcats were still on operational status. A further restriction on operations affecting the Swordfish occurred the same day when the wind speed dropped to a level that prevented a normal load of depth charges and/or rockets being lifted into the air.

However, a change in fortunes was not far away when the carrier commenced cover for the homeward-bound RA57 on 2 March, although bad weather kept the aircraft deck-bound until the morning of the 4th (as well as keeping the U-Boats

from making any interceptions). Then, on three successive days (4 to 6 March) the Swordfish crews struck home. On the 4th U-472 was so badly damaged by rockets discharged from Sub-Lt. Beresford's Swordfish that it could not submerge, and *Korvettenkapitän Freiherr* von Forstner later scuttled his vessel when fired upon by the destroyer ONSLAUGHT. Next day, Sub-Lt. Mason achieved the first of two direct 'kills' when four of the eight rockets on the Swordfish struck home against U-366. Twenty-four hours later U-973 succumbed to another 'Stringbag' piloted by Sub-Lt. Bennett, who later in the day closed upon and damaged a second U-Boat. (Both of the sunken vessels appear to have been caught on the surface and unable to operate their guns, which were probably adversely affected by icing. If the latter assertion was true, it was a fortunate break for the crews, considering the stately flying performance of the Swordfish, but this should not detract from the airmen's achievements).

The tactical lessons to be learned from this convoy was that the Swordfish had an insuperable problem in taking off with a full load other than when the wind condition was favourable, while the closing speed on a target such as a surfaced U-Boat with gun crews at the alert was dangerously slow. The open cockpit layout left the crews badly exposed to the elements, to the extent that all too often they had to be assisted down out of their positions on return. In the event –

Another Fulmar Mk.IINF/DR726 has come to grief on board RAVAGER on 23 February 1944. Both landing gear wheels lie in the center foreground One of the two-man crew is standing by the wing trailing edge. His hunched shoulders indicate resignation at what has happened – perhaps he is the pilot!

and despite confirmed evidence that the vastly superior Grumman Avenger could be safely operated off escort carriers – the Swordfish would regularly continue to operate in the Arctic until the end of World War II (Avengers however would feature as part of JW/RA58, JW/RA61 and the penultimate wartime convoy JW/RA65).

The first of these exceptions to the Swordfish's virtually exclusive wartime presence on the Russian run occurred on the very next convoy JW/RA58. One ATTACKER Class carrier, TRACKER, and the British-built ACTIVITY were assigned. The latter vessel had a restricted hangar length of 100 ft. that limited her aircraft capacity to just ten – in this instance three Swordfish and seven Wildcats of No.819 Sqdn. By contrast, TRACKER's complement from No.846 Sqdn. comprised twelve Avengers and seven Wildcats. The presence of ACTIVITY was an emergency measure since the original choice (BITER) had not been ready in time. The surface escort for what was the largest convoy to date (forty-eight merchantmen) included two specialist Groups borrowed from normal operations in the North Atlantic, and one of which was the 2nd. Escort Group led by the redoubtable Capt. 'Johnny' Walker, arguably the Force most feared by the U-Boat crews.

The voyage was in its formative stage when on 29 March, the latest addition to the 2nd. Escort Group's list of 'kills' occurred; U-961 was on passage for the Atlantic but its progress was brutally brought to a close when Walker's own sloop STARLING administered the '*coup de grâce*'. Next day, one of the 'shadowers' looming up was intercepted by ACTIVITY's Wildcats, and the Ju 88 in question was shot down. Although the successors to the Ju 88 tended to fly low down and well out of range of the warships' Mk.79B radar surveillance, this ploy was not always successful. The crew of an Fw 200 was visually sighted on 31 March and paid the price when another pair of Wildcats from ACTIVITY took their aircraft down; before the day was over a further two Condors were shot down by the Wildcats. This same day, the anti-submarine role assigned to TRACKER's Avengers paid off when U-355 was attacked and sunk by the Avenger/Wildcat pair along with the destroyer BEAGLE.

By 4 April when JW58 steamed into Kola, a further three 'shadowers' had been downed along with two more U-Boats. The second of these on 2 April was U-288, which had previously dived upon the approach of one of ACTIVITY's Swordfish. The location was marked out, and when the aircraft returned there it was to find the U-Boat surfacing off to starboard. The biplane kept contact with the target, which perhaps unwisely remained on the surface, and within the hour was under machine gun attack by the Wildcat previously called in to assist. Then the Swordfish and the Wildcat's Avenger 'partner' struck home, their combined rocket and depth charge

ordnance causing the hapless vessel to explode. The value of both a solid surface escort and air support had clearly paid off, because no losses had been incurred despite the presence of seventeen U-Boats, four of which were sunk and three damaged! Nor did the German airmen and sailors fare any better when RA58 made passage back to Britain, although flying activities on the escort carriers was severely restricted due to the windless conditions.

The third and final 'gap' in regular convoys to Russia occurred between April and August, this being due to the perceived requirement for all available escort and carrier vessels to be on hand for the impending Operation OVERLORD. One return convoy was completed in this time during April-May, when RA59 was sailed with forty-five merchantmen under strong support from sixteen destroyers and four frigates as well as two escort carriers. The latter warships were ACTIVITY bearing the same Sqdn. and complement of aircraft as used for the previous JW/RA convoy and FENCER with No.842 Sqdn.'s eleven Swordfish and nine Wildcats. On the way over three Swordfish, two from ACTIVITY's meagre collection that were being flown by inexperienced 'replacement' crews, either crashed on the flight deck or were 'ditched'. Hasty aircraft repair work was carried out between arrival in, and departure from, Vaenga on 28 April. Within the first three days, the good weather pattern now broke down into heavy seas and snowstorms, during which period one merchantman was torpedoed.

A recurring problem affecting anti-submarine operations with the Swordfish concerned the type and maximum load of ordnance. With U-Boats regularly electing to remain on the surface and use their flak guns when intercepted, the ideal counter-weapon was the rocket projectile; however, should the 'Stringbag' not be in the company of a Wildcat, the crew faced the risk of being downed before closing to firing range, although this could be maintained at several hundred yards distance. Conversely, should the U-Boat submerge before coming within range, then the depth charge, or better still the Mk.24 'homing' mine would be of far greater value. Several variations were tried during RA59's progress; these included two or more Swordfish equipped with depth charges or rockets dispatched on the same patrol, or one Swordfish calling in a target, whereupon the carriers launched a 'back-up' strike force. The bald truth was that the Swordfish was well past her operational 'sell by date' compared to the Avenger for example. In addition the lack of an accelerator combined with still wind conditions to be found in the Arctic would inhibit the aircraft's load-carrying capability to the point of virtual impotency.

FENCER's 'arcticizing' equipment proved valuable in clearing the snow-laden flight deck, whereas the lack of such equipment on ACTIVITY seriously interfered with operations.

Over a seventy-two hour period commencing 1 May FENCER kept up a virtually continuous chain of anti-submarine patrols, during which time a number of U-Boats were intercepted and attacked. Although just one was claimed as sunk, the crews were subsequently found to have under-stated the degree of success. In fact, U-277, U-674 and U-959 never returned from their patrols around RA59. In the meantime at least one Bv 138 'shadower' had failed to escape the attentions of ACTIVITY's Wildcats.

Normal Service is Permanently Resumed

The Soviet desire, if not demand, for regular supplies via the Arctic was satisfied for the last time from August 1944 onwards when convoys JW59 and RA59A were initiated. From then until late May 1945, a monthly sequence of convoys would be sailed. This regularity masked an ironic twist in the overall situation, since the Soviet dependency on outside supply sources had surely long gone, given that their internal production system since 1943 onwards was massive by comparison.

JW59 enjoyed air cover from two escort carriers and, with two exceptions, no remaining Arctic convoy would be furnished with less than this number of these specialist vessels. The current duo featured one British-built and one U.S.-built warship, being VINDEX and STRIKER respectively. The British carrier was operating as a Trade Protection vessel featured an interesting albeit obsolescent fighter design with the Sea Hurricane Mk.IIC; this was flown by No.825 Sqdn. and was accompanied by twelve Swordfish. This Hawker variant possessed a potentially fearsome degree of armament comprising four 20mm cannon and four rocket rails, with which to assail any surfaced U-Boat. Moreover, her Swordfish were Mk.III variations fitted with ASV Mk.XI equipment. No.824 Sqdn.'s complement of twelve Swordfish and ten Wildcats operated off the other carrier.

The opposition faced by JW59 took the usual form of U-Boats, five of which were deployed east of Jan Mayen Island following the convoy's discovery by a 'shadower'. U-344 achieved a lethal strike with a T5 acoustic torpedo on the sloop KITE, following which he made a 'sighting' report that drew in a further four U-Boats. However, the presence both of the carriers' aircraft and a Coastal Command Catalina ensured that this group of U-Boats were kept submerged and finally lost contact. (STRIKER's log between the 20th and 22nd recorded no less than twenty-one sightings).

Kapitänleutnant Pietsch's success with KITE was avenged by one of VINDEX's Swordfish next day. Lt. Bennett was returning to the carrier when he sighted the U-Boat and his 'stick' of depth charges straddled the submerging vessel; One of the weapons was seen to lodge in the U-Boat's bow section

and the hapless vessel disintegrated just under the surface. On the 23rd, U-354 was also hunted to its death by a combination of aircraft and surface escorts. The first sighting by another STRIKER Swordfish resulted in the U-Boat hastily submerging in the face of the aircraft rocket barrage No less than four warships joined in the hunt that finished off *Kapitänleutnant* Sthamer and his crew – the same captain who just twenty-four hours previous had torpedoed the escort carrier NABOB as she was returning from the latest mass air-strike on TIRPITZ!

JW59 arrived safely at Kola on the 25th and three days later RA59A set out for home where it arrived equally intact on 5 September. The U-Boats attempting to impede its progress not only had no success but also returned to their berths short of U-394. The vessel was unfortunate enough to have its radio transmission picked up by a VINDEX Swordfish, whose subsequent attack left its prey damaged but not sunk. However, this reprieve for *Kapitänleutnant* Borger's crew was a scant one: the Swordfish 'called in' no less than four escorts and the ensuing six-hour 'creeping' pattern of attacks finally put paid to the U-Boat.

They Also Serve

Part of an escort Group that apparently matched if not exceeded convoy JW61 in numbers comprised no less than three escort carriers NAIRANA, VINDEX and TRACKER. The sturdier riveted construction of the first two-named British-built warships compared to the welded construction of their U.S. built contemporary, along with the British vessels' appreciably greater gross tonnage, were to prove of critical importance when facing the full rigours of the Arctic storms that would now be on hand as winter approached. On the other hand the British carriers suffered several basic disabilities, the first of which related to the flight deck width of just 65 ft. on the first two-named vessels – fully 17-23 ft. less than the various Classes of U.S. carriers. This left little margin for error especially when landing at night or in stormy weather conditions. The single lift on hand compared badly in terms of aircraft movements when set against the double lift facility on the ATTACKER and RULER Class vessels. Finally, the absence of an accelerator was to prove a notable impediment when launching either heavily laden aircraft or any aircraft in minimal wind conditions.

The steady rate of U-Boat sinkings enjoyed up to convoy JW/RA60 in September 1944, when U-921 was destroyed, was destined to almost dry up as regards aircraft involvement from this point onwards. The Swordfish crews and Wildcat pilots would continue to seek out their sea-borne and air-borne adversaries in the face of often atrocious weather conditions, and with monotony as their regular psychological 'companion'

A fabric-covered aircraft was an even greater fire hazard than a metal constructed design, as depicted here. A Swordfish is rapidly being consumed by the flames following a bad landing, with the fabric already totally burnt off the fin and rudder. The attentions of the 'Hot Papa' in his asbestos suit who is running in the foreground are hopefully not needed to extricate the aircrew.

while they scanned the featureless Arctic waters. The overall experience naturally brought to mind a variation of the saying 'They also serve who only stand and wait'. In this instance, it could be said of the aircrew that 'They also served who only flew and searched'!

The need to keep the U-Boats and aerial 'shadowers' clear of the convoys was to remain the top priority for the convoy escorts. This was a function that was admirably achieved throughout the remainder of 1944 and on to beyond VE-Day. In the course of the eight convoys dispatched in both directions, merchant shipping losses were virtually nil. JW/RA61 was a prime example of this complete turn in fortunes since not a single merchantman was lost. A further measure of the importance of aircraft to Royal Navy operations was the fact that Admiral Dalrymple-Hamilton chose to fly his flag in VINDEX, the first time an Arctic convoy Escort Leader had sailed in other than a standard Naval warship.

NAIRANA's Swordfish personnel were from No.835 Sqdn., a unit that had been long established since early 1942 but whose entry on operations had been with one exception restrained for various reasons – none of which were to do with the airmen's efficiency – until the end of 1943. (The sole operational spell to that point had been on board BATTLER during mid-1943 when one north Atlantic and one Gibraltar convoy was covered). Their second introduction to combat on NAIRANA that would last almost to VE-Day was to prove not only wearisome but also often extremely hazardous, particularly during the Arctic spell of operations.

Nature's Revenge
JW61 proved no exception to these physical and climatic limitations, thanks to the mountainous seas and minimal visibility encountered as soon as the convoy rendezvous had been made. The tiredness factor on this voyage was further heightened by the seeming inability of TRACKER to operate its ten Avengers coupled to other operational limitations on board VINDEX that inhibited the use of its twelve Swordfish during the convoy's initial voyage until the weather cleared. So it was that the planned eight-hour spells for each carrier's anti-submarine complement evolved into a virtual 'solo effort' by the fourteen Swordfish based on NAIRANA!

There was little rest when off duty due to the carrier's pitching up to forty degrees in either direction. The Duty aircrews had to sit up in the darkened Ready Room for the purpose of establishing instance night vision if called to take off, so their physical lot was arguably even worse. The need for instance night vision was due to the current period of daily darkness that spanned almost twenty-two of the twenty-four hours. The limitation on Avenger operations, even in fair weather conditions, was increased by their lack of ASV equipment, whose presence was vital not only for seeking out U-Boats but also for maintaining some form of 'contact' with the convoy and the carriers in particular.

The motion of a carrier in heavy seas was a constant headache, not to say potential killer, for returning aircraft and their crews. The vessels' pitching motion could extend up to forty or fifty ft., and should an aircraft be over the deck-end as

This Avenger's hook has caught the arrester wire but the aircraft's attitude will result in a heavy albeit successful landing on the CVE's flight deck. Despite the Avenger's availability for use on Arctic convoys from late 1943 onwards, it was the Swordfish that featured as the primary anti-submarine aircraft for the majority of the convoy runs to Russia.

the carrier rose upwards, the resultant impact could easily smash its wheels and throw it out of control to skate along the deck or even over the side. A violent sideways motion was equally hazardous, as one crew on NAIRANA discovered when about to touch down. In this instance the pilot banked violently to starboard and barely missed the miniscule superstructure mass, although several mast aerials were ripped away by his fuselage or wings. A swift circuit and new landing approach was thankfully completed without further incident!

The sub-zero temperature had to be borne by the crews during each patrol whose average duration was around three hours. Two crews from VINDEX who confused a rain cloud with the convoy at the end of their patrol spent nearly two more hours before finally receiving a bearing that brought them back on board. The expression 'frozen stiff' proved to be the literal case for all four aviators who had to be cut free from their cockpits.

Diminishing Returns

VINDEX's experience on the return voyage was little short of disastrous for its aircrew although none of the losses were to enemy action. First, on 3 November, a Wildcat pilot disoriented by the poor light and lateral visibility flew straight into the sea on take-off; the pilot's recovery within less than five minutes proved too long for him to survive the cruel cold as exposure took its latest human toll. Then, the Rocket-assisted Take-off (RATOG) equipment on a loaded Swordfish failed to properly activate, causing the aircraft's loss off the bow along with its hapless crew. The third fatality later that same day involved the pilot of a Swordfish that went off to one side of the deck on landing, hung momentarily by its temporarily wire-engaged hook, before the attachment tore off to leave the aircraft plummeting into the sea.

The final act of destruction involved two 'ranged' Wildcats, whose deck-handlers were unable to secure in place when heavy seas were suddenly encountered, with the result that they 'skated' and finally slid over the side. These losses formed the final act in reducing No.811's aircraft complement from an original figure of sixteen to just six. Even this limited number was rendered useless when the carrier's lift went out of action. And so it was that NAIRANA was again forced to assume the entire anti-submarine brief as TRACKER's motion through the storm-tossed waters again rendered her Avengers out of action. However, NAIRANA's Captain, much to his aircrew's disgust, did not act upon Admiral Dalrymple-Hamilton's order for all flying to cease.

Their subsequent effort in flying fourteen separate patrols over the intervening forty-eight hours was all the more to their credit, especially as several landings ended in near disaster. Lt. Whittick was literally 'bounced' off the deck end and into the air by the carrier's vertical motion to leave the Swordfish hovering in a semi-stalled position over the crash barrier. The pilot desperately rammed opened the engine throttle and by a miracle managed to 'leapfrog' the barrier and still maintain the barest degree of flying control. The subsequent circuit and successful landing was very tame by comparison! Another pilot whose Swordfish had so far failed to engage a wire after bouncing on landing, and was heading for the raised safety barrier, was greatly relieved when the final, rigid 'Jesus Christ' wire (Presumably so named because the aircrew would by now be calling on that august person to prevent their colliding with the barrier!) was engaged, although the very abrupt stop saw the pilot's head collide with the windscreen in addition to stressing the aircraft's fuselage frame.

The inability to launch the Wildcats in order to deal with a persistent 'shadower' who was circling in the dark on 3 November was solved in a rather bizarre manner. A Swordfish crew volunteered to act in the role of night fighter and duly took off – armed with nothing more than a sub-machine gun. NAIRANA's Fighter Director Officer vectored his charge towards the *Luftwaffe* aircraft, upon which it turned away from the convoy and never regained contact. Lt. Newberry (Observer) stated caustically after landing, "It's lucky for us all cats are grey in the dark!" (Had the enemy crew possessed an inkling of the type of 'opposition' heading their way, it is certain they would not have been too bothered, and indeed might well have become the 'hunter' instead of the 'prey!').

Challenge from the Air

Another British-built escort carrier CAMPANIA accompanied convoy JW/RA61A, and this vessel was on hand for the succeeding convoy (JW/RA62, and the last of the 1944 Arctic convoys) along with NAIRANA. Over the past seven to eight months the progress of the convoys had been un-impeded as

A pair of Martlets and a second pair of Swordfish are spotted on the after flight deck of an escort carrier. The laborious duty of clearing away the coating of snow under which may well be a surface of ice was often intensified by the frigid temperatures and turbulent waters of the North Atlantic and the Arctic Oceans.

regards direct air attack, *Luftwaffe* activity having been confined to acting in the 'shadower' role. This satisfactory situation was about to be momentarily disrupted while the convoy was still west of Bear Island.

The torpedo-carrying Ju 88s of I./KG 26 were currently based at Trondheim/Vaernes and the *Gruppenkommandeur*, *Maj.* Soelter duly briefed his crews for a sortie against JW62 on 12 December. The *Gruppe* took off and separated into Staffel-strength sub-units; they then headed north in the face of constant rain and snow showers. Approximately an hour before reaching the convoy, Soelter picked up the homing signal from the convoy 'shadower' and on sighting the pack of vessels, ordered the two *Staffeln* to fan outwards at forty-five degrees and commence their attack runs, while hugging the sea surface.

During the action, several aircrews noted that some torpedoes were detonating while still some distance from the intended target. On return to Vaernes, still others stated that the safety covers on some firing pistols had been seen to be in the 'off' position before reaching the convoy, which meant the weapons in question were already armed – not very healthy for the crews concerned should the intense AA fire have struck home prior to release.

Although hits were claimed on at least two vessels, the entire convoy emerged unscathed from the attack. On NAIRANA, the radar 'plots' displayed separate formations approaching from the northeast and southeast, with an estimated figure that tallied with *Staffel*-strength units. Two Wildcats were launched as the short day faded and darkness

began to settle in, but their attempt to pick up the raiders was limited to a single encounter with a Ju 88 that promptly evaded in the thickening cloud and gloom.

The convoy's experience was that only one enemy formation was reported as making its assault run, but the combination of AA and poor light conditions seemed to have played a major part in thwarting the attack since no torpedoes found their mark. Two of the three bombers failing to return fell to Wildcats based on CAMPANIA. One of the NAIRANA Wildcats was lost but not to enemy action; instead – and despite having its navigation lights on and making its landing approach – the fighter was taken out by the gunners on a nearby escort vessel, killing the pilot in the process.

Next day, (according to KG 26 records at least) a second attack force with reduced numbers was sent out, of which an element managed to launch their torpedoes. Once again, the claims for hits on both merchant and warships proved to be in vain. Another recurring feature of the sortie lay in the premature explosions of several torpedoes. Since not all crews managed to penetrate the defensive screen, the AA reception faced by the remainder was all the more concentrated, and almost certainly accounted for the loss figure increasing over the previous day's action. To add to this failure, U-365 was caught by Swordfish from CAMPANIA and depth charged to destruction.

The Clock Runs Down

As 1945 was entered the first of the final four Arctic convoys to face a direct enemy challenge was sailed during January.

This very nasty pile-up involved two Swordfish, one of which literally 'landed' on top of the other on concluding a night-flying exercise. As far as is recorded, no serious injuries were incurred by any of the 'participants'. The incident occurred on 19 February 1944 at Arbroath, Scotland (CONDOR) that was home for the No.2 Observers School as well as similar Schools for Deck-Landing training and Naval Air Signals.

VINDEX was the sole carrier assigned but it was probably Mother Nature that provided the overall opposition. No U-Boats or aircraft made interception with the total of thirty-eight and thirty-one merchantmen constituting the separate JW and RA63 elements of the convoy. It was a different story in February for the same pair of carriers involved in JW/RA62. The Ju 88s of II./KG 26 were now based at Bardufoss with III./KG 26 located further south at Trondheim-Vaernes, this sub-unit having converted onto the refined Ju 88 version – the Ju 188 – during November.

'Shadowers' had picked up JW64 on 6 February and the first full attack came in from the Bardufoss-based *Gruppe* on the 7th. According to KG 26 records, full surprise was lost; this was thanks to one Ju 88 crew who, having failed to take off on time due to technical problems then flew straight for the convoy and arrived ahead of the formation, causing the AA gunners to be on full alert. The usual concentrated AA gunfire as well as Wildcat fighters met the twenty-five-strong force. The end result was no torpedo hits against at least three crews unaccounted for on the *Gruppe*'s return to Bardufoss. British records indicate that separate formations engaged the convoy with the second one attacking some 60 minutes later.

Another major attack was dispatched a day later according to *Luftwaffe* records, (although British accounts refer to this action as occurring on the 10th). III./KG 26 had transferred up to Bardufoss and its eighteen Ju 188s would share the sortie with fourteen from II./KG 26. The intention was to 'snare' the convoy in a pincer movement that would create problems in evading the torpedoes and also split the AA defences. The Ju 188 formation would approach from the northwest, with the Ju 88s coming in on the convoy's starboard beam. However, the westward-oriented formation's approach was detected by radar, while a sighting report had also been frantically radioed back to NAIRANA by the Swordfish crew involved.

The *Luftwaffe* aircraft skimmed in over the smooth, frigid sea surface, and headed in towards the main convoy after failing to sight either of the two carriers in what were stated to be poor visibility conditions, even though NAIRANA at least was positioned within the rear ranks of merchantmen. The ten Wildcats shared between the carriers were up and ready to take on the Ju 88s, while the AA gunners began to make their fire felt – in both positive and negative form. One Ju 88 pilot

Two 'Wrens' clad in what appear to be bulky but comfortable Sidcot Suits are securing the canvas cover over a Swordfish cockpit after conducting a radio equipment test; they are assisted in this duty by a civilian-clothed man. Note how the aircraft's control cables for the rudder and elevator are channelled into the rear fuselage via tapered 'sleeve' fairings.

Three Avengers from No.846 Sqdn. are lined up in an echelon-left formation. This unit served on several escort carriers up to VE-Day both on the North Atlantic and the Arctic convoy routes. The camouflage separation line, with the cowling area raised above the forward fuselage was a standard feature on the Grumman design while in FAA service.

gallantly flew through the wall of fire and got his torpedoes away against the front rank of merchantmen before having both engines igniting and crashing into the unyielding water.

Another bomber was engaged by Wildcats from NAIRANA, when still at a moderate altitude for torpedo release. The weapons were nevertheless jettisoned and the pilot vainly sought cloud cover; the aircraft was set on fire as it penetrated a low cloud layer and then seen to emerge on the far side in a terminal dive. Five Ju 88s in all were lost and others damaged, but the original estimate of seven 'kills' was grimly accurate. The revised figure was made up by two of the Wildcats, both of whom were downed by the AA fire, along with one of the pilots!

AA Discipline

The question of AA gunner discipline was a subject of heated debate during World War II. To those pilots and crews affected by what is now termed 'friendly fire', there was no apparent excuse for the situation to arise. Aircraft identification training should have at least taken the edge off the inability of the most unintelligent and/or ignorant sailor manning these weapons to differentiate between Allied and enemy aircraft outlines. On the other hand, the matter of aircraft recognition is that it is an art as much as a theoretical process; the 'sit' of an aircraft

in flight can be as much a feature of its specific layout as its actual shape. Then there is the question of similar outlines, an example of which is the C-47 and He 111: there is a disturbing resemblance when each is viewed from below and behind.

However, the bald truth was that the AA gunners firing from a relatively immobile platform – especially in the case of the merchant vessels tied to their convoy positions – were on the back foot compared to the twisting and weaving aerial attacker. Should an aircraft come within the body of the convoy, it was largely a case of 'fire first, and confirm later!'. This was the reverse problem for the naval fighters attempting to head off the attackers before they could do their worst, but coming under fire in the process.

On the other hand, the occasions when aircraft in the carrier landing circuit were fired upon – even after the main action was over – were basically indefensible incidents. In the case of the Arctic convoys, there was no regular involvement of *Luftwaffe* single-engine fighters, since the range was mainly too great for their presence. How, then, could AA fire be justifiably directed at the Wildcats or Swordfish? How indeed could a Swordfish be mistaken for anything else, yet still be shot at? (A secondary issue that was rarely raised was how many vessels were struck by 'friendly fire' in the heat of an action. Although vessels were reasonably spaced out, they were close enough for some of the expended ammunition to reach far enough in their direction, especially during a low-level assault).

Last Fling of the *Luftwaffe*

The various sorties launched by the *Luftwaffe* against the Arctic convoys had not proved very fruitful in terms of vessels sunk or even damaged. The last recorded sortie by KG 26, the main challenger to the Allied effort, was on 20 February 1945. A U-Boat sighting of RA64 had come in, ironically just as the vessels that had been scattered by an extremely severe gale had been re-assembled. A force of fifteen Ju 88s and ten Ju 188s was formed up consisting of the more experienced crews. (*Hptm.* Prinz (III./KG 26) recalled that the bad weather conditions were grounds enough for applying this operational restriction). The attack plan again involved a 'pincers' movement and unbeknown to the *Luftwaffe* airmen was the fact that the fighter opposition had been reduced from ten to six thanks to storm damage on board CAMPANIA that had wrecked or disabled all her Wildcats. Even so, it took a full hour for NAIRANA to range four fighters in readiness for take-off.

It was mid-morning when the radar screens picked up 'bogeys' and the fighters launched in the face of a pitching flight deck that made take-off extremely hazardous. The fighters tore into the enemy formation and along with the AA gunfire managed disrupt their adversaries sufficiently to throw most off their attack runs. *Hptm.* Prinz further recalled having

to swerve his bomber around a cruiser before releasing his two 'eels' (German slang term for a torpedo) against a merchantman; as he passed this vessel's bow he observed it to be almost at a standstill, but as his Ju 188 manoeuvered through the AA fire, one explosion was claimed to have been seen against the target's hull. No losses were actually suffered by the convoy at this stage of the voyage so the likelihood was that the blast was caused by premature detonation. Four more strikes, two of them fatal, were reported at the de-briefing session by several of the twenty-two surviving crews.

This aerial action was the last recorded against an Arctic convoy, although a straggling vessel was intercepted and sunk by a formation of Ju 88s three days later. The undoubted courage of the *Luftwaffe* crews had not been rewarded in any material way since the heyday of operations in June and September 1942. Each sortie had entailed at least four or five hours of flying low over the hostile sea surface from which there was little or no chance of survival in the event of a 'ditching'. The weather conditions were consistently bad, so that the task of finding a convoy, even with the assistance of a 'shadower's' radio guidance signal, was not always guaranteed.

Even when found, it sometimes happened that elements of the formation when breaking off to make their individual attack approach could still lose sight of the convoy. Then, the need to climb up to 200 ft. in order to release the torpedoes, exposed the aircraft to even more unhealthy attention from AA fire. The subsequent evasive action as the pilots sought to escape the deadly embrace of both AA and any fighters on the

Wearing their distinctive 'Mae West' life jackets, the three-man crew of a Swordfish Mk.II are pondering what went wrong with this failed landing attempt that shattered their 'Stringbag's' landing gear. It is 'all hands to the pump' as the deck handlers begin to bodily haul the aircraft around. Points of note are the upper wing leading edge slats and the square outline of the dinghy hatch just above the port side of the fuselage.

scene meant that it was all too easy to 'dig' a wing into the sea with almost certain fatal consequences for aircraft and crew.

The JW/RA64 convoy was to prove the last both for NAIRANA and No.835 Sqdn., with the Swordfish unit being disbanded at the end of March. CAMPANIA sailed on JW/RA65 along with TRUMPETER, while the April convoy VINDEX and PREMIER covered JW/RA66. Two merchantmen and one sloop were sunk during the March run against one frigate lost during April, while U-307 and U-826 tasted the bitter seeds of failure along with their crews during the latter operation. The final act in Arctic waters occurred directly following VE-Day but JW/RA67 was provided with a normal escort that included the escort carrier QUEEN; this was done to guard against any possibility of a U-Boat attack by one or more 'rogue' Captains, still loyal to their *Führer* and prepared to fight on.

Reflections

The cost of the forty-one outward-bound and twenty-four homeward-bound convoys to and from Northern Russia was 104 merchantmen (of which nearly a quarter were suffered during the disastrous PQ17 action) and eighteen warships, while human casualties were just less than 900 merchant and Navy seamen. These loss statistics are clearly much more favourable compared to the other major convoy Theaters, especially that across the Atlantic. However, the true test of the Arctic sailors arguably stemmed not only from their battles with the *Kriegsmarine* and *Luftwaffe* but moreover from their physical 'battles' with the uniquely cruel weather elements up on the 'Roof of the Earth'. Sub-zero temperatures and waters that could expunge life within minutes or even seconds of being immersed – Polar ice-packs – almost perpetual daylight in summer and a reverse night-shrouded experience in winter – unpredictable heavy seas and gale force winds. These were the combined factors that entitle the survivors who made the runs to Murmansk and Archangel to express a quiet, if also relieved, pride in their specific achievements.

CHAPTER EIGHT

Mediterranean Advance
1943-1944

The Overall Allied situation in the Mediterranean as 1943 was entered displayed a vastly different and positive aspect compared to even the early autumn of 1942. Then, the land battle centered around El Alamein had only been stabilised. The Italian Fleet, although still inhibited in its apparent desire to take on the Royal Navy could not be ignored especially when it was backed by sizeable elements of the *Luftwaffe* and Regia Aeronautica as well as German U-Boats. Malta was desperately in need of re-supply and faced a real possibility of going under, thereby opening up the way for almost unfettered supply of Rommel's *Afrikakorps* across the central Mediterranean, with all that this implied for its Eighth Army opponents chances of staving off defeat in Egypt and the subsequent capture of the Nile Delta and beyond.

The latter months of 1942 by stark contrast threw up a pattern of Allied success. The continued plundering of the Axis convoy routes particularly by Malta-based forces weakened Rommel to the point of virtual impotence when Montgomery attacked on 23 October. Malta's prospects had previously taken a positive turn thanks to the 'Pedestal' convoy. A second massive blow to the enemy's chances of even holding on to North Africa came with the advent of Operation 'Torch' on 8 November. Now, by 1 January the twin arms of the Allied 'pincer movement' were slowly but surely compressing the Axis forces back towards Tunisia.

The swift success of 'Torch' had been followed by a steady reduction in aircraft carrier provision once the Allied Air Forces had secured airfields ashore. By January just FORMIDABLE was still on station within Force H, based for the most part at Oran. The Albacores of No.820 Sqdn. had enjoyed a notable success on 17 November when one crew had fatally crippled U-331. Now between December and April the unit was to operate from no less than six North African airfields including La Senia, Tafaroui and Blida as well as North Front (Gibraltar), with three interim spells aboard FORMIDABLE. Nos.885 (Seafire IIC), 888 and 893 Sqdns. (Martlet IV) fighters made similar transfers between ship and shore during the same period, with airfields around Oran being selected. One other FAA Sqdn. was also on hand; No.813 Sqdn. had landed its Swordfish at Tafaroui during 'Torch' and had subsequently moved eastwards to Bone. Finally, shortly before the Campaign ended No.821 Sqdn.'s Albacores moved from Hal Far, Malta to Sfax, below Tunis and on Tunisia's eastern coastline.

Sicilian Set-Back

The North African Campaign ground successfully to its sometimes-turgid advance in mid May, and almost immediately plans were set in motion for the conquest of Sicily. The Allied Air Forces now held sufficient bases within striking range of the Island to provide overall cover for the intended Invasion Force. However, the FAA crews were not totally excluded from the Operation, thanks to the continued existence of the main Italian Fleet lurking at La Spezia and Taranto in particular. FORMIDABLE duly embarked her four Sqdns in the run up to the Invasion date of 'Operation 'Husky' (10 July) and linked up with INDOMITABLE, recently re-commissioned following her prolonged spell under repair in Britain, and bearing No.817 Sqdn.'s Albacores as well as Seafire IICs from Nos.807, 880, and 899 Sqdns.

Both carriers and their Force H fellow-warships took up station well to the east of Malta, ready to challenge any foray by the harbor-bound Italians, but no such reaction was encountered, on the surface at least. It was a very different matter as regards aerial reaction, although the circumstances involving the crippling of INDOMITABLE on 16 July were somewhat incredible. A single torpedo-bearing *Luftwaffe*

bomber made its run during the evening and planted the weapon squarely into the carrier's port side before skimming away unscathed by any AA fire. Aircraft recognition is an art as much as a process of learning the outlines of aircraft. However, the confusing of an Albacore outline with that of a Ju 88 indicates extreme lethargy in recognition ability by those personnel who reputedly made the sighting as the Axis aircraft approached! The damage was fortunately not fatal, but its scale merited INDOMITABLE's withdrawal from operational service for a second prolonged period of nearly a year.

Operation 'Avalanche'

Generals Montgomery and Patton's soldiers brought Sicily under complete Allied control by mid August, with southern Italy next on the Invasion programme. The Straits of Messina separating Sicily and Italy were stormed by the Eighth Army

Opposite
Top: The Albacore Sqdns. serving in North Africa between mid-1941 and mid-1943 faced the same basic and harsh operational conditions as their RAF contemporaries. Here a group of mechanics are gathered by bombs scattered casually on the sandstone and scrub surface that passed for a 'desert'.

Bottom: The pilot of a Swordfish Mk.II and a fellow-officer stand in front of the aircraft, while deck handlers are ready to pull away the wheel chocks. The picture was reportedly taken during Operation 'Torch' – an assertion backed by the U.S.-pattern steel helmets – but seems contradicted by the fact that no Swordfish units participated in the November 1942 Landings.

Below: A head-on view of an Albacore on a Fleet carrier emphasises the stalky landing gear struts and the bulk of its Taurus radial engine that provided 1065 hp and 1085 hp depending on whether it was the II or XII version. Two depth charges are mounted under the wings. With wings folded the Albacore fitted comfortably onto the carrier's lifts.

on 3 September but a second more ambitious element of this latest Invasion concerned the port of Naples nearly 200 miles further up the west coast. Capture of this vital location would be of incalculable benefit to further advances, as well as 'pinching off' German forces to the south. Salerno, about twenty miles south of Naples, possessed the necessary beachhead stretches on which to land the Allied troops who would be tasked with capturing Naples.

The aerial tactical situation for operation 'Avalanche' was the direct antithesis of 'Husky' Then, direct air cover had been the province of the land-based Allied Sqdns. This time round, the extended range between the nearest available Sicilian airfield and the beachhead reduced fighter cover to an unacceptably low level in terms of both time and numbers. Consequently the Fleet Air Arm was called into service. Force V had been assembled several weeks before the Invasion of Italy, and was led by Rear Admiral Sir Philip Vian; this sailor was previously involved with destroyers, and had gained fame for leading COSSACK into a Norwegian fjord in early 1940, in order to storm the prison-ship ALTMARK and release her British and Allied captives, survivors from freighters sunk by the GRAF SPEE. From his cruiser flagship EURYALUS he held charge of four escort carriers, ATTACKER, BATTLER, HUNTER and STALKER; also in support was the repair carrier UNICORN.

The four carriers possessed between them eight Sqdns. in full or Flight strength and operating nearly eighty Seafires LIIC, while UNICORN had embarked a further 'reserve' of thirty-nine LIICs split between four Sqdns. and one Flight,

three Swordfish and seventeen Martlets IV. The provision of more than 100 fighters promised sound air cover for the ground troops, as well as sufficient numbers of fighters with which to achieve this aim. The availability of the Mk.LIIC augured well for the operation. This variant of the IIC had been fitted with a Merlin 32 in place of the Merlin 46 and a four-blade propeller instead of the three-blade unit on all previous Seafire variants. With a shorter take-off run, enhanced top speed at all heights up to 25,000 ft. and a greater climb-rate than the IIC, the new Mark promised to give any Axis attacker a hard time.

Standing further out to sea off Salerno, FORMIDABLE and ILLUSTRIOUS, with a mix of Seafires IIC, Martlets IV and Albacores provided part of Force H's covering operation against Italian Fleet intrusions. It was all the more ironic that the enemy warships were destined to venture out on the 9th when 'Avalanche' was initiated – but only in a passive capacity, since they were heading for Malta in order to surrender!

Hard Knocks

On the 8th September, Force V threaded the straits of Messina and Force H steamed north and west of Sicily. In the early hours of the next morning the first range of Seafires were launched, the intention being to keep around twenty fighters constantly in the air, with each group operating for around one hour under the radar direction of a specialised Fighter Direction vessel. The planners of the land Operation had predicted virtually no German resistance, and therefore swift consolidation of the beachhead area and its large airfield at Montecorvino, into which Allied fighters could be flown. Unfortunately, the Operation immediately ran foul of hitherto undetected Panzer units and the Allied troops were hard-pressed to even stay ashore for the ensuing 24-48 hours; at one point Gen. Mark Clark even proposed a full-scale evacuation, but this was fortunately rejected.

The parallel situation for Force V was proving equally degenerative, and arose out of several operational factors. First, the flat calm produced by the fine summer weather, when allied to the slow maximum speed of the escort carriers, did nothing to assist the Seafire pilots in making sound landings. The relative fragility of the Supermarine design when faced with making contact on the short carrier decks resulted in a steady rate of attrition. Either the undercarriage failed to stand up to the landing impact, or the fighter pitched forward sufficiently for the propeller blades to literally 'peck' the deck. (On HUNTER the latter problem was solved when its Captain ordered all blades shortened by two inches, with no discernable effect upon overall aircraft performance).

A number of Seafires also 'floated' down the deck length, missing all the arrester wires and wrote themselves off either in the safety barrier or even by impacting with the preceding fighter to land. Wrinkled rear fuselages and over-strained engine bearers were other damage sources arising out of heavy

Two No.885 Sqdn. Seafires Mk.IIc are lined up along the port side of FORMIDABLE's flight deck Their airframes display the potentially corrosive effect of salt water spray. In the far distance are the two battleships NELSON and RODNEY with their distinctive aft superstructure and the Fleet carrier INDOMITABLE. The latter warship had no sooner returned from a British repair yard than she was again put out of action by an air-dropped torpedo and forced to spend another spell under repair – this time in Norfolk, VA!

A Deck Landing Control Officer (DLCO) on right of picture guides a Seafire Mk.IIc of No.885 Sqdn. in for a precise landing on FORMIDABLE. Three other Sqdn. aircraft – the nearest pair being Mk. I Bs equipped with tropical filters – are positioned with their rear fuselages over-hanging the deck edge and tail wheels fitted into out-rigger frames, thereby increasing the available deck width for flying operations. This photograph was believed taken during the Salerno Landings in September 1943.

landings. All in all the Seafire was not enjoying the best of fortunes as a carrier fighter. (Indeed, its subsequent operational career with the FAA would never fully rise to an acceptable level of efficiency in some Naval authorities' views, although there were also those who rejected such a blanket criticism).

The stationing of Force V fairly close in to the coast created a second operational limitation. The high terrain around Salerno created a 'robbing' effect on Allied radar screens, and conversely provided the defending fighters with little or no time to position themselves for enemy aircraft making their attack runs. The Fw 190 and Bf 109s in particular favored a diving approach to their intended targets while the Ju 88s were almost as fast. The relative lack of direct engagements has tended to be put down to this factor, but the radar warning-limitation provides a better reason for this seeming failure. As it was the Seafires did discourage several groups of raiders from proceeding through to the beachhead on the 9th when the aircraft concerned jettisoned their bomb-loads and headed back. A further limitation on picking out attackers was ascribed to the thick haze hanging over the battlefront that provided minimum visual warning.

The carrier's presence had been expected to last for the time it took to consolidate the beachhead and seize Montecorvino airfield, but the battle was proceeding 'according to somebody else's plan'. Four full days was to elapse before the Operation was to achieve its primary aim. In that extended time the Seafire pilots and carrier support crews

did their utmost to provide the maximum air cover. However, all were facing a logistical 'implosion' as ever more Seafires were 'written off' in the unforgiving atmospheric conditions. It is all the more to the FAA's credit that nearly 500 sorties were flown during the first two days, although the operationally available fighters were reduced to thirty-nine on the 11th; nevertheless, this seriously reduced force achieved an individual average of four sorties!

By day four of 'Avalanche', an airfield had become available, although not the original choice. When captured, Montecorvino was assessed as being too heavily damaged and in the meantime a strip had been hastily created out of agricultural fields at Paestum. It was to here that the surviving Seafires – just twenty-six in all – were flown off on the 12th. No refuelling or rearming facilities or servicing personnel were yet on hand which left the pilots to their own devices during the short twenty-four-hour occupation of Paestum. This was just as well because the thick dust condition threatened to drastically reduce engine efficiency due to the Seafire's lack of a tropical filter. Three sorties were flown up to the following afternoon, after which the presence of a mass of USAAF fighters on the airfield forced a move to another RAF-occupied strip.

During one of these patrols, the FAA formation was 'bounced' by two fighters, one of which was downed by the top cover. Unfortunately, what might easily have been mistaken for a Bf 109 turned out to be an A-36A Mustang – a design

A Seafire Mk.IIc has just come to an abrupt halt on ILLUSTRIOUS as a deck handler rushes forward to release the arrester wire from the deck cable. The fighter is equipped with an auxiliary 'slipper' tank under the fuselage. This Fleet carrier along with FORMIDABLE acted as a potential 'screen' for Force V in the event of the Italian Fleet attempting to interfere with Operation 'Avalanche'.

with an ominously similar outline to the Messerschmitt fighter! The American pilot baled out safely, but his CO raised all kinds of hell with his British contemporaries, saying "Which of you lousy SOBs shot down my goddam idiot Number Two" – a clear contradiction in terms when given the Major's equal lack of sound aircraft recognition! A final patrol on the 14th witnessed the end of Force V's involvement in the Salerno landings. Both the operational and climatic odds had been against the Seafire from the very beginning In addition, the FAA would never again carry out a fighter-based operation with just a single design on hand. In the future the Seafire would share duties with both the Hellcat and Corsair, both of which were custom-built for carrier operations.

Lessons from 'Avalanche'

The choice of the Seafire as the FAA's latest acquisition for what was regarded as a sound air superiority weapon could be regarded as enforced to some degree. By late 1942, the Sea Hurricane and Martlet had been bearing the brunt of this necessary duty. The Grumman fighter had at least been brought into existence with carrier operations in mind whereas the Hurricane was but an adaptation for seaborne activities and was more limited in terms of overall performance as well as automatic suitability for proper functioning off carrier decks. What better solution then, than to adapt the Supermarine design in a similar manner?

The original Spitfire airframe had naturally been constructed with land operations, and furthermore with grass airfield surfaces, in mind. In addition the airframe in its pure form was so well balanced out that ancillary control items such as trim tabs and horn balances were basically dispensed with. The first Spitfire variants in effect were the 'flat racers' of their era. What was required for the greater 'rough and tumble' of carrier operations was initially embodied in the Wildcat, and later (and even more efficiently) in the Grumman Hellcat and Chance-Vought Corsair, all of whom could be placed in the 'Steeple Chaser' category – in other words embodying the general performance of the Spitfire but with more robust airframe structures for the specific task at hand.

The basic problem that had afflicted Seafire operations off Salerno could so easily be ascribed to the windless weather condition and the small deck size of the CVEs, but this 'explanation' is rather simplistic. The real problem tended to lie in the art of landing aircraft on carriers. There were several performance and aerodynamic factors in this respect that were to regularly plague the operational career of the Seafire up to VJ-Day:

• The recommended maximum – or rather the minimum – speed on landing approach was barely above the power-on stall point. When this limitation is considered (along with the fact that premature tail buffeting due to disturbed

By the time of Operation 'Avalanche', the Salerno Landings in September 1943, Nos.888 and 893 Sqdns. with their Martlets Mk.IV had been embarked on FORMIDABLE. Several aircraft of No.893 Sqdn. are warming up. The three Seafires Mk.1B appear to be the same ones seen in the preceding photograph

airflow, caused in turn by poorly fitting fuselage and wing panels around the wing root section, gave the impression of an imminent stall) it was small wonder that pilots tended to keep their speed well up compared to the recommended figure.

• The recommended rate of descent onto the deck for a Seafire was set at no more than seven ft. per second; otherwise the landing gear was liable to collapse. The trouble was that a normal straight and horizontal approach

could not be indulged in, as would be the case on a land-based airfield. Here, the approach had to be made in a curve so that the pilot could sight the 'Batsman's' signals, with minimal time to straighten out prior to landing.

• The primary need to get the tail and therefore the arrester-hook to engage a wire in the relatively short deck length over which the set of wires extended meant that a three-point landing was mandatory. However, should the aircraft's speed be above the required rate, the Seafire was

The Fairey Barracuda's operational debut was during Operation 'Avalanche' off Salerno when No.810 Sqdn. embarked on ILLUSTRIOUS. This color picture picks out the dark slate grey and extra dark sea grey upper surface camouflage along with the Sky undersides applied to FAA aircraft. The forward torpedo length bears an orange shade.

The perceived operational function of the Barracuda was as a torpedo-bomber. As it transpired the bulk of the actions involving the Fairey design related to dive or glide-bombing. The 'Barra's' disconcerting tendency towards rudder imbalance was a likely factor in throwing it into an inverted spin while recovering from a dive, and which proved fatal to the aircraft and crew concerned!

The extended length of the Royal Navy's torpedo can be judged from this picture, since it takes up virtually half the 39 ft. 9 inch length of Barracuda P9926. The external carriage of the 'Barra's' offensive weaponry inevitably reduced the aircraft's overall performance to a moderate level compared with its U.S.-constructed contemporary, the Avenger.

liable to touch down on the main landing gear first; this tended to force the nose up and lead to the wings assuming a lift function – that is, keeping the aircraft aloft long enough for the arrester wires to be by-passed before the hook could make contact. Just as bad was the engagement of a wire while the aircraft was in this unfortunate configuration. The imbalanced CG effect caused by this action would often pitch the aircraft onto its nose, after which the tail would slam back onto the deck with almost certain stress damage to the rear fuselage as well as shock-loading the engine.

Operation 'Dragoon'

Shortly after 'Avalanche' had been completed the dissolution took place both of Force V and Force H. Whereas the assembly of the former-listed Force was specifically arranged for a single Operation, Force H had become a symbol of the Royal Navy's predominance in the Mediterranean; its passing into history was a sad but logical process, since the principal obstacle to Britain's control of the entire region no longer existed, but was safely disarmed and moored under the guns of Malta. And so it was that the major portion of the Navy's heavy warships and carriers dispersed to other Theaters of Operations – in particular the Atlantic. Over the intervening ten months, RAF, Commonwealth and USAAF Sqdns exercised Allied air power in the Mediterranean, as the Italian mainland beyond Rome and the Islands of Sardinia and Corsica were liberated.

Although the Allies were well entrenched in Normandy by July, the planning for a second landing in southern France was in its final stage. The area chosen was east of Marseilles and Toulon, and a Franco-American Force was to be involved in the Invasion. Once ashore the troops would carry out a northwards drive up through the Rhone valley.

As with Salerno, so the land-based Allied aircraft would be hard-pressed to provide air cover, particularly in terms of single-engine fighters, due to the distance between their Corsican bases and the beachheads. So it was that the U.S. and Royal Navies were called upon to provide the requisite air support. One major difference compared to Salerno would be the use of the Seafires, Wildcats and Hellcats. This time around, they would chiefly be used in an offensive capacity, by carrying out armed reconnaissance and strafing sorties not only over the beachheads but also along the path of the ground troops advance. 'Spotting' for the bombarding battleships and cruisers would also be indulged in.

The carrier Force allotted to 'Dragoon' consisted wholly of escort vessels, seven from the Royal Navy and two from the USN. Five of the British carriers were modified to an 'Assault' capability. This entailed expanding the fighter direction facilities to cover liaison with the ground troops, a process that required extra personnel to handle the operational telephone system and monitor the R/T and W/T equipment set up around the Aircraft Direction Room. The carriers concerned were ATTACKER, HUNTER, KHEDIVE and STALKER, with all but BATTLER following up on their experience off Salerno. In addition two 'fighter' carriers – PURSUER and SEARCHER, whose aircraft would come from No.7 Naval Fighter Wing, as were those embarked on EMPEROR – would also join in the Operation; No.4 Fighter Wing provided the fighters and pilots on three of the other four carriers, KHEDIVE being the exception.

The bulk of the Seafires in current use on the Force's arrival in the Mediterranean were Mk.IICs and LRIICs. A number of the latest LIII variant was embarked in Gibraltar when ATTACKER, HUNTER and STALKER arrived in late May. Over the ensuing few weeks all three were utilised for convoy protection, during which time a proportion of the Seafires was disembarked in North Africa and twenty-eight were then dispatched to Italy to assist the RAF in ground-support operations; their use in this way was perceived as practice for 'Dragoon' although the loss of eleven aircraft was somewhat of a drain on overall numbers for the forthcoming Invasion.

By late July, the remaining two 'Assault' and two 'Fighter' carriers were also on station. Overall control was to be exercised by Rear-Admiral Troubridge, a veteran Fleet carrier Captain sailing in the Canadian cruiser ROYALIST. Two Task Forces were created, 88.1 and 88.2 commanded by Troubridge and Rear Admiral Durgin, USN, respectively. Three of the 'Assault' and the two 'Fighter' carriers formed TF88.1, and

between them possessed fifty Seafires LIII, four Seafires LIIC, twenty-three Hellcats I and fifty-two Wildcats V or VI. TF88.2 by contrast was an Anglo-American combination, since the 'Casablanca' class escort carriers TULAGI (Durgin's Command Ship) and KASAAN BAY were joined by HUNTER and STALKER.

The FAA carriers held thirty-five Seafires LIII and six each of LIIC or LRIIC variants. The Seafire LIII was fitted with folding wings and wing tips, and even more significantly it possessed a Merlin 55 engine that raised maximum speed by twenty mph overall, while climb rate was equally superior to the LIIC. On board the USN carriers were forty-eight F6F-5 and seven F6F-3N Hellcat variants. The pilots flying the former-named variant were trained in the 'spotting' and anti-submarine functions while the seven remaining Hellcats were night-fighters.

Four years previous, the Royal navy's carriers had sat off the Norwegian coastline in the face of superior German strength and tactics, and the attendant threat of suffering severe losses in warships and aircraft. Now, the skies over the French and Italian territories belonged to the Allied Air Forces, as the rapidly withering ranks of their Axis opponents were squeezed

HUNTER was one of the five escort carriers comprising Force V, whose Seafires provided direct cover for Operation 'Avalanche'. In this picture a Seafire Mk.IIc from either No.834 or 899 Sqdn. has the arrester-hook lowered but appears to be 'aborting' its landing attempt. The still wind conditions and slow maximum speed of the carriers were major factors in creating the high attrition rate borne by these fighters, especially when landing-on.

out of serious contention. The Fleet Air Arm had truly grown into a formidable technological body since the 'locust' days of 1940, with much owed to the aircraft designs emanating from the Grumman and Chance-Vought factories. However, the aircraft were only as effective as the pilots and crews who operated on them. The rapid expansion of the FAA from its immediate pre-War strength in personnel had not witnessed any diminution in operational ability, rather the opposite.

A prolonged ten-day spell of exercises was carried out off Malta by the full Task Force in order to iron out differences in operating and tactical procedures, before the Force sailed northward for the impending Invasion, arriving on 12 August just as the 12th USAAF was indulging its four-day 'softening up' of the German defences. This process culminated on 15 August with a combined attack by bombers and TF88's aircraft along with a Naval bombardment, that preceded the Franco-American landings on three beaches between Hyeres and St. Raphael and airborne thrusts further inland – what would become known as the 'Champagne Invasion' had begun.

'Dragoon's' launch signalled the start of nine days operations for TF88.1 and a further two days for TF88.2. Operations on the first day were commenced at 0600 hours,

with TF88.1's aircraft carrying out 'spotting' duties and dive-bombing shore defences, while CAP patrols were also flown from KHEDIVE, HUNTER and STALKER. Light winds dictated either the use of catapults or maximum deck-length for safe launch of the bomb-laden fighters that naturally increased the physical effort on the deck handlers, but no accidents were recorded. The German defensive system being almost non-existent, General Patch (C-in-C, 7th U.S. Army) was encouraged to push quickly inland, whereupon the full ground-support role of the Allied fighters was brought into play.

Sorties took the form of armed reconnaissance with P-47s joining the TF88 fighters in this duty. Bridges were a natural potential 'choke-point', as were railway stations, goods yards and even tunnels, while bombs and rocket projectiles equally hammered any recognised defensive position or road convoy. Landing accidents over the first four days were initially light although EMPEROR had her complement of Hellcats reduced by four on the 16th. However, a heavy sea swell developed towards the 19th that caused created serious landing problems and resultant crashes in particular for the Seafires operating off HUNTER and STALKER.

Two Hellcats from different Navies are depicted here. A fighter of No.800 Sqdn. embarked on EMPEROR is parked on the forward deck as a U.S. Navy Hellcat from either USS TULAGI or KASAAN BAY is launched. The incident occurred while all three CVEs were participating in Operation 'Dragoon', the Invasion of southern France in August 1944.

KHEDIVE is launching one of its Seafire Mk.LIIIs during Operation 'Dragoon' in August 1944. The 500 lb. bomb slung under the fuselage will be used to harass the German defenders resisting the Franco-American Invasion troops. This aircraft was assigned to No.899 Sqdn.

Three Wildcats Mk.VI are lined up on the flight deck of PURSUER during operation 'Dragoon'. The bomb trolleys bear 250 lb. weapons with which to attack the retreating German forces as they head northward into central France. The fighter at the rear already has its bombs in place.

A compact formation of Wildcats Mk.V is accompanied by a second formation of Hellcats on the right. The escort carrier is PURSUER identified by her hull number (73) and whose deck is lined with Wildcats Mk.V or VI. Two Sqdns., Nos.896 and 882, were embarked on board between November 1943 and April 1945.

The two sections of TF88 remained off the Invasion Zone until the 19th, when landing strips were established ashore, after which its carriers steamed westward just beyond Marseilles, from where attacks were launched upon the German forces retreating up the Rhone valley. The vastly superior range and ordnance-bearing capacity of the Hellcat over the Seafire was utilised when the USN Hellcats staged a strafing assault on Toulouse airfield 200 miles to the west, that destroyed several Do 217s on the ground and three Ju 52s in the air; elsewhere the USN Hellcats encountered and shot down six more *Luftwaffe* bombers. The latter incidents comprised the first aerial appearance of the *Luftwaffe* in any form since 'Dragoon' was initiated!

Nightfall on the 19th saw all of TF88.1 but KHEDIVE (who joined up with TF88.2) retiring from operations for twenty-four hours rest and recuperation. Meanwhile the reduced Force represented by TF88.2 made up for lack of numbers by an aggressive programme that included 'spotting' for a battleship/cruiser bombardment of several positions west of Toulon. The three FAA carriers mounted numerous armed reconnaissance sorties and CAP patrols that along with the USN Hellcats destroyed or immobilised goods trains, vehicles and barges in Toulon harbor, the Rhone delta and along the river's upper reaches. The USN Hellcats again extended their activities westward and severely disrupted several road convoys. However, the increased pace of operations did incur a price, with five Hellcats and two Seafires lost in action and a further two Seafires destroyed on landing.

KHEDIVE retired 'off station' on the 21st as the other TF88.1 carriers resumed their station. The six FAA carriers within the joint TF sub-Forces dispatched well over 100 Seafires, Wildcats and Hellcats on interdiction sorties up the Rhone Valley, and the result was another large batch of motorised transport and destruction of rail facilities, at the cost of four fighters, with three of the pilots recorded as surviving their aircraft's loss. The relentless pressure on German communications was kept up over the ensuing two days, during which a rare aerial victory was scored by two Hellcats on the 22nd; the victims were three Ju 52s whose pedestrian performance provided their crews with little or no chance of escaping unscathed. It was inevitable that the pace of operations would begin to tell on aircraft and personnel. Three Hellcats from EMPEROR were lost on the 23rd, one of which 'ditched' due to battle damage, a second taxied over the side, while the

third was abandoned in mid-air when one main wheel refused to deploy. (The heavier Grumman fighters were forced to use the accelerators for take-off in light wind conditions, whereas the Seafire was not similarly inhibited).

TF88.2 finally withdrew from the Operation on the evening of the 23rd to leave HUNTER and STALKER as the sole FAA representatives. The Seafires still operational (thirty-three out of forty-seven, with no replacements available) were accordingly limited to strafing sorties, although these had petered out by the 27th with the enemy retreating beyond effective range. In the meantime a combination of CAP patrols and 'spotting' for the warships bombarding shore positions was also indulged in. The cost to the FAA was a single STALKER fighter shot down along with its pilot. The two FAA carriers finally joined up with TF88.1 at Maddalena after departing the operational zone late on the 27th. Two days later 'Dragoon' was declared completed. Between them the Anglo-American carriers had lost twenty-one (FAA) and fourteen (USN) aircraft in direct combat with almost twice that combined figure 'written off' in deck landing or other operational incidents. On the 29th Rear Admiral Troubridge led his Escort Carrier Sqdn. from Sardinia to Alexandria for rest and replenishment, after which vessels and crews stood by for their next set of operations.

Run-Down in the Mediterranean

The Germans were still in possession of the Balkan countries bordering the Mediterranean at this stage of World War II, and the intention of the Allied leaders was two-fold. The first was to see the region, particularly Yugoslavia and Greece, liberated as quickly as possible. The second more political intention was to ensure as far as possible that any vacuum left by the Axis exclusion not be filled by pro-Communist forces, but rather by political structures acceptable to Churchill and Roosevelt.

The Aegean Sea was destined to become the focus of attention for four of the escort carriers involved in 'Dragoon' – HUNTER, KHEDIVE, PURSUER and SEARCHER. The first-named pair possessed forty Seafires LIII and LRIIC in all, while forty Wildcats V and VI were shared between the other two carriers. Commencing 9 September the Force steamed north west towards the outer ring of islands that barred passage to the Aegean Sea, with Crete and Rhodes the two premier targets in mind, especially since both possessed several airfields worthy of neutralisation. While mine-sweepers cleared

a path towards the island of Kithira in preparation for its occupation, and a destroyer force led by the cruiser ROYALIST struck at shipping to the north of Crete, the Seafires and Wildcats commenced operations on the 16th by making bombing sorties against shipping laying in the Island's harbors and inlets as well as striking at road transport.

Suda Bay took a particular pounding two days later when a group of Do 24 and Bv 222 seaplanes were strafed. Rhodes harbor was struck next day by over forty fighter-bombers, including ten Hellcats from EMPEROR that had just arrived 'on station'. Heavy damage was sustained by a number of vessels that included three depot ships and a transport. The loss of sea transportation with which to evacuate the Axis garrisons caused by these depredations, as well as those inflicted by the destroyer Force, led to the reverse situation experienced over Tunisia in 1943. Then, the enemy had attempted to fly in reinforcements to a desperate *Afrikakorps*. Now a similar attempt at evacuation of key personnel by Ju 52 was made, but the presence of Beaufighters and P-38s making night patrols under control from the Fighter Direction vessel ULSTER QUEEN ensured that this traffic was severely disrupted. These longer-ranged aircraft also strafed airfield around Athens, adding to the loss of Ju 52 strength.

Neutralisation of the outer Island ring by the wholesale destruction of Axis shipping and subsequent marooning of the garrisons was judged completed within a matter of days of Operation 'Outing' Part I being commenced, and the carriers withdrew to Alexandria for rest and replenishment. Then 'Outing' Part 2 was put in motion at the beginning of October. This time round the intention was to neutralise the Dodecanese and Cyclades Island Groups restricting the sea passage up into the main Aegean Sea. Prior to this, STALKER was first 'on station' with the twin intention of providing CAP patrols for the mine-sweeper force clearing the main Kinaros Channel between the Island Groups and mounting bombing sorties on enemy facilities in the Dodecanese Islands – the same Group whose defences on Kos and Leros had overwhelmed the British Landing Force back in late 1943, when proper air support was not forthcoming and proved a fatal omission to the chances of a successful Invasion.

On 29 September destroyers supported by BLACK PRINCE steamed up the Kinaros Channel in order to invest the Cyclades Islands and destroy any shipping in the area. Almost immediately, STALKER returned to Alexandria with the BLACK PRINCE, and the carriers ATTACKER, EMPEROR and HUNTER replaced them 'on station' along with the cruiser AURORA. Initial air patrols over Crete and Rhodes confirmed a total lack of military movements. The tiny island of Levitha stood astride the top end of the Kinaros Channel. The existence of a radio station on there led to an

Several of the escort carriers involved in Operation 'Dragoon' remained in the Mediterranean for operations against the Germans in the Aegean Sea region. KHEDIVE is easing its way in to the narrow confines of Malta's Grand Harbor, with two rows of Seafires Mk.III from No.899 Sqdn., whose code letters are barely discernable, even on the nearest fighter. The wing-fold bracing struts are neatly laid out on the wings.

armed party being landed on 5 October in order to close down this source of ready intelligence for the Germans regarding Royal Naval dispositions. Next day STALKER and BLACK PRINCE appeared and the overall Force commenced operations across the breadth and length of the upper Aegean Sea. There was a continued lack of resistance to the incursions, as the carrier aircraft struck at shipping as well as rail communications bordering Greece's eastern seaboard.

EMPEROR had not initially accompanied her sister-warships, since she was held back to monitor the situation on Crete. Towards mid-October, she was ordered to take the place of HUNTER and STALKER when the latter pair was dispatched back to Alexandria. (PURSUER and SEARCHER had already departed for the UK on 1 October and HUNTER would also leave the Mediterranean by the month-end along with KHEDIVE) However, STALKER was destined to remain and share the air support element for Operation 'Manna', the landings on the Greek mainland around Athens on the 15th, with ATTACKER and EMPEROR. It was at this time that a very rare encounter with the *Luftwaffe* took place between two

Seafires LIIC off STALKER and a Ju 88. Flak did knock down several aircraft during attacks on road and rail communications but all the pilots survived. By the 24th only ATTACKER was still on hand, but before being ordered back to Alexandria her aircraft supported landing forces taking over the islands of Lesbos and Tilos.

The ability of the Royal Navy to operate within the confined waters of the Aegean demonstrated just how the power of the *Luftwaffe* had been inhibited by this stage of World War II; three years previous it had been the Navy who had been on the back-foot when operating around Crete. On the tactical side, the overall performance of the Seafire during the Campaign proved to be good. Just five were lost in action while a mere three more were damaged. Even more encouraging was the relatively small number of deck-landing incidents, none of which resulted in the aircraft concerned being 'written off'. This positive trend that had begun during Operation 'Dragoon' was a far cry from the disasters off Salerno!

CHAPTER NINE

'Tirpitz' and the Capital Ship Threat

"On land I am a Hero, at sea I am a Coward." – Adolf Hitler.
This prophetic statement was indicative of Hitler's general attitude towards the conduct of warfare. The path to military victory as far as the Fuehrer was concerned lay firmly in conquering his adversaries' territory; this was a sound initiative when applied to the conquest of the landmass of continental Europe, but not in the case of the British Isles. On the other hand, the weakness of the island nation lay in the fact that its very existence not to say prosperity was dependent upon the import of goods. Should the shipping lanes in and out of Britain be strangled then a direct invasion would not be necessary to achieve Hitler's vaunting ambition to totally dominate Europe. Britain's military and therefore its political resistance would wither away in the process.

This grim scenario for the people of the sole entity opposing the Nazis burgeoning power – at least between June 1940 and Operation BARBAROSSA on 22 June 1941 – was grimly faced up to during that year, and indeed for the ensuing two years following the Invasion of Russia. Over this extended period, Britain's Atlantic lifeline was under mortal threat, thanks chiefly to the depredations wrought upon the convoy routes by Admiral Dönitz's U-Boat fleet.

To this basic threat to Britain's very existence was added the danger from Germany's fleet of surface raiders. The 'pocket battleships' DEUTSCHLAND and GRAF SPEE had begun this secondary, but no less deadly, line of assault during 1939-1940. ADMIRAL SCHEER had sunk seventeen freighters in a five-month cruise ending on 1 April 1941 and spanning the Arctic to the Indian Oceans. The heavy battleships SCHARNHORST and GNEISENAU had additionally interdicted the north Atlantic routes during the same overall period, with a major two-month campaign ending during March 1941 that netted twenty-one freighters. Surface raiding,

although recording but a fraction of the successes being achieved by the U-Boats, had added to this attrition rate.

By early 1942 the latter two named warships had affected a daring and (for the Royal Navy) humiliating passage of the English Channel back to Germany. They were accompanied by PRINZ EUGEN that had been stranded in Brest since May 1941 after breaking away from BISMARCK in the course of what was to have been the latest surface assault on the convoy routes, but had resulted in the loss of what was then Germany's pride and joy in capital ship efficiency.

The Admiralty's attitude towards the enemy's surface raiders was naturally cautious in that their very existence demanded a viable Force of contemporary warships with which to challenge any movement into the Atlantic. The BISMARCK incident had exposed this cautionary attitude in that no less than five battleships, two carriers and a strong cruiser and escort force had been directed against the duo of *Kriegsmarine* vessels. The natural outcome from this stance was that the Royal Navy then had to assign a sizeable Force to permanent stationing in Home Waters in order to pin down their adversaries – even if the latter never moved from their moorings!

One battleship in particular was destined to highlight this logistical dilemma for the Admiralty. The TIRPITZ had been launched weeks after the BISMARCK in 1939 (ironically on 1 April) and was finally commissioned on 25 January 1941. Her gross tonnage figure of 52,600 tons was marginally greater than BISMARCK while her main armament of eight fifteen-inch guns was the same, and the largest in World War II *Kriegsmarine* service. Supplementary armament consisted of twelve 5.9-inch main and sixteen 4.1-inch secondary armament weapons, along with a veritable host of sixteen 4.1-inch, sixteen 37mm and seventy 20mm AA guns. Her hull was

An Albacore Mk.I of No.817 Sqdn. is photographed flying along an inhospitable coastline, probably that of Iceland. The Sqdn. was embarked along with No.832 Sqdn.'s Albacores on VICTORIOUS during 1941-1942. During this time both units participated on a failed strike against the battleship TIRPITZ.

encompassed by an armor belt 12 1/2-inch thick that would resist the explosive effect of even the most powerful torpedo, although the need to leave the propellers and their shafts unprotected constituted the same technical 'Achilles Heel' that had spelled the initial doom of BISMARCK.

A future intention by the Germans following the 'Channel Dash' was to sortie all four major warships into the Atlantic. However, damage caused by British sea-mines and collision had rendered the participation of SCHARNHORST and GNEISENAU out of the question for the time being. TIRPITZ had already departed northwards for Trondheim in mid-January, but only PRINZ EUGEN and ADMIRAL SCHEER were on hand to link up with her during February. This Force was a sizeable enough threat especially to the continuing PQ/QP Russian convoy system, but the torpedoing of PRINZ EUGEN on arrival, which had inflicted material damage requiring many months of attention, had diminished its ranks.

First Strike Failure

The carrier VICTORIOUS was still an element of the Home Fleet based in Scapa Flow, whose two squadrons of Albacore torpedo-bombers were keen to continue proving their value as anti-shipping aircraft. Convoy PQ12 was heading for Russia when on 5 March 1942 a U-Boat sighted it, and Hitler's permission was granted for TIRPITZ to make an interception. The British in turn were aware through interception of German radio traffic of the warship's departure and plans were put in place for the Home Fleet to carry out an interception. Between the 5th and 99h the two Forces traversed the northern waters;

the enemy warships sailed perilously close to the convoy but fortunately did not make contact after deciding to head back to port, while Admiral Tovey's calculations as to his adversary's disposition particularly on the 8th proved to be almost lethally (for PQ12) inaccurate, as his Force was too far south of the convoy to provide direct assistance should TIRPITZ have effected contact with its prey!

Poor weather conditions had not assisted the Royal Navy by restricting air-search operations until dawn on the 9th. Then six Albacores, launched in the face of low cloud and icing even at sea level, were dispatched to carry out a 'fan pattern' of individual searches. Three of the biplane crews picked up the enemy force steaming towards the central Norwegian coast and the port of Trondheim, and confirmed its location for the main attack formation split between Nos.817 and 832 Sqdns. and launched fifty minutes after the 'shadowers' had departed. – the 'hounds' had cleared the path for the 'hunters'.

The presence of the FAA reconnaissance aircraft was equally known to the German sailors, who then had adequate warning of an impending attack. The task for the torpedo-bearing Albacores was compounded by the weather and their aircraft's restricted performance especially as regards speed. The warships were first sighted at around 16 miles by Lt-Cdr. Lucas, the formation CO. However, the combination of the warships' forward speed and the wind velocity at the formation's height, when measured against the aircraft speed left no more than a thirty mph advantage! The protective cloud cover within which the Albacores were flying certainly posed an increasing risk of icing-up the longer they remained therein.

Albacore 5C of No.817 Sqdn. trails its deceptively frail-looking arrester-hook in search of a wire as it settles down on the flight deck. The Albacore's combat debut in 1940 came at a time when the biplane and fixed landing gear design was already dangerously out of date, given the quality of Axis high-performance fighters such as the Bf 109.

Physical exercise was never a great priority for Naval ratings, so it can be assumed this party assembled on a Fleet carrier's flight deck (especially the sailor in the center foreground) are nothing like as enthusiastic about the 'activity' as the PT Instructor in the left background! A single Albacore is being attended to as the carrier lies at anchor. The bleak tree-less scenery suggests picture taken at Scapa Flow.

VICTORIOUS is seen lying at anchor in Seydisfjord, Iceland, during the autumn (Fall) of 1941. On her after deck are parked the Albacores of No.832 Sqdn. along with a solitary Fulmar Mk.I from No.809 Sqdn. The latter unit had participated in the disastrous raid on Kirkenes on 30 July 1941 when it lost two of its number out of the nine dispatched; eleven of the twenty attacking Albacores were also lost.

An Albacore of No.832 Sqdn. is ranged on the flight deck of VICTORIOUS. The folded starboard wing bears the 'ashcan' shape of a depth charge. Also visible are the under-wing racks that can be used for small bombs or flares. Two Fulmars are spotted behind the Albacore. A KGV Class battleship steams in the background.

Also, before the final order to attack was given, the formation Leader had cleared each sub-flight to act independently – an action that split the resultant attack pattern into three separate elements, and arguably reduced the chances of scoring hits compared to a single mass torpedo-drop. In the event, any real prospect for success surely vanished when the attack order was given; upon clearing the cloud cover and dropping to attack height the FAA crews found themselves level with their target instead of ahead.

TIRPITZ and her destroyer escort immediately began to take an evasive course that over the ensuing ten minutes described a huge 'Z' arc. One sub-flight of three Albacores did manage to cross over from starboard to port of the warships' track before delivering their torpedoes, while a similar-strength flight, having approached from the port side was the first to discharge its 'tinfish'. The remaining six Albacores had held course on the starboard quarter and struggled on for several minutes in a bid to gain a proper beam torpedo run. Their effort was unconsciously aided by the warships' steering to port and then two to three minutes later altering course back to starboard, a manoeuvre that seemingly fell right into the airmen's trap.

In the event, only four of the six torpedoes were recorded as running, but no hits were recorded. Camera evidence of the drop carried out by the Albacore so equipped further suggested its pilot at least had miscalculated the desired distance for proper release; on the other hand, the Germans recorded some drops being made at least well within range, while one weapon narrowly missed the battleship's stern. Two of the Albacores were brought down during the frenetic but relatively brief action, and the desperately disappointed surviving crews headed back to their carrier.

What was to prove the sole opportunity to bring TIRPITZ to bay through aerial assault upon the open seas had gone. What would remain unbeknown to the Admiralty until after the War was the psychological effect that the attack had established, not upon the *Kriegsmarine* High Command but rather upon their *Führer* (Known as '*Grosfaz*', among the German military, being an abbreviation of the German for 'Greatest Fieldmarshal ever' – always expressed behind Hitler's back of course!). From this stage onwards the Nazi Leader decreed that the capital ships – at least those in the battleship category – were not to commence any sortie should the presence of an enemy aircraft carrier even be suspected, let alone confirmed!

During the remainder of 1942 and through 1943 *Kriegsmarine* plans for future incursions into the Atlantic using the several capital ships gathered in northwest Germany were beset by a combination of technical and military stumbling blocks. The RAF initiated the first of several counter-strikes during late February when Bomber Command raided Kiel. Bomb hits destroyed the entire bow section on GNEISENAU,

An Albacore formation from what is believed to be No.817 Sqdn. is seen bearing a mixture of eighteen inch torpedoes, and in two cases (including aircraft 5A), what look like practice torpedoes. The Type C1 markings indicate picture taken from mid-1942 onwards. The Sqdn. served on the Fleet carriers VICTORIOUS, INDOMITABLE and FURIOUS between 1941 and 1945, as well as in the European and Far East operational Theaters.

and following repairs to make her seaworthy, the warship was towed eastwards to Gydnia in Poland where she was fated to wither away.

During the early summer TIRPITZ and LÜTZOW along with the heavy cruiser HIPPER were ordered to intercept convoy PQ17. Despite the LÜTZOW running aground prior to departure, and the other two warships being ordered to turn back after being detected, the mere fact of their sailing had (wrongly) induced Admiral Pound in London to order the 'scattering' of the convoy to avoid its destruction – an act that tragically still bore fruit when U-Boats and aircraft achieved the same result.

In December 1942 TIRPITZ's 'partners' for the PQ17 Operation were dispatched against the latest Russian convoy but were thwarted in their intentions by part of JW-51B's escort force. The year 1943 witnessed no great advance in German capital ship operations, but did record one massive disaster on Boxing Day when SCHARNHORST's career was brought to a halt by the guns and torpedoes of the Home Fleet; the warship was literally blown to pieces and just thirty-six of her crew of 1754 survived the icy waters of the Barents Sea.

The experiences of TIRPITZ and crew during these two years varied from the boring normalcy of being moored up in various Norwegian fjords to intermittent sorties up into the Arctic; these activities were interspersed with several RAF and Royal Navy operations that resulted in varying degrees of failure and success. The first of these operations involved RAF

Bomber Command, who dispatched Halifaxes and Lancasters on two successive April nights in 1942; a combination of efficient smoke floats and the high-sided fjord led to no hits at the cost of five bombers. The 'abortive' run by TIRPITZ against PQ17 was followed in August by a sortie to bombard Russian locations in the Kara Sea.

1943 Actions

The next attempt to cripple or sink TIRPITZ occurred during October, but proved to be a total failure. Two 'chariots', two-man human torpedoes, were towed by a fishing boat across the North Sea and into the Trondheim fjord; at this stage bad weather caused the moorings to snap and both 'chariots' were lost. During the ensuing winter SCHARNHORST joined up with TIRPITZ but the sole action involving both warships did not occur until the following September when a bombardment of Spitzbergen Island was carried out. Up to now, the TIRPITZ and her crew had remained free of serious danger but this positive if unexciting existence was to alter drastically a mere two weeks following the Spitzbergen 'run'.

The Royal Navy had been developing a more sophisticated variant of the 'Chariot' human torpedo known as the X-Craft. This was a midget submarine manned by four men. Six of these warships were towed individually by full-sized submarines but only four survived the crossing that culminated on the small force penetrating through to Altenfjord on the 22nd. TIRPITZ having been moved out of her normal well-

The particularly bleak landscape of the Orkney Islands is the backcloth for this picture of two Albacores of No.817 Sqdn.; the unit was disembarked from VICTORIOUS while the Fleet carrier was undergoing repair around mid-1942. The picture angle captures the noticeable wing dihedral of the Albacore.

An Albacore from No.817 Sqdn. trundles down the flight deck of VICTORIOUS following a landing. The aircraft is passing over the safety barrier that will be immediately raised once the aircraft is past; this is because the DLCO in the background is already indicating the approach angle of a succeeding aircraft.

protected mooring and anchored further down in the open fjord waters had unknowingly heightened the chances for a positive result.

Although the Germans were to be alerted to the presence of the attacking vessels a full hour before the charges were set to go off, the time-lapse proved far too short for effective counter-measures to be taken and TIRPITZ shuddered violently under the concussion of two close-spaced explosions. The rudder, propellers and the hull suffered major damage while one main gun turret was lifted off its mountings. At long last the Royal Navy had inflicted a major blow to Germany's largest surviving battleship; many months would elapse before she was restored to a perceived state of operational efficiency – only for the Fleet Air Arm to flex its 'muscle' and deal out another bout of punishment!

1944: Operation 'Tungsten'

The continuing presence of TIRPITZ in northern waters and the threat this warship above all other *Kriegsmarine* capital units was perceived to hold, particularly in respect of the Russian convoy routes, in turn forced the retention in Home waters of an inordinate number of Royal Navy vessels in order to fully contain her movements. By March 1944 plans were

being formulated for an air strike to be initiated by the Fleet Air Arm. It was just over two years since the sadly 'abortive' attack by the VICTORIOUS-based Albacores, and the force now being assembled to make this latest sortie displayed just how vast the gap was between the numbers and quality of the aircraft operated in 1942 as compared to this stage of World War II.

On hand were two Torpedo-Bomber-Reconnaissance (TBR) Wings, comprising thirty-nine aircraft in all and operating on the Barracuda II. The Albacores had made their attack un-escorted, whereas the Barracuda crews were to be almost overwhelmed by the escort provision on hand – twenty-eight Corsairs of No.47 Naval Fighter Wing, twenty Hellcats and forty Wildcats Mk.V and eight Wildcats Mk. IV. In addition fourteen Seafires were available for CAP purposes along with twelve Swordfish for anti-submarine duties. Of course the huge increase in aircraft strength would not have counted had it not been for the parallel introduction of increasing number of escort carriers, especially during the previous year, with which to supplement the main Fleet carrier strength. No less than two Fleet and four escort carriers would be involved in the operation. One carrier in the former category was VICTORIOUS that had been involved in the March 1942

attack; here was the opportunity for the ship's crew, if not the original Albacore Sqdns involved, to gain a measure of revenge.

The Barracuda – A Royal Navy 'Folly?'

The main attack aircraft for this and subsequent 'TIRPITZ' assaults had in effect been custom-built for the FAA – that is, the design was laid out on the principle that the Observer was the key member of what was to be the latest and up-to-date

Opposite
Top: An Albacore has been flipped over onto its back on board VICTORIOUS, and is under casual inspection by several groups of the carrier's crew. There is no obvious reason for the incident to have occurred although the folded wings suggest the aircraft was not flying at the time! Two more fortunate fellow-biplanes are spotted on the rear flight deck.

Bottom: The landing gear on 4Q from No.832 Sqdn. has totally failed to survive a heavy landing on VICTORIOUS and the aircraft is almost certainly a candidate for being 'written off'. No.832 Sqdn.'s period of Albacore operations from April 1941 to December 1942 was spent entirely on this Fleet carrier, and the Fairey biplanes were finally displaced by Avengers in January 1943.

Below: A group of aircrew sporting a variety of footwear walk past Corsairs Mk.II on board VICTORIOUS following the first strike against TIRPITZ lurking in Kaa Fjord, Norway on 3 April 1944. The Corsairs that belong to either No.1834 or 1835 Sqdn. were part of the action to judge by the absence of the gun muzzle patches, intended to prevent dirt or the frigid Arctic air from entering and fouling up the precise machine gun mechanism.

Torpedo-Bomber-Reconnaissance (TBR) machine for the Navy. The high wing profile was intended to permit the fitting of large Plexiglas panels mounted in the central fuselage for the Observer. However, this meant that all ordnance had to be externally mounted. In addition, the aerodynamic quality of the tail-plane, which tended to be blanked off by the main-plane, especially when dive-brakes were deployed, was destined to be regarded as the most probable cause for a sizeable number of crashes. (Tests with the Barracuda at Farnborough had thrown up an alarming tendency for the rudder to overbalance and cast the aircraft nose downward. When the test procedure was further expanded by diving the aircraft and levelling out before kicking the rudder and retracting the dive-brakes, the instant result was an inverted spin. The test was naturally made at altitude, but since the overall manoeuvre was the recommended one for successfully delivering a torpedo and evading the flak, the chances of survival at sea level appeared to be between minimal and nil).

Other problems related to manually folded wings; this in turn, led to the fitting of retractable 'V-Pattern' loops under the wing tips so that the deck crew, who were away below the height of the wing surfaces, could reach up to engage the loops with poles in order to carry out the folding and un-folding actions! Tail-plane support struts, wing 'fences', bulged

Observer's panels and (in the case of the Mk.II onwards) ASV aerials, all tended to further inhibit the design's overall flying performance to some degree, as did the externally mounted bombs or torpedoes. The massive landing gear frames and detached landing flap arrangement also gave the Barracuda a most un-aerodynamic appearance when landing or taking off. (One observer referred to a 'Barra' on landing approach as presenting an outline not unlike a section of the Forth Railway Bridge, a famous structure near Edinburgh, Scotland!). Marcel Loebelle who had previously designed the Swordfish, Albacore and Fulmar – all aircraft with a sound aerodynamic appearance, regardless of their general performance – must have had some reservations regarding the prospects of operational success for his latest 'creation'.

Run-Up to 'Tungsten'

A loch inlet in Caithness (the author's home county) whose geographic layout bore an uncanny resemblance to TIRPITZ's Kaa Fjord mooring formed a 'dummy' range upon which the TBR crews on FURIOUS (No.8 Wing) and VICTORIOUS (No.52 Wing) practiced. This was a particularly valuable requirement for the inexperienced crews embarked on VICTORIOUS. Following a final practice session off Scapa Flow on 28 March the stage was set for 'Tungsten' to proceed.

Convoy JW58 had just set out for Russia and the main Home Fleet commanded by Admiral Sir Bruce Fraser and including VICTORIOUS along with two KGV-Class

A Barracuda Mk.II receives its 'payload' consisting of a 1,600 lb. armor-piercing bomb, which was the largest weapon in the Fleet Air Arm's inventory at the time of the TIRPITZ assaults. The large bulged windows provided an good scanning platform for the Observer, but meant that the 'Barra' had to carry its ordnance externally, so creating an extra drag in flight.

battleships set out on 30 March. Force 1's primary duty was to cover the convoy against any enemy warship sortie, but the secondary albeit important function this time round was to head for the aircraft launch-point northwest of Kaafjord. There it would link up with Force 2 containing FURIOUS and the escort carriers EMPEROR, SEARCHER, PURSUER and FENCER.

Another positive comparison between the March 1942 sortie and this assault lay in the quality of the weather. Then,

An 882 Sqdn. pilot clambers out of his Wildcat Mk.V cockpit and the deck handlers keenly await his account of the sortie, which was part of Operation 'Tungsten', the initial attack on TIRPITZ. The fighter was based on the CVE SEARCHER, which along with PURSUER, dispatched Wildcats to act in a joint escort and flak-suppression role.

A Barracuda Mk.II is seen in what seems an over-shoot judging by its height and distance along the carrier deck length. Another 'Barra' is also making a landing approach. The Fairey TBR design had a very chequered operational history but it was the primary assault weapon when conducting the series of FAA assaults on TIRPITZ between April and August 1944.

the unfortunate Albacores crews had to fight their way through low cloud and strong wing conditions. On the morning of 3 April, as the six carriers steamed along at the rendezvous point, a flat calm and bright sunshine greeted the aviators and deck handlers as the aircraft were ranged and prepared for launch, while similar clear weather conditions existed over the target area.

The FAA airmen were under no illusion as to the scale of the task facing them however. Their target was moored in a geographically awkward location, while a sizeable number of AA batteries, both on the warship and ashore and backed by smoke floats, presented a serious barrier. The *Luftwaffe* was also based in the immediate area but the influence of any of their fighters making a challenge was expected to be nullified by the Corsairs in particular; the Hellcats and Wildcats were assigned to strafing the enemy defensive positions during the two-pronged assault. Both attack waves were composed of Barracudas supported by forty-five fighters with an hour's separation between the waves.

Preparations

The exposed carrier deck was no place upon which to park aircraft for any length of time, especially when given the corrosive effect of salt water and spray. This was particularly relevant when more than the normal complement of aircraft

was borne, as now in the case of VICTORIOUS whose maximum complement of thirty-six was increased to forty-nine. The ordnance to be used in the attack comprised four types of bombs, ranging from the 500 lb. MC (medium capacity) and SAP (semi-armor piercing) and the 600 lb. A/S (anti/submarine) to the 1,600 lb. armor-piercing weapon. (Use of the anti-submarine bombs was expected to create a 'mining' effect on the warship's hull plating should these land alongside). The armorers on VICTORIOUS at least were reputedly hard-pressed to locate the appropriate aircraft on which to mount the assigned bomb-type or types, although only the Barracudas were detailed for this function. As it was the overall task was satisfactorily completed just hours before launch!

The Attack Goes In

At 0416 hours with VICTORIOUS and FURIOUS having turned into wind and increased speed, the ten Corsairs of No.1834 Sqdn. were launched, after which the Barracuda force (No.8 TBR Wing, comprised twenty-one aircraft split between Nos.827 based on VICTORIOUS and 830 operating off FURIOUS) departed from the two carrier decks along with the remaining fighters dispatched by the escort carriers. The sixty-one aircraft quickly formed up at low level and headed in towards the Norwegian coast. Then, as the coastline was

This Barracuda of No.827 or 829 Sqdn. embarked on VICTORIOUS has run into the safety barrier, and the steel wires have excised the entire radiator housing under the nose. Foam is liberally spread on the deck following its use to extinguish an engine fire. The aircraft was damaged by flak during Operation 'Tungsten' but the crew were more fortunate than two of their contemporaries who were shot down or posted 'Missing in Action' (MIA).

This Corsair Mk.II pilot, believed to be with No.1842 Sqdn. based on FORMIDABLE, begins the process of folding his fighter's wings following a safe recovery. The degree of damage to the starboard horizontal stabiliser and elevator was reportedly caused by flak during Operation 'Tungsten'.

Three 1,600 lb. armor-piercing bombs are trundled past a Corsair Mk.II of No.1841 Sqdn. on board FORMIDABLE, for loading under several of the Barracuda strike force. The occasion was either Operation 'Mascot' (17 July) or one of the series of August sorties launched under Operation 'Goodwood' against TIRPITZ. Unfortunately just one solid strike by this weapon-type (the heaviest used by the FAA against the German battleship) would be secured throughout the entire period of assault – and the bomb in question did not explode!

The same Corsair of No.1841 Sqdn. seen in the previous picture is commencing its take-off run from FORMIDABLE's flight deck. The propeller blades are creating vortices that normally appear in humid conditions. This atmospheric phenomenon was a feature on the Corsair.

almost in sight, the Barracudas rose to their attack altitude (10,000 ft.) and closed the approximately fifty mile stretch overland from the coast to the target before banking to port and beginning their final approach.

The other aircraft disposed themselves accordingly – the Corsairs angled out in a huge right-hand circuit over Kaa Fjord with the intention of heading off any fighters approaching from Bardufoss airfield, none of which did appear, while the contingent out of the twenty Hellcats of Nos.800 and 804 Sqdns. based on EMPEROR, the twenty Wildcats Mk.V from Nos.881 and 896 Sqdns. (SEARCHER) and a further twenty from Nos.882 and 898 Sqdns. (PURSUER) assigned to the first attack wave headed directly towards the TIRPITZ to begin their strafing passes.

As in the case of the X-Craft assault, the German battleship was again placed in a position of heightened vulnerability. This was due to the fact that she was being readied for the second bout of sea trials, in extended form this time round. Tugs were fussing around her and the main anchors were being weighed as the first alarm signal was sounded. Desperate efforts were made to close-up the warship and fully man the flak guns, but these vital defensive measures were still far from completed when the Barracudas swung over into their attack dives.

Lt-Cdr Baker-Faulkner as the Strike Leader witnessed the Hellcats and Wildcats making strafing runs on both the TIRPITZ's and shore-based flak positions as the Barracuda pilots maintained either a clear or marginally obscured sight of their target, thanks to the belated deployment of the smoke screen generators. Almost immediately, the warship began to take hits that knocked out communications and flak fire control equipment, the latter blow leaving the German gunners' blind' in terms of directed fire as well as decidedly vulnerable to injury or death from both bullets and bomb blast.

At least ten hits, including three 1,600 lb. Armor-piercing weapons (out of fourteen listed by the Germans arising out of the overall assault) were claimed during the scant sixty seconds that it took the attackers to deliver their loads. As the formation reassembled it was just one aircraft short, the unlucky exception being a No.830 Sqdn. machine last seen after the attack in an un-powered gliding angle. The escorts suffered no combat losses but one Hellcat was 'ditched' alongside a destroyer as the other aircraft circled to land.

The second wave of attackers led by Lt-Cdr Rance was launched around the time of the first assault. However, No.52 TBR Wing comprised of twelve No.829 Sqdn. and nine No.831 Sqdn. machines departed from the rally point short of two

A Barracuda has come to a halt on the deck of FURIOUS, whose miniscule superstructure was a distinctive recognition feature. Note the rear edge of the ramp that was fitted to the veteran carrier during the latter stages of her extended operational career. FURIOUS participated in all the TIRPITZ strikes.

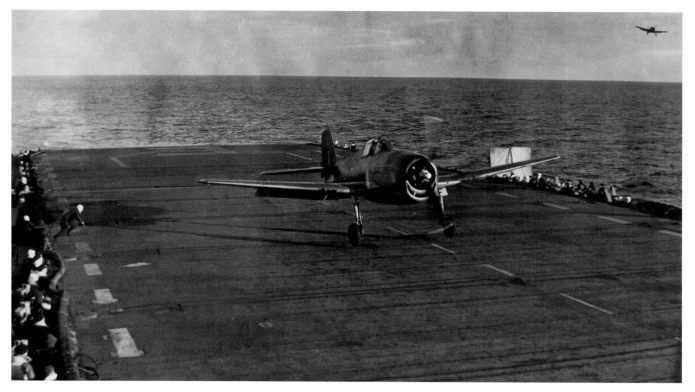

One of EMPEROR's Hellcats has returned from the initial strike on TIRPITZ. The aircraft is still in a tail-up attitude and does not appear to have yet caught a wire with its hook. However, the deck handler leaping out of the catwalk would be unlikely to do so unless its forward motion had been halted!

Barracudas, one of which was lost on launch along with its crew; one Hellcat also 'aborted' due to mechanical problems. In close support were ten Corsairs Mk.II of No.1836 Sqdn., while nineteen Wildcats Mk.V of Nos.896 (PURSUER) and 898 Sqdn. (SEARCHER) along with the nine remaining Hellcats Mk.II of No.804 Sqdn. (EMPEROR).

The element of surprise was totally gone this time round with the smoke screen clearly visible from many miles away. TIRPITZ was being manoeuvered back into her berth as the attack developed and was completed in same time-scale as its predecessor. Although the smoke was undoubtedly interfering with the flak gunners' sighting, they managed to throw up a disconcerting degree of fire that set a Barracuda from No.829 Sqdn. on fire, after which the aircraft crashed. The final sight of the battleship was of flames billowing up from a large fire amidships, believed to be the result of one of the seven strikes claimed this time round. A total of 428 sailors had been killed or injured and although the warship's deck surface had not been penetrated even by the 1,600 lb. armor-piercing bombs, the scale of damage was to prove sufficient to render her operationally redundant for several more months.

The Hellcat – A More Violent Feline

The introduction of the Grumman Wildcat or Martlet into FAA service in late 1940 had pointed the way forward for the Royal Navy's aviators in their bid to overcome the manifold technological and operational deficiencies that afflicted so many of the aircraft designs at their disposal. The Wildcat had been specifically designed with carriers operations in mind. By 1942-1943 however this trusty little fighter's limitations against the principal Axis fighters then in use was beginning to show. Fortunately, the Grumman designers had anticipated this possibility and by mid-1943 had developed and produced what was the Wildcat's replacement – the Hellcat.

The U.S. Navy's combat experience against the Japanese had been utilised in order to produce the Hellcat, and this range of practical input from the Wildcat pilots would certainly pay off following the new fighter's introduction into combat in the early autumn of 1943. Strangely enough, it was the FAA who was first to take on the Hellcat, when No.800 Sqdn. bade farewell to their Sea Hurricanes in July and made the necessary conversion; in December the unit embarked on the CVE EMPEROR.

Power was provided by the 2,000 hp R-1800-10 Double Wasp radial with eighteen cylinders so it is not surprising that, compared to the Wildcat's 1,200 hp output from the fourteen cylinder R-1830-86 Twin Wasp, the speed factor for its successor was increased by fifty mph from sea level upwards. The climb rate revealed an increase of around 25%, and the maximum range figure was increased by a similar margin. On the other hand the Hellcat's service ceiling was only marginally better.

All these advances in performance were achieved in spite of the Hellcat's much heavier weight compared to the Wildcat. The same combat technique as used by the Wildcat pilots especially against the 'Zero' meant that tight turns were avoided; instead the Hellcats out-did their opponents by using 'dive and zoom' manoeuvres, depending upon the striking power of the six .50 machine guns to literally tear the lightly constructed Japanese fighters apart.

A revised wing position lower down the fuselage permitted the mounting of the landing gear within the wings. This change provided a much wider track than the fuselage-location on the Wildcat. In an unusual move, the landing gear bays were aligned fore-and-aft, with the gear struts retracting back and turning through ninety degrees in order to lie flush with the wing interior. The cockpit interior was enlarged and the view from there with its more open-framed windshield and canopy was judged to be better.

The superiority of the Hellcat over the Seafire as a carrier-friendly aircraft during its World War II service with the FAA was to be amply demonstrated following its first sea-borne experience with No.800 Sqdn. on board the CVE EMPEROR. Between then and VJ-Day the Hellcat would be assigned to fourteen Sqdns., three-quarters of whose sea service would be spent on the greatly confined deck lengths of CVEs as opposed to the more generous Fleet carrier equivalent. The Grumman

These two Barracudas embarked on FURIOUS participated in the 3 April 1944 strike on TIRPITZ. Both machines bear the code letters for No.830 Sqdn. The wing radar aerials and the 'V' frames at the wing-tips for folding and unfolding the wings are points of note. One of the three escort carriers taking part in the Operation steams a parallel course in the background.

fighter was to take everything in its stride and come away with a non-combat attrition rate, especially in the deck-landing category, markedly down on that 'enjoyed' by its structurally frail British contemporary.

Operation 'Mascot'

The TIRPITZ saga was rolling almost inexorably towards its violent conclusion, but this desired scenario was still months distant. In the meantime the FAA aircrew were to continue

'The Men behind the Men who made the News'. This expression aptly sums up the situation for the mechanics who serviced the FAA aircraft or operated in the deck handling role. This group are probably involved with the Barracudas that one seaman has used as a photographic 'perch'. The massive bulk of the 'Barra's' wing is seen to good effect.

This Corsair Mk.II has already assumed a tail-up configuration within what is a short take-off on a CVE's wooden deck. Note the 'clipped' wing tips involving the removal of an eight-inch section; this was carried out in order to fit the design into Royal Navy carrier hangars.

The cloud layer through which the blinding sunshine is spurting over the waters off Norway is in contrast to the grim task at hand. A Hellcat is in the landing circuit with its arrester-hook deployed and a second Hellcat has just landed and is taxiing forward. Both have just participated in one of the TIRPITZ strikes. A 'County' Class cruiser is outlined on the horizon.

This Corsair had wiped out its landing gear and displays the blackened effect of a fire, probably caused by its ruptured auxiliary tank. The fact that the lift shaft is open suggests the fighter originally over-turned; the hawsers attached to the airframe would then be used to pull their load up and over using the lift space for the purpose of dropping the aircraft's nose into the gap.

At first sight this picture is recording the recovery of a damaged Barracuda on board one of the three Fleet carriers involved in the series of TIRPITZ strikes between April and August 1944. In fact the aircraft has been deemed too badly damaged to be repaired and is being lowered over the side into the sea.

with the efforts, although the next raid was only launched on 17 July, two previous sorties during May having been postponed thanks to adverse weather conditions. This time round, no escort carriers were involved in Operation 'Mascot'; instead the fleet carriers FORMIDABLE, and INDEFATIGABLE supported by the veteran FURIOUS were assigned the task.

Once again the Barracuda was the core of the direct assault effort, with Nos.820 and 826 forming No.9 TBR Wing and flying off INDEFATIGABLE; the other two 'Barra' Sqdns. comprising No.8 TBR Wing were Nos.827 and 829 both of whom had participated in the April raid and were now stationed on FORMIDABLE, as were the eighteen Corsairs of No.1841 Sqdn. FURIOUS possessed twenty Corsairs Mk. II from No.1840 Sqdn. as well as three Seafires Mk. LIIC and three Swordfish from Nos.880 and 842 Sqdns. respectively. A further twelve Seafires Mk. FIII of No.894 Sqdns. for CAP duties were embarked on INDEFATIGABLE as well as No.1779 Sqdn.'s twelve Fireflies Mk.I making the Fairey design's operational debut in a fighter-bomber role.

Although the attack force was marginally larger than on the preceding occasion, the overall provision of fighters or support aircraft seemed well down – forty-eight compared to eighty-eight – but this comparison was to prove deceptive since just a single thrust out of the two planned would be delivered on this occasion compared to April's double-strike.

The overall force of forty-eight Barracudas was initially reduced to forty-five operationally prepared and loaded machines and this number was further reduced when one aircraft failed to get airborne during the launch sequence that commenced at 0040 hours. The entire Force was assembled and on its way in under an hour but the high expectations for a good strike on TIRPITZ were to be thwarted. The main problem arose out of the fact that the Germans had more than sufficient warning of the aircrafts' inward progress thanks to good radar surveillance, in order to 'close up' the warship and activate the smoke screens around Kaa Fjord.

Consequently, none of the Barracuda crews could gain even a basic sight of their primary target other than by the streams of tracer shells that were being fired equally blindly. The same visual disability faced the escort element assigned to strafing the target area. The majority of the Barracudas released their bombs into the smoke-shrouded fjord while the strafing fighters either fired blindly or took on a range of targets positioned clear of the smoke zone. As the Force withdrew (less one Hellcat of No.1841 Sqdn.) it was fired upon by flak batteries based on shore and on destroyers, but no further losses were sustained at this stage. However, two Barracudas were ' ditched' on return to the carriers.

Operation 'Goodwood'

Whereas the two previous FAA operations against TIRPITZ had involved a single day's action, the final bid to at least cripple the massive warship was to be mounted over eight days during which time four separate sorties would be launched. In addition the carriage of bombs would be extended to the Hellcat and Corsair Sqdns., both designs being capable of bearing up to two 1,000 lb. bombs on centerline racks. The largest available armor-piercing weapon in FAA service (1,600 lb.) was still allocated to the Barracuda Sqdns.

An added refinement to the 'Goodwood' action was the inclusion of Avengers from No.846 Sqdn. based on TRUMPETER and No.852 Sqdn. on NABOB. These aircraft would be used to lay sea mines at the neck of Kaa Fjord as

A Barracuda is at full throttle as it trundles down the flight deck of a Fleet carrier. It bears an unequal bomb load of two weapons under the starboard wing and a single example under the port wing. In the left background is the wing of a second 'Barra' whose pilot is being motioned forward by a deck handler.

A Barracuda Mk.II is canted up at a sharp angle on the very edge of an escort carrier's flight deck and with the engine still functioning seems in imminent danger of 'going over the side' in an inverted manner. Should that occur, the chances of the three-man crew escaping would be seriously if not fatally compromised.

The distinctive shape of FURIOUS with its extended lower flight deck and miniscule 'island' superstructure is seen here as she launches what appears to be an Albacore. Several Sqdns. operating this design were embarked on the carrier between July 1942 and July 1943. The veteran carrier was on regular World War II operations until September 1944 when she was withdrawn into reserve, and finally scrapped in 1948.

The extra dark sea grey and dark slate grey top camouflage on a Hellcat are clearly defined in this close-up aerial view. The fighter's undersides are finished in 'Sky S'. Full Type C1 markings along with Type B upper wing roundels are applied but missing codes indicate aircraft is still to be assigned to a Sqdn.

'One foot in the grave'. This is NABOB with her bows canted in the air as she staggers laboriously back to Scapa Flow. On 22 August 1944 she was torpedoed by U-354 and barely managed to remain afloat. In spite of the scale of damage she still managed to fly-off and recover several of the Avengers seen perched on her flight deck. The scale of damage was sufficient for her to be permanently withdrawn from service.

well as depositing the weapons around TIRPITZ – a very dangerous proposition in the case of the crews allotted to the latter duty, even with the presence of the anti-flak fighters. As it happened the low cloud conditions on 22 August prevented the Avengers use; then when NABOB was torpedoed the same day, TRUMPETER was part of the Force assigned to escort the seriously crippled carrier back to Scapa Flow.

As for the main force of FAA aircraft, the same weather conditions forced those Barracudas of Nos.820 Sqdn. (INDEFATIGABLE), 826 and 828 Sqdns. (FORMIDABLE) and No.827 Sqdn. (FURIOUS) assigned to the sortie to 'abort' along with their Corsair escort from Nos.1841 and 1842 Sqdns. (FORMIDABLE). The Fireflies of No.1770 Sqdn., the Hellcats from No.1840 Sqdn. accompanied by eight Seafires FIII of No.887 Sqdn. – all based on INDEFATIGABLE – managed to press on through the conditions. The Supermarine fighters attacked Banak airfield and a seaplane base, the Fireflies took on flak positions around the fjord and the nine Hellcats delivered their 500 lb. SAP bombs. That same evening, a small force of INDEFATIGABLE – based aircraft made a second run; seven Hellcats dropped 500 lb. SAPs None of the bombs were later confirmed as striking the battleship, however. The overall cost was a single Barracuda 'ditched', and one Hellcat and Seafire MIA. TIRPITZ was seemingly weathering the storm of FAA assault.

The extended presence of the Fleet off the Norwegian coast over the next seven days and the reverse threat of aerial counter-attacks was recognised by the scale of defensive aircraft, with no less than fifty-six Seafires embarked on the three Fleet carriers. Once again, the *Luftwaffe* failed to materialise, and their absence permitted elements of the Seafires to be assigned a more positive role as witnessed by No.887 Sqdn. on the 22nd. Two days later, all four Barracuda Sqdns. dispatched thirty-three aircraft between them, bearing 1,600 lb. APs. This time round, every one of the twenty-four Corsair escorts mounted 1,000 lb. APs while the ten Hellcats carried 500 lb. SAPs; the latter weapons were reportedly to be used to attack flak positions along with No.1770 Sqdn.'s Fireflies, while eight Seafires again headed for Banak airfield.

Although the initially poor weather conditions that had delayed an attack in the morning had given way to clear skies by the mid-afternoon launch, the steady approach pace of the Barracudas in particular permitted adequate time for a smoke-screen to form up and block off visibility over Kaa Fjord. The Barracudas dived to around 4,000 ft before releasing their bombs in to the solid pall of smoke, and the Corsair pilots added their weight to the direct assault.

Post-operation analysis suggested a single strike by a Hellcat while two of the APs were also adjudged to have found a mark. This was to prove positive as well as negative in one

NABOB was steaming back to Scapa Flow when she received her near-fatal torpedo strike. This photograph was taken from her fellow-escort carrier TRUMPETER whose forward flight deck supports two Avengers and a single Wildcat Mk.V of No.846 Sqdn.

of the latter cases. The 'positive' aspect came from the weapon in question having fulfilled its purpose of punching through five decks to lodge in the warship's innards. The 'negative' aspect of this strike lay in the fact that the bomb did not explode! (The German reaction to what had happened was initially sceptical but was later revised to acknowledge that very serious consequences would have arisen had the detonation taken place). The cost this time round was shared between the Corsairs (three) and Hellcats (two) MIA and a fourth Corsair 'ditched'.

So far TIRPITZ had been sorely battered but not materially affected by the series of FAA assaults, and this pattern of frustrated endeavour for the aircrews was to reach its culmination on the 29th. FURIOUS had by then been dispatched back to Scapa Flow but the two remaining Fleet carriers bore sufficient theoretical 'punch'. Once again the weather pattern on the 29th progressed from poor to good by the afternoon when the strike was launched. The target-approach was altered from a north westerly to a southwesterly angle. Twenty-six Barracudas bearing 1,600 lb. APs and just two Corsairs with 1,000 lb. APs were allotted to the main assault, while three Hellcats carried 500 lb. MCs. A total of twenty-five Corsairs and Fireflies flew along for flak-

The circumstances of this incident are not as critical for the crew of the up-ended Avenger seen here. Lt/Cdr Bradshaw (No.852 Sqdn. CO) had been on an anti-submarine patrol, having taken off from NABOB's angled-up deck. On return the aircraft was involved in a crash-landing but the crew emerged unscathed. This picture is taken after the aircraft was cast overboard.

Below: The raised windscreens on FURIOUS enclose a parked Seafire LIII whose inner wing surfaces are being used for the stowage of spare wheel-blocks. The rear section of the carrier's flight deck ramp, which had been added to improve take-off facilities can be seen on the left side of the picture.

The starboard wing cannon barrel covers, and the recoil spring unit on the inner mounted weapon have been detached by the servicing party working on a Firefly Mk.I. The nose-mounted radiator scoop and the clear-framed pilot's canopy cannot fully disguise the Fairey Company design's development from its Fulmar predecessor. Note the twin aerial masts located on the cowling and central fuselage; the latter unit is actually angled to the right.

A Corsair landing on FORMIDABLE has made a particularly poor job of the act and has slewed round as the pilot braces his arms against the windshield frame. The engine cowling has struck a solid object to judge by the large dent in the lower rim. Nos.1841 and 1842 Sqdn. were embarked on this Fleet carrier from June and August 1944 respectively; the single code letter was a feature on No.1842 Sqdn. Corsairs during the first months of operations up to March 1945, when numbers were substituted.

The veteran carrier ARGUS was utilised during World War II for deck-landing training. No.768 Sqdn. was equipped with a variety of aircraft types from 1941 when it was formed and given the codes M2. Here a Swordfish Mk.II photographed sometime after mid-1942 when the Type C1 national markings were introduced, has just caught an arrester-wire.

suppression duties. As in the case of 'Mascot' and the foregoing 'Goodwood' sorties, the force came in over its target that was smoke-shrouded, and although a further four Hellcats had been allotted a target-marking role, the fifty-two tons of bombs dropped achieved little or nothing by way of any, let alone lethal, damage. Two of the escort force was culled from the ranks of the attack force.

The Firefly – Catching up with Naval Aviation Progress

The presence of the two-seat Fairey Firefly on the final TIRPITZ Operation was in fact the debut for this design. Not only was it originally ordered by the Admiralty, but also its appearance and overall performance provided a promise of solid returns much greater than that achieved in the fighter-reconnaissance role by its Fulmar predecessor. The basic Fulmar outline had been refined particularly in respect of the wings that were more elliptically shaped but the real advance lay in the choice of the Griffon IIB engine; the 1,730 hp output contrasted with the Fulmar's Merlin VIII that produced 650 hp less. (Later introduction of the Griffon XII raised maximum output to 1,990 hp!) Maximum speed rose by nearly forty miles to 316 mph, and the climb rate increased from 1,200 ft. to 2,000 ft. per minute.

An equally vital aspect of the reconnaissance function (range) saw a leap from 800-1,300 miles. Four 20mm cannon replaced the eight machine guns, while the mounting of rocket rails or bomb racks that could bear a bomb weight up to 1,000 lbs. materially added to the Firefly's striking power. Yet another improvement lay with the Fairey-Youngman flap system. When deployed they provided a stable platform if flying at cruising speed, as well as reducing the turning radius of the aircraft, which boded well for avoiding unwelcome enemy fighter attention. Here at long last was a reasonably effective British-built design for future Fleet Air Arm operations.

Lessons

Unbeknownst to its airmen the Navy had finished in practice with its bid to neutralise or sink TIRPITZ. Two factors probably militated against the hoped-for result by the FAA crews. The first concerned the use of the main strike-aircraft. The Barracuda was not the perfect instrument, especially given its relatively slow airspeed. There again the maximum armor-piercing bomb weight of 1,600 lbs. was probably no more than adequate to achieve the desired purpose, especially in the light of subsequent RAF Bomber Command attacks with immeasurably heavier weapons.

Then too, the repeated pattern of FAA target-approach – climbing to bombing altitude on approach to the coast while still well distant of the target – was open to criticism since it largely provided the Germans with too much leeway in advanced radar detection with which to prepare an effective defence. Use of the Hellcats and Corsairs as fighter-bombers was indulged in but never with the 1,600 lb. AP; this begs the question of whether their much-enhanced performance compared to the Barracuda could have proved a more effective method of striking at TIRPITZ by surprise, and catching the defences before the smoke screen could be properly deployed.

On the other hand, their maximum load of two 1,000 lb. bombs was hardly sufficient to deal a lethal blow.

Beginning with the X-Craft attack in September 1943, the Royal Navy's underwater and aerial resources had literally 'pecked away' at their formidable adversary, with the RAF administering the coup de grace fourteen months later. The submarine-inflicted damage was regarded in some post-war circles as being so severe that this invalidated the primary concerns of the Allied authorities on future operations by TIRPITZ. Furthermore, the repeated FAA attacks and Intelligence interpretation of the results also added to the supposition that the battleship was so crippled as to no longer constitute a serious threat. On the other hand the bald truth

was that as long as TIRPITZ was upright and afloat nothing could be taken for granted, and she remained the core of a 'Fleet in being' that pinned down major units of the Allied Navies better deployed elsewhere.

The fact that the single 'Tallboy' strike off the second RAF raid had so devastated the bow section that the battleship was effectively neutralised in terms of sea-going operations, and was relegated to a floating heavy gun battery could not absolutely be confirmed at the time. Also, the fact that during the second of the three Lancaster raids the warship had basically managed to absorb the blast of a weapon several times the capacity of the Navy's 1,600 lb. AP equivalent also casts doubts upon a similar positive outcome for the FAA attacks

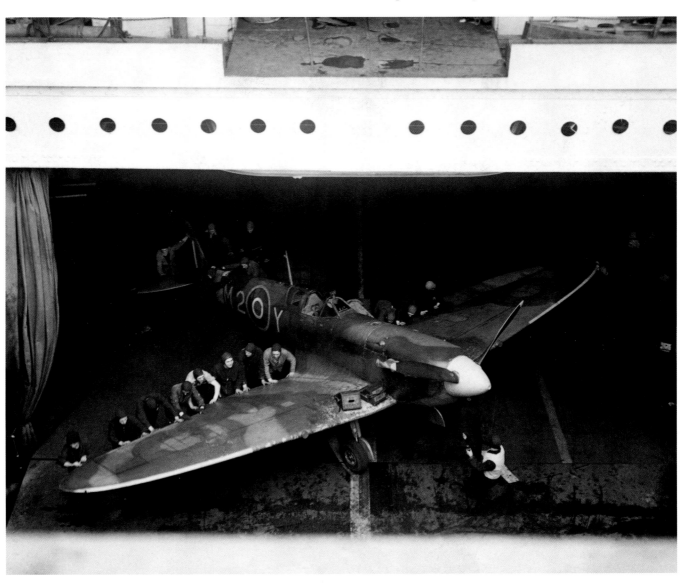

No.768 Sqdn. was based on several airfields around the Clyde Estuary, Scotland, and its aircraft were used for deck-landing training on ARGUS. Among those designs operated during 1943 were Spitfires Mk.Va and Vb, but only the latter variant was fitted out with arrester-hooks. M2:Y reflects its exposure to salt water and sea wind conditions with the paint worn off the wing roots and inner leading edges.

Although the Barracuda with four depth charges dominates this scene, the true significance of the picture lies with the airmen. During World War II the FAA was dependent upon the ranks of the Royal Naval Volunteer Reserve for the rapidly expanding bulk of its pilots and Observers. This salient fact is confirmed by the presence of just one regular RN officer (the Lt/Cdr. in the middle wearing the Mae West) from among those officers whose rank is visible; the others all bear the insignia of the 'Wavy Navy'.

through the use of the latter bomb-type, unless a concentration of these could have been delivered onto the open deck areas of TIRPITZ.

Finally, the FAA fliers had generally been frustrated by the effective use of smoke screens, (thereby destroying any chance of the fore-going bomb-concentration) as were the Lancaster crews on the first two assaults. It took a combination of clear weather and minimal smoke screen cover on 12 November 1944 for the RAF bomb-aimers to be able to accurately focus their bomb-sights and deliver the final blow, apart from which at least two direct hits and several clustered around the warship's mooring appeared necessary to bring about her demise.

CHAPTER TEN

Atlantic Victory
1943-1945

The outlook for the Allied cause in the crucial Battle of the Atlantic as 1943 commenced was poor and in the period up to March was becoming ever bleaker. The toll of merchant shipping particularly in the 'Black Zone' in the North Atlantic, where air cover was currently almost absent, showed every sign of increasing to the critical point where the monthly tonnage lost would be greater than that needed to sustain the Conflict from British shores. Dönitz's U-Boats were still managing to get the better of the available surface escorts while maintaining their own losses at a reasonable level. In the second half of 1942 nearly three million tons of Allied merchant shipping had been sunk at a cost of thirty-two U-Boats; however, over half of the *Kriegsmarine* losses were due to aircraft, which was an ominous portent should air power come into its own across the entire breadth of the North Atlantic.

The first sign of a long-term change in Allied fortunes had appeared in the autumn of 1942 with the transfer of No.120 Sqdn. RAF with its Very Long Range (VLR) Liberators to Iceland. From there, the aircrews could rendezvous with convoys and hold position overhead for several hours. One of the crews led by S/Ldr. Bulloch was to leave its specific mark upon the U-Boat Force, but in the main airborne 'sightings' of the *Kriegsmarine* submarines were not too frequent. However there was a negative but nonetheless important aspect to the Liberators' presence around the convoy, namely their 'deterrent' value. The mere presence of an aircraft regularly proved sufficient to keep a U-Boat submerged and therefore likely to finally lose contact with its targets. Indeed, on more than one occasion the enemy Captains were reporting that they were unable to effect their attacks thanks to the numbers of aircraft present – a situation all the more gratifying for the single Liberator crew that was normally on hand!

For example, during 'Gap' cover for Convoy HX217 in December, S/Ldrs. Bulloch and Isted had in the course of their separate patrols sighted or attacked thirteen U-Boats; the subsequent action-analysis at U-Boat HQ cast up the impression of overwhelming air cover Unfortunately, the small numbers of VLR bombers available resulted in an interrupted pattern of convoy coverage, which in turn provided the U-Boats with the chance to strike home with virtual impunity when faced only by the Allied Escort warships, who were limited in numbers and often lacking fully effective detection equipment and equally effective depth-charges.

Although weather patterns in January were violent enough to hold off the main assault although twenty-seven ships were sunk, while February's total of losses was nearly double (forty-six), bringing the overall tonnage figure to some 450,000 tons. In March the Battle continued its familiar and negative form, at least as regards the action between the surface and underwater Forces. The tonnage sunk rose to just under 1/2 million tons. Two massive Convoy assaults (SC122 and HX229/229A) accounted for twenty-one of the ninety-seven vessels failing to survive their voyages during the month; even more disturbing was the fact that many had been destroyed while sailing within the very Convoy system that was designed to provide them with the maximum degree of security compared to sailing in isolation!

As it was, the increased availability of the one specific aircraft design, the Consolidated B-24 Liberator in its Very Long Range (VLR) variant – albeit still in relatively small numbers – did at last begin to bite into the U-Boats hitherto unrestricted freedom of movement. No.120 Sqdn., along with No.86 Sqdn. flying from Northern Ireland, was capable of providing cover in the 'Atlantic Gap'; it was therefore all the more frustrating that their services were not seemingly called

A Swordfish Mk.II displays the inevitable ravages of operating from the exposed deck of an escort carrier. The topside camouflage pattern is limited to the area in front of the pilot and the upper wing surface. The lighter colors on anti-submarine aircraft assisted in concealing their presence to surfaced U-Boat observers much more than was the case with fully camouflaged machines.

This is a Swordfish crew's view of their landing approach to an escort carrier, in this instance recorded as SMITER. The DLCO's bats are angled slightly down to the right as seen here; which instructs the pilot to raise his port wing. A Second Swordfish has just lifted off the flight deck. This carrier was used for training purposes only during World War II.

Above: A reverse view of an escort carrier is afforded by this picture taken from the rear cockpit of a Swordfish. A second Swordfish is ranged and ready for take-off. The aircraft in flight is banking to port but normal procedure was to bank to starboard in order to minimise the turbulence effect on succeeding aircraft take-offs.

Right: In what seems like a posed picture, a Swordfish crew run their pre-flight checks. The TAG is sighting his .303 machine-gun placed on a High-speed Gun mounting. The Observer is also sighting through the compass in the starboard circular base, while the pilot prepares for take-off.

upon for the afore-mentioned two Convoys as the 'Gap' was first being traversed.

The counter-measure weapons at hand had also greatly expanded in numbers and efficiency by the end of March 1943. To the standard depth-charge with its more effective explosive content and more accurate depth-setting, was now added the ship-mounted 'Hedgehog' that fired up to twenty-four mortars ahead of the warship. In the air, the first rocket projectiles were being provided, while just arrived in Britain was the Mk. 24 Mine, also known as 'Wandering Annie' or 'Fido'. This was an acoustic-directed weapon of particularly lethal proportions, designed to 'home in' upon the cavitations from the U-Boat's propellers. (The dropping of this particular weapon was usually delayed until the U-Boat in question had submerged in order to ensure that its existence was kept secret from the enemy Authorities).

Escort Carrier Expansion

The provision of sizeable numbers of smaller escort carriers with which to protect the still sorely-pressed Atlantic convoys had gathered steady if sometimes frustrating pace during 1942. The three 'Avenger' Class warships had come into service during mid-1942, but 'ARCHER's progress towards operational duties was regularly bedevilled up to early 1943. Two major sources of U.S.-constructed supply were to be the 'Attacker' and 'Ameer' Classes of which eleven and twenty-three would be commissioned in RN service by February 1944. The 'Attackers' were part of the American 'Bogue' Class transferred under Lend-Lease terms and were conversions from merchant ships. Their flight deck dimensions were 440 ft. by 82 ft. compared to the 438x88 ft. dimensions of the 'Ameer' Class, which were constructed as aircraft carriers. All thirty-four were equipped with two lifts and their aircraft complement was twenty. By the time the Battle of the Atlantic was boiling up to its March/May climax, all but one of the 'Attacker' Class had been commissioned.

Enter the Fleet Air Arm

The travails of the merchant vessels and their escorts occurring during March did not bode well for the immediate future, but the immediate Crisis posed by the severe losses was to fade away at an accelerated rate over the ensuing two to three months. During this time the first of the CVEs to participate in the Battle came on the scene. HMS BITER commenced her Atlantic service during April with eleven Swordfish Mk.II and three Wildcats Mk.IV of No.811 Sqdn. This unit was one of several provided with such a mixed complement of strike aircraft and fighters. The venerable but reliable 'Stringbag' could deliver depth-charges and rocket projectiles with deadly accuracy, but its very deliberate pace left it vulnerable to counter-fire from a surfaced U-Boat. The presence of the Wildcats was designed to keep the heads of the *Kriegsmarine* gunners down, if not render them out of action, during which time the Swordfish crew could make their attack with impunity.

The use of the projectiles was potentially as deadly as, if not more deadly than, the depthcharge; in the former instance the aircraft did not have to pass over its victim but could to some degree adopt a 'stand off' position, given that the rockets had a range of several hundred yards. The normal technique was to fire the rockets in groups, using the first or second group for 'ranging' and landing the remainder upon the U-Boat's hull, this procedure being necessary due to the weapon's notable gravity-drop.

Into Action with the CVE

The benefits accruing from BITER's presence soon surfaced when on 25 April U-203 became one of twelve U-Boats to be sunk during the month; the success was shared with HMS HARVESTER. The CVE's involvement in the May joint Convoys HX237 and SC129 was to yield further success, but

This Swordfish Mk.II of No.842 Sqdn. demonstrates how even the sturdy landing gear on the 'Stringbag' could not always absorb the hard impact with a carrier deck. The nearside gear leg can be seen forced back and up, in between the wing trailing edge and the fuselage. The Sqdn. was based on FENCER between October 1943 and June 1944. The carrier's aircrew set a record for U-Boat sinkings (three) during one Arctic convoy in May 1944.

The use of Rocket-assisted Take-off (RATOG) equipment with which to shorten the launch run of Seafires was tested on board ILLUSTRIOUS during January 1943. The starboard half of the equipment is seen located on the inner wing section of what appears to be a Mk.Ib to judge by the three-bladed propeller. Although the tests were satisfactory, the Seafire made no operational use of RATOG.

at a price. First, U-403 that was 'shadowing' the convoy lost contact after an inconclusive encounter with a Swordfish. Then, on the 12th another Swordfish that had followed HF/DF bearings directed onto a U-Boat's transmissions, approached U-230 but crashed when almost overhead. The depthcharges exploded and killed the airmen, but left their victim intact. Finally, the same day U-89 was spotted ahead of the convoy by another Swordfish, whose subsequent directions on behalf of two escort vessels led to a successful depthcharging of the enemy warship. Next day the convoys had passed into the zone of land-based air cover. The hoped-for success by the thirty-six-strong U-Boat Force had not materialised; instead just one more merchantman (five) had been lost compared to U-Boat losses.

Worse still was the fate of the attackers as they attempted to disrupt SC130 and ON184, two more of the ten convoys sailing in May up to the 24th. By that date less than 1% of the 370 merchantmen involved had been sunk, compared to thirteen U-Boats. It was then that Admiral Dönitz ordered a general withdrawal from mid-Atlantic to France with a new Group from among his Force re-assembling off the Azores. However, any chances of easier pickings in that zone were to be short-lived. Commencing in March 1943, the U.S. Navy had switched its warships from the North Atlantic to bring this region within its total command. In addition its tactic of using 'Hunter/killer' groups of warships that included a CVE to stalk the U-Boats was to yield solid dividends. The net was

drawing around *Kriegsmarine* operations in every reach of the Atlantic Ocean and the initiative was destined to pass steadily but permanently to the Allied Naval and Air Forces.

The second Royal Navy CVE to join in the Battle was the long-suffering ARCHER. Her complement of Swordfish Mk.II and Wildcats Mk.IV (the latter added in July) came from Nos.819 and 892 Sqdn. respectively. The operational career of this carrier was to extend over a short three-month period up to July after which she was destined to be withdrawn from front-line service, but in that time-span one of her aircraft was to score a 'first' for the FAA. On the 23rd May, U-752 was sighted by a rocket-bearing Swordfish whose weapons led to the demise of the U-Boat in the short encounter that ensued.

Just one other CVE was to be called upon for the Atlantic convoy routes, and this was TRACKER. The carrier's service extended between September 1943 and June 1944 but the twelve convoy actions and two Anti-Submarine sweeps she was involved in were split between the Atlantic, Arctic and Gibraltar routes. No.816 Sqdn. provided the nine Swordfish Mk.II and six Seafires LIIC and 1b that were embarked up to the end of 1943; these were exchanged for twelve Avengers Mk.I and seven Wildcats Mk.V from No.846 Sqdn. that comprised her complement up to June 1944.

The MAC Ships Take Over

A practical alternative to the standard aircraft carrier design had been proposed during 1942, namely the adaptation of grain carriers – and latterly oil tankers – by having their superstructures removed and replaced by a flight deck. In this manner, the vessels concerned could still carry out their vital function of bringing supplies into Britain, while providing equally vital air cover for themselves and their fellow-merchantmen within the convoy.

The relatively short hull lengths of most merchantmen did not allow for flight deck lengths that were any more than adequate. In the case of the six grain carriers and four oil tankers within the 'Empire' Class, the flight decks were 400ft. in length for the first category and 450 ft. for the remaining four; the standard deck width was sixty ft. The fitting of a hangar proved only possible with the grain carriers, whose cargo could be filled via internal trunking spaced at intervals around the flight deck edges and provided with flush-fitting deck covers that did not intrude upon safe flying operations.

The hangar lift was 42x22 ft. in pattern and the hangar height 24 ft., and its interior could accommodate up to four aircraft that were to come from the Swordfish design. The miniscule island superstructure contained Type 271 M surface and Type 79 air warning radar equipment. Defensive armament consisted of a single four inch gun at the stern, with two 40mm and four 20mm weapons mounted in sponsons on the hull sides on the grain carriers. The armament provision on the oil tankers retained the 4-in gun but eight 20mm weapons were fitted in a similar hull-mounted 'spread'.

A second MAC-Ship Class was created from oil tankers belonging to the Anglo-Saxon Petroleum Company. The initial Admiralty resistance to these vessels' use in this revised and supplementary role was based on the danger of a bad aircraft crash and fire on the deck spreading to the cargo and causing a total loss. Such doubts were largely quelled and the scheme

This Swordfish of No.842 Sqdn. hangs precariously over the flight deck. The starboard lower wing is swung back and the engine is partially dislodged from its bulkhead. It is likely the aircraft will not be salvaged but will end up in 'the greatest dustbin (garbage can) in the World!' after all available spare parts have been detached.

went ahead. Removal of the bridge and after superstructure, and venting off the engine gases so that they discharged at the sides of the hull, was followed by the fitting of a steel girder frame on which the flight deck of 460 ft. length and sixty feet width rested. An interesting variation concerned the 'cargo' destined to be carried by the seven vessels in what was the RAPANA Class; it was oil fuel that was often provided to the convoy escorts, who were duly refuelled at sea! (An added reason for the choice of this product was said to trace back to the Admiralty's fear of an accidental conflagration, in that the oil fuel constituted a reduced hazard in this respect).

Operations from what became the Merchant Aircraft Carrier (MAC) were to involve Nos.836, 840 and 860 (Royal Netherlands) Sqdn., with the former two units providing the

No.842 Sqdn. operated a mix of Swordfish and fighters, with the latter acting in the flak suppression role when U-Boats were attacked. This Wildcat V is caught at the point of engaging the arrester-wire on FENCER. The Wildcats took over in March 1944 from the original Seafires Mk. Ib and LIIc that had been embarked the previous July.

Left: A Wildcat Mk.V is snapped standing on its nose and about to slam over onto its back following a failed landing on FENCER. This escort carrier served in the Atlantic and Arctic waters between August 1943 and October 1944. Right: The same over-turned Wildcat Mk.V on FENCER is surrounded by deck personnel, doubtless concerned for the pilot trapped in his cockpit. In fact the fighter's occupant suffered no serious injury thanks to the strong airframe on the Wildcat. In addition, none of the other Wildcats appear to have been damaged in the incident.

A Seafire Mk.Ib or LIIc has landed on FENCER but does not appear to have 'grabbed' an arrester wire with its hook. In addition the port main landing gear is disintegrating with the wheel shooting off towards the deck edge.

Two white-helmeted deck handlers hastily scurry for cover inside FENCER's 'island' as a Swordfish Mk.II careers along the deck with the starboard lower wing-tip scraping the deck. The second picture shows how the aircraft finally fetched up against the 'Island' with damage seemingly avoided even to the lower wing section, as the crew scramble out.

The final variant of the Sea Hurricane to come into FAA service was the Mk.IIC, which was equipped with four 20mm Hispano cannon. The example being launched here is the prototype airframe as denoted by the yellow letter P in a thin yellow circle behind the fuselage roundel. The circular ammunition drums required elliptical fairings to be fitted on the upper wing surfaces.

STRIKER operated on the Atlantic and Arctic convoy routes between October 1943 and October 1944. In that time she embarked the Sea Hurricanes Mk.IIc (later replaced by Wildcats Mk.V) and Swordfish Mk.II of No.824 Sqdn. Two of the 'Stringbags' are already airborne as the single Sea Hurricane is about to lift off the carrier deck. The fighter will serve in a flak-suppression role should a surfaced U-Boat be encountered; alternatively its pilot will challenge any incursion by enemy aircraft.

bulk of the aircraft to seventeen of this group of vessels, and the remaining unit supplying the two other vessels that were assigned to the Dutch Navy; each carrier was allocated three or four Swordfish. The first commissioning involved EMPIRE MacALPINE on 14 April 1943, and early the following month L/Cdr. Slater completed the inaugural deck landing in his 'Stringbag'.

The RN personnel serving on the MAC ships were to exist in a different world, in that they all had to sign ships articles in order to place them under the control of the ship's Merchant Navy Captain. Officers held dual RN/MN rank and the ratings signed up as deckhands. The clothing worn reflected the more relaxed world of the civilian sailor, but on some vessels there was segregation practiced in the dining saloon. (A visible sign of this FAA 'double existence' was to be seen on numerous aircraft, with the 'Royal Navy' stencil on the aircrafts' rear fuselage changed to 'Merchant Navy'!).

By the time EMPIRE MacALPINE sailed on her first Atlantic convoy at the end of May, the Battle had swung against the *Kriegsmarine*'s underwater Fleet. Two more of her sister-ships, EMPIRE MacANDREW and EMPIRE MACRAE were also 'on station' by September, but little or no action was generally encountered from the enemy during this time. However, the U-Boats were operating their latest refined weapon, the 'Gnat' acoustic torpedo. An immediate counter-measure against this German equivalent to the Mk.24 Mine was the 'Foxer', a propeller-sounding device, which was towed behind escort vessels. The 'Gnat' was designed for use against medium to fast-paced vessels, a category into which the majority of the escorts naturally fitted. In the course of Convoys ONS18 and ON22 progress westwards during September, no less than three escorts were reported as sunk and one damaged by these weapons, along with four merchantmen. The air and surface defences retaliated by destroying three U-Boats but this figure might have risen to four.

On the 22 May EMPIRE MacALPINE launched two of her three Swordfish in very clear conditions, following the heavy fog that had previously surrounded the convoys. The first flown by Sub/Lt. Barlow carried two depth charges, but when he sighted a U-Boat on the surface he held off from attacking, since his aircraft was likely to get the worst of any encounter with the fully alerted enemy crew. Radio failure prevented the U-Boat's location being relayed to the escorts, but one warship did hove in sight and was contacted by Aldis Lamp.

Soon after, Sub/Lt. Gifford in a rocket-bearing Swordfish appeared and both pilots headed up-sun before commencing their still-risky assault. Gifford went in first but his projectiles under or over-shot, while the twisting course adopted by the U-Boat probably threw Barlow's aim off, since his depth charges fell well clear. The intense flak directed at both aircraft fortunately did little or no damage. On the other hand, the presence of a Seafire or Wildcat fighter acting as a flak suppressor could have permitted much more accurate and potentially lethal attack runs to have been made. At least the U-Boat's approach to the convoy had been reversed when she was last seen. (The total absence of fighters from the MAC ships complement is surprising, when it is considered that they did successfully operate off escort carriers during World War II).

Closing the Final Atlantic 'Gap'

In March 1943 the operational control of convoys in the northern reaches of the Atlantic that had hitherto been largely an Anglo-American affair changed. This was due to the U.S. Navy deciding to concentrate its efforts further south, so

No.842 Sqdn.'s use of the Seafire extended between July 1943 and March 1944 when the Wildcat took over. This is a good example of a perfect landing attempt by the Supermarine fighter as it comes to an intact halt on FENCER. The Sqdn. operated both the 1b and LIIC variants but the detail shown here is insufficient to confirm which variant is present here.

Above: The weather patterns through which the convoys plied their Atlantic routes sometimes threw up sunny, cloudless conditions. A Wildcat V of No.842 Sqdn. squats on FENCER's flight deck, while its pilot sits at cockpit readiness under the shade of an umbrella.

Right: The mangled remains of a Swordfish Mk.II or III are viewed just as they are jettisoned over the side of the carrier. Holes punched into the fabric will accelerate the rate of submersion.

leaving the Royal Canadian Navy (RCN) to take up the vacated position. The American's directed a greater degree of concentration towards 'Hunter/Killer' Groups of warships with which to track down U-Boats. On the other hand, up to October 1943, there was a sizeable 'Air Gap' existing in their region of the central Atlantic. B-17s and B-24s could reach out eastwards in an arc extending from Florida up to Greenland, but even the B-24 could not extend southwestward from Britain or directly west from North Africa in order to bisect the U.S.-based pattern of range.

The Azores Island chain lying nearly 700 miles out in the Atlantic from southern Portugal belonged to that country, but at this time its government was neutral. Gen. Salazar had resisted British pleas for air bases on the Azores, while an American-inspired plan for occupation did not sit well with their principal Ally. Fortunately, in August 1943 the Portuguese Dictator did accede to the requests and on 8 October Operation 'Alacrity' saw FENCER arriving off the Islands as part of the 8th Escort Group. Over the next three days the Seafires Mk.Ib of No.842 Sqdn. flew patrols, before the Sqdn's embarked Swordfish complement was flown off to Lagans airfield to provide anti-submarine sorties in the immediate vicinity of the Azores under Seafire cover. The aircraft were all back on board FENCER by the 24th by which time Hudsons were in position to take over the same duty; Fortresses were also on hand for long-range patrol duties. The 'Southern Gap' had been duly closed and now the entire Atlantic Battlefield was under Allied aerial supervision.

Into 1944

The carrier ACTIVITY had come into service as a deck training vessel during 1943 but was currently serving on the North Atlantic and Gibraltar routes, as much as a refuelling source for the escorts as in her primary role. Along with NAIRANA, she had originally covered convoy OS66/KMS70 on the south-bound route; now on 5 February she was acting as an oiler for Walker's redoubtable 2nd. Escort Group. This duty had recently been completed when the 'Asdics' began their ominous 'pinging' – ominous not for the convoy but for the

U-Boat in question that was all too soon overwhelmed by a train of depth-charges!

The bulk of U-Boats sunk by the Royal Navy in World War II were taken out by the escorts. But a steady toll was to be exacted by the FAA aircraft. On 10 February FENCER and STRIKER were covering ON223. FENCER's Swordfish were ranged on the deck when to everyone's amazement, U-666 surfaced directly astern. Two 'Stringbags' were shot off at the double and were over their target before anyone on board even became aware of their extreme peril; they were given no chance to reflect or indeed to survive as the depthcharges fulfilled their lethal function. This was but the first 'kill' out of four for the carrier's aircrew, which was to be a phenomenal record by any standard.

The Swordfish, willing 'workhorse' that it was proving to be for the FAA, nevertheless began to face operational limitations in both its Mk.II and III forms. The carriage of the three-man crew, a full fuel load, along with depth-charges, rockets and even on occasions the Mk.24 Mine, was creating difficulties during take-off; this was especially the case when the carrier was steaming through ocean stretches enjoying windless or light wind conditions. (The added weight and drag of the ASV Mk. XI radar pod under the forward fuselage on the Mk.III made that variant just as prone to the problem. On the other hand its rear cockpit had been expanded to permit a better layout of the equipment that in turn would permit the Observer to also take over the function of the TAG). Rocket-Assisted Take Off Gear (RATOG) would finally be fitted to the 'Stringbags' in order to permit maximum weight take-offs from the all-too-minimal CVE deck lengths.

The Swordfish crew just visible in this picture were very fortunate to survive both their Swordfish's crash and subsequent immersion – especially since this occurred in December 1943, and the airmen spent around twenty minutes in the especially frigid water before being fished out! Lt. Bill Penlington was landing on FENCER when the carrier pitched and the aircraft struck the superstructure before plummeting into the deceptively calm Atlantic waters.

The Gibraltar Run

Although the North Atlantic was arguably the primary source for the sea-borne delivery of Britain's supplies during World War II, there was a supplementary trade route that was of equal importance to the Nation's commercial and military survival, namely that running down into the Mediterranean or past West Africa and round into the Indian Ocean. In the former case, the presence of Axis Naval surface warships along with aircraft drastically hindered merchant shipping movements up to the winter of 1942-1943. The need to transport military equipment to its Armed Forces in the Middle and Far East Theaters, as

A tragedy is about to unfold as this Wildcat rears up and banks to port. The pilot Lt. Kay a New Zealander was practicing landings on FENCER in the Firth of Clyde. His fighter struck the carrier's 'round-down' (Deck-end) and went out of control. Seconds after this picture was taken the aircraft exploded, killing Kay instantly.

well as to ensure the import of goods from its major Colonies within these regions, placed these trade routes under the same danger from air and U-Boat assault.

The Bay of Biscay laying off the French and northern Spanish coastlines had to be traversed by the convoys, whose first destination southwards or last northwards was the Fortress of Gibraltar. Here was concentrated much of the Royal Navy's warships, both for action in the western Mediterranean and for covering the afore-mentioned convoy route. So it was that the seamen and ships involved in fighting the cargoes through to their British or Colonial destinations came to talk about 'the Gibraltar Run' because it was across this stretch of ocean that the Royal and Merchant Navies had to face the full might of the U-Boat assault. The Bay of Biscay was the crossing point for U-Boats moving to and from their French ports to take up their stations in the Atlantic. The convoys skirting the Bay were accordingly at even greater risk since their freedom of movement was more constrained than their contemporaries out in the much wider stretches of the North Atlantic. In addition, the convoy routes' closer proximity to the U-Boat

bases permitted those enemy crews assigned to patrol the Bay an extended time 'on station' and a smaller area in which to seek out their prey.

The CAM-Ships Sign Off

The almost total lack of carrier air cover in the Bay up to 1943 – apart from AUDACITY's short and intense but sadly fatal period of operations in late 1941 – had witnessed the convoys being regularly decimated. The sole crumb of comfort had been provided by the CAM-ships and their catapult-mounted Hurricanes. Now, by mid-1943, the overall picture was beginning to look much brighter, as ever more CVEs and MAC-ships were making their welcome if belated appearance. On the other hand, CAM-ship operations, that had been officially declared redundant n June, signed off with a flourish in late July, when the last two vessels (EMPIRE TIDE and EMPIRE DARWIN) sailed back to Britain out of Gibraltar as part of a convoy. With no other ship-borne aircraft on hand, the prospects for the *Luftwaffe* and *Kriegsmarine* might have appeared good.

This rocket-laden Swordfish Mk.II seems to be in imminent danger of slipping over the side of STRIKER as the escort carrier heels over to starboard. The engine is still running as the crew are clambering out. Cables attached to the landing gear legs and fuselage underside may be in position to pull the 'Stringbag' from where the starboard wheel has probably gone over the flight deck edge. One of the deck handlers is beginning to fold the port wing,

TRACKER embarked the Swordfish Mk.II and Seafires Mk.Ib from No.816 Sqdn. during the second half of 1943. Here, a DLCO who is well-padded against the Atlantic chill, gives the 'cut engine' signal to a 'Stringbag'. The aircraft still possesses its full load of eight rocket projectiles, which indicates an uneventful anti-submarine sortie.

Three days out from Gibraltar, a Fw 200 *Kondor* was sighted, followed next day by several more sightings. During mid-evening, F/O Stewart was dispatched from EMPIRE DARWIN in response to an Fw 200 that had manoeuvered into an up-sun position. An interception was quickly made well out from the convoy, but both aircraft were observed to disappear. In fact, Stewart survived the incident and was later picked up out of the water. One hour later F/O Flynn on the other CAM-ship was sent off against yet another Fw 200 flying ahead of the convoy. Flynn's interception was equally swift and he commenced his initial run from the left quarter and followed this up with five approaches from an up-sun angle. Strikes were recorded around the cockpit and both top gun turret positions with a view to reducing the persistent flow of return fire, and one engine commenced smoking. By the time Flynn ran out of ammunition, the Fw 200 was still flying but had released its bombs and was turning away while losing height. Flynn then orbited the convoy ready to bale out after the action. He jumped clear and floated down into the water; having then released his parachute and inflated his dinghy he

calmly awaited the arrival of one of the escort vessel's whalers whose crew duly picked him up. For both pilot's the day's activity had provided their first combat experience.

Escort Carriers in 'the Bay'

Between May and June 1943 three Gibraltar convoys enjoyed the unique protection from a non-CVE source, namely UNICORN. This British-built warship displacing 16,550 tons was designed to serve in the secondary but vital role of a depot ship, and over the next two years would fulfil its function during Operation 'Avalanche', the Landings at Salerno and Operation 'Iceberg' in the Pacific. Prior to her first main Operation she provided air cover with the Swordfish of Nos.818 and 824 Sqdns. along with the Seafires of No.887 Sqdn.

BATTLER was the first of four Assault escort carriers bound for Mediterranean operations in 1943 that would be involved in convoy protection either prior to or after their spell of duty in that Theater. She was ready for combat on 4 June when she accompanied two slow convoys down to the 'Rock'.

No.835 Sqdn.'s Swordfish Mk.II mounted anti-submarine patrols, while the Seafires LIIC of No.808A Sqdn. stood by to challenge the *Luftwaffe*. On the 11th, two Seafires were launched to investigate a 'bogey' that ended up as an RAF aircraft with an inoperable 'Information Friend or Foe' (IFF) set. On the return voyage, better fortune attended the Flight CO and his Wingman on the 22nd when a Fw 200 that was hovering around the convoy paid the price, being intercepted and shot out of the sky in a welter of cannon shells and bullets.

By the end of 1943 three more escort carriers TRACKER, FENCER and STRIKER had joined in at various dates on the Gibraltar 'Run'. In this time no recorded 'kills' of *Luftwaffe* aircraft were recorded but a potentially deadly threat to both the merchantmen and escorts appeared in late August in the form of the Henschel 293 radio-controlled bomb. II./KG 100 based at Cognac in southwest France attacked destroyers with uncertain results. Two days later the sloop EGRET was not so fortunate and was sunk by one of the missiles. In October the He 177s of II./KG 40 based at Bordeaux-Merignac commenced similar operations, this time against Atlantic convoys in an apparent bid to make up the leeway on behalf of the U-Boat Force whose numbers had been seriously reduced thanks to the effective Allied counter-measures. As it was, no direct interference with the Gibraltar convoys was made, and both units transferred their efforts to the Mediterranean by the year-end; some of the III./KG 40 *Kondors* were modified to accommodate the weapon and made occasional sorties, but mainly against RN escorts.

CVEs – The British Connection

VINDEX, NAIRANA and CAMPANIA were to prove the main exception to U.S.-provided escort carriers for the Royal Navy. All three were originally laid down as fast cargo liners, and as such were twin-screw, riveted-plate hull designs. The latter feature provided a sturdier sea-going frame compared to the all-welded hulls from American sources, and would prove its value especially in the storm-tossed Atlantic and Arctic Oceans. The steel flight deck was 495x65 ft. and the single lift had generous dimensions of 45x34 ft. The island superstructure followed the general escort carrier pattern of a narrow 'box' shape that was completely offset from the flight deck. Total aircraft complement was set at twenty-one, split between fifteen strike and six fighter airframes. All three were to serve on the Atlantic, Arctic and Gibraltar convoy routes between February and June 1944 onwards.

NAIRANA, along with ACTIVITY (Another British-built escort carrier with similar construction format and flight deck dimensions to its companion carrier, but with a reduced aircraft complement of ten) took part in supporting Convoy OS66/KMS70 at the end of January; also on hand was the 2nd. Escort Group commanded by Capt. 'Johnny' Walker, who were to fulfil their usual 'Hunter/Killer' function. Although the U-Boat disposition was currently concentrated on the Western Approaches to Britain, elements of the remaining Force were attempting to challenge the convoy's movements along all the major routes. NAIRANA was probably fortunate not to be torpedoed on what was her first-ever operational launch of

No.736 Sqdn. was formed at Yeovilton from May 1943 as the unit for the FAA's School of Air Combat where the techniques of air combat were passed on by veteran fighter Leaders. Three Seafires Mk.1b are flying a neat 'V' formation. The leading fighter appears to have darkened sections to the wing leading edge panels and light-colored elevators.

aircraft, when one of Walker's warships informed Capt. Taylor that a U-Boat had been picked up by Asdic in a prime position to attack the carrier! Soon after, U-592 was hunted to her destruction, using Walker's favorite tactic, the 'creeping attack'.

The subsequent southbound convoy witnessed a rare air battle-involving PURSUER, one of the Fighter Carriers, and her twenty Wildcats split between Nos.881 and 896 Sqdns. On 11 February, the day's flying was completed and the fighters being 'struck below' when radar plots indicated 'bogeys'. Four Wildcats were 'scrambled' and swept up and into the attack against a mixed Force of seven Fw 200s and He 177s, with the latter bearing Hs 293 radio-controlled bombs. At least two of the bombers were reported downed by the fighters, and the remainder soon gave up and retired back to their airfields. Four days later, over convoy OS68/KMS42, another Hs 293-bearing bomber – this time a Ju 290 – was taken down by two Wildcats of No.811 Sqdn. embarked on BITER.

VINDEX in Triumph and Tragedy

L/Cdr Percy Gick was Commander (Flying) on VINDEX and was a veteran of some standing, having served on ARK ROYAL and participated in the attack on BISMARCK. Thanks to his rather covert efforts his carrier had been appointed to be the first night-flying CVE. On 9 March 1944 she set sail along with STRIKER to cover Convoy OS70/KMS44. The twelve Swordfish of No.825 Sqdn. would over the intervening twenty-three days (or rather days and nights) record 122 sorties entailing 275 hours flying, but their experiences would mirror

The Royal Navy meets the Merchant Navy; Lt./Cdr. Slater (left) shakes hands with First Officer Campbell on the flight deck of the converted grain carrier EMPIRE MACALPINE. The occasion was the first ever FAA aircraft landing on a MAC-ship in May 1943, with the Swordfish in the background making the sortie.

Below: ANCYLUS was one of the seven oil tankers, one of which (ALEXIA) was originally constructed in a Bremen shipyard, that were converted to MAC-ship standard. Her hull is heavily weathered and two of her small Swordfish complement are parked precariously on the forward edge of the flight deck. These RAPANA Class carriers possessed no internal hangar space.

An Avenger Mk.I maintains its surveillance against U-Boat assault on a Gibraltar convoy sometime during the first half of 1944. The large bulkhead behind the pilot and the good overall view enjoyed by the Observer are outlined here. Aircraft belongs to No.846 Sqdn. embarked on TRACKER, who is sharing this particular convoy with BITER steaming in the background.

No.846 Sqdn. transferred from TRACKER to TRUMPETER in July 1944. While based at Scapa Flow this Avenger Mk.I failed to maintain flight immediately after its launch and crashed. The TAG on Sub/Lt. Thomas's crew can be seen exiting his gun turret and all three crewmembers were picked up.

An Avenger has come to an undignified stop on the flight deck of an escort carrier. The landing gear has completely collapsed and the propeller blades have been thoroughly twisted in the process. As the deck handlers run into position, the Observer can be seen emerging from the opened side-hinged cockpit section.

A Sea Hurricane Mk.IIc heels sharply to the left as its pilot applies full power to the fighter's Merlin engine. The pair of Swordfish Mk. II has also started up, and all three aircraft will shortly take off for a joint anti-submarine patrol. The combination of cannon shells and rockets borne by the respective aircraft could prove a lethal threat to any surfaced U-Boat.

STRIKER has just dispatched both Swordfish Mk.II, and the Sea Hurricane Mk.IIc closely follows these. The presence of the 20mm cannon-armed fighter would either keep the heads down of, or disable, the flak gunners on any surfaced U-Boat that might be encountered during the ensuing patrol. The Sqdn. involved was No.824 that was embarked between October 1943 and October 1944.

The Mk.24 Mine mounted under the fuselage of a Swordfish Mk.II from No.824 Sqdn. was a particularly effective weapon in the Allied anti-submarine armoury. The device was actually a torpedo that homed onto a vessel's propeller cavitations. It was normally dropped on submerged U-Boats in order to prevent knowledge of its existence from getting back to the German military authorities.

the rigours of carrier operations in the Atlantic for both aircrew and ship's personnel.

Heavy weather as the sortie began contributed to the loss of two seamen. The open carrier deck naturally had no permanent guard-rail system as fitted to all other warship designs, since this would have seriously intruded upon safe aircraft operation. Consequently, one hapless deck handler faced little chance of survival, other than tumbling into the narrow catwalks flanking the deck sides, when propeller wash swept him overboard. The other seaman also disappeared overboard but in less clear circumstances.

The ordeal for the aircrew, particularly those assigned to fly the twelve Swordfish on hand, soon followed up. On the 11th two 'Stringbags' sighted and attacked a U-Boat; the latter escaped destruction but return flak fire was encountered that accounted for one of the TAGs. Then several days later during a patrol, Sub/Lt. Sharrock's aircraft suffered engine failure thanks to water-contaminated fuel and 'ditched' although all three crewmembers were picked up by an escort vessel. Sub/Lt. Webb had the first of two brushes with danger when his 'Stringbag' failed to pick up a wire and smashed into the safety barrier.

This litany of failure was somewhat balanced out on the seventh day out (15th). Sub/Lt. Couch's crew made radar 'contact' with a U-Boat, and marked out the location. The crew of U-653 were unknowingly up against it, because the escort called in to the attack was the sloop STARLING, one of the warships from Capt. 'Johnny' Walker's formidable 2nd. Escort Group, and her depthcharges summarily dispatched their submarine. Four days later, yet another Swordfish crashed into

the sea, with fuel contamination recorded as the cause. Sadly, the foggy conditions initially prevailing undoubtedly contributed to Sub/Lt. Varley's crew not being spotted in spite of intensive searching by his fellow-airmen. However, the discovery of an empty dinghy and pieces of wreckage provided a fair indication that nobody had actually survived the impact.

Before the carrier had completed two of her scheduled three weeks at sea, three more incidents had occurred, one of which could have had severe consequences for the vessel's survival. First, gale conditions forced the 'striking down' of all aircraft into the hangar. The weather had barely moderated when Sub/Lt. Sharrock was sent out on a patrol that ended as quickly as it started – the downward sweep of the carrier's bow as the 'Stringbag' lifted off sent it straight into the storm-tossed waters! Given these conditions, it was a miracle that all the crew not only survived the crash and the subsequent wash of water coming off the ship's bow as it swept off to one side, but managed to withstand the chilled water temperature long enough to be fished out of their partially-inflated dinghy. Another Swordfish crew were very fortunate when their take-off run saw one set of wing tips ripped off after contact with the island superstructure; superb flying skill by Sub/Lt. Ward was the reason why the aircraft flew a circuit and landed safely back on board.

The final incident again involved Sub/Lt. Webb, when on the 24th a night landing onto a pitching deck resulted in the arrester wires being missed, and the landing gear being sliced off by the safety barrier, whereupon the 'Stringbag' ground to a halt on the forward deck and caught fire. This was bad enough but to add to the danger was the presence of two depthcharges

The final operational variant of the Swordfish was the Mk.III, which was equipped with centimetric radar (ASV Mk.XI) housed in a cover under the forward fuselage. Rocket-assisted Take-off (RATOG) pipes were another regular feature on the Mk.III. The extra power was deemed necessary to guarantee a safe launch when the aircraft was fully loaded.

No.736 Sqdn. was commissioned in May 1943 at Yeovilton and assumed duties as the School of Air Combat; in doing so the FAA severed its previous dependence upon the RAF's Fighter leader's School. It later transferred to St. Merryn where it served as the Fighter Combat School element of the School of Naval Warfare. Here a Seafire Mk.Ib is moving along the runway at one of the two-named airfields.

under the wings. The crew scrambled clear and although hoses were played upon the flames, at least one of the weapons 'cooked off', blowing a large hole in the deck surface. Mercifully, only one seaman was killed; ironically he was not on the deck but directly below the explosion.

VINDEX – Seeking the 'Weatherman'

During VINDEX's March convoy duty, a number of radio and compass failures among her Sea Hurricane complement had restricted their operational use. In the interim period up to late April, these faults had been rectified. In addition, L/Cdr. Gick had ordered the adaptation of five of the fighters for the carriage of rocket racks while a sixth Sea Hurricane among the remaining three carried marine markers in place of two of its cannon. Also on board were eight Mk.III Swordfish bearing ASV Mk.XI radar pods and five Mk.IIs.

A regular feature of U-Boat operations was the presence in mid-Atlantic of several submarines whose brief it was to report weather conditions back to the central U-Boat HQ at Lorient in France. VINDEX was attached to the 6th Escort Group whose task it would be to hunt down and sink one of these enemy warships. Heavy seas, rainsqualls and limited visibility accompanied the Force as they headed out for the reported area. Before the warships were in the required search zone, yet another Swordfish crew had fallen victim to fuel contamination. On the 5th one of the Sea Hurricanes launched immediately came down in the sea through engine failure, and its pilot drowned or died of exposure prior to being picked up.

The next day yielded the anticipated result, however, when a cluster of depth-charges ejected by a sloop brought U-765 to the surface. By the time L/Cdr. Sheffield (No.825 Sqdn. CO) was beginning his attack run the *Kriegsmarine* crew were

Numbers of Swordfish Mk.II were converted from a three-man to a two-man crew function, the purpose being to provide a dual-control function in order to instruct new pilots to the 'Stringbag'. Both cockpits are fitted with prominent headrests – doubtless for absorbing the shock of a heavy landing by the trainee pilot! The aircraft taking off is a Percival Proctor communications machine.

The danger to an airman's life and limb, as well as the security of his aircraft, was not restricted to time spent aloft. In this case, One Corsair Mk.I from No.1835 Sqdn. has smashed the fin and rudder of a second Mk.I during ground handling operations during the unit's time at Brunswick, Maine. The damaged fighter displays the framed 'birdcage' canopy fitted to this initial Corsair variant.

A Petty Officer is being handed radio equipment out of an Albacore's rear cockpit by a 'Wren', who is standing in the open area between the hinged canopy frame and the sliding hatch cover. Other points of note are the entrance door and the dinghy hatch immediately behind the sliding hatch.

manning their flak guns and pouring out a hail of fire that damaged the diving 'Stringbag' but did not prevent its two depth-charges pitching into the sea on either side of its target. The resultant explosions literally blew the U-Boat in half to leave a handful of survivors swimming for their lives.

Continued water contamination of the aviation fuel tanks inevitably slowed down refuelling operations, while a major problem with the lift mechanism resulted in almost twenty-four hours where the alternative of manual cranking adversely affected the pace of aircraft 'ranging' and 'striking down'. Then on the 11th occurred the latest tragedy involving aircrew. The Webb crew had survived two serious crash-landings on the deck during March and during the early hours this day were to be involved in a third incident; this time round the outcome would be fatal. A Force Seven gale was causing VINDEX to carve a torturous path through the Atlantic waters, as Webb was manoeuvered his 'Stringbag' in over the carrier's stern. Just then, the vessel pitched violently upwards, and the impact between deck and aircraft smashed the landing gear. On the previous occasion this had happened, the aircraft had slithered to a halt. On this occasion, a combination of the carrier's motion and the aircraft's action in slewing to one side saw the latter drop over the side and into the watery maelstrom. All three airmen were never seen again and were presumed to have drowned; even had they survived the enforced 'ditching', death by exposure in the darkened Atlantic void would soon have followed.

One positive result arising from VINDEX's latest sortie was the solving of the fuel contamination problem. The aviation fuel tanks were surrounded by compartments containing cold water, by way of reducing the hazard of fire and/or explosions. The fuel was pumped out to the aircraft refuelling points using compressed air, which by its very nature tended to heat up – until it entered the tanks, when it rapidly cooled down and condensed! Here was the source of the contamination.

The Chief Engineer's remedy, recommended to (and ultimately accepted by) the Admiralty, was to first dispense with the coldwater protection facility. A three-stage operation would then be initiated: 1.) Prior to filling the tanks with fuel, seawater would be pumped in, in order to dispel all the air; 2.) When filling up with fuel, a separate outlet would be opened, with which the seawater would be expelled as the fuel poured in; 3.) On commencing refuelling operations, the sea water would be re-admitted. Since the seawater was of greater density it would not mix with the aviation fuel in a similar manner to fresh water, but would merely force its onward movement to the refuelling points.

The Swordfish Aircrew's Travails

The regular threat of U-Boat attacks on the Atlantic convoy routes had largely faded into the background by mid-1944, and the CVEs were detached to other Theaters of Operations, leaving the nineteen MAC-ships to fulfil escort duties. By VE-Day, such was the control exercised by the Royal and Canadian

Aerodrome Dummy Deck Landing (ADDL) facilities were created at several airfields. These enabled pilots to practice deck landings in a much more easy-paced set of circumstances before advancing to the full test of landing on a carrier. The Albacore in the foreground has made a neat approach, but the following aircraft seems to be too close and is banking away to make a second approach.

A MAC-ship positioned within the ranks of the convoy it is escorting has turned across the path of the merchantmen in order to steam into wind. The Swordfish Mk.III is about to touch down in good order as the 'Batsman' swings his bats down. The risk to the 'Batsman' of being struck by an aircraft was always high, especially on the MAC-ships, whose flight deck width (60 ft.) was not greatly in excess of a Swordfish's wingspan at 45 ft.!

The U.S. carrier RANGER was 'loaned' to the Home Fleet during late 1943 as a replacement for ILLUSTRIOUS, then operating in the Mediterranean. The US Navy warships' SBD Dauntlesses and Avengers attacked Norwegian targets inside Bodo harbor on 4 October, destroying five merchantmen and damaging a further five in the process.

The personnel for the initial group of Avenger-equipped Sqdns. were dispatched over to the United States during 1943 in order to work-up on the aircraft prior to becoming operational. Two Petty officers with white-topped peak caps are supervising a pair of ratings working on a .50 machine gun. The Avenger behind is already bearing British roundels.

Navies that no recorded attack on a convoy under MAC-ship cover was to be noted. Conversely, there were to be but a handful of occasions during the 4,000 individual sorties flown by the FAA aircrew when a positive U-Boat sighting and follow-up attack was made.

The open cockpit arrangement on the Swordfish was hardly the best environment in which to conduct flying operations at any time of the year or in the majority of the Theaters of Operation during World War II. While in flight the already windy effect of the aircraft's slipstream was swiftly turned into a frigid atmosphere that inevitably took its toll on even the fittest of airmen. Controlling the aircraft, attempting to plot a course or carrying out TAG duties all too often became a grim struggle against the elements, whether in the form of wind and gales, lashing rain, sleet or snow – conditions regularly experienced over the Atlantic and Arctic Oceans in particular. It was little wonder that numerous crews on return to their carrier had to be virtually hauled out of their cockpits

To the sheer monotony and discomfort accruing from these sorties was added the manifold dangers inherent in operating over the ocean. For a start, the aircraft were not flying from a fixed land base but from a mobile platform, a fact that increased the pressure upon each Swordfish Observer, who literally had

This posed picture shows a Lt/Cdr in full No.1 Dress uniform standing on the wing of a Hellcat. In fact the full length jacket, although very smart in appearance, proved to be an impractical item of wear for the rough and tumble of combat flying and was replaced during World War II by a shortened battledress design similar to the "Ike" Jacket.

Below: Two Swordfish Mk.II are being ranged on the deck of TRACKER; both belong to No.816 Sqdn. and are bearing the lighter color scheme introduced around 1943. This was largely white with the top fuselage and upper wing surfaces in dark slate grey and extra dark sea grey. The engine inertia-starter handle is in place on the nearside aircraft's cowling.

Two lines of Seafires Mk.Ib are gathered near the hangars at Yeovilton, home for the No. 1 Naval Air Fighter School. The party of four 'airmen' on the right are in fact civilian teenagers from the RAF youth organisation, the Air Training Corps (ATC). The Seafires belong to No.736 Sqdn., which transferred to St. Merryn in September 1943 to become the Fighter Combat School element of the School of Naval Air Warfare.

to navigate for his and his crew's life. Navigation at sea possessed a potentially grave disadvantage compared to operations conducted over land, namely that there were no geographic features on which to make a visual confirmation of one's position. Radio silence was tightly applied in order to conceal a convoy's presence, so this medium for confirming the carrier's position was discouraged, even in an emergency. (Short Morse Code transmissions could be made by the TAG on each leg of the patrol's triangular course, but this was the normal limit of transmission traffic).

The advent of ASV radar did provide a crude means of identifying the convoy, which would register as a large 'blip' at distances up to thirty miles, but with the aircraft heading away up to sixty miles on two of the three legs of the triangle, the chance of a navigational error creating the grounds for a missed rendezvous was always lurking in the background. Then, the wind condition could vary at any time, a factor that was to cause the loss of several of the 'Stringbags'. The pedestrian speed of the aircraft approaching from behind and battling against the combination of a headwind and the convoy speed could and did result in its running out of fuel before even visual contact had been made, so consigning the crew to sad, watery oblivion.

Cloud or mist over the carrier on a successful return overhead would also render attempts to gain visual contact in vain. The ultimate option of baling out would, unlike their land-based contemporaries, almost certainly prove fatal; the twin option of 'ditching' was not much better, unless effected in the near vicinity of either a merchantman or escort, since there was a good chance of dying from exposure in the often chilled Atlantic waters before being picked up.

Landings on the ' postage stamp' sized decks of the MAC-ships was never easy, even with the Swordfish. A sizeable number of the 'Stringbags' smashed their landing gear whenever the carrier pitched too violently at the point of landing, or dislodged the engine when the aircraft over-shot the arrester-wires and impacted with the safety barrier. Other aircraft went over into the catwalks or overboard when their 'airfield' inconveniently rolled under the influence of the sea.

All in all, the FAA aircrews lot was a particularly hard one, and deserving of full respect from their RAF contemporaries, no matter how difficult the latter body's tasks were perceived to be!

Final Victory

The final twelve months of Allied Naval/Air operations in the Atlantic produced relatively little 'excitement' in the way of encounters with single U-Boats, let alone any prospect of mass assault upon the convoys, many of whom were formed out of three-figure Forces of merchantmen. Indeed, such was the dominance factor over the entire region that a proportion of the MAC-Ships were relieved of their duty by the end of 1944.

The *Kriegsmarine*'s hold had been thoroughly wrested away from this operational Theater and was never to regain the slightest semblance of its mid-War threat to Britain's (and by extension Allied) advancement towards a Final Victory in Europe. During 1944 a very small number of merchantmen (thirty-one) were culled from the convoy ranks by the U-Boats whose use of the Schnorkel air-intake system did reduce their overall time spent on the surface; on the other hand, the Allied aircraft and surface escort vessels kept up a relentless pressure to add no less than 111 U-Boats to their lethal tally of sinkings. A similar scale of merchantmen to U-Boat losses (nineteen to seventy-one, with the latter figure including sixteen crews in transit from Germany to Norway) occurred up to the onset of VE-Day.

One of the final victories in the Atlantic initially involved Swordfish embarked on EMPIRE MCALPINE. On 12 April an SOS call from a torpedoed merchantmen was subsequently responded to by three crews from No. 836 Sqdn's Y Flight, one of whom picked out the tell-tale 'feather' trail left behind by a Schnorkel frame and released his two depth charges, although with no apparent result. However, later in the day, the surface escorts picked up a 'contact' that finally evolved into U-1024; the U-Boat surfaced and its *Kapitän* surrendered himself and the crew. The warship was boarded and secured for towing into a British harbor.

Although VE-Day occurred on 8 May 1945, a state of operational alert was maintained for several weeks thereafter. This was deemed necessary in order to ensure all surviving German warships – in practice this meant U-Boats – were confirmed as accounted for and secured under Allied control. The MAC-Ship contribution to Victory was concluded on 21 May when No.836 Sqdn. that had formed the nucleus for all Swordfish embarked was disbanded. However, the final aircraft sortie occurred on 28 June with the arrival in a British port of EMPIRE MACKAY.

The statistics recorded by the MAC-ship Swordfish crew were excellent; upwards of 200 convoys escorted, slightly over 9,000 hours operational flying that involved just over 4,000 individual sorties. The primary risk to the aircrew had largely arisen from the treacherous weather elements existing in the Atlantic rather than from the flak batteries on the U-Boats, since very few of the enemy warships were ever sighted let alone attacked. This fact in no way diminishes the overall effort put in by the aviators and their equally hard-working support staff on the MAC-Ships in what was a successful bid to ensure the safe delivery of the convoys plying the North Atlantic routes – a 'victory' to stand alongside any of the offensive Actions undertaken by the Fleet Air Arm in World War II.

CHAPTER ELEVEN

D-Day to VE-Day in Europe

The long-term and detailed preparations for the Invasion of Western Europe meant the wholesale involvement of the Allied Air Forces, which in Britain's case encompassed both the RAF and the FAA. However, the latter Force's units would operate both off carriers and from airfields allocated within Southern England. In the case of the Avenger, and Swordfish-equipped Sqdns those involved in Operation 'Overlord' would be assigned to General Reconnaissance Wings of RAF Coastal Command operating out of four airfields. Manston and Hawkinge in Kent were to accommodate Nos.155 and 157 Wings; No.848 Sqdn. (Avengers) and No.819 Sqdn. (Swordfish) came under No.155 Wing while No.157 Wing (Hawkinge) initially played host to Nos.854 and 855 Sqdns. (both with Avengers). The other pair of airfields was located in the southwest, at Harrowbeer and Perranporth. Their FAA allocation was No.838 Sqdn. (Swordfish) at Harrowbeer, and Nos.816 (Swordfish), 849 and 850 (Avenger) Sqdns. at Perranporth.

Those Sqdns. based in Kent were to make numerous sorties along the coastline between France and Holland with a mix of anti-shipping strikes and anti-submarine patrols being completed on either side of D-Day. Their contemporaries further west were to be involved in an up-to-date and virtually watertight version of 'Channel Stop'. This title originally referred to the ultimately humiliating attempts to 'bottle up' the three *Kriegsmarine* Capital ships in Brest, whose successful 'Channel Dash' in February 1942 witnessed a tactical nadir for both the RAF and Royal Navy Forces assigned to this function. Now, in 1944, the boot was to be very much on the other foot, with any attempts by German surface or underwater warships to gain access to the mass of Allied shipping crossing over to the Normandy beach-heads being literally 'killed off'.

Several FAA fighter Sqdns. were also involved in the planning. No.24 Naval Fighter Wing (NFW), with its Seafires III of Nos.887 and 894 Sqdns. took up the duty of escorting Typhoon sorties in the April-May run-up to D-Day, before embarking on INDEFATIGABLE. Meanwhile, No.3 Naval Fighter Wing (NFW) consisted of Nos.808, 885, 886 and 897 Sqdns. FAA, plus Nos.26 and 63 Sqdns. RAF and VCS-7 of the U.S. Navy. The basic brief for these units, who were brought together as an Air Spotting Pool, was to act as 'spotters' for the Naval bombarding Force during and immediately after D-Day: tactical reconnaissance operations were also to be carried out.

Based at Lee-on-Solent on England's south coast near to the huge Naval Base at Portsmouth, the pilots were thoroughly instructed in the 'spotting' duty. Two primary methods were to be indulged in:

• 'Ship Control'. This consisted of working on the 'clock' system with noon towards the north to provide the appropriate direction indicator to the gunners. Distance information was provided in yards.

• 'Air Control'. This consisted of the direction pilot telling the gunners to raise or lower range in yards, using the bracket principal of zeroing in on a target. When satisfied the target was 'zeroed in' the pilot would say 'Fire for effect'. This was in order, provided the gunners kept to the directions while firing a sequence of broadsides. However, if the initial salvo was still off range the pilot generally could not get himself heard until all firing had ceased – hence an inordinate and unnecessary ordnance waste would have occurred in such an event – with the

The split-level hangar arrangement on FURIOUS is shown to advantage in this picture. Two Seafires Mk.LIIc belonging to Nos.801 or 880 Sqdn. occupy the upper deck, while directly below, the massive bulk of a No.830 Sqdn. Barracuda Mk.II is rolled forward onto the lift platform; note the RAF airman standing to the left.

blame for the miscalculation seemingly placed on the pilot's head, regardless!

The forty-eight aircraft comprising No.3 NFW's strength were Seafires Mk.LIII, which possessed several advantages for the low to medium-altitude operations intended to be flown over Normandy. For a start this variant had the Merlin 55M fitted with a 'cropped' blower that did not absorb the engine power to no purpose at low altitude. The resultant energy saved meant that the aircraft could go faster and further on the same fuel capacity. Another alteration involved the 'cropping' of the wing tips by two feet; this increased the Seafire LIII's roll-rate but did not adversely affect the fighter's turning circle, while the marginally reduced wing area added to the maximum speed factor. With a lighter fuselage (200 lbs.), plus more weight loss with the deletion of the outer MGs, (As well as an increase in 200 hp compared to the Spitfire Mk.IX), the LIII could out-turn, out-climb and out-roll its RAF contemporary below 10,000 ft. Also, the GGS IID replaced the fixed GM Mk.II gun-sight. The new sight had two 'rings' – a fixed four-degree unit for those wishing to adhere to the former GG Mk.II's use and a second unit that altered its aiming point in a manner that enabled the pilot to automatically allow for the correct deflection, provided he kept it upon the target.

The Tribulations of 'Spotting'

The indifferent weather conditions on D-Day fortunately did not materially interfere with the 'spotting' sorties, and Lt. Crosley's (No.880 Sqdn.) experience this day was fairly typical. He and his No.2 – the latter acting as cover against being 'bounced' – flew three sorties, acting on behalf of the battleship WARSPITE. Each sortie lasted some two hours, and the primary targets were German coastal defence batteries. During the first sortie, these still remained in action despite an accurate bombardment by the RN gunners, and tended to confirm the solid nature of the concrete emplacements that were probably only vulnerable to a direct hit. (The physical and psychological pressure on the Germans arising from the constant pounding effect could not be discounted, and played a part in the ultimate Allied success, even if the batteries were not always destroyed). Also, the ship's gunners during the second sortie were only ready to operate when the Seafires were virtually at the stage of having to head home; before turning back, the two pilots went down and strafed road transport. On both occasions, the R/T connection from the warship was intermittent, and this problem was destined to persist throughout the entire period of 'spotting' activities. (The third sortie was finally 'aborted' when Crosley discovered his replacement fighter's drop tank would not jettison and his guns would not work).

By nightfall on 6 June, four FAA pilots had either been shot down or force-landed due to the persistent low cloud base that kept the aircraft dangerously exposed to enemy flak. On the other hand a latent, more insidious danger to the 'spotters' survival was to come from the Allied CAP Force. These pilots, sighting aircraft at low level, especially ones with seemingly 'square' wing tips that tallied with Fw 190 or even Bf 109 outlines, would naturally descend on what they took to be

Two officers from No.819 Sqdn. stand by a Swordfish Mk.III at Manston, Kent. This unit was then part of No.155 Wing based at the airfield around D-Day. Duties included anti-submarine patrols as well as the laying of smoke screens over the Invasion Fleet on 6 June. The overall black colour applied to the aircraft is broken by the White D-Day stripes applied just ahead of the Invasion date of 6 June 1944.

A Corsair from an FAA Sqdn. training-up in the United States is snapped in the act of 'cleaning up' its landing gear. The main struts are turning through ninety degrees to lay fore-and-aft in the wing bays. The bottom of the tail-wheel tire would extend through the rectangular recesses in the door covers.

Luftwaffe fighters. For the Lead pilot in each 'spotter' Section, the problems of working with folding maps in the already cramped confines of a Seafire further restricted his ability to pay attention to other than the task at hand – hence the absolute necessity for the No.2 to keep his eyes peeled for any aerial attacker.

The virtual absence of the *Luftwaffe* over the D-Day beaches was followed up next day (7th) by an almost similar lack of aerial challenge to the Invading Forces. Lt. Crosley was on his first daily sortie and seeking out suitable bombardment targets near Caen when he observed a single 'bogey' flying on a reverse course and in a gentle fashion. Before its identity could be absolutely confirmed it had disappeared into cloud. A short time after, a second 'bogey' was picked up and this time Crosley used his extra height to tuck in behind. The need to see the identifying Black Crosses of a *Luftwaffe* aircraft should have proved unnecessary since the machine was not bearing D-Day stripes and therefore had to be 'hostile'. As it was a short burst of cannon fire put paid to fighter and pilot as they fell down to impact with the Normandy soil.

'Friendly Fire' 1

On 8 June, Lt. Crosley was flying an early morning sortie at moderate altitude. He and Lt. Keen were carrying out a 'sweep' inland to search out reported enemy airfields, prior to carrying out their basic function, the associated warship not being yet prepared for action. The absence up to now of the *Luftwaffe* had created a dangerous sense of ease that any other aircraft sighted would be Allied machines. Therefore when a bunch of

fighters were seen, Crosley assumed they were Spitfires – that swiftly evolved into Fw 190s! It was then that a combination of the sound turning radius of the Seafire Mk.FIII and the pilots' wearing of Franks Suits that kept the resultant combat from ending in the Germans favor.

The Franks Suit was an 'anti-G' piece of outer clothing that used a gallon of water with which to apply all-round pressure to the body and prevent blood flow from feeding down to the lower limbs when engaged in tight turn or similar high-stress manoeuvres. The benefit of this facility had been proved from the Suit's introduction in late 1942 and was proved again on this occasion, because the two FAA pilots successfully held off their numerically superior adversaries for fully twenty minutes.

On a later sortie the same day these two pilots again experienced the 'bounce' as the Section flew over beach-head, this time by Spitfires They had previously been advised to contact RAMILLES due to WARSPITE being rendered out of action when they again came under attack. This second air combat lasted almost as long as the morning experience with the Spitfires' fire coming uncomfortably close, but the FAA fighters' superior turning radius, especially in the climb, again saved the day and the RAF finally pilots slunk away unfulfilled, as had the true adversaries earlier on.

The twin success of this Section in evading being shot down was not always matched by their fellow-FAA colleagues. Between 7 and 8 June at least four other FAA or RAF 'spotter' aircraft failed to survive being 'bounced' by the *Luftwaffe* although all the pilots managed to escape with their lives. Two more fighters were successfully engaged by enemy flak

A Swordfish Mk.II or III has come to an undignified end in a Belgian field sometime between November 1944 and February 1945. In that period a No.819 Sqdn. Detachment operated out of two airfields in Belgium, Maldeghem and Knokke-le-Zoute. The all-black finish had been retained by this particular aircraft.

Below: The D-Day stripes on this trio of rocket-armed Swordfish Mk.II operating with No.816 Sqdn. stand out clearly against the wing camouflage. Note also that the stripes positioned on the wings of the central Swordfish are further inwards than on either of the other two aircraft. This Sqdn. operated from southwest England as part of No.19 Group, RAF Coastal Command up to August 1944 when it was disbanded.

This Avenger Mk.II had its port stabiliser shot off by flak during a June 1944 anti-shipping sortie off the French coast. The strike killed the Observer and wounded Sub/Lt. White (P) and the TAG. In spite of the severe degree of damage and White's wounds, the aircraft was brought back and landed safely. Note how a thin black line separates the D-Day stripe from the camouflage pattern.

This picture highlights the Fleet Air Arm's general dependence on American aircraft designs from 1943 onwards. The escort carrier's deck holds five Grumman Avengers and two Wildcats. Overhead five Corsairs are banking to port.

The stubby outline of a Wildcat Mk.V is further highlighted by the application of a full set of black-and-white D-Day stripes. The rear fuselage stripe has been amended to take account of the lettering and aircraft serial number.

The New England landscape is seen beneath a line-abreast formation of six FAA Corsairs. The pilots are becoming accustomed to flying the huge fighter off an airfield, after which they will commence deck-landing practice. Two of the aircraft have their individual numbers applied against a white rectangular background.

King George VI stands in the center of a group of Senior Naval staff while in the course of inspecting the crew and facilities on board a Fleet carrier. To the monarch's immediate right is Admiral Sir Bruce Fraser who became C-in-C of the British Pacific Fleet in late 1944. The escort carrier in the background is SEARCHER.

King George VI is now being escorted round the facilities on board SEARCHER on the same day as his inspection of a Fleet carrier. The nearest Wildcat V bears the codes for 898 Sqdn. that was embarked on this escort carrier between December 1943 and the unit's disbandment in the following July.

The Grumman Avenger's bulky shape concealed a sound all-round performance for carrier operations that included its take-off and landing capabilities, even on the reduced flight decks length of a CVE. In this picture, an aircraft from No.846 Sqdn. lifts off TRACKER with a comfortable margin of deck still remaining.

batteries and crash-landed, one of which was flown by Lt. 'Dicky' Law, the No.886 Sqdn. senior pilot. The bulk of his Franks Suit having been discarded, Law collected the still-secret Gyro Gun-sight among other equipment items of importance and hiked his way along to the nearest Allied Beachhead.

'Friendly Fire' 2

A second self-inflicted danger came from Allied AA batteries on warships and even landing craft. The plethora of cannon-caliber weapons currently on hand could throw up an almost impenetrable weight of firepower, that was all the more lethal thanks to the recent introduction of 'proximity-fused' shells on the 40mm guns that did not need to impact directly with their target in order to bring them down. It mattered not one jot that Gen. Eisenhower had prior to D-Day issued his famous statement relating to air power; "When you see aircraft overhead they will be ours". The shipboard gunners worked on the not unjustified premise that since their static vessels were at a disadvantage to any encroaching aircraft they would fire first – regardless of its Nationality!

L/Cdr. Bailey (No.886 Sqdn. CO) had arrived over the beaches to commence his 'spotter' duty on the 8th but received unwelcome attention from Allied AA fire. He banked away and came in at a deliberate pace in order to confirm his 'friendly' status – only to be again engaged, this time with fatal results for his Seafire. The fighter lurched downwards as Bailey desperately struggled to get out from the plunging machine. All his efforts had failed and he had given up hope of surviving. Then, in a final bid to escape his looming fate he pulled the parachute ripcord. His next recollection was of laying in the water edge of a beach with a badly dislocated

shoulder, but the exact manner of how he had cheated Death would never be known.

He had landed in an American sector, and to add insult to injury was not greeted as an Ally when confronted but was instead taken along to a temporary POW 'Cage'; it appeared that the black flying overalls he was wearing and a lack of personal identity convinced his 'captors' that he was German! It was some hours before Bailey could clarify who he was, but even then an air of suspicion seemed to linger in the minds of those U.S. personnel who interrogated him following his release from the 'Cage'.

From 16 to 20 June, the Allied Armies advance was such that the ships' gunners were increasingly firing at maximum range. On 25 June the penultimate phase of ship-to-shore bombardment was initiated, this time further west on the port of Cherbourg. The quayside facilities had made the town a priority target for early occupation by the U.S. Army, but the German garrison had mounted a stiff resistance The fortress installations located there were targeted and duly hammered although once again the 'spotters' observations indicated that a good degree of the fire was spread outside the area. Finally, at the month-end the two major battleships NELSON and RODNEY were shifted back to the east to support the British advance on Caen.

Over the entire period since D-Day 'spotter' pilot complaints were voiced about the R/T links between them and their assigned warships. These had often proved to be indifferent to poor in quality and were probably a contributory factor in the indifferent to poor results arising from the shelling, at least as observed. However, the comments of the German Commanders in the Field as to the stultifying effect of the shelling – as well as the bombing assault – on their efforts to

A Corsair Mk.II appears to be in danger of running out of available flight deck on an escort carrier before getting airborne. The code letters are those for No.1841 Sqdn. but this unit only operated off an escort carrier during its transit from America to Britain, after which it served on FORMIDABLE until the end of World War II.

Left: NF588 was a Seafire Mk.III, one of a 1944 Westland-produced batch. The failed deck landing has been attempted on board SMITER, an escort carrier that was retained in a training role until mid-1945. The Seafire's rear fuselage displays a clear wrinkling of the skin. Note the deck handler who is wielding a fire extinguisher, ready to extinguish the flames should a fire occur. Right: The escort carrier RAJAH was commissioned in January 1944 but was primarily employed in a passive role as an 'aircraft-ferry' vessel. In this picture her deck is crowded with Hellcats destined not for the FAA but the U.S. Navy.

properly mount a counter-offensive confirmed that material damage was being regularly inflicted. One Chief of Staff also reported how some of the Panzer units were literally blown onto their sides even by near misses! No.3 Wing casualties were thirty-two aircraft with eleven of the pilots KIA, in return for which 2,500 sorties were flown.

Up North

Hitler's fixation as to the likelihood of a second Invasion Front opening in Norway had been assiduously fed prior to D-Day by the creation of a fictitious 'Army Command' in Scotland. One consequence of the *Führer*'s obsession had already resulted in the stationing of a massive Wehrmacht Force throughout that Northern outpost a good proportion of which could have been far better utilised on the other major Fronts,

particularly in Russia. Now that France had been invaded, even the German Leader was forced to consider re-deploying these troops as reinforcements. The road routes in Norway were few and limited in terms of quick traffic movement and so to carry out the transfers, the Germans also had to use shipping down along the Norwegian coastline, after which further ship transportation across the Skagerrak to Denmark would be required.

There were other current and subsequent considerations for mounting a sustained Naval Campaign against Norway. The first involved the continuing presence to the Allied convoy routes posed by the battleship TIRPITZ. As it was a further five months would ensue before the warship was finally put out of permanent commission by Nos.9 and 617 Sqdns. Lancasters on 12 November. The major U-Boat Bases at Brest,

No.766 Sqdn. served in a number of support roles during World War II. By July 1943 it had transferred to Inskip where its Swordfish Mks.II and III were operated as part of No.1 Naval Operational Training Unit (NOTU). This Mk.II bears a full rocket load under the wings. Note how the aircraft code letters are placed within a black-edged rectangle.

St. Nazaire and Lorient were quickly cut off from their main supply routes over land and by the beginning of August were coming under direct siege. The impending loss of these key U-Boat 'outlets' into the Atlantic consequently forced the *Kriegsmarine* to consider operations from Norwegian ports, in particular Bergen.

The interdiction of German shipping all along the western European coastline had commenced in 1940/41 with the efforts of No.2 Group RAF's Blenheims to hinder traffic through low-level attacks, a process that had proved as costly in aircraft and crews as in registering solid figures of vessels sunk. This policy had also been reinforced over the same time-period by the laying of sea-mines, with RAF Bomber Command playing the leading role. ACM Harris's 'heavies' had sowed copious numbers of these weapons as far down as the Franco-Spanish border, into the Baltic and up along Norway's seaboard. In the latter case, the FAA had joined in this form of Offensive from March 1944 onwards. However, prior to this in the middle of 1943 three brief excursions – two Royal Navy and one U.S. Navy – had been directed against northern Norway; the first two were 'sweeps' involving FURIOUS, UNICORN and ILLUSTRIOUS that were designed to draw German attention away from the impending Invasion of Sicily, while USS

From 1943 onwards, to the threat to U-Boats of their being damaged or destroyed by depth charges or homing torpedoes was added that posed by the rocket projectile. Two of these three-inch weapons are being carried by the two sailors and are probably for fitting to the Swordfish directly behind. The 'Stringbag's' rocket rails were mounted in two groups of four under the wings.

Below: No.816 Sqdn. was one of the Swordfish-equipped units that were tasked with closing off the English Channel to U-Boats and surface warships attempting to interdict the cross-Channel Allied build-up in Normandy from D-Day onwards. Note the engine inertia-starter handle protruding from the cowling, whose operation was physically draining on the individual unfortunate enough to be assigned the duty!

Seafires and Fireflies for a major mine-laying sortie in the Leads at Alesund south of Trondheim. The mines were to be released by Nos.852 and 846 Sqdns. Avengers flying off the CVEs NABOB and TRUMPETER. The Fireflies attacked flak positions while the Seafires provided top cover and also strafed an airfield housing Bf 110s, six of whom were destroyed. The Avengers got their mines away in the face of ultimately fierce flak that claimed one Avenger along with its crew and one Firefly.

A month later another large-scale mine-laying sortie was laid on at Aaramsund close to Alesund. This assault involved the CVE TRUMPETER and FURIOUS, the veteran carrier's three decades of valuable RN service being brought to a close with this Operation. The limited space on the first-named carrier restricted her complement to eighteen Avengers of Nos.846 and 852 Sqdns., the latter-named Sqdn.'s machines being 'borrowed' from the now permanently de-commissioned NABOB, following her near sinking on 22 August. Fighter cover in the form of Nos.801 and 880 Sqdns. Seafires was embarked on FURIOUS; also on hand were the Barracudas of No.827 Sqdn. to provide anti-submarine duties as well as a second strike wave.

The attacking Force was off the Norwegian coast on 11 September and commenced launching the aircraft for the planned low-level sortie. The correct landfall was made and the Avengers adopted the briefed formation pattern of three-plane columns with which to carry out the drop. However, the channel stretch that was chosen to be 'sown' and expected to be absent of shipping was now occupied by several vessels, whose combined flak weaponry along with shore-based units opened up. The frantic weaving of the Seafires around the strike formation as the latter streamed down to engage the defences did not prevent an accurate mine-drop pattern. The enemy vessels did not escape unscathed from the strafing runs, with a minesweeper and a small merchantman reported as sunk, and a large merchantman left burning. Given the circumstances it was fortunate that just one aircraft was lost, this being a Seafire of No.801 Sqdn. along with its pilot.

The operational debut of the first Fairey Fireflies during July and August provided the FAA with another means by which to interdict shipping in particular, namely the rocket. The Firefly was able to mount under-wing racks bearing a total of eight three-inch weapons. No.1770 Sqdn. on board INDEFATIGABLE had put these to use during the second and final series of strikes on TIRPITZ although the emphasis was upon flak-suppression in the surrounding area of Kaafjord. During November and December IMPLACABLE participated in two anti-shipping sorties that opened her World War II operational career. Her Firefly Sqdn. (No.1771) escorted by Seafires enjoyed a particularly good haul on 26 November when a convoy with heavy flak-ship cover was pounced on. When the action was over the cannon and rocket fire from both strike and fighter escort three of the flak-ships were knocked out or sunk and one of the merchantmen forced into a situation where her Norwegian Captain drove her ashore, where she later sank.

A Kingfisher floatplane has its engine running up as the pilot prepares to taxi forward off the slipway and into the sea. The Vought-Sikorsky design was aerodynamically more advanced and enjoyed a superior performance to the FAA's veteran Walrus. However, the Walrus maintained its pre-eminent position on board Royal Naval battleships and cruisers throughout World War II. In addition the Kingfisher entered FAA service at a point when catapult aircraft were no longer as necessary thanks to the expansion of carrier numbers.

Several FAA aircraft types are seen 'struck down' in the hangar of the escort carrier RAVAGER, a vessel that saw regular service as a deck-landing trainer. A Fulmar Mk.II occupies the right foreground, and directly behind is a Barracuda Mk.II. A single Hellcat is in the center foreground, while behind and to its left lurk two Avengers.

A Barracuda just landed off a strike against shipping targets near Bodo in northern Norway on 26 April 1944; several merchantmen in the convoy attacked were sunk. The 'Barra's' inner-rear wing sections are being folded upwards, after which the wings will also be folded backwards in the same manner as the aircraft in front.

The deck handler squatting on the right watches the departure of one of EMPEROR's Hellcats for a sortie against targets in Norway. The carrier embarked Nos.800 and 804 Sqdn. between December 1943 and June 1944. What appears to be the letter E on the fighter second from left would identify it as being assigned to No.800 Sqdn.

A Seafire has just been fired off the flight deck through the use of a 'cradle' frame. The frame was collapsible and was erected under and attached to each succeeding aircraft. This was a procedure that was probably slower than the later method of launching aircraft with a strop and deck-mounted catapult 'shuttle'. Launching in a tail-down attitude was also regarded as better for gaining immediate stability in flight.

The weather conditions prior to this strike had kept the aircraft deck-bound for some seventy-two hours as mountainous seas added to the discomfort afforded by the already chilled temperature, and having moderated sufficiently for launch on the 26th promptly deteriorated again. The Gale Force 11 illustrated the fact that deck handling of aircraft was ever a very dangerous proposition, especially when attempting to manoeuver the aircraft on a tilting and slippery spray-soaked surface. The man in the cockpit had to be ready to hit the brakes quickly and two others with wheel-chocks equally ready to place these in position when needed, otherwise the aircraft was liable to slip off into the catwalk or worse still disappear with its 'pilot' over the side. At least one Seafire tipped up on its nose and splintered the propeller tips due to the carrier rolling at an inopportune moment as the wheel chocks were being inserted; this braking action only exacerbated the situation since the aircraft was pointing 'downhill'! As it was the second sortie by the carrier had to be cut short due to the battering she had received from the seas having damaged the bow area so much that it was another two months before she was again declared operational. Mother Nature had once again shown she was the equal of any human adversary.

Tightening the Noose

The series of FAA assaults on the Norwegian coast continued into the New Year. An interesting variation in interdiction of enemy shipping traffic arose during February, and brought to mind the earlier Mediterranean experiences of Force K the Malta-based group of cruiser that harried Axis traffic between

On 26 November 1944 IMPLACABLE launched Fireflies along with Seafires and Barracudas off the Norwegian coast. A convoy near Rorvik was attacked and much damage inflicted. One of the Fireflies from No.1771 Sqdn., presumably having completed its strafing run, is seen crossing above this large merchantman, which is shrouded in smoke.

Italy and North Africa in 1941-1942. On the 10th the cruisers NORFOLK (Of BISMARCK fame) and DIDO set out with destroyer escorts to strike at any vessels encountered on the shipping route south of Trondheim. A separate Force consisting of the cruiser DEVONSHIRE and her destroyer escort accompanied two CVEs. One was PREMIER bearing Avengers and Wildcat IVs from No.856 Sqdn. The other was PUNCHER, the second such warship bearing a Canadian crew but with Royal Navy Sqdns. – in this case No.821 with Barracudas and Wildcats VI. This second Force was heading further south for

During World War II the Fairchild Argus entered limited service with the FAA as a communications aircraft. The large bulk of the design seems almost too much for the small two-bladed propeller to hold it in the air.

A party of sailors are tugging or pushing on the surfaces of a Wildcat Mk.V while the Petty Officer in the cockpit revs the engine in a bid to free the fighter from the clogging effect of the thick carpet of snow. Picture was taken at Yeovilton in 1945 and the aircraft belongs to No.759 Sqdn.

Haugesund near Stavangar. (The apparent absence of air cover for the Trondheim Force was misleading since it would arrive off its designated area by night before steaming south to link up with the other Force by daylight). The actual mining sorties on the 12th and 13th were carried out by the Avengers under strong Wildcat cover, with all but one mine secured in place, the exception being borne by an aircraft that 'aborted' the first sortie.

The pressure on shipping movements was maintained a week later when a twin-pronged operation initially involved the 'sweeping' of a German minefield believed to have been laid off southern Norway. This action was supplemented twenty-four hours later (22nd) by the latest mine-laying operation in the same coastal stretch. Nine Barracudas lifted

off PUNCHER and headed for the drop zone at Haugesund under escort by the carrier's Wildcat contingent as well as a further eight from PREMIER. Unexpectedly heavy flak took out two of the 'Barras' and inflicted varying degrees of damage on the other seven but the survivors made perfect drops in the selected Channel. At the same time the escorts indulged in strafing runs in Stavangar harbor.

One of the strikes launched during March (26th) involved PUNCHER, QUEEN and SEARCHER with mine-drops in the stretch between Trondheim and Kristiansand also involving seeking out suitable shipping targets. Up to now, the absence of the *Luftwaffe* in challenging this type of operation was surprising, but this scenario presented itself here. The Bf 109s of *Stab*/III. and III./JG 5 were then based at Trondheim, Gossen

A Hellcat has used up the bulk of the aft flight deck before finally engaging an arrester wire but has still tangled its landing gear with another wire. The wires sometimes snapped under the sheer weight and momentum of the aircraft, to provide a mortal threat to any deck handler unlucky enough to be in the way.

A group of FAA officers display a cheery manner as well as a very casual range of uniform dress. The majority wear battledress jackets and trousers, all but one of which is in dark blue. Shirts are conspicuous by their absence with polo-neck pullovers and/or scarves the majority choice. One officer (extreme right) sports flying boots while his immediate companion favours standard boots and gaiters. These men are almost certainly RNVR personnel.

Those 'Wrens' trained as air mechanics were not restricted to remaining on the ground if the equipment they were working on, such as radio or radar gear, required an air-test. This 'Wren' wearing a parachute harness above her flight overalls is walking away from the Barracuda, having probably carried out this stated duty.

An Avenger makes a sharp nose-up launch off TRUMPETER. The Ruler-class escort carrier was commissioned in late 1943 and participated in the last ever FAA strike against Norwegian targets (Kilbotn on 4 May 1945) when her Avengers of No.846 Sqdn. sunk U-711. The vessel also saw service with the BPF.

and Herdla and it was almost certainly elements of the *Gruppe* that engaged the FAA formation as it was strafing shipping. The resultant air battle between the estimated ten-strong *Luftwaffe* Force and the two Wildcat Flights ended with claims for three Bf 109s shot down; conversely, JG 5 records indicate just one pilot (*Fw*. Jäger of 9./JG 5) being declared MIA.

The weather effectively closed down a projected four-carrier assault on targets at Narvik in early April, but there was no such hindrance when what proved to be the final FAA strike on Norway was mounted on 4 May. The CVEs QUEEN, SEARCHER and TRUMPETER held the Avengers of Nos.853, 882 ad 846 Sqdns. Forty-four of the Grumman aircraft were dispatched against shipping targets at Harstad along with Wildcats acting in a flak-suppression role. The actual location at Kilbotn contained the Olsen Line's BLACK WATCH now impressed into German service as a Depot-ship. Moored alongside this vessel was a U-Boat, later confirmed as U-711, while nearby was a second merchantman. When the brisk action was over, all three vessels were sunk or sinking, at a

logistical toll of one Avenger and one Wildcat. The more insidious effect of the FAA mine-laying operations, in concert with the even more frequently pitched rocket strikes by the RAF's Strike Wings of Beaufighters and Mosquitoes against the Scandanavian coastlines, had ensured that the enemy was kept under almost relentless pressure in this northern Zone of Operations from late 1943 onwards.

WRNS – The Vital Female Factor

The vital part that the women of Britain and the Commonwealth played in the winning of both World Wars cannot be understated. The production of war material was as, if not more, dependent upon their effort, especially since the ranks of their male contemporaries had been greatly reduced thanks to the demands of military service.

However, the presence of women within the Armed Forces was arguably of equal value, as was evidenced by the three Service organisations – the Womens Auxiliary Air Force (WAAF), The Army's Auxiliary Territorial Service (ATS) and

A Wildcat Mk.VI has ended up 'ditched' and the pilot, having survived the sharp impact with the sea, is ready to scramble clear. The fighter's code letters indicate assignment to No.882 Sqdn. at a period commencing in early 1945 when the unit was embarked on the escort carrier SEARCHER for operations off Norway.

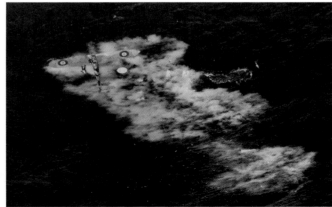

A Barracuda pilot has carried out a perfect 'ditching' into a mercifully smooth sea surface. The dinghy is attached by a lanyard to the fuselage as the three-man crew prepare to abandon their aircraft. The Barracuda was embarked on one of the four COLOSSUS-Class Light carriers at the time.

the Womens Royal Naval Service (WRNS) or 'Wrens'. As it was the latter Service did not come into being until June 1939, and there was a chauvinistic element spreading downwards from the Admiralty who regarded their very presence, let alone their ability to function efficiently in their ultimately manifold roles, as respectively unnecessary and unlikely. (In effect this attitude was; "The Navy is a Man's Service!").

The initial range of trades probably reflected a degree of this attitude in that it included 'office' functions such as secretaries, typists and clerks, although transport driving and accountancy and de-coding duties were also made available to the WRNS. The culinary profession was not ignored and sizeable numbers of women joined their male cook counterparts. The posting of qualified staff to the majority of Home Naval Bases and airfields was well in hand within the first two years of the Service's creation, and overseas postings commenced in late 1941, albeit in a shocking manner; all twenty-two personnel bound for Gibraltar lost their lives when their vessel was sunk en route.

The clear ability of women to match up to the demands of the tasks at hand was further acknowledged by the mid-period of World War II. By then, 'Wrens' were able to function in a vast range of trades extending from radar operators and photographic reconnaissance and meteorology staff to Intelligence and Operations duties. Direct activities with aircraft were also by now regularly carried out on Naval Air Stations all across the Globe. This included 'Wrens' acting as engine and airframe fitters, handling ordnance and radio equipment and packing parachutes. By 1944 the strength of

Ropes have been attached to the tail-wheel strut of an errant Seafire that has nosed over on landing, but appears to be structurally intact apart from a probable bent propeller. However, there is a risk of seriously fracturing the rear fuselage if the lowering process is not achieved in a very careful manner and the aircraft makes a heavy impact with the flight deck.

the WRNS was estimated at 75,000 officers and ratings, and the chauvinists put squarely 'in their place'.

'The Wavy Navy'

During World War II the Royal Naval Volunteer Reserve (RNVR) was destined to be affectionately or irreverently known as 'The Wavy Navy'. This was primarily due to the curving braid designs of the officers' rank badges, in contrast to the straight patterns applied to the uniforms of the Royal Navy's 'regulars'. Just as the expansion of the WRNS Service

A Barracuda Mk.II is ready to be launched from the Light Fleet carrier VENERABLE while steaming off a snow-capped landscape, probably Scotland. Picture was taken during April 1945 when the carrier was training-up for operations with the BPF. The curving white line on the aircraft's rear fuselage is the dinghy-release lanyard. The vertical shapes outboard of the wing Yagi aerials are the outer wing section locking plungers.

proved of inestimable value to the Navy's progress during the Conflict, so did the RNVR play an equally important role in advancing the future for both the surface and FAA elements of the 'Senior Service'.

The FAA was ill-prepared for taking on its Axis adversaries, particularly in the case of the Germans. There was barely sufficient numbers of middle and senior-ranking officers available in September 1939 and their numbers were to be seriously eroded over the ensuing two to three years. This ominously developing shortfall in operational expertise was initially balanced out by the thousands of often very youthful but enthusiastic 'volunteer' airmen who in effect could be regarded as a 'citizens FAA' in terms of their background. The vast bulk of them regularly treated the traditions of the Royal Navy in a casual manner that did not sit well with that eminent Body's hierarchy. As one among their number was quoted as saying, "We needed a much longer War, and the time therein, in order to learn about Kings Regulations and Admiralty Regulations!" What was not in any doubt was their desire to fly and to play their part in first arresting and then obliterating the worldwide onrush of Fascism.

By 1944, numerous Establishments on both sides of the Atlantic were catering for this human 'production line', with a sizeable proportion of officer pilots and Observers (as well as ratings accepted for Telegraphist/Air Gunner (TAG) duties) being trained out in the more open and combat-free expanses

At first sight the Swordfish from which this picture is taken has the approaching U-Boat at its mercy as it is about to complete its attack without apparent flak opposition. In fact VE-Day has already taken place and the *Kriegsmarine* vessel, like dozens of its submersible contemporaries, is sailing towards a rendezvous point where its crew will then be escorted into a British Naval Base.

of Canada and the United States. The officers training also included a short period at the Naval College, Greenwich in London where what were described as 'Officer-like qualities' were (hopefully) absorbed. For example, the proper procedure for 'dining-in' nights was outlined, an aspect of Naval tradition that separated a Gentleman from a Peasant – in the eyes of

'The cow is killed.' A Swordfish over-flies two rows of U-Boats moored in an Irish or Scottish loch. It is mid-May 1945 and the Battle of the Atlantic has been brought to its prolonged and bloody conclusion. Merchant shipping losses were more than 2,500 vessels and 30,000 seamen killed or drowned, while the Allied Navies and Air Forces had also suffered heavy warship, aircraft and personnel losses. U-Boat attrition was even greater with nearly 800 vessels sunk and four out of every five of the *Kriegsmarine*'s 40,000 submariners killed!

Although Avenger C2:Y/FN795 is fully armed defensively, the armament is deemed redundant, since World War II had concluded prior to No.711 Sqdn. converting onto the Grumman design. The Sqdn. was an Operational Training Unit based at Crail, Scotland at the time the aircraft was photographed, but it was soon disbanded in late 1945.

This is one of two Swordfish based in Britain that are maintained in flying condition, and is photographed at the Biggin Hill Airshow. The D-Day stripes are not appropriate since the colour scheme and the Type A1 national markings were phased out by late-1942. The 5A code relates to No.825 Sqdn. when operating off VICTORIOUS during the pursuit of the battleship BISMARCK in May 1941.

The duo of airworthy Swordfish are seen together. The torpedo-bearing aircraft is marked as the CO's machine from No.810 Sqdn. when embarked on ARK ROYAL in the immediate run-up to World War II. The other 'Stringbag' by contrast bears a more modest color scheme introduced around 1943 for anti-submarine operations, with a view to making the aircraft less visible to the lookouts on surfaced U-Boats.

Their Lordships, if no one else! In the event a goodly percentage of the 'Wavy Navy' aviators upon surviving the War, did apply for and receive permanent commissions in the Royal Navy, subsequently advancing to middle and senior command rank and taking the places of their unfortunate predecessors from the Pre-War era in the process.

Combat Fatigue

One insidious problem that beset FAA aircrew, whether Regular RN or RNVR during World War II, was that of combat fatigue. This developing danger to an airman's efficiency and ultimately to his chances of surviving operations, had long been recognised by the RAF who applied limits of around 300 hours for fighter pilots and between twenty-five and thirty-five 'Operations' (Missions) in Bomber Command, as examples. No such limiting factor was apparently even considered by the Admiralty, who may have regarded the

relatively low scale of FAA active involvement with enemy air or sea Forces as a sufficient justification for their inertia in introducing operational flying limits. As it was, the mere fact of flying over the ocean, coupled with an inability to literally get away from either the carrier or one's fellow-airmen when at sea, must have induced a form of mental frustration coupled with the boredom engendered by little or no operational activity. This in turn would stealthily but surely take the edge off the sharpness needed for operational flying to a potentially (and sometimes actual) lethal degree. Unfortunately the practice of tying down an Air Group's existence to that of the carrier on which it was embarked ensured that the combat fatigue factor would never be satisfactorily resolved before the end of World War II. It is likely that all too many fatal incidents, for example when taking off or landing, were conveniently or unknowingly ascribed to 'pilot error' when the real villain was mental fatigue.

CHAPTER TWELVE

Eastern Fleet/East Indies Fleet
1944-1945

The Naval war in the Far East and Pacific during 1943 had almost wholly involved the titanic struggle between the Forces of the United States and the Empire of Japan within the western stretches of the Ocean. As the Americans advanced sometimes painfully but ever remorselessly forward in the face of dogged enemy resistance, the Japanese in turn diverted little of their attention to operations in the Indian Ocean.

The appearance of the escort carrier BATTLER towards the end of 1943 was not made in response to any upsurge in Japanese surface Naval activity but rather as a counter-measure to the Axis U-Boats in the region who had taken a steady toll of merchant shipping during 1942-1943. These losses had occurred mainly as a result of merchantmen sailing alone as opposed to being in convoy. As it was, a continuing tendency to concentrate their attacks upon merchantmen sailing in isolation provided an almost impossible task for the carrier's aircraft to seek the U-Boats out following the warship's assignment to the protection of convoy traffic. However, the potential 'Achilles Heel' in U-Boat operations lay in the regular use of several supply ships steaming around the Indian Ocean, who provisioned the underwater predators during their patrols, and whose destruction would seriously inhibit operations.

Admiral Somerville turned a 'Nelson's Eye' towards the Admiralty's insistence on close convoy escort, and commenced to roam the Ocean along with his destroyers escorts in a 'Hunter/Killer' function. Inside a period of two weeks during March 1944 both the CHARLOTTE SCHLIEMANN and BRAKE were intercepted and sunk. Somerville's initiative had paid off handsomely, although 'Ultra ' intercepts had almost certainly contributed to the speedy tracking-down of both vessels. A knock-on effect from these vessels loss was to inhibit the overall period of U-Boat patrol; their main base was at

Penang in Malaya, so causing them to face a protracted period prior to arriving at their patrol areas and the absence of the supply ships cut down their time 'on station' even further.

During late January 1944 the nucleus of a Fleet carrier Force was commenced with the arrival in Ceylon of ILLUSTRIOUS accompanied by three Capital ships. The coincidental transfer of five Japanese battleships and three major aircraft carriers from their Pacific Base at Truk in the Carolines across to Singapore naturally raised fears of a second, and equally lethal, enemy incursion into the Indian Ocean. In fact the transfer was a necessary measure to avoid total annihilation at the hands of the U.S. Navy, apart from which Singapore possessed sound dockyard facilities.

Cometh the Corsair

The operational presence of the Chance-Vought Corsair and the Grumman Avenger were potent reminders of just how much the FAA had developed since its 'locust' entry into combat on 3 September 1939. Then, its motley collection of biplanes and minimal-performance monoplanes had regularly placed the aircrew assigned to fly them at the mercy of the Axis ground and air Forces. The arrival of the Corsair was one of several aircraft designs – nearly all American – that were to transform the combat situation in favor of the FAA during the course of the last two years of the Conflict.

The Corsair's combat debut, following the working up of several Sqdns. within the United States during 1943, had actually occurred two weeks before the Sabang sortie (and halfway around the world) when twenty-eight aircraft serving with Nos.1834 and 1836 Sqdns. on board VICTORIOUS participated in Operation 'Tungsten' the initial FAA assault upon the battleship TIRPITZ. This massive creation weighted in at an All-up weight (AUW) of 13,846 lbs. Top speed was around 400 mph at 24,000 ft., its climb rate was 2,000 ft. a minute and maximum range was 1,100 miles with an attendant flight endurance of over five hours; the latter feature was a very healthy improvement in one leading FAA fighter pilot's eyes, since "with this worth of fuel in your tanks you had little worry as to whether or not you would get back on board!"

Other technical advances were down to the hydraulic system, which spread and folded the wings, lowered and retracted the arrester-hook and landing gear and loaded and cocked the four .50 machine guns, with their massive striking power and ammunition capacity. (The Mk.II possessed six machine guns as well as provision for carrying up to 2,000 lbs. of bombs or an auxiliary drop tank with a capacity of 175 U.S. Galls. on a centerline pylon; an alternate to the single drop tank was two tanks with a total capacity of 274 U.S. Galls under the wings).

Initial carrier operations with the U.S. Navy during 1943 were be-devilled by landing accidents that were basically attributed to a built-in oleo 'bounce', whereupon the aircraft were relegated to operations from land bases, until the problem had been solved. This was ultimately achieved by fitting air valves to the top of the oleo legs. Prior to this amendment, the oleo shock absorbers, with their content of air on top of oil, properly absorbed the shock of landing; however, the air, having no means of escape, immediately forced the oil back down – hence the 'bounce' effect. Now the air would be released as the oil pushed up in the shock absorber unit without any immediate reverse effect. When the fighter next took off, the weight release on the landing gear would permit the valves to induce air into the oleo leg, ready for the next landing.

One major drawback concerned the long engine cowling that presented the pilot with visibility problems in particular when making a carrier landing approach. (The original 'birdcage' framed canopy was replaced by a 'bubble' shaped unit but in the eyes of one U.S. aviator this increased forward visibility from 'poor' to indifferent'!) The daunting appearance of the Corsair on the ground so scared one of the FAA pilots training-up in the States, that in his words; "They were the most dangerous bloody looking things I had ever seen", and he was not ashamed to admit that he actually made out his will; in fact Lt. Hansen of No.1833 went on to command the Sqdn., so confounding his initial doubts! (A subsequent very

A Vought Kingfisher Mk.I from No.703 Sqdn. is recovered from the Indian Ocean using a net-covered sled, prior to being secured and hoisted aboard the Armed Merchant Cruiser (AMC) CILICIA. The retention of European-style National markings is unusual; normally, the red color was deleted in order to prevent confusion with the Japanese 'Rising Sun' marking.

The narrow rectangular forward lift on ILLUSTRIOUS contains a Barracuda Mk.II of No.810 Sqdn. that has completed a sortie to Port Blair in the Andaman Islands on 21 June 1944. The picture angle depicts the complicated manner of the 'Barra's' wing-folding procedure. The flaps and wing rear section moved upward and forward before the main wing area was aligned with the fuselage. The carrier also embarked the Corsairs of Nos.1830 and 1833 Sqdns.

Aircraft servicing facilities in the Far East were often simple if not basic as depicted in this photograph. A Fulmar has been divested of its Merlin VIII engine and is now being pushed clear of the tri-cornered rig from which the powerplant is suspended.

serious crash with his aircraft did not resurrect Hanson's doubts since he continued on operations during the entire spell of ILLUSTRIOUS's BPF service). All in all, the Corsair was a quantum leap in overall performance compared to the Sea Hurricane and even the Seafire, in terms of range and endurance at least.

Japanese Response

As it was, just the one sortie of any material strength was launched by the Japanese in March, when three cruisers steamed up off the Cocos Islands and sank two merchant vessels. A counter-sweep by ILLUSTRIOUS made in the hope of intercepting these warships drew a blank, but the planned rendezvous with the USS SARATOGA (sent on short-term detachment to the Royal Navy), duly took place and both warships then steamed back to Trincomalee to prepare for combined operations off Sabang Island located on the extreme northern tip of Sumatra.

It was during this Operation that the 'volatility' of the Corsair airframe was brought home to the No.1833 Sqdn. personnel. First, one pilot's uncertain landing attempt landed him and his fighter over a gun sponson. Then Sub/Lt. Vickers bounced over the arrester wires and slammed into the crash barriers, although he too emerged unscathed. (A separate tragic loss involved a Barracuda whose practice torpedo run ended in a fatal high-speed stall). Vickers lease on life was to run a

Above: This nubile young lady was a member of a Variety show party touring the Far East. She is sitting astride the cowling of a Seafire named in her honor. The sailor at the top right seems more interested in her lower anatomy than the 'christening' ceremony! The picture was taken in Ceylon in 1944-1945.

Opposite: The camera-bearing aircraft is making a low pass along the flight deck of VICTORIOUS. The central deck area is liberally covered with sixteen Corsairs. Eight Barracudas, three with wings unfolded, take up the rear deck area. Picture was taken in 1944, during the carrier's operational period in the Indian Ocean.

Below: The retention of centerline auxiliary fuel tanks was a regular feature of FAA fighter operations, and one that was fraught with risk should a tank fall off or be otherwise ruptured during a landing. Such an occurrence has involved a Corsair Mk.II on VICTORIOUS, after the aircraft touched down on return from the Sigli strike of 18 September 1944. Fortunately neither the pilot nor his mount was affected.

mere twenty-four hours, however. Next day, he did not follow the DCLO's instructions to 'go round again' and his aircraft ended up tangled with the first crash barrier. Two medical staff and another officer rushed over to assist the seemingly unconscious pilot out of the cockpit.

They were all clustered around the center fuselage when without warning the Corsair's main fuel tank erupted into flame. The blast hurled one man into the sea, from where he was picked out with horrific and fatal burns, ejected a second onto the deck with equally horrific, but survivable, burns and consumed the pilot and the third man. Three seamen in a compartment directly below the wreckage were also badly burned by fuel that seeped into their area. All attempts to extinguish the fire quickly failed when the rear of the engine block formed from magnesium alloy also caught fire and proved impossible to control. A final potentially lethal action by the dying Corsair occurred when the ammunition for the six .50 weapons 'cooked off', spraying the superstructure with bullets.

Anglo-American Cooperation

Following two weeks of intensive planning and rehearsal, a large Force of nearly thirty warships sailed south on 16 April and three days later were positioned off Sabang. The two carriers between them launched eighty-three aircraft – Nos.810 and 847 Sqdns. Barracudas and Nos.1830 and 1833 Sqdns. Corsairs from ILLUSTRIOUS and the Hellcats, Avengers and Dauntlesses from SARATOGA. There was a disappointingly degree of shipping in Sabang harbor and just one small freighter was sunk, but oil storage tanks and harbor installations were destroyed or heavily damaged in the face of flak. A number of aircraft were additionally strafed and destroyed on the island's airfields at the cost of one Hellcat whose pilot baled out and was then rescued by a RN submarine. A belated attempt at air assault by G4M 'Betty' bombers came to naught when the Hellcat CAP circling the warships 'splashed' all three.

The second and last operation involving SARATOGA was launched in the course of that warship's return to America for a re-fit. The targets were aviation fuel stores at Soerabaya on the eastern edge of Java, an island landmass laying directly southeast of Sumatra. The Force actually sailed past Java as far as Exmouth Gulf on the northwest corner of Australia, where it re-fuelled before doubling back on its tracks. The point of launch was reached on 16 May, around 200 miles south of Soerabaya. Avengers of Nos.832 and 845 Sqdns. had replaced the Barracudas and they shared the attack with SARATOGA's Avengers and Dauntless, while under the joint escort of Corsairs and Hellcats. Once again the defenders were caught by surprise but equally the results were poor, with just one small vessel sunk and marginal damage done to the fuel

This Hellcat of No.888 Sqdn. based on EMPRESS has been 'snapped' at the point of doing a 'head-stand'. The pilot is bracing himself for the impact that will end in the fighter either slamming back onto its tail or flipping completely over. The wrinkled skin on the fuselage suggests the aircraft's structure is adversely affected and may even be broken.

A Corsair Mk.II has lost most of its starboard wing after it jumped the arrester-wires and slammed into the safety barrier. The pilot has already made his exit and foam is being sprayed on the wing stump and engine to prevent fire breaking out.

A Hellcat serving on an EIF carrier has its hook deployed ready to snatch the first available arrester-wire, although his landing angle is somewhat tilted to port. The white South East Asia Command (SEAC) identification bands on the forward engine cowling and centerline of the wings stand out. This aircraft is equipped with four rocket rails under each wing.

stores. So ended the U.S. Navy's carrier involvement in the Indian Ocean.

Solo Effort

The Andaman Island chain was aligned north and south some 200 miles off the Burmese-Malayan border, and Port Blair with its harbor and airfield was selected for assault in June. ILLUSTRIOUS was assigned the solo air function, and the battleships RICHELIEU and RENOWN went along to add the weight of their massive artillery to the attack The Barracudas and Corsairs took off on the morning of the 19th and came in over their targets as the dawn was breaking. The fighters' heavy armament played havoc with the aircraft's collection of aircraft and surrounding buildings, while a subsequent assault on what was a radar station yielded equally sound results. Elsewhere, the Barracuda crews were not so successful due to the small number and size of the vessels in the harbor. This 'solo' effort by an 'ILLUSTRIOUS' Class carrier would not be repeated during the remaining period of Far East and Pacific operations.

On preparing to land, Sub/Lt. Shaw from No.1833 Sqdn. discovered that his Corsair's landing gear would only partially descend, and he had no choice but to bale out. His initial attempt to drop out by inverting the fighter failed and so he came back into an upright position and clambered over the side. The watching Sqdn. personnel on ILLUSTRIOUS recoiled in horror as their fellow-pilot's body tumbled un-arrested towards the sea; only at the last instant did the white canopy burst into life and deposit its human load safely. (Back on the carrier when asked why he had delayed pulling the ripcord, Shaw replied that the sensation of almost floating through the warm air had relaxed him so much that his mind had almost not concentrated on the vital task at hand!)

Over 90% of the available Force of fifty-seven aircraft had participated in the attack, which fact placed a particular onus on the deck personnel to operate swiftly in order to get all the aircraft safely down before the last elements were faced with fuel shortage. The initial responsibility for effective control rested directly in the returning formations spacing themselves out. Should a succeeding aircraft approach too close behind its predecessor, the DCLO would have little option but to wave him clear to proceed back into the circuit. Conversely, too great a spacing would swallow up valuable time.

The deck handlers had to move equally swiftly and efficiently. As each aircraft (hopefully) engaged the wires and halted intact, the hook was dis-engaged and the safety barrier lowered to enable the pilot to taxi forward into the forward deck 'park', after which the safety barrier was resurrected. Below decks the wire operator had to reel in the arrester wire that had been engaged and extebnded by the aircraft and re-set it. If all went well, a rate of landing-on at less than one aircraft every thirty seconds could be achieved. (The other advantage arising from efficient recovery or launch procedure came from ensuring that the carrier's divergence from the primary course being steered by the overall Force – should the wind direction be at variance with this – was also kept to a minimum period of time).

'Pairing' Service Resumed

VICTORIOUS arrived 'on station' in early July along with INDOMITABLE; between them, the two Fleet carriers possessed eighty-three aircraft, of which around two-thirds were Corsairs or Hellcats, with the remainder Barracudas. In fact at this stage of the War in the Far East the FAA aircraft inventory on the Fleet carriers was increasingly arriving from American sources – Corsairs, Avengers and Hellcats – and this trend would only be marginally altered with the appearance in January 1945 of Seafires and Fireflies carried on board INDEFATIGABLE and the later presence of Seafires on IMPLACABLE, the Barracudas having been dispensed with in the meantime. (A similar trend was also to affect the CVEs of the East Indies Fleet from late 1944 when the Swordfish was finally displaced and only HUNTER and STALKER retained their Seafires up to VJ-Day).

The maximum bomb load of an Avenger was 2,000 lbs. In this case four 500 lb. weapons are hoisted into position, and an armourer attends to the fuse on the left-rear example. The Avenger could not carry the standard Royal Navy torpedo.

ILLUSTRIOUS and VICTORIOUS were dispatched to repeat the assault upon Sabang, but this time round three battleships, whose heavy guns were to provide the firepower, accompanied the carriers. So it was that just nine Barracudas of No.810 Sqdn. were recorded as being retained by ILLUSTRIOUS and six of the eighty-one Corsairs on hand 'spotted' for what was assessed as an effective bombardment

A Seafire Mk.FIII belonging to No.894 Sqdn. based on INDEFATIGABLE is making an extremely heavy landing on its nose, with the wire-less arrester-hook dangling forlornly in mid-air. The propeller blades are snapped off and the engine cowling is sprung, while the inner wing trailing edge is badly wrinkled.

Yet another demolition job on a Seafire Mk.LIII of No.894 Sqdn. is being accomplished. The starboard landing gear is almost totally destroyed and the safety barrier wires are tangling with the propeller. The Seafire was basically too gentle a design to withstand the rigours of carrier operations.

The first of two pictures captures a deck-landing disaster in the making. The airborne Swordfish has failed to engage a wire and is hovering perilously close to a companion 'Stringbag' parked on the forward flight deck. The Observer can be seen leaning out and surely apprehensive about his chances of surviving what seems to be an impending crash. In the second picture of this incident the 'offending' Swordfish has managed to retain flying speed and clear the other aircraft but its arrester-hook has gouged holes in the starboard upper-wing fabric on the parked machine, which can be quickly repaired; no structural damage was apparently suffered.

of both port and oil refinery facilities' An element of the other Corsairs indulged in strafing attacks on Sabang airfield prior to the battleship 'shoot', after which main activity 'targets of opportunity' were sought out; in 1833 Sqdn.'s case this took the form of a large merchantman. The remaining Corsairs mounted CAP patrols. The latter activity succeeded in netting several Japanese aircraft, including two Ki-21 'Sallies' and at least four 'Zekes' that made belated appearances as the Force withdrew.

ILLUSTRIOUS now sailed for South Africa for refitting purposes while the next sortie was set in motion during late August. VICTORIOUS and INDOMITABLE held ninety-seven aircraft, nearly half of which were Barracudas from Nos.815, 817 and 822 Sqdns., who constituted the Strike Force. Sumatra possessed a key cement works at Inderoeng and this location, along with the harbour at Emmahaven, was attacked on the 24th. The result varied from 'good' at Indaroeng (Production being halted for several months) to 'poor' at Emmahaven (Two medium-sized vessels damaged). The days of Barracuda service were drawing to a close with a penultimate attack on a rail center at Sigli, also on Sumatra, on 18 September. The same three Sqdns. from the 24 August sortie duly delivered the assault but once again the results were regarded as barely acceptable by the Senior Naval Commanders. (Admiral Somerville had been replaced by Admiral Sir Bruce Fraser around August, and the new C-in-C would subsequently lead what became the British Pacific Fleet in November 1944).

Right: An over-shoot by this Hellcat PR Mk.II of No.804 Sqdn. on board SHAH sometime during April 1945 has left the offending fighter perched high on its nose, while its forward motion has thoroughly mangled the Hellcat parked on the right. One of the camera apertures fitted to the photo-reconnaissance machine is seen directly under the fuselage roundel. The aircraft's SEAC markings are fully applied along with white Identification bands on wings, stabilisers and fin-and-rudder.

The use of the FAA carriers in the Indian Ocean continued to be of a rather desultory nature as well as being somewhat intermittent. This was a pattern that continued during October when the VICTORIOUS/INDOMITABLE pairing headed for the Cap Nicobar Islands for Operation 'Millet'. Two attacks on the 17th and 19th were delivered against shipping in Nancowry harbour as well as several airfields. For the first time Japanese fighters in the shape of the formidable Ki-43 'Oscar' challenged the FAA attackers and while two Corsairs and one Hellcat were shot down, the enemy suffered the loss of seven aircraft. Flak also claimed one Barracuda and two Corsairs.

BPF Operations in the Indian Ocean

It was fully two months before the newly titled British Pacific Fleet (BPF) carried out its latest operation. During this time, the Barracuda Sqdns had converted onto the Avenger. While the Grumman design was clearly superior in performance and carried greater ordnance loads internally, the fact that it would deliver its attacks in a glide rather than a dive dictated a switch

over from pure escort duties for the Corsairs and Hellcats to one that added the suppression of flak batteries to their overall role. A change of far greater import concerned the type of target that would be the focus for FAA attention in the region.

Oil was the life-blood of all the World War II combatant Nations. In Japan's case, occupation of the East Indies and Sumatra in particular had provided its Forces with key sources of oil production at Pangkalan Brandan and the even larger oilfield complex of Palembang. On this initial occasion the former location in the northern sector of Sumatra was selected for assault. For whatever reason, only the carriers ILLUSTRIOUS and INDOMITABLE, were assigned to the operation that was launched on 20 December – and then only twenty-seven of the forty-two available Avengers and twenty-eight out of the sixty-five Corsairs and Hellcats actually took part. As it so happened the Japanese received a temporary reprieve due to poor weather conditions that blanketed the Primary target. Low cloud and heavy squalls were also present over the Secondary (the port of Belewan Deli) and little direct damage was inflicted there either. It was little consolation that the escorts strafed several aircraft to destruction on airfields at Sabang as the Force withdrew.

Before 1944 was out, the latest Fleet carrier to join the BPF came 'on station'. INDEFATIGABLE, in contrast to the early 'Illustrious' Class warships, was provided with two hangars, which noticeably increased her aircraft capacity. The number of aircraft carried for her first operation (seventy-one) included six Hellcats PR II of No.888 Sqdn. The three carriers departed on New Year's Eve from Trincomalee and four days later were off the Sumatran coast. A departure from the normal attack procedure was made in that it was split into two sections. The first consisted of a 'Ramrod' offensive sweep by a small Force of Corsairs and Hellcats that attacked several airfields and destroyed a number of Japanese aircraft in the process, including two in the air. Ninety minutes after the 'Ramrod' pilots had departed, the Main Fore was launched. The thirty-two Avengers and Fireflies were bearing a load of bombs and rockets respectively, both of which were suitable forms of weaponry for destroying vulnerable targets such as oil cracking plants and storage tanks as well as electrical installations. Although the Japanese Air Force were alerted to some degree by the 'Ramrod' preliminary attack, the few 'Oscar' fighters that did clash with the FAA Force had nothing to show for their efforts, while nearly half were claimed as shot down. The almost total absence of flak over the target area was a

A Petty Officer is standing by the side of this Barracuda's cockpit as he carries out an engine run-up check on the aircraft. The removal of the cowling reveals the large radiator 'drum' shape. Also noticeable is the 'inverted L' duct along which the exhaust gases are channelled. The oriental location of the carrier is confirmed by the SEAC pattern fuselage roundel in the background.

Right: The Barracuda's operational career in the Far East concluded during October 1944 over the Cap Nicobar Islands, after which it was displaced by the Avenger. Here, two armorers are operating the wing-positioned bomb-winch and three more mechanics steady the 500 lb. bomb for a 'Barra' embarked either on VICTORIOUS or INDOMITABLE. Note how the 'Yagi' ASV aerial is angled outwards.

welcome relief but this positive factor would not be so prevalent next time around.

1945

The BPF now possessed four Fleet carriers and a formidable Strike Force of over 230 aircraft as 1945 was entered. To the 160 aircraft carried by the other three carriers was added INDEFATIGABLE's expanded strength, consisting of twenty-four Seafires FIII of 887 Sqdn. and sixteen Seafires LIII of No.894 Sqdn. along with twelve Fireflies Mk.I of No.1770 Sqdn. and twenty-one Avengers of No.820 Sqdn. The departure of the BPF for the Theater of Operations within its title was finalised in mid-January. In the event the Force would have to bypass Sumatra en route, in which case a second attack on the Palembang complex was planned. The 1st. Aircraft Carrier Sqdn. (1st ACS) was ready to repeat Operation 'Lentil' under the revised title of 'Meridian'.

Two separate attacks were to be launched but the first was delayed for two days until 24 January by bad weather. Once again only about half the actual Avengers Force of eighty-four aircraft was deployed along with No.1770 Sqdn.'s twelve

Fireflies. A similar proportion of the fighters went along as escort – sixteen Corsairs from VICTORIOUS as Top Cover, a further sixteen Hellcats and eight Corsairs from INDOMITABLE as Middle Cover and eight Corsairs from ILLUSTRIOUS as the Low Cover. The attack against the Pladjoe refinery involved four Avengers and part of the escort simultaneously interdicting the surrounding airfields and destroying numerous aircraft as the Main Force struck home. The efforts of the Secondary Force to neutralise the four airfields around the target area were of vital importance to ensure minimum interference from Japanese fighters, who could create havoc among the Avengers should they get through in any numbers.

The slow speed of the Avengers proved dangerously inhibiting on the escorts' room to manoeuvre in the face of Japanese fighter attacks, since they were wallowing along at the same pace. L/Cdr. Hansen (CO, 1833 Sqdn.) was concerned enough to order his pilots to open their throttles and adapt a weaving pattern in their Low Cover role; he was also concerned at the absence of the Fireflies whose pilots were supposed to serve the same function. (Why the Firefly, whose general

Air combats between the FAA and Japanese Air Force were rare. Sub/Lts. Bedding (left) and West-Taylor embarked with No.808 Sqdn. on KHEDIVE ran into a Ki-48 'Lily' with two Ki-43 'Oscars' as escort. During the ensuing dogfight one of the escorts was downed by Bedding. Date of the action was 15 April 1944.

No.756 Sqdn. was based at Katukurunda, Ceylon from October 1943. Its primary function was to provide deck landing training and refresher flying, using Fulmars Mk.II and later Barracudas Mks.II and III. The Swordfish Mk.II also served with the Sqdn. from March 1944 as represented by this aircraft.

The snow-encrusted flight deck of RULER houses a sizeable group of Fireflies in the foreground with Avengers and Hellcats further back. The picture was taken in Glasgow, Scotland and both the carrier and its cargo are bound for the Far East. RULER served with the British Pacific Fleet in 1945 and operated all three types of aircraft shown here while serving in the Assault and Fighter carrier roles.

A No.807 Sqdn. Seafire Mk.III is nosed-up on the flight deck of the escort carrier HUNTER. Full Sqdn. code letters have been applied in the unusual manner adopted by the FAA, namely by splitting the unit numbers/letters on either side of the roundel instead of placing them together. (D5, not 5L denotes the Sqdn.). The white Identification bands on the wings do not extend onto the ailerons. Note how the machine-gun apertures are also outlined in white.

Whereas D5:L of No.807 Sqdn. has probably sustained a degree of reparable damage, this is not the case with aircraft X from the same unit. The landing gear has been thoroughly mangled as well as the lower edges of the flaps, leaving the aircraft ready to be 'written off'. This Sqdn. served on HUNTER at regular intervals between January 1944 and VJ-Day.

performance was well below that of the other FAA fighters, should have been assigned such a function seems surprising).

The steady climb to altitude and the 100 miles landward approach to the target evidently permitted the enemy radar screens ample time to record the Force's advance; in addition the Secondary Force was not able to prevent a number of fighters from being 'scrambled' and making interceptions as the target was sighted. An 'Oscar' closed in behind L/Cdr. Hanson but not only misdirected his fire but also over-shot – right in front of several Corsairs, whose massed gunfire blew off several sections and sent it down in smoking ruin. Several other enemy fighters were challenged and their attentions towards the Avengers thwarted both during the main assault on the refinery and as the Force was withdrawing.

Flak was surprisingly light with no fighters making interception at this point. However, the presence of barrage balloons ascending to various heights provided a nasty jolt to the crews although with no effect upon their successful arrival and departure. The withdrawal phase did not go so smoothly, however, because the chosen location was unknowingly occupied by a sizeable number of flak guns that fatally damaged two Avengers and seriously damaged a number of others; one of the downed crews was in fact later rescued. Seven fighters were also declared MIA or otherwise 'written off' but fourteen Japanese aircraft were claimed as 'kills'. (Among this latter MIA figure was two Corsairs of No.1833 Sqdn., one of which was flown by the same Sub-Lt. Shaw, he of the nearly lethal 'free-fall' incident on 19 June 1944. Both survived their aircraft losses, but along with seven other FAA survivors, were then summarily executed by their captors).

L/Cdr. Hanson's Corsair was one of the aircraft losses and he was very fortunate to survive the incident. His landing approach was already proving difficult due to a basic inability for the fighter to slow down. In addition, he was at a dangerously low height but was still being beckoned on to land by the Batsman, when another Corsair cut in on Hanson's run. The resultant slipstream effect threw the heavy fighter into a steep slide-slip and before full recovery could be made it struck the sea. Hanson was rendered temporarily unconscious, but recovered and managed to exit the submerged cockpit; his initial attempt at escape failed due to the partially opened canopy that trapped his parachute pack and forced him to drop back inside to release the item before again ascending to the surface. Even then, an inability to breathe properly due to swallowing copious amounts of salt water was nearly his undoing in the seeming interminable spell before a whaler from a picket destroyer finally fished him out.

The post-mortem on the Pladjoe attack threw up several criticisms, the central one being the lack of escort cover between the target and the Rendezvous Point, that left the Avengers dangerously open to fighter interception, with several crews fortunate to survive the resultant attacks – a criticism that did not seem to include No.1833 Sqdn. at least. The approach to the target was deemed to be too deliberate in both the climb and descent stages, giving certain rise to premature radar detection. Another adverse comment by an Avenger Sqdn. CO concerned the seeming reluctance of some of his crews to complete their runs until such time as the barrage balloon cover had been satisfactorily reduced – something that was not basically achieved, and led only to these crews hanging about

A Corsair landing on a Fleet carrier has suffered a collapsed starboard landing gear. The auxiliary tank is perilously close to the deck surface and if ruptured through contact is liable to burst into flames.

in the target area for longer than necessary. Finally, R/T discipline was adjudged to be rather poor, and tending to seriously intrude upon any call for assistance.

The second phase of 'Meridian' took place five days later, when the refinery at Soengi Gerong was the focus for assault. The number of 'strike' aircraft was almost the same but with some changes in procedure. This time round, the Fireflies were launched in front to carry out a 'Ramrod' function, and the post-attack Rendezvous Point was selected over terrain believed to be free from flak guns. The Japanese responded by having fighters airborne and in a position to intercept the incoming Force; this situation for No.849 Sqdn.'s Avengers was worsened by the absence of their escorts when so intercepted. Several Avengers were shot down by fighters while two more remained behind in the target area; one of the latter aircraft was flown by L/Cdr. Mainprice (No.854 Sqdn. CO off ILLUSTRIOUS) who sadly failed to survive impacting with

a barrage balloon cable. A higher than average loss factor (Sixteen aircraft over the target area and nine others elsewhere) was experienced by the FAA Force, but no less than thirty-nine Japanese aircraft were destroyed on the ground while the escorts had a field day with a further thirty claimed aerial 'kills'.

Some of these enemy losses related to post-sortie attacks on the 1st ACS warships. A seven-strong formation of Ki-21 'Sallys' was totally wiped out by Seafires of No.24 Fighter Wing, a Corsair and a Hellcat. (The latter fighter was subsequently heavily damaged by AA fire from King George V, so demonstrating the risks inherent in attacking aircraft over and around the warship defensive screen! In addition two 5.25 inch shells fired by the cruiser EURYALUS struck ILLUSTRIOUS to cause slight external structural damage. Unfortunately, two Avengers being man-handled right where the shells struck were set on fire and a number of the personnel

A Martlet Mk.V of No.890 Sqdn. is being catapulted from the deck of ATHELING. The launching strop has just become detached and is seen just above the deck and directly behind the main landing gear. The original small-size tailwheel strut replaced on the Mk.II to IV by larger units has been restored on this penultimate Wildcat variant.

killed outright). The attack on the refinery proved a serious reverse for oil production, which was reduced by over one-third for at least two months and never fully resumed normal production levels.

East Indies Fleet in 1945

During the course of the second half of 1944 the CVE strength of the EIF had built up to between four and five carriers. BATTLER had started this pattern back in November 1943, when it arrived bearing a typical FAA aircraft-mix for convoy protection duties – in this instance, twelve Swordfish and six Seafires IIC of No.834 Sqdn., although the Seafires were later replaced by Wildcat Vs during the following May. One of the four other CVEs to arrive (ATHELING, bearing the Seafires FIII of No.889 Sqdn. and Wildcat Vs of No.890 Sqdn.) spent less than three months in the Theater before departing. The remaining three CVEs all arrived in July or August; BEGUM, SHAH and AMEER had embarked Nos.832, 852 and 843 Sqdns. respectively, each with twelve Avengers and either four Wildcat Vs, or six in SHAH's case. The trade protection function had proved to be a successful but boring activity for the aircrew, in that no U-Boats were encountered making a direct contact with a convoy. The occasional anti-submarine 'sweep; did at least throw up one success. The action involved the Avengers on SHAH and BEGUM while they were operating off the Seychelles in August 1944; the unfortunate submarine happened to be U-198 whose destruction was shared between the aircraft and two frigates.

On One's Own Again

The beginning of 1945 witnessed another temporary downturn in carrier strength for the EIF. The 21st Aircraft Carrier Sqdn. (ACS) was intended to be the EIF's air striking element but the carriers forming its core were still on their way out to the Indian Ocean when Admiral Powers assumed command of the Fleet in January. At this time only three CVE were 'on station', being AMEER (now with Hellcat IIs of No.804 Sqdn.), and SHAH and EMPRESS carrying Avengers. In fact it was to be March before four of the UK-dispatched carriers were also 'on Station'. Two arrived during February – KHEDIVE and EMPEROR bearing the Hellcat Sqdns of No.3 Wing. The following month HUNTER and STALKER completed the voyage having respectively embarked Nos.807 and 809 Sqdns. with their Seafires. LIII and FRIII that made up No.4 Wing.

In this interim three-month period, the available CVEs were tasked with beginning what would be the first of two future operational trends for the 21st ACS, namely the support of Gen. Slim's Fourteenth Army in Burma; the other was the containment of Japanese Naval units comprised of a cruiser Sqdn. based in Singapore. AMEER was the first carrier to be

A Corsair Mk.II has not only suffered a serious fracture of its port main landing gear but, worse still, has become inverted and about to smash down onto VICTORIOUS's flight deck. The fighter was from No.1836 Sqdn. and the T8 codes were carried between January and March 1945.

called upon during the latter part of January. The 14th Army columns were advancing steadily through central Burma and a key objective was the seizure of Akyab on the coast. The coastal islands of Ramree (Operation 'Matador') and Cheduba (Operation 'Sankey') laying to the south of Akyab were to be invaded as part of the overall exercise and AMEER's Hellcats were called upon to provide air support for the troops through strafing and dive-bombing; in addition the pilots of No.804 Sqdn. provided the CAP for the bombarding battleship QUEEN ELIZABETH and cruiser PHEOBE in the course of the former-named Operation.

Over the ensuing seven months the EIF CVEs were to be involved in seven more operations, at least three of which involved an element of photo-reconnaissance by the Hellcats PRII of No.888 Sqdn. The first PR exercise was carried out with the intention of preparing the way for the capture of Malaya. Code-named Operation 'Stacey' it involved SHAH and EMPRESS with a total of thirty-one Hellcats and eight Avengers embarked in all. The Force sailed on 22 February and was back in port on 4 March. The northern Malayan sector from the Kra Isthmus down to Phuket Island was covered in this initial bid to determine both the state and extent of the Japanese defensive provisions. Japanese interference with the carrier's progress only occurred on 1 March but the air attacks achieved nothing at the cost of a single Ki-46 'Dinah' and two Ki-43 'Oscars' – the first recorded 'kills' for fighters operating off the CVEs.

'Sunfish'

It was fully five weeks before Vice-Admiral Walker departed Trincomalee with Force 63 to launch Operation 'Sunfish', the second PR sortie. This time round the area to be reconnoitred photographically was to be centered on Port Swettenham some 200 miles north of Singapore and well within the Malaccan Straits. However, the PR function was but a part of the overall operation. On hand within Group 1 were two battleships (QUEEN ELIZABETH and the French RICHELIEU) who were to carry out bombardment duties while supported by the cruiser LONDON and three destroyers; Group 2 comprised EMPEROR and KHEDIVE, the heavy cruiser CUMBERLAND and two destroyers. No.808 Sqdn. on KHEDIVE had seconded four of their twenty-four fighters to EMPEROR; No.851 Sqdn.'s Avengers were also on board.

The PR exercise commenced on the 14th and was completed by the 16th in the face of indifferent weather conditions that did not prove conducive to good photographic quality. In addition one Hellcat was forced to 'ditch' in the Malaccan Straits with the fatal loss of its pilot. By then No.808 Sqdn. had also lost two Hellcats with their pilots in landing accidents; the second of these had also swept a parked Hellcat into the sea along with its companion, while three deck handlers were also killed.

First contact with the Japanese Air Force occurred on the 11th when one of seven Ki-43 'Oscars' was rash enough to follow Lt. Foxley after he had disengaged from combat with the formation; the FAA pilot first eluded his pursuer, then, used cloud cover to close in on his adversary and shoot him down. Later that same day a Ki-46 'Dinah' on a reconnaissance sortie was taken down by three of EMPEROR's No.808 Sqdn. contingent. At last the FAA fighter pilot of the EIF were proving they could more than hold their own against their Japanese opponents.

More success followed on the 16th when Sub-Lts. Bedding and West-Taylor climbed almost into the stratosphere to intercept a high-flying Ki-46 'Dinah' and its two escort 'Oscars'. The bomber finally escaped the resultant encounter but one of the 'Oscars' was not so lucky. The Avengers joined in the action on the 16th when their crews sought out shipping in Emmahaven in northern Sumatra, while part of their No.808 Sqdn. cover decided to descent on Padang airfield and make strafing runs that netted several aircraft destroyed or damaged. Yet another aerial 'kill' was registered by S/Lt. McNee, who added an 'Oscar' to No.808 Sqdn.'s tally. As it so happened he had been fortunate to escape the previous lethal intentions of a second 'Oscar' whose bullets badly damaged the Hellcat. The landing back on KHEDIVE was fraught with risk since the fighter's hydraulic system had been disabled but fortunately all went well with the attempt.

Two lines of Corsairs Mk.II are lined up and ready to take off, although one pilot is still in the act of unfolding his fighter's wings. Nos.1830 and 1833 Sqdns. were embarked on ILLUSTRIOUS at this time and the A6 codes visible on the two forward aircraft identify the last-named unit. The danger to the deck handlers from the mass of whirling propellers is fairly evident

An Avenger from No.845 Sqdn. on ILLUSTRIOUS has engaged an arrester-wire and will make a good if bumpy landing. The original wing and fuselage roundels can still be seen but they have been dulled-down and replaced by small-diameter SEAC markings. The carrier was operating off Indonesia at this time in May 1944.

Two Avengers of No.854 Sqdn., one of which is being 'ranged' on the forward lift, are joining six Corsairs Mk.II from either No.1830 or (in the case of the left-hand fighter) 1833 Sqdn. The date is 20 December 1944 but the briefed oil refinery target at Pangkalan Brandan on Sumatra was 'socked in' by clouds, so the harbor at Belawan Deli was attacked instead.

'Dracula' and 'Bishop'

By the time of 'Sunfish's' completion, plans were being formulated for the EIF to be involved in Operation 'Dracula', the capture of the Burmese Capital, Rangoon. The possibility of this Operation being adversely affected by the monsoon season that was due to break in early June was clear; a parallel and serious logistical factor was the likely withdrawal of nearly 50% of the USAAF transport aircraft by 1 June and their redeployment in support of the Nationalist Chinese Army.

Four of the 21st ACS Force of CVEs – HUNTER, STALKER, KHEDIVE and EMPEROR – were assigned a CAP role over the assault convoys. EMPRESS and SHAH were to be part of Force 63, whose brief with its pair of battleships, four cruisers and five-destroyer 'screen' was to cruise in the Andaman Sea and by so doing ward off any attempted enemy interference, particularly by the Singapore-based Second Diversionary Attack Force. (The original complement of two battleships had steamed back to Japan in February, but the two heavy cruisers HAGURO and ASHIGARA still present were a reasonably potent Force; two other cruisers TAKAO and MYOKO were on hand at Singapore but had arrived there in a disabled state).

The Rangoon assault convoys moved in on their target on 28 April and the landing commenced four days later in the face of a deep Depression that threw up heavy cloud, thunderstorms and sudden squalls. In that ninety-six-hour

This Barracuda Mk.II from No.810 Sqdn. must have made an extremely heavy landing or struck a deck obstacle in order to have the starboard landing gear crumple up in this manner. The Walrus amphibian with folded wings bears a Type C1 fuselage roundel with the red center deleted.

Below: The badly battered airframe of a Hellcat Mk.II belonging to No.804 Sqdn. is poised on the edge of the flight deck. The mobile crane is advancing to give the wreckage a final push into the ocean. The picture was taken between December 1944 and May 1945, during which time the Sqdn. served on several escort carriers.

interim period Force 63 had bombarded and strafed the airfields on Car Nicobar Island before moving on to interdict Port Blair on South Andaman Island. Meanwhile the four CVEs providing CAP sorties left Akyab with their complement of forty-four Hellcats and fifty-four Seafires LIII and FRIII. The anticipated strong Japanese resistance to the landings was destined never to materialise since the invading troops (doubtless to their relief) discovered what was an almost deserted city with few troops on hand to put up a fight.

The heavy sea that was running by now caused the CVEs to pitch dangerously and this factor combined with rain that blurred the fighter's windshields undoubtedly contributed to at least two Seafires and one pilot lost from No.807 Sqdn. embarked on HUNTER. With no further need to stand off Rangoon, the four CAP carriers headed south and on 6 May STALKER's Seafires LIII escorted a Hellcat strike on Port Victoria and surrounding airfields. EMPRESS and SHAH were also continuing to play their part in what was Force 63's Operation 'Bishop' by attacking shipping off northern Arakan and strafing airfields round Port Victoria.

HAGURO Incident

One day before Operations' Dracula' and 'Bishop' were completed several radio transmissions using the call sign of the Japanese heavy cruiser HAGURO had been picked up by a destroyer accompanying EMPRESS and SHAH. Any

prospects for an attack by the Avengers of No.851 Sqdn. would have had to be limited to 500 lb. bombs since British torpedoes would not fit in the Grumman design's bomb-bays. The transmissions quickly stopped, and with no further action taken by the two CVEs, they along with the other Allied warships finally steamed back into port on the 9th.

Scarcely were the vessels berthed when orders were issued for a sailing to be made early next morning. 'Ultra' intercepts had confirmed that a Japanese heavy cruiser would sail north to Port Blair and remain overnight on 12-13 May before returning to Singapore. What was titled Operation 'Diadem' involved a very strong Force comprising many of the warships from Operation 'Dracula'; the carrier element was formed of HUNTER, EMPEROR, KHEDIVE and SHAH, but only the Avengers of No.851 Sqdn. (hastily transferred over from SHAH to EMPEROR when the former CVE suffered fuel contamination that reduced her maximum speed to a figure well below safe launching speed) were felt to be in a position to hand out truly serious punishment to the enemy warship, and then only through the use of bombs.

An RN submarine had sighted the cruiser and her escorts proceeding up the Malacca Straits, but its attempt to fire a spread of torpedoes failed when the Force altered course. Force 61 on arrival between the Andaman and Nicober Islands took up position to await its adversary's arrival. However a Japanese aircraft then sighted Force 61 and its report caused the

The pilot of this Hellcat was fortunate to escape serious injury or even death after the fighter failed to engage an arrester-wire and smashed onto its back, probably after 'snagging' the safety barrier. The Hellcat on the right has been involved in the incident because its tail-plane section is twisted to one side. The World War I battleship QUEEN ELIZABETH steams in the background.

The key Burmese city and seaport of Rangoon was recaptured by the British in early May 1945. During the operation one of the escort carriers received an unusual 'visitor'; this was an Auster 'spotter' operated by the Royal Artillery. The pilot has landed off-center and the deck handlers on the aircraft's port side seem to be ensuring the light aircraft does not go over the side!

The distinctive outline of SARATOGA with its separate bridge and funnel structures is photographed from ILLUSTRIOUS when the U.S. Navy carrier finished its short spell of duty with the EIF during April-May 1944. Her crew are lined up on deck as the warship prepares to return home for a refit.

HAGURO's Captain to reverse course. Over the next forty-eight hours or so a 'cat and mouse' game took place. The Japanese Force was intended to provide cover for a large troopship evacuating personnel from the Islands to Singapore. The troopship was later sighted by one of No.851 Sqdn.'s Avengers but this aircraft was damaged by return fire and forced to 'ditch'. Four other Avengers were then launched but achieved no success in locating the troopship before having to head back through dwindling fuel reserves. However, L/Cdr. Fuller then ran across the troopship and escort, quickly followed by his sighting of what was the Force containing HAGURO – but all bombs had been jettisoned! All Fuller could do was to 'shadow' as long as possible and radio back his position for Admiral Walker's Force 61 to close in and intercept.

Several hours later, three more Avengers were launched and, after rendezvousing with Force 63's destroyer element, commenced a square search that ultimately succeeded. Diving from around 10,000 ft the three attackers encountered a stiff flak barrage that slightly damaged two aircraft; their bombs impacted all around the cruiser but caused no discernable damage. A further strike was cancelled on the grounds that the No.800 Sqdn. Hellcats assigned the task would find themselves out-ranged. No further air contact was made, and in fact it was to be the destroyers of Force 61 that would finally ambush HAGURO inside the Malacca Straits in the early hours of 16 May and despatch her with a succession of torpedoes.

Diminuendo in the Far East

Just three more operations of any major significance were to be conducted by the EIF prior to VJ-Day. Operation 'Balsam' involved further photo-reconnaissance activity over southern Malaya between 16-18 June, as well as strikes upon Sumatran airfields. A total of forty-four Hellcats from Nos.804 and 808 Sqdns., as well as the PR Mk.IIs of No.888 Sqdn., and twenty-four Seafires LIII of No.809 Sqdn., carried out the operation from AMEER, STALKER and KHEDIVE. Then, between 5 and 11 July, Operation 'Collie' involved Hellcats embarked on AMEER (896 Sqdn.) and EMPEROR (800 Sqdn.) standing off the Nicobar Islands to strike at targets there while also providing cover for a minesweeping Force. Finally, AMEER and EMPRESS embarked the Hellcats of Nos.804 and 896 Sqdns. respectively for Operation 'Livery', when a minesweeping Force carried out its role off Phuket Island;

On 11 April 1945 four Hellcats embarked on EMPEROR engaged a seven-strong formation of Ki-43 'Oscars'. One of the Japanese fighters inflicted this slight damage to Sub/Lt. Foxley's aircraft. After the main combat was over and the FAA pilots were heading back, the New Zealander sighted a single 'Oscar' closing from behind; he took this latest adversary on and shot him down with a quick burst of fire. Nos.808 and 888 Sqdns. were on board EMPEROR at this time.

strafing attacks were also indulged in. The Japanese were in retreat across the broad spectrum of their conquests, so resistance to these assaults was desultory.

The EIF's final act was completed in the immediate aftermath of Japan's Surrender, when British and Commonwealth Forces completed the re-occupation of Malaya and the city of Singapore. Between 8-10 September, Operation 'Zipper' saw KHEDIVE, EMPEROR, AMEER, EMPRESS, HUNTER and STALKER steaming into what had been Britain's Naval bastion prior to 7 December 1941

CHAPTER THIRTEEN

British Pacific Fleet

In the Beginning

The presence of the Royal Navy in the Pacific during World War II was largely limited to the period from March until August 1945. Up to then, the massive Ocean had been the natural preserve of the U.S. Navy as it grappled with its Japanese adversary. Britain's maritime involvement in the Far East had hitherto centered upon the Indian Ocean. As it so happened, however, the Royal Navy had been involved in Pacific operations well before what was titled the British Pacific Fleet made its 1945 'debut'. That involvement although centered round just one Fleet carrier VICTORIOUS occurred at a still-critical time for American fortunes at sea.

By late 1942 the U.S. Navy's main carrier Force was seriously depleted, with four of its major warships, LEXINGTON, YORKTOWN, WASP and HORNET, all sunk. Just two carriers, SARATOGA and ENTERPRISE, were currently operational. Calls for assistance from the Royal Navy were finally, if belatedly (at least in the view of some Senior American minds), responded to by the dispatch of VICTORIOUS during December. The protracted voyage would be via the Panama Canal but before that point was reached the carrier would call into Norfolk Navy Yard, VA. During her time there, the Albacores of No.832 Sqdn. were replaced by Grumman Avengers. The appearance of the Fairey biplanes as they landed at Norfolk NAS inevitably drew some ribald comments from the American observers as to whether they were fighting in World War I or World War II! As far as the FAA crews of No.832 Sqdn. were concerned the switchover to the Avenger must have been more than welcome.

The Avenger Approacheth

By this mid-period of World War II the Fleet Air Arm was steadily emerging from the parlous state of aircraft equipment with which it had entered the Conflict. The first Seafires were on hand and along with the Sea Hurricane and the tried and trusty Martlet/Wildcat, were forming a sound core of fighter strength. Now, with the advent of the Grumman Avenger in FAA service arose the opportunity for an enhanced prospect of striking back against enemy submarines and shipping, as well as surviving the experience in the process. The basic contrast between the Fairey Swordfish and Albacore, which were currently providing the primary 'strike force' numbers for the FAA, and the Avenger, was almost stark. The new design's monoplane structure, the retractable landing gear and the internal carriage of ordnance signified an overall performance that was almost out of sight. For example, the maximum speed of 259 mph was almost double the 139 mph and 161 mph for the Fairey duo. Other basic performance comparisons were as follows:

	Avenger	*Swordfish*	*Albacore*
Range (Maximum load)	1,000 miles	550 miles	930 miles
Climb-rate (Feet per minute)	1,600	500	750
Service ceiling	25,000	10,000	20,700
Ordnance load (maximum)	2,000 lbs	1,610 lbs	1,610 lbs

One distinct advantage over the Swordfish lay in the fact that the cockpit was totally enclosed and fully appointed compared to the windswept open area and the Spartan layout on the British biplane. The internal carriage of ordnance was in contrast to the drag inevitably created by the external carriage of bombs, torpedoes or rockets on the Swordfish or Albacore. Finally, the Avenger's strong structure was ready-made for

Two Fireflies of No.1770 Sqdn. have landed on INDEFATIGABLE. The wing-folding procedure on the forward aircraft is complete while this action is being effected on the nearside machine. The retention bar for the starboard wing is slotted into the fuselage. The other end will engage the recess with a hinged cover located behind the wing roundel. The manual wing-folding operation required several deck handlers to manoeuvre each wing.

making trouble-free deck landings, whereas the Swordfish and even the Albacore on occasions were prone to coming to grief when attempting landings in other than relatively calm sea conditions. The controls tended to stiffen up in a dive or when taking evasive action following a torpedo-drop, but the FAA's use of the Grumman aircraft was to be principally as a bomber.

The Avenger's landing approach was particularly sound with a good view over the engine cowling; the 'sting' type arrester hook positioned under the end of the fuselage virtually ensured that a landing wire would be caught while the parallel ability of the main landing gear to absorb a severe descent up to 16 ft. a second further added to the chances for a safe landing.

(All four major U.S. Navy designs in FAA service during World War II encapsulated the principal of the rear-positioned arrester hook. The British designs by contrast had their hooks located ahead of the tail wheel, which did not permit the pilots to 'scrape' their tail wheels along the deck and so provide a good guarantee of securing a landing wire; the chance of missing the wires was enhanced, especially if the main landing gear wheels made the first contact with the deck).

Pacific Preparations

The aircrew were lectured on U.S. Navy deck-landing procedure, which was a vital requirement especially as regards

INDEFATIGABLE was the penultimate ILLUSTRIOUS-Class carriers to be constructed and was commissioned in May 1944. She is seen passing through the Suez Canal on passage in late 1944, first to the Indian Ocean and then to the Pacific with the BPF. The Seafires Mk.III on the forward flight deck belong to No.894 Sqdn.

instructions from the DCLOs or 'Batsmen'. The American 'Batsmen' used their bats to indicate the aircraft's current approach attitude in relation to the required attitude (in other words, the signals were 'mirror images' of how the pilot should adjust his aircraft's approach), whereas the RN Batsmen signals were instructing the pilot what to do. In addition, U.S. aircraft were literally flown onto the deck by cutting the engine throttle and then 'dumping' the machine from anything up to fifty ft. above the deck. In contrast, RN aircraft were flown onto the deck in a nose-high attitude, with the engine throttle cut just prior to touching down; this was a more gentle action that reflected the less sturdy nature of British-built FAA aircraft compared to their U.S.-built 'cousins'.

Although the Martlet Sqdns. were to suffer the loss of several aircraft during exercises involving actual deck landings on a USN carrier, no such difficulties affected No.832 Sqdn. Finally, on 3 February 1943, with Nos.882, 896 and 898 Sqdns. Martlets and No.832 Sqdn., VICTORIOUS raised her anchors and sailed for the Panama Canal, through which she passed (with the odd scrape) by mid-month. Before reaching Pearl Harbor problems arose with the inability of the forward-mounted arrester-wires to prevent the much greater weight of the Avenger from dragging them sufficiently to make contact the safety barrier. Only while at Pearl could suitable modifications be carried out. A second adaptation applied at Norfolk and linked to the landing-control system had involved the replacement of the 'round down' at the stern for a

The ceremony of 'Crossing the Equator' was a feature of Naval activities when the occasion permitted during hostilities. A central part of the action involved immersing those personnel whose first experience of line-crossing it was in a large water tank; this was achieved by sitting them on one of the seats and then tipping it backwards. The Commander in full Naval tropical kit would naturally be free from such treatment, even if he were also a 'novice'!

conventional flat section; this permitted the addition of arrester-wires to the current number on hand, which in turn provided the Avengers in particular with a greater chance of catching an early wire.

With fifty-eight aircraft on board the RN carrier slipped her moorings on 7 May and headed southwest for New Caledonia accompanied by SARATOGA and the U.S. battleship NORTH CAROLINA. After ten days the Force

A U.S. Navy Hellcat holds a fairly close formation with an FAA Avenge. The latter aircraft design is identified by the 'inverted L' pitot mast protruding above the port wing and the fixed leading edge slot outboard of the BPF insignia. The auxiliary tank on the Hellcat was generally not jettisoned when the fuel content was exhausted; this could lead to a serious fire hazard if the tank was ruptured thanks to a bad landing and contact with the flight deck.

Seafires Mk.III are scattered along the flight deck of IMPLACABLE either during the final weeks of World War II or shortly following VJ-Day. The letter N denotes the carrier in question while the number system on the aircraft denotes either 801 Sqdn. (Nos.111-151) or No.880 Sqdn. (Nos.111-122). However, there is no clear way of confirming which Sqdn. the visible aircraft bearing numbers between 111 and 122 belong to. Note the folding wingtips and colored fin on aircraft 11+3 in the background.

Lt. Cole the Senior Pilot on No.1830 Sqdn. is in a perilous position with his Corsair Mk.II. The crash barrier is raised but it seems as if the fighter's flight attitude may well take it over and into the forward flight deck of ILLUSTRIOUS.

arrived at Noumea, and three days later what was titled Task Force 14 commenced a sortie into the waters north of the Solomon Islands. Japanese Fleet movements out of the key Naval base at Truk had been reported on a northerly course, an action that could have been swiftly reversed; in the event nothing transpired, and the Force finally sailed back to Noumea. The joint exercises made by both carriers during this time elicited the suggestion from the U.S. Navy that VICTORIOUS should serve as a pure fighter carrier and SARATOGA operate all strike aircraft including No.832 Sqdn. A prime reason for the switch lay in the well-founded Fighter Direction system on the RN warship, and from which the US Navy drew much benefit for its future carrier-based Operations Rooms, or Combat Intelligence Centers (CIC).

A planned American landing on New Georgia in the Solomon Islands constituted the background to what was to be TF 36.3 and the sole other Operation involving the Anglo-American carriers. While direct air support was provided by aircraft operating from Guadalcanal just south of New Georgia, the Naval Force was to be acting as a 'screen' between the Invasion Force and any Japanese Naval intervention, but it would stand off well to the south in the Coral Sea. Rendova Island was assaulted on 30 June, but all that happened before TF36.3 sailed back to Noumea nearly four weeks later was limited to a single occasion, when a G4M 'Betty' bomber was unsuccessfully intercepted by an SBD dive bomber!

By mid-1943 four of the new 'Essex' Class of fast carrier, including YORKTOWN and LEXINGTON, and a similar number of 'Independence' Class CVLs, had been commissioned and were ready to assume combat duty. The immediate crisis period for the U.S. Navy was deemed to be over and VICTORIOUS was duly released back to RN operational use. No direct contact with Japanese fighting units had been made during the period of detachment, and indeed the sole enemy individuals encountered were two POWs! Expressions of appreciations for the carrier's presence, as well as hopes for a more active future meeting in the Pacific – hopes that would be realised nearly two years hence – were received from Admirals Nimitz and Towers. By mid-September the carrier was back in Liverpool's Gladstone Dock to begin an extensive refit over the next six months

British Pacific Fleet Operations in the Pacific in 1945

The arrival of the BPF in Australia was effected by early February but a combination of technical problems and difficulties with the Dock Workers Union meant that it was almost another three weeks before the Fleet stood out from Sydney and headed north for its Forward Base at Manus in the Admiralty Islands. A similar time period then elapsed before

A Seafire LIII hangs over the edge of a carrier's flight deck following a failed landing and the port wing has been totally ripped off in the process. The stencil for locating the wing tip trestle can be clearly seen.

Lt. Cole's aircraft in fact ended up on its nose and hard up against the 'island' superstructure. The dark shape directly ahead of the engine cowling is probably the propeller, which has detached itself. Note the over-scale national marking on the fuselage. The incident occurred – on the 13th of the month! (April 1945), and was the second in quick succession to befall the veteran combat flier.

replenishment at Manus was completed, after which the warships sailed further on to Ulithi in the Carolines; here it became Task Force 57 and was placed under operational control of the U.S. Navy's Fifth Fleet commanded by the Victor of the Midway Action in June 1942, Admiral Raymond Spruance.

The presence of the BPF in this American 'lake' was as much a political as a military fact of life. The U.S. Navy had more than sufficient human and logistical means with which to defeat the Empire of Japan on its own. Consequently, the Royal Navy's contribution was not vital to the progress of the Conflict. However, the decision to use the BPF as a part of the U.S. Navy's operations meant that the U.S. Joint Chiefs of Staff had rejected Gen. McArthur's parallel call for the BPF to supplement his CVE Fleet ahead of amphibious operations against Borneo and Mindanao. As it was, the BPF carriers and supporting warships were destined to be utilised in somewhat of a secondary, albeit still useful, role during the impending Invasion of Okinawa.

Admiral Nimitz, C-in-C Pacific's, reported use of the BPF carriers as a 'flexible reserve' might also have been based on the fact that all four possessed armoured decks, and might be required to be substituted for their wooden-decked U.S. contemporaries should numbers of the latter be knocked out of action by the now regular Kamikazi assaults. Prior to Operation 'Iceberg', two U.S. carriers had been sufficiently damaged by Kamikazi strikes to preclude their use in the initial Okinawa Action while USS FRANKLIN was nearly sunk and rendered out of action for the rest of World War II.

Okinawa was the last geographic hurdle on the approach to the Japanese mainland, and would certainly be defended literally 'to the death' by the enemy. Approximately 300 miles to the southwest of Okinawa lay the huge Island of Formosa (now Taiwan), and roughly halfway between these two major Islands and military bases lay the Sakishima Gunto. This small group of islands possessed six airfields positioned on Ishigaki Shima and Mujako Shima. The neutralisation of these airfields

This Seafire III has suffered the virtual loss of its landing gear while all four propeller blades have also been completely broken away. The Seafire behind with its ninety-gallon auxiliary tank in place seems to have suffered similar damage. Both fighters have folded wings, so a third fighter making a failed landing-on attempt probably caused the damage. The incident occurred on IMPLACABLE.

was the main duty for the BPF aircraft in order to prevent any likely reinforcements from Formosa to Okinawa taking place.

Phase 1 of 'Iceberg'

By 26 March, ILLUSTRIOUS, VICTORIOUS, INDOMITABLE and INDEFATIGABLE were laying 100 miles off to the south of the Gunto; in support were the battleships KGV and HOWE, five cruisers and eleven destroyers. The Force was by now well versed in the U.S. Navy's signals pattern, tactical doctrine and carrier operating technique. Far less satisfactory was the full provision of a Fleet Train for regular replenishment while at sea. The Force of

This Seafire Mk.XV is reportedly stationed at Trincomalee in mid-1945 and bears the codes for No.802 Sqdn. However, this unit actually passed through Ceylon in mid-1946 en route to embark on VENERABLE in Australia. The arrester-hook protruding from the lower area of the rudder and the retractable tail wheel were recognition features on this Seafire variant.

The Corsair was produced in four variants but only the Mks.II and IV were equipped with support pylons for bombs or auxiliary fuel tanks. In this case a No.1830 or 1833 Sqdn. Mk.II embarked on ILLUSTRIOUS is having a 500 lb. bomb winched up into position on the port wing pylon. The Corsair could carry up to 2,000 lbs. of bombs.

A Seafire LIII 'curtsies' sharply to the right as its propeller blades lose their battle with the safety barrier wires and the remnant of the starboard landing gear folds under and crushes the radiator cover. INDEFATIGABLE's aircraft complement will surely be reduced by one after the incident.

oilers, supply and store, and repair vessels on hand was never to prove more than adequate compared to the U.S. Navy. In fact several CVEs had to be used in large measure for some of these functions.

On hand for air operations were eighty-four Avengers, and twelve Fireflies, whose bomb and rocket loads were to provide the main source of assault. A further twenty-nine Hellcats and eighty-eight Corsairs could also inflict heavy punishment through 'Ramrod' strafing action, while also fulfilling their primary escort role. Finally, CAP duties were maintained by the forty Seafires on hand. The series of attacks over the two-day period of operations – known as a 'Serial' – witnessed the Avengers dropping 500 lb. bombs on the runway surfaces as well as airfield hangars and other structure, while the Fireflies struck at flak emplacements with their rockets and cannon shells. Airfields, on the face of things, might appear to be particularly vulnerable targets with paved runways being susceptible to permanent loss.

However, craters can soon be filled in and the runways restored to use. In the case of the Gunto runways, which were formed out of crushed coral, the rate of recovery was even faster than with a standard surface; in addition the lack of nocturnal interdiction over the airfields by the BPF crews meant that the Japanese could carry out the repairs totally un-impeded. A secondary problem for the attackers lay in picking out flak positions for destruction. Not only were these hard to pin down; the Japanese were able to set 'ambushes' for the strafing aircraft through the use of 'dummy' or disabled aircraft in whose immediate vicinity were flak guns. By the evening of the 27th BPF strength had been reduced by sixteen machines either MIA or 'written off' in deck accidents and nine aircrew lost in action. A total of 548 sorties had been flown with sixty-

four tons of bombs and 151 rockets released on two of the main airfields. The Fleet then withdrew for refuelling and replenishment purposes before returning 'on station' on 31 March.

This second 'Serial' spell for the BPF was destined to introduce the warships and their crews to the 'Kamikaze' threat. Japanese bombers had begun to seek out the Fleet and attack in conventional manner. However, on 1 April Sub/Lt. 'Dick' Reynolds of No.887 Sqdn. was orbiting the Fleet in his Seafire FIII when he encountered a 'Zeke' single-engine fighter, one out of twenty attackers. The FAA pilot manoeuvered to close in as the two fighters challenged each other. Suddenly, the Japanese pilot broke away into a dive that saw the 'Zeke' smash itself against the base of INDEFATIGABLE's island structure. This was the first and effective demonstration of the armoured deck's resilience, and a vital factor in making up for the crew's extreme discomfort at working and living within its solid protective cover while serving in the extreme tropical heat. Far from rendering the carrier out of action, the deck was literally swept clear and became available for operations within one hour. (The subsequent landing-on by Sub/Lt. Reynolds during this time was fraught with risk thanks to the scattered debris, but he got down in good order!). This was the sole successful Kamikazi strike inflicted on the BPF prior to withdrawal on the 2nd.

The third 'Serial' commenced on the 5th and was to extend over three days, with the same pattern of airfield assault – and further Kamikaze intervention. By now, not only the Avengers were equipped with bombs, but the Corsair Sqdns. were adding to the destruction of the runways and other airfield facilities by carrying 500 lb. bombs on their centerline racks. A rather horrific addition to the arsenal of offensive weapons involved the use of the fighters' drop tanks. These had containers of Naplam inserted inside, with the tanks being jettisoned on suitable locations, which disappeared under the 'rain of fire' created by the impact.

As regards the Fleet carriers, it was as well they were fitted with armoured decks, due to the relatively meagre defensive firepower compared to their U.S. Navy contemporaries – and even those immeasurably better provisioned warships in this respect had proved they were far from invulnerable to Kamikazi assault. The supporting BPF warships did maintain close station and thereby bolster the overall firepower strength as attacks developed. On the 6th one of the determined enemy pilots did penetrate the AA barrage to plant his aircraft onto ILLUSTRIOUS's island base but with the same extremely limited restriction in that carrier's operational capability.

Diminishing Returns

For the FAA aviators, to the strain of flying combat operations was added the physical restrictions of not being able to get away from the pressures, since they were literally 'on the scene' all the time. This situation contrasted sharply with their land-based contemporaries who could vacate their airfield whenever the chance arose, and seek comfort and relaxation elsewhere. Physical and mental lassitude contributed to the growing number of incidents; forgetting to put the gun switches on 'SAFE' after landing, and triggering off a fusillade when about to climb out of the cockpit; making too fast and/or too high an approach, or failing to close the throttle on landing, with drastic effects ranging from crashing onto the deck, striking the barrier or careering overboard; failing to open up the throttle when approaching 'stall' speed and crashing into the sea.

L/Cdr Hanson on ILLUSTRIOUS made one precipitate take-off run before the carrier was fully into wind. The result was that the wind effect pushed his Corsair sufficiently to the left for the wing flaps on that side to impact with a metal stanchion, as well as for the left wheel to strike the raised edge of a 4.5-inch gun turret. The flap damage meant that whenever a subsequent landing approach was attempted, the imbalance caused by the left-side flaps only partially lowering tended to throw the fighter into an incipient roll. The final landing approach was of necessity made without the retarding presence of flaps and at an ominously high pace for a positive conclusion. Fortunately the arrester hook caught the final wire ahead of the crash barrier, leaving the pilot with no more than a strained neck arising out of the incident.

The pace of operations inevitably affected the mechanics' scale of efficiency no less. On one occasion a 'scramble' warning was responded to by L/Cdr Hanson jumping into a seemingly serviceable Corsair. In fact a new set of plugs was needed to restore the fighter to proper flying status – a fact only discovered after take-off when the engine's performance resembled that of a road-roller. A safe if frantic emergency circuit and landing was achieved but relations between the pilot and his Sqdn. Maintenance Chief were at least temporarily cool. The latter explained the circumstances of the aircraft's

Two Fireflies Mk.I display the revised tail markings adopted by the BPF in 1945, when individual letters denoting the carrier (in this instance N is for IMPLACABLE) replaced the fin markings. U.S.-style national markings are clearly outlined, as are the wing auxiliary tanks. Aircraft belong to No.1771 Sqdn.

continued deck presence, stating that the chance to 'strike down' the fighter into the hangar had been due to the lift not being available.

Formosan Variation

The knocking out of effective action of a fourth heavy carrier USS HANCOCK by Kamikaze means on the 8th led to a request by Admiral Spruance for the BPF to switch operations to Formosa; the Admiral was of the opinion that airfields in the north of the Island were harbouring sizeable numbers of the Kamikaze aircraft. So it was that the Fleet was again 'on station' off Formosa on the 11th, although weather conditions hindered operations for twenty-four hours. Even then, the initial Force of forty-eight Avengers and forty Corsairs were largely hindered by low cloud conditions from attacking the intended Primary targets.

The Avengers turned their attention to port facilities at Kiirun and inflicted heavy damage there as well as to an adjoining chemical plant. A handful of the Corsairs did strafe one airfield but better fortune attended the later strike; a thorough bombing and strafing assault on the airfield in question resulted in much damage to the runways and building, while the fighters added to enemy aircraft losses with strafing runs. In what was to prove a rare encounter with Japanese aircraft (other than over the Fleet itself), two Firefly crews of No.1770 Sqdn. had the good fortune to intercept five 'Sonias' heading toward Okinawa, four of these fixed-landing gear monoplanes were duly harried and pursued to their destruction. During the evening an intended air attack on the Fleet was totally thwarted by a mixed CAP of Hellcats and Corsairs, who brought down four and damaged several more.

The sole Japanese raid that did get through during the next few days consisted of just four raiders (13th) and the AA barrage was sufficient to either ward then off or take them down. By the time the BPF completed its Formosan 'variation' its aircrews had inflicted much destruction on several airfields as well as road and rail communications and port facilities. Sixteen Japanese aircraft were claimed as 'kills' against a total cost of three aircraft MIA and two 'written off'.

Operation 'Iceberg' was not proceeding to plan. It so happened that to the depredations being wrought upon the U.S. Navy by the Kamikazes was added the cunning counter-measure adopted by the Island's defenders. The Japanese had established themselves in the northern section of Okinawa; the Invasion Force encountered little or no initial resistance, but this positive situation was already being turned round as

"One more for Davy Jones' Locker". A Seafire from IMPLACABLE describes a headstand. The propeller blades are already stationery while one landing gear unit along with the P-40-pattern auxiliary tank are thrown backwards by the impact. The retractable tail wheel, engine cowling 'bulge' and absence of the lower rudder section are indications the aircraft shown here is a Mk.XV, but records show the Fleet carrier never embarked this Seafire variant during World War II.

the American soldiers and Marines encountered the series of dug-in defensive positions that had to be rooted out and that was causing serious casualties in the process.

Between 16-17 April and 19-20 April the BPF aircrews resumed their assault on the Japanese facilities within the Sakishima Gunto. By the latter date the need for both the Fleet and its supporting Train of supply vessels to seek a logistical respite was imperative since the range of material from aircraft

Right: One of the oil tankers from the Fleet Train servicing the British Pacific Fleet is photographed in the process of replenishing supplies for one of the destroyer escorts. The photograph is taken from FORMIDABLE on whose forward flight deck can be seen three Corsairs with full BPF national markings. The wing/fuselage bracing bars can be seen on all three fighters.

and aircraft spares to fuel and ordnance had almost dried up. On 21 April, the Force withdrew south to Leyte for one weeks rest and replenishment. Although nearly fifty aircraft had been lost during the month-long period of operations, the total of over 2,400 sorties had involved the dropping of over 400 tons of bombs while the Fireflies had discharged over 300 rockets.

The presence of an efficient rescue service comprised of U.S. submarines and PBY flying boats – to which the FAA's Walrus's had been added – ensured that the human toll was limited to around thirty aircrew killed or MIA. During this time the Fleet carrier FORMIDABLE arrived and exchanged places with ILLUSTRIOUS; the latter warship had suffered a greater degree of structural damage from the Kamikaze strike than was first thought, and the decision was taken to return her to the UK for repair. So far five of the six ILLUSTRIOUS or IMPLACABLE Class of Fleet carriers had served, or was about to see service, in the BPF and the sixth carrier IMPLACABLE would soon join in the action.

Phase 2 of 'Iceberg'

The carriers resumed their positions off the Gunto on 4 May, with the crews probably glad to escape the humidity of San Pedro Bay, especially since their warships were not equipped with air-conditioning. Both battleships were deployed to shell the base on Miyako while the aircraft went after Ishigaki. While the extra punishment handed out by the fourteen-inch guns was welcome, the absence of both warships along with their AA armament placed inordinate pressure upon the AA gunners

on the main Force warships when two separate groups of Kamikazes headed towards them. Fortunately the combination of shipboard gunnery and CAP fighters ensured that just two machines from the first wave were able to penetrate the defensive screen.

As it was the duo split their effort between INDOMITABLE and FORMIDABLE. In the former instance the Japanese pilot only managed to impact on the after deck before skidding off and into the sea. A more solid result was achieved on FORMIDABLE, which was struck alongside the island. Although metal fragments did temporarily place one of the boiler-rooms out of action, fires were started, and the carrier's forward pace was temporarily inhibited to around eighteen knots, operations were only halted until a two-foot dent in the deck plating had been levelled off using quick-drying cement! This latest example of the British carrier's virtual immunity from even serious damage, let alone destruction, caused one U.S. Navy Liaison Officer to state; "When one of our carriers is struck by a Kamikaze, it is generally a case of six months in a repair yard – with the British it is a case of "all hands to the brooms and sweep the deck clear!" (The second wave appearing later in the day enjoyed no success at all, and the total cost to the Japanese of fourteen aircraft was dearly bought, since just eleven FAA fighters were 'written off' on FORMIDABLE's deck).

Five days later, during the current 'Serial' commenced on the 8th, FORMIDABLE was again the focus for Kamikaze attack. Once again the operational delay was less than one

An Avenger embarked on one of the BPF Fleet carriers is 'flaring out' as it is on the point of crossing over the flight deck 'round-down'. The U.S.-pattern fuselage marking stands out even more against the gloss blue finish that replaced the original camouflage layout on Pacific-based FAA aircraft during the final months of World War II.

Two escort carriers, bearing Hellcats (SPEAKER) and Corsairs (unidentified) on the right and left respectively are battering their way through choppy seas. The sharp rise and fall of the flight deck as seen in this picture would present serious problems in attempting a landing-on with any FAA aircraft, in particular those with high performance characteristics.

hour but the logistical cost was eighteen Avengers and Corsairs, and less than twenty aircraft were then available for operations. Two further strikes both affected VICTORIOUS; the first close to the forward lift, caused damage to this facility and fires were started. During the efforts to extinguish the blaze a second Kamikaze struck home but although this act destroyed four Corsairs, the attacker ended up in the sea.

Around this stage of the Okinawa Invasion two more heavy carriers off Okinawa were so disabled that they took no further part in World War II operations to add to the five CV and CVE carriers affected temporarily or permanently since Operation 'Iceberg' had been initiated. This contrasted badly with the six strikes on four of the BPF carriers that had with one exception – ILLUSTRIOUS – not prevented operations from being hindered by more than several hours. The armoured deck, for all its attendant physical discomfort for the Royal Naval personnel on board, had proved its worth.

However, the fact that the terminal velocity of an aircraft was nothing like as great as that of a freely released bomb has to be taken into account when making the comparison between steel and wooden decks. The case of ILLUSTRIOUS on 10 January 1941 proves this point, and in fact had the *Luftwaffe* used a weapon greater than the 500 kg. that day, not even the presence of the armoured deck would have stood up to the penetrating force. (A similar situation was faced by FORMIDABLE in May 1941 and by INDOMITABLE during the 'Pedestal' convoy to Malta in August 1942; once again the carriers survived but were virtually useless as an aircraft-operating platform until repaired over many months).

Further 'Serials' were initiated up to 25th May, after which the BPF Force sailed back to the Admiralty Islands. Since 31 March more than 5,300 sorties had been flown during which

around 1,000 tons of bombs and nearly 1,000 rockets had been dropped or discharged. Eighty-five aircrew and carrier crewmembers were killed or MIA along with almost exactly double that figure in terms of aircraft lost in action or otherwise 'written off' in accidents or Kamikaze strikes.

FORMIDABLE had suffered the attentions of the Kamikazes twice and had come through virtually unscathed in terms of her own structure. However, there was a third serious incident that was self-inflicted. During hangar maintenance on 18 May the guns on one of the aircraft had been triggered off, setting fire to other aircraft and precipitating a series of sympathetic explosions that threatened to engulf the hangar space. Worse still, was the reported inability of the water from the sprinkler system to escape in sufficient quantity through the scuppers, thanks to the litter of debris blocking the way. The resultant water build-up could easily have led to the carrier facing the fate of capsizing if the mean level over the entire hangar floor had exceeded more than the permitted depth of just a few inches! Thankfully, either the fires were brought under control in time or the scuppers were sufficiently un-blocked in order to avoid this lethal situation. Thirty aircraft were 'written off' and two days later when the next 'Serial' was commenced the damaged carrier could only provide CAP sorties with its available fighters

Final Operations by the BPF

Arrival back at Manus at the end of May and from there to Sydney as June opened signalled a spell of several weeks in port while repairs and replenishment of the BPF carriers was indulged in. The arrival in the region of IMPLACABLE meant that this fresh carrier and her aircraft could be dispatched as part of Task Force 111/2 for an attack on Truk in the Carolines.

In the course of this planned action, the Avengers of No.828 Sqdn., Fireflies of No.1771 Sqdn. and the Seafires LIII and FRIII flown by Nos.801 and 880 Sqdn. would be able to 'work up' prior to linking up with the BPF when next called upon. Truk Atoll had become treated as the 'Gibraltar of the Pacific' since it housed a huge Naval Base facility that was believed – at least by the British – to still be active and therefore likely to present a major defensive obstacle for any attacking aerial Force. Also on hand for Operation 'Inmate' was the CVE RULER, which carried only a single ASR Walrus and was to be utilised as a spare deck for returning aircraft.

The U.S. Navy had been battering Truk since mid-1944 and by now the bulk of the defences, as well as the mass of warships formerly moored there, had greatly shrunk into virtual impotency or been sunk or dispersed respectively. The two days of sorties 0n 14 and 15 June cast up little for the FAA aircrew to get their teeth into; some 200 sorties were flown involving several photo-reconnaissance efforts by No.880 Sqdn. Just one Seafire was actually lost, and this was thought to have been as much due to Nature as to the enemy defences; the extremely heavy rainstorms existing over the area had struck as the fighters headed for their target and the pilot concerned may well have become disorientated and spun out. In addition one Seafire crashed on landing while the third loss occurred when an Avenger was catapulted off and went into the sea. Three further Avengers ended up in the 'drink' through problems with their engines. These latter losses were to add up to over ten before the problem was traced to an 'own goal' in respect of the wrong type of spark plug having been fitted!

(Earlier, on board IMPLACABLE and INDEFATI-GABLE, the intrusion of salt water onto the sparking plug

The aftermath of a 'Kamikazi' strike on a Fleet carrier is illustrated by this picture of the blackened superstructure, and crumpled remains of an aircraft. The value of the armoured deck is also illustrated here, since flying operations were recommenced at most within a few hours following the series of strikes on BPF carriers. The scale of damage would have rendered a wooden-decked contemporary out of action for a prolonged period, or even led to the warship's loss.

harnesses, allied to the high humidity that caused the spark to earth on some of the mountings, had seen many of the Avenger pilots literally staggering around the circuit after take-off, barely managing to stay airborne, and frantically seeking a landing with the partial power available to them!). The sense of frustration at the lack of suitable targets was probably more than offset by a sense of relief that the brief action over Truk had not created any notable degree of loss among the aircrew.

Task Force 37 off Japan

On 16 July what was designated the 1st Aircraft Carrier Sqdn. (ACS) linked up with the U.S. Third Fleet for operations

The BPF National marking on this Corsair's fuselage stands out against the dark camouflage scheme. The picture angle also displays how poor forward vision would be when landing. The tail letter P identifies VICTORIOUS but the number 120 is too low for that used by No.1836 Sqdn. and the other two Sqdns. to embark with Corsairs (Nos.1837 and 1838) used different code forms.

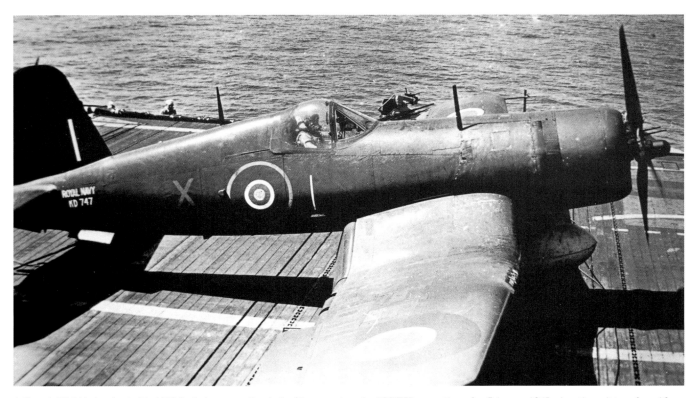

A Corsair Mk.IV belonging to No.1843 Sqdn. is seen on the deck of the escort carrier ARBITER, some time after February 1945 when the unit transferred from the Mk. II. Type D wing roundels are carried along with an unusual five-ring variation of the fuselage roundel. The Sqdn. saw no action in the Far East before VJ-Day.

The deck of the escort carrier SMITER holds two lines of RAF Spitfires Mk.XIV bearing full SEAC national markings and white identification bands. Aircraft code letters are for No.132 Sqdn. In fact World War II was over by this time, since the fighters were being delivered to Hong Kong following its reoccupation.

A total of six FAA Sqdns. were equipped with the Fairey Firefly during World War II. No.1770 Sqdn. was the first and embarked on board INDEFATIGABLE in May 1944. This damaged Firefly is being manhandled onto the forward flight deck. The pilot appears fortunate not to be seriously injured or killed to judge by the shattered remnants of his cockpit canopy.

against the Japanese mainland. FORMIDABLE (Nos.1841 and 1842 Sqdns. Corsairs and No.848 Sqdn.'s Avengers) had taken the place of INDOMITABLE as Admiral Vian's Flagship while the latter warship was being re-fitted; six Hellcats of No.1844 Sqdn. normally embarked on this carrier were transferred to the Flagship for PR and night-fighter duties. Also on hand were VICTORIOUS (Nos.1834 and 1836 Sqdn.'s Corsairs and No.849 Sqdn's Avengers) and IMPLACABLE (Nos.801 and 880 Sqdn.'s Seafires, No.1771 Sqdn.'s Fireflies and No.828 Sqdn.'s Avengers). This grand total of over 250 combat aircraft was to represent the pinnacle of FAA air power during World War II.

In support was the Fleet Train (Task Force 112) and five CVEs comprising the 30th ACS, whose joint duty was to replenish the aircraft and spares stock on the Fleet carriers and to provide CAP patrols for the Fleet Train. Back at Manus there was now an aircraft repair and assembly facility; also on hand were the carriers UNICORN and PIONEER, each of

which also functioned as aircraft repair warships. The Conflict in the Pacific had just one month to run at this point, but its violent conclusion through the advent of Atomic power could never have been foreseen. As far as the Allied Military was concerned, the Naval assault was but the prelude to many months of vicious, casualty-laden operations against an obdurate opponent prepared to literally 'fight to the death'.

FAA Operations Commence

Third Fleet operations had already commenced on 10 July off the central point of Honshu Island and the Force would shift position over the ensuing weeks to various sectors along the multi-hundred mile length of what was the central Japanese mainland. The existence of a typhoon in the area did not deter the RN carriers from commencing operations on 17 July, in the 'Right of the Line' element of the sixty-mile front along which the three U.S. Navy and single RN Task Groups were to operate. Corsairs from VICTORIOUS and FORMIDABLE managed, despite solid cloud cover, to penetrate this barrier and attack airfields on both the seaward and landward coastlines. Politics reared its unfortunate head next day when major Japanese warship units gathered in Yokosuka Naval Base were exclusively attacked by the US Navy aviators, despite the availability of their British and Commonwealth contemporaries, who were at least dispatched to other targets. (The U.S. Navy assaults were carried out on three further days up to the 28th).

Adverse sea and weather conditions now held up FAA operations for five days. On the 24th the final destruction of the Japanese Navy was marginally added to when aircraft from all four carriers (INDEFATIGABLE (Nos.887 and 894 Sqdn.'s Seafires, No.1772 Sqdn.'s Fireflies and No.820 Sqdn's Avengers) having just arrived 'on station', after sorting out mechanical problems in Sydney) came across the light carrier KAIYO moored in the southern Honshu water stretch called the Inland Sea. Although she was still afloat when the combined assault was completed, her decks and hull were knocked totally out of commission in respect of her intended Naval function. What was to prove the penultimate spell of FAA operations off Japan commenced on the 28th for three days. In that time Naval facilities around the Inland Sea were assaulted. However

fog around the Tokyo region on the 30th prevented effective attacks on airfields and alternate targets on the coast were sought out.

Seafire Crescendo

The presence of the Seafire Sqdns. on IMPLACABLE would provide their pilots with the chance to prove that the design was not 'short-legged' in terms of range and therefore of true offensive capability. Cdr. Evans (Commander Flying) on IMPLACABLE and L/Cdr. Crosley (CO, No.880 Sqdn.) had sought out suitable auxiliary tanks with which to really extend the Seafire's range. Nothing was available from British stocks but a consignment of rusting ninety gallon tanks previously used by USAAF Kittyhawk fighters had come to light. These were adapted and slung under the Seafires, to provide a 'seven league boot' boost for the Supermarine thoroughbred – the days of pure CAP operations were over!

In the case of IMPLACABLE the two Seafire Sqdns. comprising 30 Wing (Nos.801 and 880) were to operate in a joint CAP and 'Ramrod' function, as would the Seafires embarked on INDEFATIGABLE. The latter role was generally carried out in an independent manner, with a range of targets being strafed along the length of Honshu. Airfields were a

A Corsair IV of No.1846 Sqdn. barrels down the flight deck of COLOSSUS, her propeller throwing off a spiral of air. The carrier was one of four warships along with VENGEANCE, VENERABLE and GLORY that were constructed to a Light Fleet category, but which entered service too late in 1945 to see action during World War II. However, GLORY was subsequently on active duty during the Korean Conflict of 1950-1953.

A Barracuda pilot is doing his level best to give grey hairs to the two crewmembers in the foreground as he rakes his aircraft in a sharp upward bank to starboard. The COLOSSUS-Class carrier's deck width is unrestricted compared to the larger Fleet carriers, whose twin-gun turrets cut into the overall deck width. Picture taken in the Pacific after VJ-Day.

particular item of interest, with the attack runs being made from several directions in order to disperse the effect of flak fire, that proved to be disturbingly persistent. The difficulty of separating genuine aircraft from 'dummies' was increased by the lack in quality in the PR photographs and the consequent lack of confirmation that what was being assaulted was worth the effort. In addition, relatively few of the aircraft were seen to catch fire but this might have been due to an overall lack of fuel.

With the carrier Fleets sitting generally between 100 miles and 150 miles offshore, the benefit of the Kittyhawk auxiliary tanks was of vital importance to these Seafire operations. On the other hand, a serious and sometimes terminal problem began to arise that was primarily caused by the very presence of the tanks. The main internal fuel tank supply pipe was placed close to the supercharger casing. The casing naturally heated up and caused the pipe to also do so. By the time the pilot was ready to switch over from the auxiliary to the main tank the pipe temperature had risen well above the boiling point of the fuel. The switching of the main tank supply cock to 'ON' could easily result in a vapor 'lock' situation arising through the fuel boiling; the centrifugal pump would then run dry and overheat, and the engine cut out and catch fire.

Kamikaze tactics had been altered to take account of returning Allied formations in an attempt to infiltrate and gain unfettered access to the warships. With this in mind, the Allies had extended their outer screen of smaller vessels to pick up aircraft at a greater distance; then in cooperation with the CAP to 'delouse' the incoming formations. A further refinement to Japanese tactics was to dispatch 'Leader' groups of aircraft that were not intended to function in the Kamikaze role. Instead, they would front the genuine attackers as the entire formation approached at low level. When well within radar surveillance distance, the Leaders would deliberately climb to altitude, the intention being to decoy the CAP patrols away. Meanwhile the Kamikazes would make their attacks runs, hopefully free of aerial interference.

One of the final aerial encounters for the TF38 aviators occurred as dusk fell on the 25th. A radar sighting of 'Bogies' at nearly 100 miles range was responded to by the vectoring of the four-strong Hellcat CAP Patrol off FORMIDABLE towards the source. Any lingering doubts as to a positive outcome from this action were dispelled when the FAA fighters intercepted the same number of B7A 'Grace' torpedo bombers; in a brief clinical exercise, three of the attackers were 'splashed' and the survivor damaged and forced away.

This Firefly Mk.I has nosed over into the catwalk on its parent Light Fleet carrier GLORY. The incident represents the degree of 'action' experienced by the carrier and its aircraft, since both arrived in the Pacific too late to see active service against the Japanese. The tip of the letter Y that was GLORY's callsign can just be seen on the vertical fin. The aircraft bears full American-pattern markings.

Final Triumphs – and Tragedies

A combination of adverse weather and sea surface conditions, as well as a temporary suspension of operations after the first Atomic bomb was dropped on 6 August to allow the Japanese to consider surrendering, prevented active operations being recommenced until the 9th. By then TF38 had steamed further north and the aircraft were launched to attack shipping, particularly in Onagawa-Wan Bay. Lt. Robert Gray (RCNVR) was leading the Corsairs of No.1841 Sqdn. from FORMIDABLE. This Senior Pilot was an aggressive aviator who had already won the Distinguished Service Cross for his conduct during Operation 'Iceberg'. Today his fighter was bearing a 1,000 lb. bomb as the 'Ramrod' Force of eight sought out suitable targets.

Suddenly, as the coast was being skirted, flak opened up from the decks of the well-camoflaged destroyer AMAKUSA lurking close inshore. Gray's immediate response was to bank towards the warship and initiate an attack that ended with the enemy crew fighting for their lives as the ship crumbled below their feet. Tragically, Gray's success in striking home with his bomb was 'equalled' by his death as a result of return fire bringing down the Corsair into the sea. (Over three months later, the posthumous award of a Victoria Cross to Gray was announced – in one respect a bitter-sweet event, since the war was really over by 9 August, although not yet officially conceded by the Japanese).

Between the 10th and 15th August, three further day's operations were conducted, although by the 13th just INDEFATIGABLE was still 'on station', the other Fleet carriers having withdrawn to Sydney to make preparations for the anticipated Invasion of Japan. On the latter date, an Avenger strike was intercepted by up to twelve A6M 'Zeroes', but the enemy pilots came off worse; the Seafire escort pilots proved the overall superiority of the Mks.FIII and LIII on hand by bringing down no less than eight of their adversaries. This stunning success was achieved at a cost of one Avenger and a Seafire of No.894 Sqdn. whose pilot was forced to bale out but landed safely on the mainland.

What transpired next in respect of the latter FAA pilot proved just how necessary it was to defeat the Japanese by all means available at the time – including the Atomic Bomb. Sub/Lt. Hockley was captured and a few hours later, led out and shot, so becoming the last fatal operational casualty of the Far East and Pacific Campaigns. His death was just as, if not even more, tragic than Lt. Gray's since the Japanese Government had actually agreed Surrender terms that very morning.

Summary of Operations

The blood-letting of the greatest recorded Conflict in History had finally ended with no adding to the estimated 55 million casualties already sustained throughout the World. This final involvement of the FAA between 17 July and 15 August had run up a tally of around 2,800 sorties that had been flown in the course of just ten days operations. Over 400 Japanese aircraft had been destroyed, almost all by strafing and bombing, while the estimated tonnage of shipping sunk was 356,000 tons. The cost was set at forty-two aircraft lost on direct operations, again almost all through flak along with thirty-five personnel. A further fifty-two aircraft were 'written off' thanks to deck-landing incidents.

The Fleet Air Arm was now a potent Force in its own right, even if its aircraft complement was to be noticeably- if temporarily – reduced by the need to scrap the bulk of the American aircraft on hand that had been supplied under the terms of the Lend-Lease Bill! The era of the battleship representing the Capital element of the World's major Navies was largely over, and only the United States would retain several of its monster 'Iowa' Class post-War, for intermittent use off Vietnam, the Lebanon and in the Gulf of Arabia.

The contrast in the Fleet Air Arm's fortunes between now and the onset of World War II was staggering. The handful of Naval Air Stations then existing (six) had expanded in the UK alone to over fifty that were mainly or fully assigned to the organisation with a further sixty-plus RAF airfields providing some degree of 'lodger' facility to its Senior Service partner. Expansion overseas had been equally dramatic with seventy-eight listed locations spread around the globe.

The handful of Sqdns and their equally slim numbers of aircraft in position on 1 September 1939 was simply dwarfed in August 1945. Fully 217 Sqdns. had been commissioned and seen service during World War II along with a commensurate huge complement of aircrew and aircraft. The original 'passive' concepts of spotting for the battleships, reconnaissance and defending the Fleet had given way to the more aggressive functions of torpedo, bomb and strafing assaults upon the enemy surface and submarine Forces as well as land targets. In addition, these activities had been indulged in by a range of aircraft not only custom-built for such duties but more able to withstand the rigours of operations from the often waywardly mobile carrier flight decks. The initial World War II dependence on the RAF for training aircrew had also largely elapsed by 1945 with the FAA carrying out its own training-up courses.

Appendix A
Color Aircraft Profiles

Profile 1: Blackburn SKUA Mk.II, s.n. L 2889 - A/C "G" of 803 Sqdn. aboard HMS *Ark Royal*, and Hatston airfield in the Orkney Islands in the Norwegian campaign counter offensive, April 1940. A/C "G" displays the new upper camouflage although its original light grey undersides have not been repainted in 'sky' as yet. Aircrew and eventual fate of "G" are unknown.

Profile 2: Fairey SWORDFISH Mk.I, s.n. V 4515 - A/C "4A" of 813 Sqdn. aboard HMS *Victorious*, fitted with long range fuel tank fit in the observer's bay for the historic Taranto harbor torpedo attack of 11 November 1940. Pilot and crew unknown. A/C lost to unknown cause in February 1943.

Profile 3: Fairey SWORDFISH Mk.II, s.n. unknown - A/C of 816 Sqdn./155 Wing based at RAF Manston as anti-sub support for the Allied invasion fleet in Operation Overlord, June 1944. Aircrew unknown.

Profile 4: Fairey FULMAR Mk I, s.n. N 1880 - A/C "M" of 806 Sqdn. aboard HMS *Illustrious* as part of the earliest eastern Mediterranean campaign. Archives suggest "M" may well have been one of the A/C assigned to Lt.Com. C.L.G. Evans' four-plane section whose pilots accounted for twenty-six confirmed axis aircraft shot down before the end of their 1940 deployment.

Profile 5: Fairey BARRACUDA Mk.II, s.n. LS 550 - A/C "4R" possibly of 831 Sqdn. aboard HMS *Furious* as part of No.52 TBR Wing missions in 1944 against the Norway coast, including Operation Tungsten against the battleship *Tirpitz*. Illustrated previously as "4A", the A/C is correctly shown here as "4R" with its white wingtips and overpainted lower observer windows. Neither its squadron, nor its aircrew, can be confirmed.

Profile 6: Fairey FIREFLY Mk.I, s.n. DT 934 - A/C "4K" of 1770 Sqdn. aboard HMS *Indefatigable* in their highly successful venture with the U.S. Navy's Task Force 57 in the Pacific. The squadron readily introduced the Firefly to service and followed on in proving its airborne firepower of four 20mm cannon and eight 60 lb. HV rockets as displayed here.

Profile 7: Fairey FIREFLY Mk.I, s.n. MB 444 - A/C #278/N of 1771 Sqdn. who replaced 1770 Sqdn. aboard HMS *Indefatigable* June 1945 for operation with the U.S. Navy Task Force 57 against the Japanese mainland. On July 10th, FIREFLYs from *Indefatigable* in these late war tactical markings were the first Royal Navy aircraft to fly over enemy home islands.

Profile 8: Grumman TARPON Mk.I (TBF-1 Avenger), s.n. FN 802 - A/C "4M" of 846 Sqdn. aboard HMS *Tracker* during their combat deployment in the North Atlantic campaign of 1944. The aircrew, nor the fate of TARPON "4M" in this premier sub-hunting squadron, unfortunately, is unknown.

Profile 9: Hawker SEA HURRICANE Mk.Ib, s.n. Z 4550 - A/C "(6)G" of 800 Sqdn. aboard HMS *Indomitable* during the Operation Pedestal convoy escorts to Malta in mid-1942. "Six-G" is shown with its full display of tactical yellow markings, plus a personal thistle emblem beneath the windscreen. It was used on numerous sorties by Lt.Com. W. Bruen to account for several aerial targets both damaged and destroyed.

Profile 10: Grumman Marlet Mk.I (Wildcat F4F-3) s.n. AX 730 - A/C "L" of 805 Sqdn., originally aboard HMS *Formidable* in the eastern Mediterranean campaign of late 1941. Their September 'desert diversion' included adopting eight former Greek air force F4F-3 kites that were hastily repainted in a variety of dark earth, middlestone above and azure beneath. Refitted as a

MARLET Mk I, this composite unit of FAA landlocked pilots added critical tactical air support until their relief in July of 1942. Several pilots sortied in the redoubtable "L" shown here which was one of the few to survive the desert campaign.

Profile 11: Grumman WILDCAT Mk.VI (FM-2) s.n. possibly JV 683 - A/C "V" of 881 Sqdn. aboard HMS *Pursuer* during Operation Dragoon in support of the August 1944 Allied landings in southern France. Some speculation persists in the interpretation of the red cowlings, as well as a consistent A/C code display for this premier FAA tactical carrier-borne unit. Wildcat "V" displays its portside 250 lb. ordnance used against all manner of reinforced German emplacements confronting the Dragoon beachhead. And again, its pilot was unidentified.

Profile 12: Voight CORSAIR Mk.II - s.n. JT 410 - A/C T8•H of 1836 Sqdn. aboard HMS *Victorious* in the Indian Ocean offensive of January 1945. Corsair "H" is purported to have been the A/C used by Sub.Lt. D.J. Sheppard in achieving four aerial victories en route to reaching sole 'Corsair ace' status in the FAA. A heavy landing in February by another flyer relegated "H" to substantial repairs in Australia, and by June, it was lost in obscurity.

Profile 13: Grumman HELLCAT Mk.I (F6F-3) - s.n. unknown - A/C "E•F" of 800 Sqdn. aboard HMS *Emperor* in mid-1944. Grumman's 'new generation Cat' provided the veteran 800 Sqdn. aircrews with a true air superiority carrier borne fighter. HMS *Emperor* became the eyes of the admiralty in flying strike aircover and artillery spotting throughout Operations Overlord and Dragoon. Photos display a wide variety of D-Day stripe patterns, as well as either white or red A/C code letters, and possible red cowl rings and prop hubs. Ironically, British radios apparently effected the removal of most antennae wires from the HELLCAT when deployed in combat.

Profile 14: Grumman HELLCAT Mk.II - s.n. JX 686 - A/C B•8H of 896 Sqdn. aboard HMS *Empress* in the Indian Ocean operations of early 1945. Fierce weathering on its dark grey and slate camouflage foils the white tactical marking for FAA Carrier A/C in the late war Burma-Malaya campaign. Although the Mk II was fitted with zero-length rocket stubs, British ordnance required the typical rail mounts for the 80 lb. HV rockets shown here which further enhanced the tactical punch of the superlative HELLCAT.

Profile 15: Vickers-Armstrong Supermarine SEAFIRE Mk.IIc (Mk.V conversion) s.n. MB 183 - A/C 7•T of 880 Sqdn. aboard HMS *Indomitable* in the Mediterranean operations of mid-1943. Despite a 20% attrition rate in failed carrier landings alone, the lightweight SEAFIRE elements of 'H Force' capped the Allied landings, first in Operation Husky over Sicily, and most dramatically two months later in Operation Avalanche over Salerno, where Mk.II and Mk.III equipped squadrons were the sole beachhead protectors. Pilots rarely flew the same A/C on consecutive missions, and thus, neither the pilot nor the fate of "7T" is known.

Profile 16: Westland-Supermarine SEAFIRE Mk.IIIc - s.n. NF 520 - A/C H•6Y of 894 Sqdn. aboard HMS *Indefatigable* in January 1945. Fit with folding wings and 'slipper' ninety gallon drop tank for better range, A/C "Y" displays the abbreviated insignia marking typical of fleet A/C in the Indian Ocean operations. 894 Sqdn. produced their sole ace in Lt. R. Reynolds, but none of his victories are attributed to A/C "Y," and he surely was not the aviator who "caught a late wire" and thus rendered A/C "Y" to category "E".

Profile 1

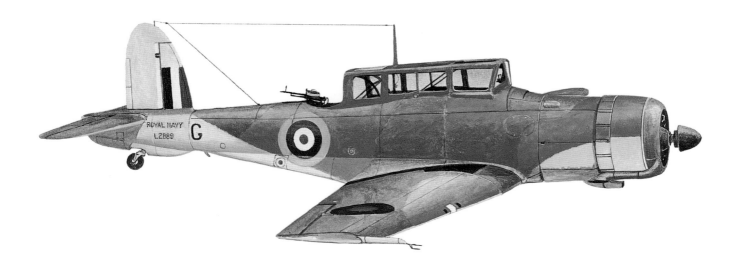

Profile 2

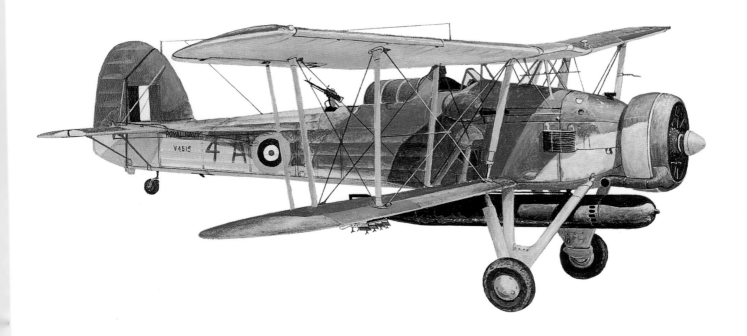

Profile 3

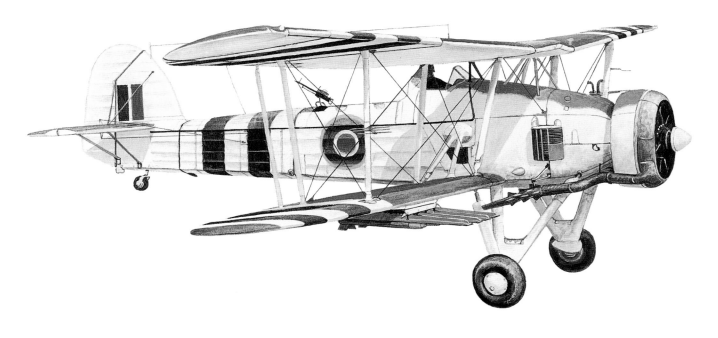

Profile 4

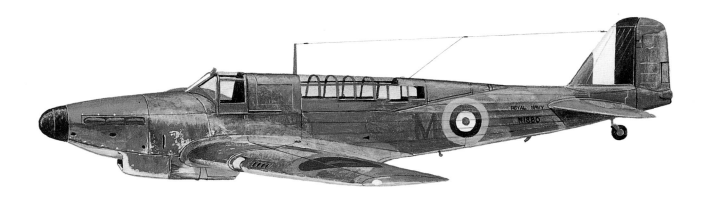

Profile 5

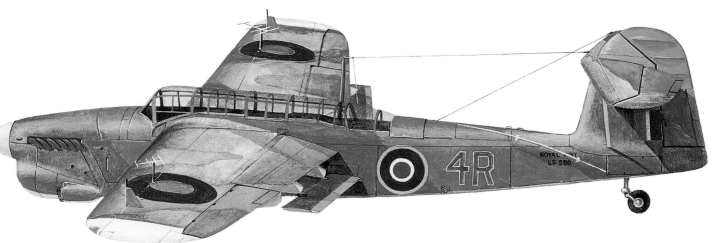

Profile 6

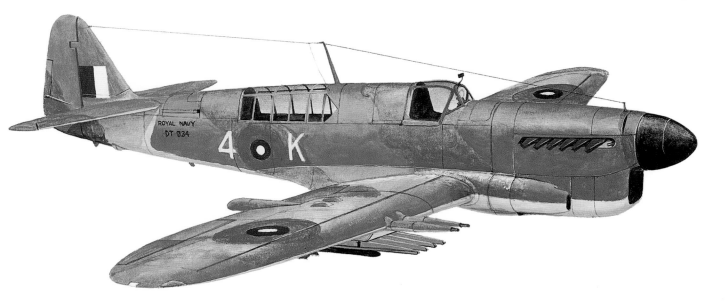

Profile 7

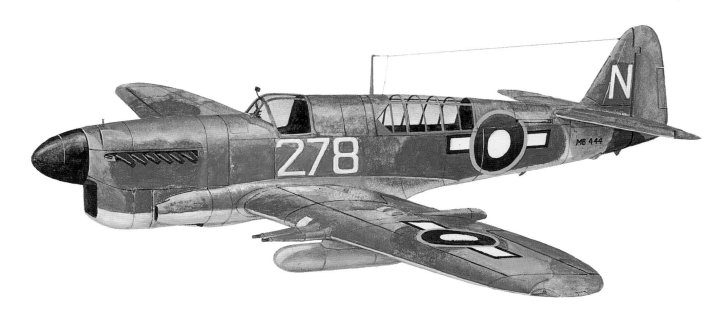

Profile 8

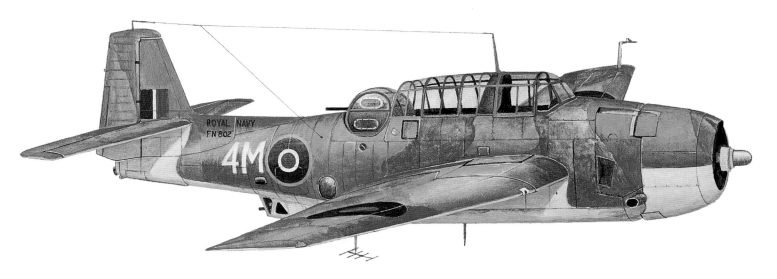

Profile 9

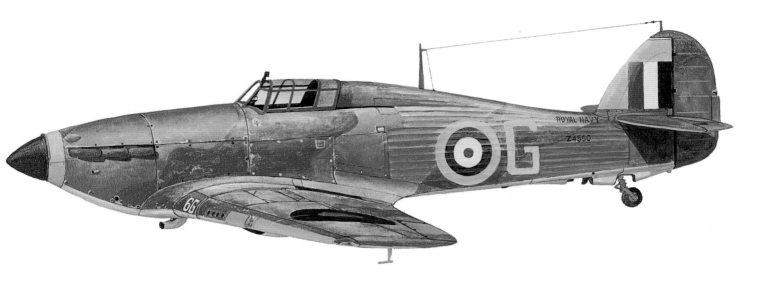

Profile 10

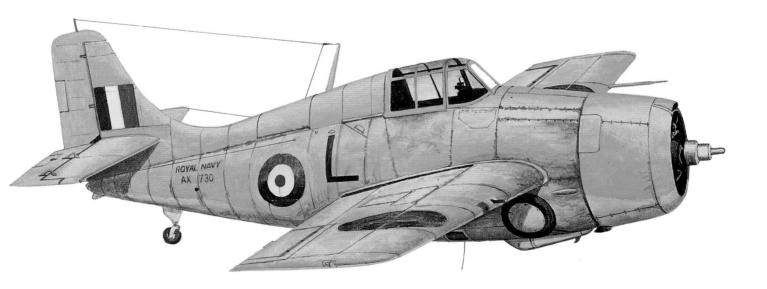

Profile 11

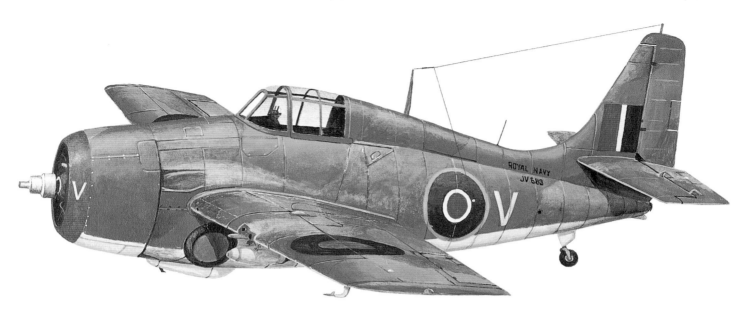

Profile 12

Profile 13

Profile 14

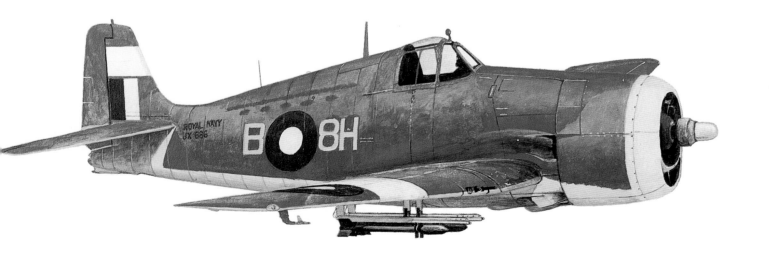

Profile 15

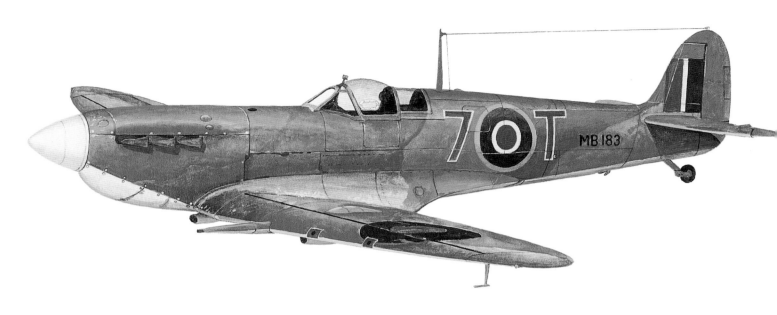

Profile 16

Appendix B
UK Naval Air Stations

Opened	Name	HMS	Function(s)
1939			
24 May	Lee-on-Solent	Daedelus	Front-line Sqdns. formed here Naval Air Ratings Depot Seaplane Base
24 May	Donibristle	Merlin	Aircraft repair yard
24 May	Ford	Peregrine	No.1 Observer School Reserved storage for biplanes
24 May	Worthy Down	Kestrel	No.1 Air Gunners School School of Aircraft Maintenance
1 July	Eastleigh	Raven	Shore Base, Safety Equipment and Air Medicine Schools and Naval air Radio Installation Unit. Also fire-fighting training.
7 July	Lympne	Daedelus II	RN Aircraft Training Establishment (until 23 May 40, when transferred to Newcastle under Lyme)
2 Oct	Hatson	Sparrowhawk	Shore Base for Home Fleet
1940			
15 May	Sandbanks	Daedelus II	Seaplane satellite base for Lee-On-Solent
19 June	Arbroath	Condor	No.2 Observers, Deck Landing and Naval Air Signals Schools
1 June	Yeovilton	Heron	No.1 Naval Air Fighter School and the Aircraft Direction Center Naval Air Fighting Development Unit
10 Aug	St. Merryn	Vulture	School of Naval Air Warfare. Also had a bombing/gunnery range.
1 Oct	Crail	Jackdaw	Air Torpedo Training Unit
Nov.	Stornoway	Mentor II	Seaplane Base
1941			
1 Jan	Twatt	Tern	Satellite for Hatston
1 Apr.	Campbeltown	Landrail/ Landrail II	Transit airfield for Clyde-based carriers
15 Jun	Machrihanish	Landrail	As for Campbeltown, from where it was transferred
15 July	Dundee	Condor II	Satellite to Arbroath
18 Aug.	Haldon	Heron II	Satellite to Yeovilton until May 43.

1942

1 Feb	Lawrenny Ferry	Daedelus II	Seaplane Base controlled by Lee-on-Solent until 24 Oct 43 (decommissioned)
1 Jun	Stretton	Blackcap	RN Aircraft Maintenance Yard
21 Jun	Sydenham	Gadwall	Disembarked Sqdns from USA/Canada Aircraft Maintenance Yard Overseas aircraft shipments
11 Oct	Fearn	Owl	TBR Sqdns working up
15 Dec	Dunino	Jackdaw II	Satellite for Crail/reserve aircraft storage

1943

1 Jan	Charlton Horethorne	Heron II	Satellite for Yeovilton
1 Apr	Henstridge	Dippper	No.2 Naval Air Fighter School
1 May	East Haven	Peewit	TBR (Part II) d deck landing training DLCO and aircraft handling training
15 May	Angle	Goldcrest	
15 May	Inskip	Nightjar	No.1 Operational Training Unit
14 Jun	Hinstock	Godwit	Beam Approach School and Naval Advanced Instrument Flying School
15 May	Eglinton	Gannet	Sqdns working up for Atlantic operations
15 Aug	Grimsetter	Robin	Satellite for Hatston
1 Sep	Burscough	Ringtail	Disembarked/working up Sqdns, and radar training
7 Sep	Dale	Goldcrest	Airfield for Kete, which held the RN Aircraft Direction Center
20 Sept	Abbotsinch	Sanderling	Aircraft storage/maintenance yard

1944

1 Jan	Maydown	Shrike	HQ for MAC-ship Flights Anti-submarine School Refresher/operational training
7 Sep	Anthorn	Nuthatch No.1	Aircraft Receipt and Despatch Unit
4 Sep	Ludham	Flycatcher	HQ, MONAB until Feb 45.
9 Oct	Evanton	Fieldfare	Aircraft Maintenance Yard
20 Oct	Ayr	Wagtail	Fleet Requirements Unit Bombardment Training School Calibration Flight
31 Oct	Rattray Head	Merganser	TBR Training (Part II) Operational Training (Part III)

1945

16 Feb	Middle Wallop	Flycatcher	MONAB HQ from Feb 45 Maintenance Test Pilots School
28 Feb	Peplow	Godwit II	Satellite for Hinstock
7 Apr	Woodvale	Ringtail II	Satellite for Burscough
18 May	Zeals	Hummingbird	Satellite for Yeovilton Fleet Requirements Unit Fighter conversion facilities.
1 June	Drem	Nighthawk	Night Fighter School Fleet Requirements Unit
1 June	MacMerry	Nighthawk	Satellite for Drem
11 July	Nutts Corner	Pintail	Fighter Sqdn use.
17 July	Ballyhalbert	Corncrake	No.4 Naval Air Fighter School
	Weston Park	Godwit II	Satellite for Hinstock

Overseas Naval Air Stations

Aden

Date	Name	HMS	Function
1939	Khormaksar	Sheba	Lodging facilities from RAF Australia
29 Jan 45	Bankston	Nabberley	MONAB 2
1 May 45	Jervis Bay	Nabwick	MONAB 5/ Satellite for Nowra
2 Jan 45	Nowra	Nabbington	MONAB 1
Feb 45	Schofields	Nabthorpe	MONAB 3
2 Apr 45	Manus	Nabaron	MONAB 4 (Admiralty Islands)
1 Jun 45	Maryborough	Nabstock	MONAB 6
9 Aug 45	Meendalen	Nabreekie	MONAB 7

Canada

Date	Name	HMS	Function
Sep 40	Dartmouth	Seaborn	Lodging base for Swordfish/Walruses From 1943, shore base for MAC-ship Swordfish.
1 Jan 43	Yarmouth	Seaborn (1.7.44)	No.2 Telegraphist/Air Gunners School
1 Aug 42	Halifax	Canada	RN Shore Station

Ceylon

Date	Name	HMS	Function
1 Oct 43	Colombo Racecourse	Bherunda	Fleet Requirements Unit Assembly of aircraft shipped from UK Recovery of crashed/damaged aircraft
15 Oct 42	Katukurunda	Ukassa	RN Aircraft Repair Yard/aircraft storage
1 Dec 44	Maharagama	Monara	RN Aircraft Training Establishment for Singalese recruits
1 Feb 43	Puttalam	Rajaliya	Reserve aircraft storage/facilities for EIF visiting aircraft
1 Jan 44	Trincomalee/ Clappenburg Bay	Bambara	Lodging facilities/ Control of Addu Atoll RN Aircraft Maintenance Yard
1942	Addu Atoll	Haitan/ Maraga (1 Jan 44)	Airstrip under Trincomalee's charge/ EIF refuelling base.

East Africa

Date	Name	HMS	Function
1939	Kilindini	Kipanga	Shore Base at Mombasa, handling FAA Sqdns.
1939	Port Reitz	Kipanga II	TBR Pool/aircraft erection facilities
1939	Voi	Kipanga II	Facilities for disembarked FAA Sqdns
1939	Mackinnon Road	Kipanga II	Reserve Aircraft Storage and same facilities as for Voi, plus fighter training.
1939	Nairobi	Korongo	RN Aircraft Repair Yard and Reserve Aircraft Storage.
1 Oct 42	Tanga	Kilele	Accommodated visiting aircraft assembly of crated aircraft

Egypt

Date	Name	HMS	Function
16 Sept 40	Dekheila	Grebe	Mediterranean Fleet transit Base FRU
15 May 41	Fayid	Phoenix	Aircraft storage depot and RN Aircraft repair yard

Gibraltar

Date	Name	HMS	Function
26 Sept 40	North Front	Cormorant II	Airfield transferred from RAF until 1 Aug 41 (then lodger facilities only) FRU from 1 Jan. 44

Gold Coast

Date	Name	HMS	Function
1 Oct 42	Komenda	Wara	Airfield for aircraft to be assembled for transit flights to North Africa#

Iceland

	Huitanes/Kaldarnes	Baidur	Facilities for disembarked aircraft from Arctic convoy carriers

India

1 Feb 45	Cochin	Kaluga	Aircraft erection depot/ facilities for disembarked aircraft (Lodger airfield)
1 Oct 42	Coimbatore	Garuda	RN Aircraft repair Yard/ assembly of aircraft from USA and UK
1 Feb 45	Sulur	Vairi	Potential aircraft storage facility.
1 July 44	Tambaram	Valluru	FRU and aircraft maintenance yard

Malta

1 April 45	Ta Kali	Goldfinch	FRU

Sierra Leone

22 Mar 43	Hastings	Spurwing	Airfield facility

South Africa

	Simonstown/ Wynberg	Afrikander	RN shore base
31 Mar 44	Stamford Hill	Kongoni	FRU (Lodger airfield from the SAAF)
15 Mar 42	Wingfield	Malagas	Air station/Aircraft repair yard for EIF

United States

1 Oct 42	Lewiston/ Quonset Point/Dartmouth	Sakar II	U.S. Base on loan. Also took over HMS Asbury's operations @ 31 Mar 44
1 Oct 42	Quonset Point Rhode Island	Asbury	Used for FAA Sqdns working up until decommissioned 31 Mar 44.
1 Oct 41	Washington	Sakar	Accounting/Administrative center for FAA in North America. Also controlled loan airfields at Squantum NY and Brunswick, Maine.

West Indies

	Bermuda	MalabarII/ Malabar III	Seaplane base
1 Aug 41	Palisadoes	Buzzard	Airfield handling disembarked Sqdns and provided reserve aircraft storage
6 Nav 40	Piarco	Goshawk	No.I Observer School

Mobile Naval Air Bases (MONABs)

In June 1943 an Order was issued by the Admiralty concerning the creation of Mobile Naval Air Bases. These self-contained structures were to be put in place in order to prepare and also repair aircraft and their components for the FAA. A total of ten MONABs were envisaged, of which all were commissioned, but the last MONAB (No.10) never actually functioned before decommissioning in October 1945. A Transportable Aircraft Maintenance Yard (TAMY) was also created.

MONAB No.1 contained the organisation's HQ and was set up in September 1944, first at Ludham and then at Middle Wallop, England. However, the existence of the British Pacific Fleet and the perceived need to operate FAA support services for this Force independently from American supply sources in the Pacific led to a steady transfer of the MONABS out to Australia. This process commenced in November 1944 and was not fully completed until October 1945. Before VJ-Day occurred MONAB Nos.1 to 7 were in operation. (Nos.8 and 9 arrived in July and October, but were assigned to operate out of Hong Kong and Singapore respectively following these Bases reoccupation).

Sources

Apps, Michael, *Send Her Victorious*, Military Book Society, 1971

Barrington, Alone on a *Wide, Wide Sea*, Cooper, 1995

Brown, David, *Carrier Operations, WWII*, Vol. 1, Royal Navy, Ian Allen, 1968

Chesneau, Roger, *Aircraft Carriers of the World, 1914 to the Present*, Brockhampton Press, 1984

Crosley, Mike, *They Gave Me a Seafire*, Airlife, 1986

Hanson, Norman, *Carrier Pilot*, PSL, 1979

Lamb, Charles, War in a Stringbag, Cassell, 1977

Mackay, Ron, *Fleet Air Arm, 1939-1945*, Squadron/Signal, 2001

Poolman, Kenneth, *The Catafighters*, William Kimber, 1970

— *Allied Escort Carriers WWII*, Blandford, 1988

Price, Alfred, *Aircraft versus Submarines*, William Kimber, 1973

Roskill, Capt. Steven, *The Navy at War, 1939-1945*, Wordsworth Editions, 1998

Smith, Peter C., *Eagle's War*, Crecy, 1995

Sweetman, John, *Tirpitz – Hunting the Beast*, Sutton Publications, 2000

Sturtivant, Ray and Balance, Theo, *Squadrons of the FAA*, Air Britain, 1994

Sturtivant, Ray, *British Naval Aviation, 1917-1990*, Arms and Armor, 1990

Thetford, Owen, *British Naval Aircraft*, Putnam, 1962

Winton, John, Find, *Fix and Strike; FAA At War, 1939-1945*, Batsford, 1980

Wragg, David, *Fleet Air Arm Handbook*, Sutton Publications, 2001

Index